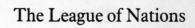

The League of Nations

F. S. NORTHEDGE

The League of Nations
its life and times
1920-1946

Holmes & Meier   New York

First published in the United States of America 1986 by
Holmes & Meier Publishers, Inc.
30 Irving Place
New York, NY 10003

Copyright © Leicester University Press 1986

Designed by Douglas Martin
Phototypeset by Bottom Line Graphics Ltd
Printed in Great Britain by the Bath Press, Avon

Library of Congress Cataloging in Publication Data
Northedge, F.S.
Bibliography: P
Includes index
1. League of Nations—History.   1. Title
JX1975.M78 1986   341.22'09
85-21989

ISBN 0-8419-1065-0

Contents

Foreword

Was the 'failure' of the League of Nations inevitable? Was any general collective security system, under which many states unite their efforts to control *any* state *anywhere* which breaks the peace, bound to be an impracticable enterprise?

Professor Northedge, who completed the manuscript of this study only a few months before his sudden death in March 1985 which so shocked his colleagues and many friends throughout the world, concludes, perhaps somewhat reluctantly, that it was. In a brilliant analysis of the pre-1914 international system 'The World before the League' he looks back rather nostalgically to an era in which traditional balance-of-power practices made the use of force more tolerated but more limited. Practices such as these were, in his mind, more in 'accord with the psychology of those who have to operate them' than experiments for the collective maintenance of peace as embodied in the Covenant or the Charter of the United Nations. This is Northedge, the perceptive political analyst of *The International Political System* (1976) and the enthralling lecturer on the *Psychological Aspects of International Relations*. For him, pacifist though he was, the traditional international political system based upon the balance of power 'has its faults, but it may have fewer faults than any alternative upon which the world could agree' (1976, p. 323).

In the very nearly 40 years which Fred Northedge spent in the Department of International Relations at LSE, first as a student, then as Lecturer and from 1968 as Professor, he never substantially shifted from this position. It was a position rooted in the historical perspective from which he viewed international relations and reflected in his impressive volume on British foreign policy in the inter-war period, *The Troubled Giant* (1966), and in *A Hundred Years of International Relations* (1971). For him history was at the very core of international relations studies: 'how can we think or talk about the nature of international relations except on the basis of our experience of the past, that is *all* we have to go on.'

In the present volume it is Northedge the historian who is concerned to explain why the League as a security system failed. To one engaged in a similar enterprise Wittgenstein once exclaimed: 'Tell him first to find out why wolves eat lambs.' Northedge would have recognised the aptness of this reaction. Yet for him failure stemmed not so much from the rapacity or pusillanimity of political leaders in the 1930s, as from a fundamental flaw in the system itself, namely, that under Article 10 it was wedded to preservation of the world's territorial and political *status quo*. Protagonists of the Covenant had supposed that the inevitable challenge to the *status quo* would emanate from only one quarter at a time and that the overwhelming majority of states would be in a dominant position to deter or defeat it. Manchuria exposed the fallacy of that presumption.

Abyssinia was, however, as Northedge rightly claims, the decisive test for the League's system, for it highlighted the extent to which a League collective security system of collective sanctions against Italy could run counter to a balance of power policy in which Britain and particularly France were desperate to retain Italian suport to provide an effective counterweight to a resurgent Germany under Hitler in the West and a militaristic Japan in the East – the latter being a factor which is often inadequately stressed. The dilemma was a painful one, especially for France, but the consequent vacillations in the Anglo-French handling of the crisis effectively alienated Italy and destroyed the League. Was failure inherent in the system, as Northedge claims, or was it mainly a failure in leadership, a failure – not shared either by Hitler or the mass of public opinion in Britain – to perceive the crucial importance of the issues at stake and the disastrous consequences of 'falling between two stools'? Effective coercion of Italy would have saved the League and maybe helped to constrain Hitler; conciliation of Italy along the lines of the Hoare-Laval pact might have saved the Stresa front. Dithering between the two earned the worst of both worlds. But inevitable? – Truman over Korea and Eisenhower over Suez?

To raise such questions is not to question Fred Northedge's masterly handling of his material; the argument throughout is cogent, well documented, commendably lucid, elegantly deployed and above all humane. For Fred Northedge was not only a scholar of distinction and a brilliant teacher, but a person of great sensitivity and humanity. One can feel in the text his wish to be as fair as possible to the League and to recognise the reality of its achievements, as in its economic and social activities. These qualities shine through in his reminder that for all its helplessness in the late 1930s Madame Curie could still write that the League 'has a grandeur that commands our support'. It is his sense of the grandeur of the enterprise, as well as the excellence of his scholarship, that has enabled Fred Northedge to bequeath such a splendid memorial to his life's work.

GEOFFREY GOODWIN

Preface

This book is an account of a world-wide organisation, the League of Nations, which came into existence in January 1920 and held its last meeting in April 1946, and its efforts to preserve world peace in one of the most tempestuous periods in modern history. The League failed, and some of the reasons for this are given here. Nevertheless, during the Second World War none of the countries ranged against the Axis Powers doubted that after the war the struggle must be taken up again, this time with the United Nations Organisation, the headquarters of which, appropriately, were to be in New York. Yet today, after forty years, in which peace has been precariously maintained, the United Nations is almost as much a lost cause as the League was in the late 1930s. Its non-political work for economic and social co-operation, for aiding the developing countries, for health and education, drug control, and so on, continue, as did that of the League until the bitter end. But, as instruments for the collective maintenance of peace, the world now relies upon methods which the League and the UN were intended to supersede.

Is there something basically false in the idea that the nations can combine their efforts to smother threats to world peace from whatever quarter they come? Must we rest content with a system (if indeed it be a system) of collective defence and balance of power which failed to prevent war in 1914 and again in 1939, and which, if it failed again, could hardly ensure the survival of our civilisation? This book examines the reasons why collective security in the period between the two world wars failed, and tries to assess how far this was a failure in the formula for collective security devised at the Paris peace conference in 1919, or of the inclemencies of the epoch in which the League existed, or of its human instruments, the men and (more in the background of affairs in those days) women who sought to make the system work, and, in some cases, to defeat it.

The book therefore attempts to be more than a historical record, though it uses primary historical sources, especially on the British side, Britain having been, at all times, the most important League member and the country to which responsibility for the League's experience chiefly attaches. It is the study of an experiment, the failure of which shook the world. The book cannot hope to do more than examine the more important of the League's activities since the League's story is that of the world, in a truer sense than is that of the United Nations. But its subject is the collective maintenance of peace, and the League's work is always regarded from that perspective. For all its helplessness in the late 1930s, the League of Nations, wrote one of its most fervent supporters, the physicist Madame Curie, 'has a grandeur that commands our support'.

The London School of Economics and Political Science, January 1985

F. S. NORTHEDGE

1 The world before the League

The League of Nations, an international organisation having as its members almost all the fifty-odd states of its day, was founded at the end of the First and wound up at the end of the Second World War.[1] Its purpose was mainly to keep the peace, but it was also intended to serve as an umbrella under which a more orderly management of all world affairs, political, economic, financial, cultural and so on, would develop. The League was a child of the First World War in that its constitution, the Covenant, formed the first twenty-six articles of the peace treaties imposed on Germany and her allies by the Allied and Associated Powers after their victory in 1918. This arrangement was insisted upon by the American President, Woodrow Wilson, the most enthusiastic exponent of the League idea among the war leaders, since he thought that his European partners were more likely to take the League seriously if it were part and parcel of the peace settlement for which they had paid so high a price. It had the drawback, however, that in later years the League tended to be regarded as the guardian of treaties which were hateful to the defeated states and were disowned by one of the victors, the United States, and by large sections of public opinion in another, Britain.

The League was also a child of the First World War in that it was launched on the tide of revulsion, not only against the war just ended, but against all war, which swept the world when the fighting stopped in November 1918. The war of 1914-18 was the first total war; for the first time in history the entire resources of the belligerents, human and material, were mobilised for the conflict, or, if any of them escaped mobilisation, were exempted only by leave of the governments. During the struggle, neither side seemed to be satisfied with anything less than the total destruction of the other. Since the war was fought in a confined space in a small land-mass, Europe, and the mass production methods resulting from the Industrial Revolution were devoted, for the first time, to the manufacture of weapons, the loss of life was unprecedented. The Allied Powers mobilised 42 million men and lost 5 million; the Central Powers, Bulgaria and Turkey mobilised 23 million and lost 3½ million. The wounded numbered an estimated 21 million and about 10 million civilians died through starvation, civil war or disease. As the war losses mounted, it became clear that the only way in which they could be made to seem tolerable was to use the peace settlement to ensure that a disaster on such a scale would never recur. The first total war became the first 'war to end all war', and on both sides the belligerents' war aims, which, when the war began, were limited to territorial claims and demands for reparation and restitution, were extended at its end to include the pledge to establish peace for all time. The formation of an international agency to prevent future wars was enrolled among the war policies of all the major states in the conflict. President Wilson, when he came to Europe in December 1918 to attend the peace conference, was acclaimed as a Messiah.

The anti-war feelings which launched the League, like the incorporation of the Covenant into the peace treatie , was at once a strength and a weakness. It made the League a passionate force for those who believed in it. If loyalty to the League ever flagged among its partisans, it was revived by memories of the 'doomed, conscripted, unvictorious ones who fed the guns'. At the same time, much of the anti-war sentiment which clung to the League had more than a tinge of pacifism of an unconditional variety about it: many of those enrolled in the League cause (and the League *was* a cause, in a sense in which its successor, the United Nations, never became) so hated war that they never wanted to fight another, not even a League war, a war to defend the Covenant. Such a war they considered to be a contradiction in terms, a commission of the sin the League was supposed to eliminate. In this way, League supporters, or some of them, became in the 1930s, perversely enough, the victims of those who used the prevailing dread of war to undermine the international order and the League with it.

But there was another consequence of the First World War for the evolution of international organisation, namely, that it led the generation which fought the war to realise, perhaps for the first time, that there surely must have been some system for managing the relations of the various states before the war, and they could hardly fail to think that it must have been criminally faulty for a disaster such as the war to occur. Yet the very fact that the system was practically unknown to the people at large in the different countries implied that it must in reality have worked fairly well; people are not usually conscious of their bones until they ache. And it had worked well. There had been wars in the hundred years before 1914, but they had been few, far between and limited in scope, hardly any of them involving the greatest Powers. Since the defeat of Napoleon Bonaparte in 1815, the great Powers had never fought each other, except in the largely futile Crimean War at mid-century, the minor Franco-Austrian war in Italy in 1859, and the brief, though politically momentous wars of Prussia against Austria in 1866 and against France in 1870-71. Prussia had also fought with Denmark in 1864. Only the Franco-Prussian war had left the fires of vengeance smouldering – until 1914, in fact.

Outside Europe, blood on a considerable scale had been shed, and the map had been radically changed as a result: this was true in the overseas empires of the European Powers, in the United States during the civil war between 1861 and 1865, and in the Russo-Japanese war of 1904-05, with its vast political effects. But in Europe, notwithstanding its being the scene of political, economic, cultural and technological changes without parallel in history, there was tranquillity, disturbed only by the hum of factories. So little did international conflict affect ordinary life that the educated élite in Europe, outside the small world of government and diplomacy, took hardly any interest in the doings of nations. The Fabian Society in Britain, for instance, founded in 1883-84, a powerful force in the creation of the Labour Representation Committee, from which the Labour Party sprang, earnestly probed into every aspect of national life, but international affairs were not on their agenda.

The war which broke out in Europe in August 1914 was a bolt from the blue, unlike the war of September 1939. Seen from London, the war clouds were gathering over Ireland, not over the continent. If war was expected between the great Powers anywhere, it was believed that it would be short, a 'jolly, little war', as William, the Emperor of Germany, put it, like the swift campaigns of Bismarck, fought for German unification. When the war came and turned out to be a monstrous horror, people considered that, to build a League of Nations capable of preventing another, the elements of international organisation which existed before 1914 must be looked at again, though few knew what they were and almost everybody suspected that they must have been highly defective. Or, rather, perhaps there had been no organisation at all, only 'international anarchy', and not merely anarchy in the sense of an absence of government and an effective system of law, but Miltonian chaos.[2]

II

How then had international affairs been conducted before 1914? Who had run the system, and what flaws in their methods of managing those affairs, or even perhaps in their moral constitution, had determined that it should break down, bringing tragedy to so many millions?

To begin with, the system was European, and Europeans, white, Christian, generally male and for the most part aristocratic, or at least upper-middle class, had run it. The United States stepped into the picture by its victory over Spain in 1898 and by acting as host for the peace conference which ended the Russo-Japanese war in 1905, but it was distinctly a minor Power until the First World War. America was about on the same level as a factor in the international system at the end of the nineteenth century as Japan, which emerged from age-old seclusion in 1868, and then amazed the world by its alliance with the most powerful of the great Powers, Britain, in 1902 and by its overthrow of another great Power, Russia, three years later. The score of Latin American states which had freed themselves from Portuguese and Spanish rule with British encouragement in the early 1820s hardly appeared on the international stage until the twentieth century, though after 1920 they played a prominent role in the League of Nations. As for the rest of the world, including the teeming millions of China and other Asian countries, and the people of Africa, all that was the object of European diplomacy and enjoyed only as much of an independent existence as the European Powers allowed. Even Turkey, with a shrinking foothold in Europe, was only admitted into the inner circle of the European great Powers after the 1850s, and then only as an ailing, elderly relative, the 'sick man of Europe', whose property was rather more of a concern to the great Powers than was his personal condition.

The principal European Powers which ran the diplomatic system before the 1914-18 war were Austria, which formed a dual state with one of its former provinces, Hungary, in 1867, to become Austria-Hungary; Britain, the *primus inter pares*, the greatest sea Power and ruler of the most extensive land empire; France, restored to membership of the managerial hub of European Powers in 1818, after having held the rest of Europe at bay for twenty-three years of war until Napoleon's final defeat at Waterloo; Prussia, which forged the thirty-nine states of the German Bund of 1815 (except for Austria) into modern Germany in 1871; and Russia. The Italian states and provinces which coalesced into a national state under the House of Savoy in the middle years of the nineteenth century joined the inner circle of the great Powers in the late 1860s, a status confirmed when Italian unification was complete with the addition of Rome in 1871.

This pentad, or hexad, of Leviathan states, which controlled the wealth and commerce of the nineteenth century, which ruled the seas and dominated almost all the world outside Europe, was for the most part governed by monarchs who exercised the real executive power in their countries, notwithstanding any façade of parliamentary legislatures that might exist. They were buttressed by landowning aristocracies fortified by wealth drawn from industry and trade as the Industrial Revolution spread. Britain and France were exceptional as representative democracies with legislatures for the most part independent of the Crown (France finally became a republic in 1871), but the franchise in neither country was universal until the twentieth century. The European monarchs looked upon the resources of their countries rather as personal property, great landed estates to be disposed of as they pleased. In Britain, for all its democratic pretensions, the question was raised as late as the 1930s whether the cession of territory in East Africa to another country would require the consent of the Crown, and some eminent constitutional authorities held that it would.

The thrones of Europe were linked with one another by a network of marriage ties, many of which led to London, Queen Victoria often being spoken of as the 'grandmother of Europe', and this helped create a sense of the Powers forming a family, as they were generally collectively known. New states formed as the century proceeded, like Greece, which broke away from the Ottoman Empire with British and Russian support in the 1820s, and Belgium, which revolted in 1830 from Holland, with which it had been joined in 1815, were given monarchs from the principal ruling families of Europe. The monarchs would communicate among themselves by paying each other personal visits, to take the waters at fashionable resorts or to see military manoeuvres, often mixing business with pleasure. But, for the conduct of their day-to-day affairs with each other, they employed a corps of professional agents, or diplomats, originally merely messengers between one ruler and another. By the nineteenth century, diplomatic practice had undergone much regularisation and was the subject of a developed international legal code, and yet the diplomat's work was essentially simple, though calling for many special personal qualities for its successful performance. It was to represent the ruler at a foreign court, to collect information (sometimes by espionage) about the country to which he was accredited and send it back home, perhaps with his own interpretations, and to negotiate agreements between the two courts. The diplomat, who would be quartered in a permanent embassy or mission in the other country and provided with immunity from the laws of the host state, was generally a personal appointee of the ruler, almost always an aristocrat, perhaps a court favourite. Not until the twentieth century did the recruitment of professional diplomats by competitive examination and their regular financing on a salary basis become anything like the normal rule in Europe.[3]

But it was also a well-established diplomatic practice to transact international business collectively, with representatives of several or perhaps all five or six great Powers present, and the spokesmen of other states when the Powers thought their participation would be useful. This was called a congress when the representatives of the Powers were heads of state or government or their chief Ministers, and when the subjects under discussion were of a general nature, and a conference when the representatives were diplomats and the subjects specialised or technical in nature. This difference in title, however, was by no means always observed in practice, the Paris peace conference in 1919, for example, being an outstanding example of a meeting which would probably have been called a congress forty or more years earlier. During the life of the League of Nations the term 'congress' tended to fall into disuse.

The congress or conference system has been described as an 'informal institution which enjoyed no more than intermittent existence'.[4] It was more common in the early nineteenth century than after 1871, when Bismarck, who disliked multilateral conferences, was a powerful force on the international stage. The historian, Sir Charles Webster, counted only eight heads-of-government and Foreign Ministers' conclaves throughout the nineteenth century, and only eighteen meetings of diplomats under the chairmanship of a local Foreign Minister during the same period.[5] The right to attend a congress or conference was almost always limited to the five or six European great Powers, although the United States attended European conferences in Madrid and Algeciras in 1906 when the subject was the Moroccan question. Small countries were rarely admitted to meetings of the great. On one occasion, at a conference in London in 1831 to deal with the Belgian issue, the King of the Netherlands, who until the 1830s ruled over Belgium, was kept waiting in an ante-room, and when he complained was told that he would be sent for when he was wanted.

Congresses and conferences, to which by the mid-century there had been given the grandiose name of the Concert of Europe, met, not at regular intervals, but when it was agreed by the participants that some question demanded a meeting. They were a 'spasmodic phenomenon with no permanent existence',[6] and it is significant that, on occasion, the fact that agreement was reached on the calling of a conference was regarded as a setback for one great Power or another, rather than as marking progress towards more continuous international organisation: this was the view taken in 1878 by Russia of one of the most famous international gatherings of the nineteenth century, the Congress of Berlin, since it revised the Tsar's treaty of San Stephano with Turkey of the same year, which was highly favourable to Russia. The place of meeting, which could be a matter of considerable political importance, was generally one of the capitals of the Powers, though not St Petersburg, which was considered too remote. The host country would provide the chairman and the secretary, or protocollist, who kept a record of the decisions reached at the meeting, though not usually of the arguments used by the participants. As a rule, congresses and conferences tended to be called on one or other of three sorts of occasions: at the end of a war to draw up a peace treaty; to meet some sudden emergency; or perhaps to deal with some question which had been germinating over a period and was now regarded by one or other of the Powers as 'ripe' for treatment. But for most of the century before 1914 there was nothing like a rule for determining when a congress or conference should be held. They were called together by mutual agreement whenever the Powers felt like it, and on whatever subject they felt like discussing.

At the beginning of the nineteenth century a serious attempt was made to give the conference system a regular form, but it failed, and the reasons for its failure are of the greatest significance. When the four allies who had defeated Napoleon – Austria, Britain, Prussia and Russia – met in Paris after the adventure of the Hundred Days, they drew up and signed a Treaty of Alliance and Friendship, otherwise known as the Quadruple Alliance, on 20 November 1815 'to facilitate and to secure the execution of the present Treaty' (that is, the revised peace treaty with France) 'and to consolidate the connections which at the present moment so closely unite the four Sovereigns for the happiness of the world'. By the sixth of the seven articles of this agreement, the parties undertook

> To renew their Meetings at fixed periods, either under the immediate auspices of the Sovereigns themselves, or by their respective Ministers, for the purpose of consulting upon their common interests, and for the consideration of the measures which at each of those periods shall be considered the most salutary for the repose and prosperity of Nations and for the maintenance of the peace of Europe.[7]

Four conferences under this provision were held, at Aachen (Aix-la-Chapelle) in 1818, at Troppau (modern Opava) in 1820, Laibach (modern Ljubljana) in 1821, and Verona in 1822.[8] Perhaps the greatest achievement of these meetings was to reintegrate France in the European system at the Congress of Aachen in 1818, and this had the incidental effect of providing Britain with an ally in her struggle with the three East European courts which finally broke the Congress system.

The issue which split Britain from Austria, Prussia and Russia, the states of the Holy Alliance, was whether the congress system should have a policy, in the sense of a definite, continuing attitude towards the questions it was intended to deal with, and, if so, what that policy should be. The East European Powers argued that it should, and that the policy should consist of upholding the principle of legitimacy, in the sense of the hereditary rights of rulers and their thrones against revolutionary forces within their own countries, and, in the case of the Latin American possessions of Portugal and Spain, of imperial Powers against colonial nationalism. They also contended that the congress system had a right of intervention in other states in defence of the principle. The British Foreign Secretary of the day, Viscount Castlereagh (1769-

1822), and, even more forcefully, his successor, George Canning (1770-1827), maintained that Britain, a constitutional democracy, could not bind itself to support in advance any general line of policy at an international conference, least of all one so illiberal. The attempt to formalise the congress system therefore yielded, after a few years, to the total informality of the Concert of Europe, and Canning's cry 'God for us all and the devil take the hindmost' became the axiom of nineteenth-century unilateralist diplomacy.

In the congress and conference system, the unanimity rule was normal in matters of substance, in accordance with the time-honoured principle that a sovereign state cannot be legally bound without its express consent. Talking between the Powers would continue, accompanied by the application of more or less discreet pressures, threats and bribes away from the conference table (if indeed there was anything so formal as a table at all), until a meeting of minds was reached, and if one was not reached, the parties would return home and perhaps renew their endeavours later. The summoning together of one's party, as though in preparation for a departure, could in itself constitute an inducement on the others to modify their policies in the interests of a consensus. In matters of procedure, however, where a decision of some sort had to be arrived at for the conference to get started, the point at issue might be decided by counting heads, though only on condition, as a rule, that no precedent was being created. Such agreements as were reached in congresses or conferences were embodied in highly formal documents known variously as agreements, treaties, final acts, conventions, declarations or protocols, together with a number of subsidiary instruments intended to place on record a state's attitude to some of the matters in dispute, an agreement between some or all of the parties on the interpretation of certain parts of the main treaty, or the reservations of some of the parties to the agreements reached. It was strictly understood that all these agreements bound only the signatory states, known as the High Contracting Parties, and usually only after ratification by their constitutional processes, and only for the specified duration of the agreement. Every care was taken to ensure that the congress or conference was understood as an essentially isolated transaction, with no necessary connection with anything which preceded or followed it, unless specifically so stated.[9]

By no stretch of words could these arrangements, even if dignified with the name 'system', be described as a legislative process. They were all highly intermittent and *ad hoc*; such regulations as issued from them were specific in the extreme, and almost invariably bore no general reference, in the sense of binding the parties in similar situations in future; and there was hardly any sense that the affairs of a community were being regulated by them. Some change in this state of affairs occurred as the nineteenth century became the twentieth. On 24 August 1898 Nicholas II of Russia startled the world of officialdom by proposing a general international conference to consider two general subjects, disarmament and the peaceful settlement of international disputes, and on 18 May of the following year representatives of twenty-six states, including the United States and Mexico, duly assembled at The Hague, the first conference to have some resemblance to an international legislature.

The Hague conference's efforts to make progress with multilateral disarmament were a dismal failure – the first of an endless succession of failures – but a convention was adopted on the laws and customs of war (the launching of missiles from balloons was placed under a ban, though needless to say, without provision for enforcement), arrangements were set in motion for commissions of inquiry (entirely voluntary, it goes without saying) when disputes arose between states – it was under this procedure that the serious dispute between Britain and Russia arising out of the firing by Russian naval vessels on British trawlers on the Dogger Bank in October 1904 was settled – and, most importantly, a framework for arbitration in the resolution of international differences was agreed. The latter, the greatest achievement of the conference, took three forms: the spelling out of the general rules of arbitration; the formation of a Permanent Court of Arbitration, in reality a panel to which each signatory state was to nominate four judges to serve for six years, and from which states in dispute could select two judges each to act in a particular case, and the four judges would then appoint a fifth to serve as an umpire; and the establishment of an administrative bureau, with a council to supervise it, and a permanent staff to keep records and conduct correspondence. The bureau was to be situated in the Dutch capital and the permanent staff was an early contribution to the development of an international civil service.

A second world conference, this time consisting of representatives of forty-four states, including sixteen countries which now joined Mexico to form a Latin American contingent, met at The Hague from 15 June until 18 October 1907, and

discussed such questions as the banning of force in the collection of
international debts (a matter of great interest in Latin America,
Venezuela having been the victim of a notorious debt-collecting
expedition in 1902), the establishment of an international court of
appeal in prize cases, the immunity of private property at sea in
wartime, and the formation of a standing court of arbitration with
regular sessions to supplement the panel of arbitrators created at
the 1899 meetings. On a large number of these issues, of course,
including the last, a consensus did not appear. However, it was
intended to hold a third Hague conference in 1914, but the war
intervened.[10]

Although these tentative first steps towards a continuing
legislative process in the international system were halted by the
First World War, it should not be forgotten that the war itself,
being an act of international relations of a most violent form, also
gave a considerable impetus to international organisation, as it was
bound to do. The fact that it was a world war, that it was waged on
several fronts and in several countries at the same time and
involved the belligerents in efforts to deny the seas all over the
globe to the other side, and that it was carried on for a number of
years by coalitions of nations which combined all their resources
for the struggle, imposed on the war-making nations a degree of
confederation unknown to previous history. Complex agencies
had to be established on both sides for co-ordinating strategy and
the efficient use of resources. It took time for this co-operative
machinery to be established and the habit of running the nation's
affairs unilaterally died hard. But by 1918, certainly on the
Entente side, international organisation was well advanced. At the
head stood the Supreme War Council, with its various committees
and sub-committees, created in December 1917, on which sat
Ministers, including heads of government, of Britain, France,
Italy, and, on occasion, the United States and Japan. The military
forces of the Entente were integrated under one supreme
commander-in-chief, Marshal Foch. The Supreme War Council
became the Supreme Council with the transition to peace, and
this, together with a parallel body, the Conference of Ambassadors
of the Allied Powers, carried the conference system into the 1920s
as the Entente states grappled with the problems of implementing
the peace they had made and guiding the war-torn world back to
recovery.

The various inter-Allied agencies and commissions formed to
supervise the distribution of scarce resources during the war did

not, however, survive the conflict, and neither did the organisations set up within the belligerent states to control their wartime economic systems. De-control became the watchword at home and abroad once the fighting stopped. One of the most important of the wartime international agencies was the Allied Shipping Control, managed by an executive council representing the Entente Powers, which sat in London and exercised exclusive control of all Allied maritime transport during the war and rationed it out in accordance with an internationally determined scheme of priorities.[11] No merchant vessel belonging to a national of the Allied Powers during the war could move an inch without the Shipping Control's agreement. Never had the international management of the resources of several countries been developed to such an extent.

managing int. vessels

III

possible thesis

This was internationalism forged by the heat of battle, most of it lasting no longer than the actual emergency. The nineteenth-century system, as we have seen, was a slower growth and the elements of it which survived the war consequently more enduring. The congresses and conferences through which it expressed itself intermittently produced agreements which enjoyed the status of international law, with all the limitations of that legal system. The principle of the equal sovereignty of states, certainly of the great Powers, was central to it: they could not be bound without their express consent, and that consent had to be interpreted in the most restrictive sense. There was no question of sanctions in the event of an agreement being violated. All that the violator would suffer as a rule was the temporary withdrawal of the goodwill of other states, and perhaps some reprisal from the state the rights of which had been violated, though both could be considerable penalties. There was no standing court of law to which alleged infractions of international law could be referred, and no enforcement agencies for implementing the awards of such irregular tribunals as existed, these being entirely dependent upon the will of the states party to them. It is remarkable in these circumstances that international legal engagements were complied with as much as they were. Indeed, the record of states for conformity with their international legal obligations was on the whole probably better before 1914 than it was at any time afterwards, one reason for this being the absence in the pre-war system of any great state committed to the overthrow of the social order in the rest of the world, like Soviet Russia after 1917 or Nazi Germany in the 1930s. The violation by Germany in August 1914 of the Treaty of London of April 1839, which guaranteed the integrity and neutrality of Belgium, was greeted with a sense of horror in the 'civilised world' (that term still being in general usage) which would have been considered unusual at almost any time since then. The admission by the German Kaiser that he had broken the treaty, but that he did so owing to the force of necessity, would sound positively old-fashioned today, though Allied public opinion at that time believed that it symbolised the very barbarism they had taken up arms to fight.

When disagreements arose between the Powers about points of law, or about anything else, there were devices which could be resorted to for settling the issue before the 'sword was unsheathed'. There was the routine process of diplomacy, perhaps supplemented by a meeting of Ministers of the two states. There could be an appeal to other states, or to a distinguished international figure, such as a King or a President, to provide their good offices or to act as a mediator, with the possibility of their guaranteeing the settlement, when accepted by the two parties, and of taking appropriate action if it was later disturbed. Or the disputing parties could resort to arbitration, a quasi-judicial proceeding which developed continuously throughout the nineteenth century, especially in the Anglo-Saxon world, until it culminated, as we have seen, in the foundation of a permanent court of arbitration (though that name is highly misleading) at the first Hague conference in 1899.[12]

Arbitration is quasi-judicial in the sense that the arbitrator chosen by the two states was generally a qualified and distinguished lawyer, or a team of lawyers, but he did not have to be. The parties could choose anyone. In July 1896 Queen Victoria accepted the office of arbitrator if the need arose from Argentina and Chile and in November 1898 the two states submitted a boundary dispute to her, whereupon she appointed a tribunal, which included one judge. When the Queen died in January 1901, the task was taken over by Edward VII, who issued an award in November 1902. It is significant, however, that in 1964, when Argentina and Chile made another appeal to Britain to arbitrate a boundary dispute in accordance with Article 5 of their General Treaty of Arbitration concluded in 1902, the appeal was to the British Government, not to the Queen personally, though the

14

award itself, when issued in 1966, was in the Queen's name. The British Government, again, appointed an arbitral tribunal, consisting of lawyers and geographers.[13]

Arbitration is also quasi-judicial in the sense that the rule to be applied is traditionally 'respect for law', and not necessarily law itself. The authoritative Institute of International Law, founded in 1873, promulgated a widely accepted set of model rules for arbitral tribunals two years later, in which international arbitration was defined as having for its object 'the settlement of differences between states by judges of their own choice' – that is to say, not by a formal or standing court of law – 'and on the basis of respect for law'. The latter phrase has generally been interpreted to mean that the arbitrator's award should not be at variance with international law (unless the parties explicitly charge him with proposing changes in the law, which, if accepted, might become valid, though only as between the parties); but, if the law was vague (and it almost always was, and, to a large extent, still is), the arbitrator was considered free to interpret it in the light of natural justice and equity. But, of course, this must be said always in the light of the overriding principle of international arbitration before 1914, namely, that it was always dependent upon the will of the parties, which is another way of saying the will of the more intransigent of the two parties.

There could be no question of arbitration at all unless both parties consented, and unless they agreed on the rules to be applied, on the point to be submitted to the arbitrator, and on the status of his award when it was finally rendered. Above all, the parties had to agree on who the arbitrator would be; even after the establishment of a general panel of arbitrators at the Hague conference in 1899, there was nothing to prevent states going outside it and choosing others. And there was no suggestion that the arbitrator's award, when the whole process ended, should be ipso facto mandatory. The parties had still to decide what to do with it, though they might if they wished bind themselves in advance to regard it as mandatory. As a general rule, it was a recommendation only, and moreover it referred only to the particular dispute in question. Whereas in England, for example, the law is considered to be that which the courts have decided, before 1914 the great Powers vehemently denied (or would have denied had anyone been foolhardy enough to put the question to them) that their hands were tied by what their arbitrators had decided. If that had been the position, it is doubtful whether they would ever have gone to arbitration, and whether there would have been any arbitration.

But there was, and the volume of it grew throughout the century. By 1914 one hundred arbitration treaties were in force; in the twenty years between 1880 and 1900 alone, ninety arbitration treaties between different states were signed.[14] The biggest contributor by far was Britain, with its vast diplomatic and commercial contacts with other countries, all fertile soil for altercation. Next came the United States, a country of law and lawyers par excellence, a neutral throughout almost all the century and hence involved in many disputes with different belligerents about the rights of neutrals, and having endless controversies with Latin American countries about the security of the persons and property of its own nationals in those countries. The United States was an active participant in the two Hague conferences, President Roosevelt taking the place for a time of Nicholas II of Russia in calling together the second Hague conference. It concluded a score of agreements with other countries before the First World War, the so-called Bryan Treaties, named after President Woodrow Wilson's Secretary of State, not, strictly speaking, for arbitration, but for the creation of standing International Commissions of Inquiry empowered to issue reports on disputes between the United States and the other country, which, however, the parties, in accordance with the universal rule, were not obliged to accept.

As early as 1794, the United States concluded a General Treaty of Friendship, Commerce and Navigation with Britain, the so-called Jay treaty, after the then American Secretary of State, John Jay, and during the following ten years questions between the two countries left over from the War of American Independence were settled by arbitration. Similarly, the Treaty of Ghent of 1814, which ended the war between Britain and the United States which began in 1812, provided for four arbitrations on territorial questions. The most celebrated arbitration between the two countries, however, was the *Alabama* Claims case, in which a composite tribunal sitting in Geneva in 1871 and 1872 fixed British liability for damage done by vessels which had escaped from British ports during the American civil war and had been fitted out elsewhere as Confederate cruisers. The *Alabama* case gave the most powerful impetus to arbitration as a method of settling disputes between nations. It should be said, however, that by the mid-century many minds were turning more and more towards the problem of giving more regular form to procedures for resolving international disputes without resort to force. One interesting example of this was the protocol of the Treaty of Paris, signed in April 1856 between Austria, Britain, France, Prussia, Russia, Sardinia and Turkey, which concluded the Crimean War. This was in the form of a wish that 'States, between which any serious misunderstanding may arise, should, before appealing to Arms, have recourse, as far as circumstances might allow, to the Good Offices of a friendly Power'.[15] It is significant that this provision was suggested by the British Government, and at the end of a war in which, for the first time in modern history, the sufferings of soldiers who became casualties were brought home to the public by the press.

IV

The machinery we have described, such as it was, for the management of international affairs in pre-war years was complemented, especially after 1860, by a proliferation of international gatherings and of more or less permanent associations, some formed by governments, but most of them resulting from private enterprise, such as that of businessmen, traders and professional people, as contacts between states developed and trade multiplied, especially with the rapid improvement in transport and communications. In the century following the final defeat of Napoleon at Waterloo, no less than 450 private, non-governmental organisations, many of them short-lived, came into being, as compared with thirty formed by governments. The growth of international fairs and exhibitions, like the Great Exhibition in London in 1851, gave a strong fillip to such unofficial internationalism. Between 1840 and the outbreak of war in 1914, 2,897 international gatherings, the overwhelming majority being private in sponsorship, were recorded.[16] Not surprisingly, some of the most important continuing organisations of this kind were in the communications and transport field. Their typical pattern of organisation was threefold – the periodic conference, the permanent committee or commission, and the bureau, with a small permanent staff, in some convenient international centre, such as Berne, Brussels, London or Paris. *La vie internationale* of industry, trade and the arts thrived and multiplied, while the great Powers, who were to make the ultimate decisions, surveyed each other through their visors, like medieval knights in the jousting field.[17]

In Paris in 1865 a conference of twenty states met to draw up a convention to bring together the telegraph administrations of signatory countries; it was revised at a meeting in St Petersburg in 1875. An administrative bureau was set up in Berne in 1869, and by 1911 the convention, which aimed at co-ordinating the telegraph services of member-states, recommending uniform charges and regulations, and so on, embraced forty-eight states and colonies, though not the United States, where telegraph services were not under federal control. Radiotelegraphy was dealt with by an international convention concluded at Berlin in 1906. By far the greatest achievement in this field, however, was the establishment of the General Postal Union on 1 July 1875 by a convention adopted by a Postal Congress at Berne in October 1874. The General Postal Union, which became the still surviving Universal Postal Union in 1878, had the effect of creating a 'single postal territory for the reciprocal exchange of correspondence', which in effect meant the abolition of national frontiers as far as postal services were concerned. It has been said that the Postal Union 'marked a successful invasion of the jealously guarded territory of national sovereignty. And this invasion was successful because the services which the union provided were so valuable that no state with any pretensions to civilisation could afford to stay outside'.[18] That is undoubtedly true, although those who looked on the UPU as a model which the world might follow in other fields tended to overlook the fact that postal services are without the emotional overtones affecting the great political issues from which the collisions of nations spring.

[handwritten margin note: mail is not emotional or political. not a formula for int. co-existence]

Similar enterprises, though not always with the special advantages which made for success as blessed the Postal Union, appeared in the field of rail, road and river transport. In 1890 a 'convention internationale sur le transport de marchandise par chemins de fer' was signed by nine states, though Britain was not one of them, applying to goods traffic only. An international meeting on automobile transport was held in Paris in 1909 and made arrangements for the issue to drivers of certificates permitting them to travel from one country to another. As for rivers, as far back as 1815 the Congress of Vienna, in Article 109 of its Final Act, laid down the principle of freedom of commerce on international rivers, though many difficulties arose in its practical implementation. Two conventions were agreed for the Rhine: the Convention of Mayence of 1831, followed by the Convention of Mannheim in 1868, which survived after the First World War, though not without many complaints about discrimination against them of non-riparian states. The Treaty of Paris in 1856 dealt in Articles 15 to 19 with freedom of navigation on the Danube, which could not have been the subject of international legislation earlier since its lower reaches were controlled by Turkey. Two commissions were created to operate the regime agreed for the river. As for the Congo, this was the subject of a special act of navigation formulated at the Berlin conference in 1884, and by means of this, similar arrangements for ensuring freedom of use of the river and its general maintenance were to be supervised by the five Powers having jurisdiction over territory along the banks of the Congo.

These examples of international administration in the field of transport and communications – and the same applies to such bodies as the influential Permanent Sugar Commission established in 1902 by fourteen sugar-beet producing countries and Britain to restrict subsidised sugar-beet production in the interests of cane sugar producers – existed on a plane apart from the high politics of the great Powers which were enacted in the congresses and conferences discussed earlier in this chapter. The same is true of all the private international organisations, from commercial to academic, political to philanthropic, which sprang into being in Europe in the 1880s and 1890s. It was not that monarchs and their Ministers shut their eyes to the vast expansion of buying and selling, the moving of goods, people and money across national boundaries, which was transforming Europe into a single community. Such matters as international cables and, later, radio had unmistakable diplomatic and strategic implications which governments could not ignore. But the rule in the nineteenth century, by and large, was for politics to run in one channel and business in another. The businessman, in a period of prosperous, expanding production and trade, did not welcome government interference, even that of his own government, in his affairs. Much less did he want international conferences, swarming with foreigners, doing so. He might want to form business connections with Frenchmen or Germans, but that would be a matter strictly under his own control, and theirs. Moreover, in Western Europe the political writers known to the business community, if not always read by it, the philosophers, for instance, of the 'Manchester School', taught that manufacturing, trading, making money, formed the essence of the 'real' world, whereas the political arena was an impostor, a relic from the remote ages of war and militarism, which would in due course 'wither away' before the logic of modern technology, as that enemy of capitalist business, albeit a child of nineteenth-century liberalism, Friedrich Engels, forecast.

This separation of the world of politics from the world of business which characterised the international system before 1914 was possible because the European economy was for the most part self-managed and successful, and as yet needed no assistance from the state, or at least very little. There were, of course, exceptions. In Germany in the 1880s, the state did involve itself in the protection of industry from foreign competition and in the provision of social insurance. The Germans thought that the full rigours of *laissez-faire* were only for the successful, who, like the British, had made an early start in the industrial race. But, in the main, and until the depressions of the late 1880s, the economic system was steered by a 'hidden hand'; or at least that was the prevailing orthodoxy. This was the age of the Gold Standard, when countries losing gold through an excess of imports over exports automatically contracted their internal purchasing power through discreet action by the banking authorities, and countries gaining gold as a result of an excess of exports over imports automatically expanded internal purchasing power through equal and opposite action of their banking authorities. The effects were that debtor countries sold more abroad because their prices fell, and bought less, because they had less money to spend, and creditors did the opposite, and righted their balance of payments for the opposite reasons. The system worked as a rule because the adjustments called for to redress the imbalances lay within margins of the practicable. Ministers and diplomats, from Talleyrand and the Duke of Wellington at the beginning of the hundred years between 1815 and 1914 to Sir Edward Grey and Bethmann Hollweg at the end of it, did not need to talk to each other about trade and employment because such matters created no problems, and in any case neither businessmen nor workers were as yet well enough organised to make difficulties about them even if they did.[19]

V

Such was the machinery of international affairs in Europe, the only theatre of those affairs, before the League existed. After 1918 it was almost universally condemned as fragmentary, intermittent and irresponsibly voluntaristic. But the politics carried on by means of this machinery were condemned even more, and often for reasons which later generations come to think of as strengths rather than weaknesses. It was socially exclusive through and through, and, what was more, élitist. The ordinary man or woman might bellow patriotic songs in music-halls when the war drums sounded, or gape at foreign rulers when they came visiting, but the affairs of nations were carried on in throne rooms and Cabinets, in embassies and chancelleries, without regard to them, and without much regard either for the minor members of the international cast, the smaller states. These might enjoy a purely titular equality but were in reality merely pawns in the game, shielded from the rapacity of one great Power only by becoming totally subservient to another. Even educated people in the big European states (outside governing circles) were uninvolved in high diplomacy, and had no wish that it should be otherwise. The business world seemed to go on well enough on its own, until it all collapsed in 1914. The work of the decision-making elites was not thrown open to public scrutiny. International agreements were not disclosed as a matter of course, even when they committed the people of a country to lay down their lives in hypothetical circumstances known only to the monarch. On occasion, a ruler or Minister might see fit to use the newspapers to disseminate information, true or false, which he thought might serve his ends. Bismarck's use of the famous touched-up Ems telegram in 1870 to stir German opinion against Napoleon III is a notorious example. But no-one imagined that monarchs or their servants had any obligation to tell their people anything about their international affairs. The agreements reached between Britain and France on military co-operation before 1914 were not even disclosed to the British Cabinet.

The system also rested on that other exclusive principle, national sovereignty, which meant that every government, whatever the internal constitution of the country, was absolute master within its own territory, the borders of which were guarded with hoops of steel. The sharpest distinction was drawn between internal and external affairs, and the former was the exclusive preserve of the sovereign. At the beginning of the nineteenth century, as we have seen, disagreements on this principle arose between the three Eastern Courts, on one side, and Britain and France, on the other; the former argued for a right of intervention in states in which the monarchical system was threatened, the latter disagreed. But the Eastern Courts never wished to elevate intervention into a general principle which might at some time operate against themselves. They wanted to intervene in other states in order to prevent them (or revolutionary regimes which might take them over) intervening against themselves. In any case, Austria, Prussia and Russia lost the argument, and Britain, the dominant Power for most of the century, helped to establish the general rule that the state is a house with doors locked against the outsider, unless he is expressly permitted to enter.

The state's independence, theoretically asserted in the doctrine of sovereignty, was in practice ensured by two instruments: its own armed forces, nourished by the country's economic strength and supported by the skill it showed in diplomacy, and the resources of its allies. The use of force to defend a state's independence, to discourage attack and strengthen the state's point of view in argument with other states, was not regarded as wrong or retrogressive by the ruling circles of the day, however much it might be condemned by the peace societies which burgeoned in Europe and the United States in the late nineteenth century.[20] On the contrary, it was the normal, time-honoured practice, to which prestige and a sense of almost knightly honour was attached. War still had glamour about it, and the Powers did not hesitate to 'draw the sword' if interest or reputation demanded it: the military uniforms of the day, splendid and colourful, symbolised the custom of war. To fight effectively, however, and to deter when it was not expedient to fight, allies were necessary, and so, as the century before 1914 drew to a close, Europe was divided into the great armed coalitions which eventually slithered into the pit.

Prominent in the great alliances of the times was the Dual Alliance of Germany and Austria-Hungary, formed in 1879 and joined by Italy in 1882 to create the Triple Alliance, then reverting to its original form when Italy withdrew and joined the Entente forces ranged against her former friends in 1915. On the other side stood the formidable Franco-Russian alliance of the early 1890s, cemented with French loans and intended to hem in Germany from two sides. And there was the extraordinary Anglo-Japanese alliance of 1902, renewed in 1905 and again in 1911. For the first time, a European great Power, the greatest of them all, Britain, reached out across the world and made an agreement with an Asian state, totally unknown until then in world affairs, in order to redress the balance in Europe. For the first time, conflicts between the Powers in Europe could not be resolved by any rearrangement of the weights in the balance in Europe itself. Well might the observer in 1902 have concluded that he had seen the beginning of the end of the European system.[21]

The fact that the European alliances formed in the last two decades of the nineteenth century provided limbs of the confrontation which constituted the First World War utterly discredited the alliance system in the eyes of the generation which fought the war. The alliance system, and the principle of the balance of power through which the alliance system worked, were widely held accountable for the tragedy of the war. Viscount Cecil, one of the best known supporters of the League of Nations in Britain, wrote that,

> The Balance of Power was purely negative. It did not aim at improving the common life of nations. It accepted the proposition that every nation was the potential enemy of every other nation, and it merely sought to limit the consequences of that disastrous assumption.[22]

Only through the root-and-branch renunciation of the alliance system and the balance-of-power principle could peace be secured.

Yet the balance of power, evil though its name became, was originally a commonsense, even inevitable arrangement. If there are five (or six) great Powers of roughly equal strength, it is inescapable that none of them should want to feel isolated, whatever it wishes to achieve in its foreign policy. A state may not want to impose its will on another, but it must strive at all costs to avoid having the will of another state imposed on itself. This can only be done by having friends, and this in its turn led to the golden rule of nineteenth-century foreign policy: avoid being one or two out of five, try to be three or four out of five. That is what the balance of power, in its simplest terms, means, and in order to form the three or four, or merely the two (if one has to be satisfied with being two), alliances, embodied in a solemn treaty, and perhaps with provision for military co-operation, are practically unavoidable. The trouble is that the structure of alliances tends to become ossified, and friends grow to think that they must stick together, even when prudent considerations point in quite another direction.

In the revulsion against the system of international management described in this chapter, which followed the end of hostilities in 1918, two assumptions about it were made which could be questioned, though in fact they rarely were. One was that the arrangements for managing the business of states before 1914 were woefully patchy and unfinished, and that they had disastrously failed in 1914 for that reason. The other was that the system maximised divisiveness and conflict between the Powers. By reserving the management of international affairs exclusively to a few states, and a minority within those states, the system placed a premium upon ambition, intrigue, acquisitiveness, plotting and planning with the object of advancing one state to the detriment of another. In the words of the Swiss international lawyer, William E. Rappard, writing after the war,

> Whatever future historians may finally decide about the notorious war-guilt question, which so dangerously continues to poison the international atmosphere even today, one thing is certain: the real culprit, whose historic responsibility will always overshadow the vanity, the stupidity and the wickedness of individual statesmen, is the pre-war system of international relations.[23] *pre-emptive strategy*

These were grave charges, providing much of the intellectual basis of the League idea after 1918, especially in the liberal-democratic states. It is doubtful, however, whether more or better machinery for international co-operation could in itself have prevented war in 1914, or could have prevented the war that broke out then from being as destructive as it was. The long peace of the nineteenth century, it seems, rested on certain political and economic foundations which made such adjustments as were necessary between the different states relatively easy to achieve, even with the rudimentary machinery that existed for making them. One of these foundations was the vast economic expansion of Europe, giving men and women, for a time at least, even more exciting things to think about and do than war, and the previous war, waged with revolutionary France from 1792 until 1815, was still too fresh in the memory for most of the century to make another one welcome just yet. Another factor was the all-pervasive, *Britian* thoroughly bourgeois influence of Britain, with its huge stake in *cutting down* peace and stability, its determination to cut adventurous rivals *rivals* down to size and its control of the financial resources to do so, its = naval forces reaching all over the world, its fingers in every pie *fear* everywhere. It was factors like these which made such machinery for international relations as there was work, not the other way round. And if the great Powers ever wanted more machinery, they could easily have created it: at the time they felt they had all the machinery they wanted. It was not machinery which was lacking in 1914 but the willingness to use it. The British Foreign Secretary, Sir Edward Grey, called for another meeting of the Concert of Europe to deal with the crisis of 1914, but Germany, for one, would not listen.

When war came in 1914, factors far more important than the lack of international machinery led towards that result: the over-topping growth in German power, which the European equation of forces was unable to contain, and the vein of reckless bravado in Germany's ruler; the long- nurtured lust for vengeance in France, the zeal of Russia to redeem itself in the Balkans; the filling in of many of the open spaces overseas, where the great Powers used to compensate one another by cessions of territory and so ease the tensions between them; the boiling conflicts of nationalism in the Balkans and the Austro-Hungarian Empire; the social hatreds engendered by industrialism; the slowing down, and in some countries the temporary arrest, of economic expansion; the decline and end-of-century harassments of Britain, the great pacifier, leading to her fear of isolation and scurrying into alliances. Such developments placed a strain on the system, just as the peace-biassed forces of nineteenth-century Europe kept the system in balance before 1914, despite the paucity of machinery.

But was the old system so wicked after all? It was permeated with privilege, certainly: privileged rich against unprivileged poor, privileged Europeans against the rest of the world. It was tolerant of the use of force, even glorifying the martial arts, though in its defence it could be said that the force then available to states was minuscule, compared with the unleashed fury of the Great War. It did not, as a rule, mix moral fervour with politics: statesmen seemed more frank, at least between themselves, as to what they feared and what they sought, and they worried rather less about the rights and wrongs of it. At the same time, governments knew that the game they played was for limited stakes. The objects of diplomacy were usually confined to the 'rectification' of a frontier or the 'recovery' of a lost province. The age of building a thousand-year Reich or leading humanity into its final inheritance of peace and freedom was not yet. Yet men were, in a strange way, more hopeful, and also less hateful when their hopes were not realised.

2 Framing the Covenant

As the First World War settled down into a seemingly endless 'blood test' and minds turned towards the creation of some effective machinery to prevent a repetition of the holocaust, it was realised that, in Europe at least, philosophers, and sometimes statesmen, too, had entertained visions of leagues and pacts to stop war since the fall of the Roman Empire. But these had been for the most part insubstantial dreams which offered little in the way of practical guidance. Inevitably, if a start was to be made after the war on forming some permanent agency to keep the peace, the existing machinery, unsatisfactory as it was, would have to be taken as a starting point. As a result, three ideas were bound to dominate wartime thinking about the future maintenance of peace. First, the system of arbitration would have to be made more effective, if possible by the provision of some kind of penalty or sanction against states which resorted to force without submitting their disputes with other states to arbitration or without complying with an arbitral award which had been given. Secondly, the intermittent conference system of the nineteenth century would have to take on a more formal and on-going character, and perhaps be used as a means of third-party settlement in international disputes for which arbitration was for one reason or another unsuitable. And thirdly, these two systems must be exploited for bringing about a pause or delay in the development of a dispute, so as to prevent that kind of helpless slithering into war which many believed had occurred in August 1914. Enthusiasts might want to go further than this and mould the new 'league of nations' into a 'parliament of man', the institutional framework for the interdependent community which had grown up in Europe in the late nineteenth century, but these three principles were the irreducible minimum, and it was on these that discussion centred as the Great War went on.

Study of the problem began, significantly, among private individuals and organisations in the Anglo-Saxon world in 1915, and even when the League idea was adopted and given material form by governments, it remained essentially an Anglo-Saxon affair. A meeting of American professors initiated by Hamilton Holt and William B. Howland at the Century Club in New York on 25 January 1915 began the argument about a future League by laying down two principles: that of 'insisting upon and guaranteeing the amicable settlement of disputes between member-states,' and that of 'guaranteeing the territorial integrity and the sovereignty of League members as against outside parties'.[1] Thus, from the very outset, a basic divergence between the American and the British approach to peace-keeping manifested itself, in that British protagonists of the League were never happy with the transatlantic insistence upon the exchange of guarantees of the *status quo* implicit in the second of these principles. This did not prevent the American group forming contacts with their counterparts in Britain, however, especially with a study group in London led by James (Viscount) Bryce, formerly Chief Secretary for Ireland in the Liberal government of 1905 and ambassador to Washington from 1907 until 1913. Bryce's London group, an outstanding member of which was G. Lowes Dickinson, produced a plan for a League which drew the famous distinction, which the New York group accepted, between justiciable and non-justiciable disputes: the former were to come before a new international legal tribunal, the latter before a Council of Conciliation, a refurbished form of the old Concert of Europe. The Bryce proposals were adopted by the British League of Nations Society, founded in May 1915, and became the centrepiece of its programme.[2]

On 9 April the American group took a major step forward in proposing that the new world organisation should use force, though how that was to be organised and applied was left undefined, to compel a disputant state to go to court, though, strangely, not to enforce the court's award.[3] Two months later, at a meeting in Independence Hall, Philadelphia, the group constituted itself as the League to Enforce Peace, thus incorporating the sanctions idea in its title.[4] Its first president was William Howard Taft, a former President of the United States.

Efforts were at once made to secure the support of Woodrow Wilson, elected President of the United States in November 1912 and again in 1916, but he held aloof, though known to be a fervent supporter of the League idea. On 27 May 1916, however, while America was still at peace, he at length gave his blessing to the League to Enforce Peace by addressing its meeting in Washington, thus becoming the first world statesman to give the idea of a League of Nations after the war his official approval.[5]

At the end of 1916, with a new term of office before him, Wilson stepped into the ring at the beginning of his campaign for the new world body. On 8 December, he issued his famous appeal to the belligerents in the war for what he called 'soundings', that is, indications of their objects in the conflict, which he claimed had never been made clear.[6] The Entente Powers, in their joint reply of 10 January 1917, gave their support to the League idea, provided its constitution was protected by forcible sanctions, and that seemed a direct bid for Wilson's sympathy. It is a curious fact, however, that, despite his passionate commitment to the League idea and his demand that it should form an integral part of the peace settlement, Wilson never took the lead in framing detailed proposals for the new organisation. He was more skilled in re-shaping other people's plans, couching them in felicitous language and throwing behind them his immense authority.

Accordingly, the first officially sponsored draft of the Covenant of the future League (though the word 'Covenant' was characteristically Wilson's brainchild) was in fact produced in Britain. Shortly after the formation of the coalition government under David Lloyd George in December 1916, the Minister of Blockade in that administration, Lord Robert Cecil of Chelwood, suggested to Foreign Secretary A. J. Balfour the setting up of a small committee to inquire, 'particularly from a juridical and historical point of view, into the various schemes for establishing by means of a League of Nations, or other device, some alternative to war as a means of settling international disputes', and, if they thought fit, 'to elaborate a further scheme'. The conspicuous pragmatism of these terms of reference was in the British tradition: the League was to stop war, not to try its hand at running world affairs.

When the committee was finally appointed – it was not until February 1918 – it turned out to be unsurprisingly conservative and legal both in composition and outlook. Mr Balfour did not want intellectual fireworks or ambitious schemes of international reform and did not get them. The committee's chairman, Sir Walter (later Lord) Phillimore, who gave his name to the committee, was a judge known for his authority in international law but not otherwise distinguished. The other members included Professor Pollard, a constitutional historian, two naval historians (perhaps reflecting the government's concern about the possibility of losing control of the fleet to the new League), and three Foreign Office heavy-weights, Sir Eyre Crowe, Sir William (later Lord) Tyrrell and Cecil (later Sir Cecil) Hurst, the Office's legal adviser.

The Phillimore committee's recommendations, which were completed by 20 March, were in accordance with its composition: they were conservative, orthodox and minimal. They were also in line with the British view, so much at variance with that of the country's continental neighbours, that the war was an accident due to miscalculation and could have been avoided had there been procedures for inquiry and delay. Accordingly, Article 1 of the Phillimore plan formed a commitment by signatory states not to resort to war without submitting the matter in dispute to arbitration or to inquiry by a 'conference of Allied states', or until an arbitral award or report by the conference had been issued, and in any case not to go to war against any state which complied with the award or report. These commitments, which by that time were part of the common stock of ideas about the peaceful settlement of disputes on both sides of the Atlantic, clearly did not rule out war in all circumstances. War would still be legal if no agreed award or report was issued, or if waged against any country which did not comply with an award or report if one were issued.

Article 2 of the plan then contained the proposals for sanctions in the event of a breach of the first article, that is, in the event of an illegal resort to war. A signatory state making war in these circumstances would be deemed *ipso facto* to be at war with all other members of the organisation, and they would be bound to take all the necessary financial, economic and ultimately naval and military measures to bring the emergency to an end. The plan then went on to specify how it was to be decided which disputes should go to arbitration and which should be referred to the conference procedure, in other words which should be considered 'political' and which 'legal'. In doing so, the plan gave birth to the famous definition of legal issues which later found its way into the League Covenant. This classified such issues as involving 'the interpretation of a treaty, any question of international law, the existence of any fact which, if established, would constitute a breach of an international obligation, or the nature and extent of reparation for any such breach'. It was conceded in the following article (Article 4), however, that, if for any reason arbitration is not practicable, any state (and this could conceivably refer to a state not actually involved in the dispute) should have the right to refer the matter to a conference of allied states. The phraseology is not entirely clear, but the meaning would seem to be that a party to a dispute could, if it wished, opt to bring its dispute before the conference rather than a panel of arbitrators, thus rendering arbitration 'not practicable'.

This scheme for a League bore not the slightest resemblance to a super-state: it proposed the minimum interference with the traditional rights of sovereign states in the form of a slight extension of the existing practice of arbitration and the conference system. Member-states would not entirely renounce the right of war. The 'conference of Allied States' was not even to have regular meetings; as in the pre-1914 system, it was to be summoned as occasion required. By Article 8 of the plan, resolutions of the conference were to have recommendatory force only. The arrangements for sanctions did indeed suggest centralised action against wrong-doers, but they were not in the form of a sort of police power over and above the states. Sanctions would come into effect, in the event of an outbreak of illegal war, in the form of member-states blackballing one of their number who had happened to break the rules. The notion of a well-run club was persistent; the spirit of Pall Mall permeated the Phillimore report.[7]

In May 1918, after an interval for study, the British government forwarded the report to Washington, but did not present it as their own plan; in fact, at no time did Britain officially present any plan of its own for a League of Nations – the Phillimore proposals were supposed to be merely a 'basis for discussion'. The French government, on the other hand, was less self-effacing in throwing its full weight behind a plan of its own committee, which was presented to Wilson at the same time. In particular, the French government left no doubt that it stood foursquare behind its committee's insistence upon effective sanctions and the creation of an international force to implement them; for this, the French committee's chairman, the ageing and distinguished jurist and former Prime Minister, Léon Bourgeois, was later to fight so tenaciously, though unsuccessfully, at the Paris peace conference. President Wilson did not warm to the idea of an international force, which would raise almost impossible constitutional problems for the United States. With democratically responsible governments in all major states in the future, Wilson thought, the peace-biassed pressure of world public opinion would be a powerful enough restraint against aggression, and if it was not, the economic sanctions which were proving so effective in Entente hands against the Central Powers would do the rest. But neither did the President much like the Phillimore scheme, which he said 'did not at all meet the requirements of the situation', despite the fact that elements of the scheme were embodied in all the four draft plans for the League Covenant which he later prepared.

The Phillimore scheme displeased Wilson mainly because of its omission of the mutual guarantees which formed the core of his own conception of the League. It is surprising that the British authorities, who were willing to satisfy practically all Wilson's other wishes in the matter of the League, should evidently not have foreseen his objections to any proposals which left out his own most important requirement, the mutual exchange of territorial guarantees. After all, he had made it well enough known. The culmination of his famous Fourteen Points address before Congress of 8 January 1918 was the statement that 'a general association of nations must be formed under specific covenants for the purpose of affording international guarantees of political independence and territorial integrity to great and small states alike'. He had repeated and elaborated the point in many other pronouncements. Moreover, the idea of guarantees accorded with the arrangements he had proposed to make with the Latin American states in the form of a General Pact of Peace, had the European war not intervened. This is not to say that, as a world-wide scheme, it would not raise overwhelming questions for the United States. Would it mean, for example, that in the sort of League Wilson desired European countries would join in a general guarantee of the independence and territory of states in the Western hemisphere, and, if so, how would that affect the Monroe Doctrine of 1823, which forbade European intervention in the Americas? But such questions did not seem to shake the President's determination to make the guarantee system the core of his League proposals.

The British never liked the idea of general guarantees and studiously omitted it from all suggestions about the future League which the government endorsed. In Lloyd George's speech to Labour delegates at Caxton Hall in London on 5 January 1918, the first detailed outline of war aims to be given by a senior British

Minister, delivered three days before Wilson's Fourteen Points address, there was a vague reference to 'some international organisation after the war', which would have as its task 'to limit the burden of armaments and diminish the probability of war'. But the idea of Britain, then the greatest world Power, underwriting the *status quo* all over the globe was never in prospect. Britain would have far too much on her hands looking after her dispersed and now restless empire, which was likely to increase with the peace settlement, to take on the protection of every other country. Many new states were likely to come into existence, especially in Eastern Europe, with the defeat of the Central Powers, and it was most unlikely that Britain, who had found herself in one terrible war as a result of her guarantee to Belgium in 1839, would want to guarantee all these unknown countries, with their as yet unknown frontiers, against aggression from an unknown quarter. Besides, life was continually in flux and the League, a wholly untried experiment, could hardly begin its existence with a pledge to keep things exactly as they were on the day of its birth.

This last difficulty about guarantees seems also to have occurred to Wilson's aide and confidante, Colonel House, his former campaign manager, when Wilson asked him in the summer of 1918 to draw up a scheme for a League of Nations in view of the President's dissatisfaction both with the Phillimore plan and the French proposals. The plan drafted by House, called 'Suggestions for a Covenant of a League of Nations' and dated 16 July, contained, as the twentieth of its twenty-one articles, the guarantee system indispensable to Wilson's philosophy, though surprisingly late in the plan: this stated that the Contracting Parties would 'unite in several guarantees to each other' (the word 'several' no doubt being intended to suggest that each signatory would be bound to act whatever the others did) 'of their territorial integrity and political independence'. This provision, however, was made subject to 'such territorial modifications, if any, as may become necessary in the future'. This phrase, in its many later reformulations, became the point of reconciliation between Wilson's guarantee system (which the French, for obvious reasons, supported from the outset) and adamant British opposition to it. And the House plan had other features which later found their way into the eventual Covenant.

In Article 5, for instance, it stated the overriding principle, later defined by the Soviet delegate to the League, Maxim Litvinov, as the 'indivisibility of peace', that 'any war or threat of war is a matter of concern to the League', ultimately to be embodied in Article 11 of the Covenant. It recommended a permanent secretariat (Article 9) and a permanent international court of fifteen judges, which would consider cases submitted to it by consent of the parties (Article 10). As in the Phillimore report, international disputes which were not settled in the ordinary course of diplomacy would be referred to arbitration or to the court (Article 13), and states which failed to comply with this requirement would be cut off from economic relations with other signatory states and a blockade would be organised against them (Articles 14 and 15). There was no provision for military or naval sanctions, however, nor, strangely, for the reference of non-justiciable disputes to political settlement. The House plan was also notable for the stress it laid on the disarmament of all signatory states 'to the lowest point consistent with safety', a delegate conference being given the responsibility of drawing up a disarmament plan, which would only bind those states expressly accepting it. Along with this went a requirement puzzling in its origin in a capitalist country, namely that 'munitions and implements of war' should not in future be left to private enterprise to manufacture. The House scheme was prefaced by four highly idealistic general axioms, soon to be discarded, except that they found a pale reflection in the Covenant preamble, which referred to the 'prescription of open, just and honourable relations between nations'. These axioms called for 'the same standards of honour and ethics' in international as in other human affairs; required that officials of all Powers should 'act honestly'; deprecated 'secret inquiries' conducted by one state into the affairs of another; and dismissed as 'dishonourable' all attempts by any state to 'influence' another state against a third country.[8]

Wilson took the House plan and made it the basis of his first draft of the Covenant. In essence, the ideas were much the same as House's, though phrased more felicitously. Language now began to appear which survived the many later debates in the United States and Paris, as for instance Article 4, which became the basis for Article 8 of the eventual Covenant, and which called for 'the reduction of armaments to the lowest point consistent with domestic' (later amended to 'national') 'safety and the enforcement by common action of international obligations'. As in the House plan, the essential penalty for resort to war without complying with the provisions for the peaceful settlement of disputes was to be the interruption of economic relations with the other signatory states. The President, however, added to the House proposals by developing somewhat the proposed machinery for the League: there was now to be a 'Body of Delegates', consisting of ambassadors and Ministers accredited to whichever state eventually became the seat of the League, while the day-to-day work of the League was to be carried on by a smaller Executive Council, these two bodies later becoming the League Assembly and Council respectively. Wilson added, too, a preamble to the House plan, discarding House's rather naive four principles, and this was substantially the form of words which were later to introduce the twenty-six articles of the Covenant.[9]

II

Meanwhile, things had been moving forward on the British side. By mid- November 1918, when the war had come to an end, a lengthy memorandum on the future League had been worked out by a special section of the Foreign Office presided over by Lord Cecil, who had by this time resigned from the government after a disagreement about Welsh affairs. This document was shortened on Cecil's instructions and combined with the chief recommendations of the Phillimore committee. It was then presented to the Cabinet on 17 December as the 'Cecil draft', and on 1 January 1919 shown to David Hunter Miller, President Wilson's chief legal adviser on League affairs, after the American mission had arrived in Paris for the opening of the peace conference on 18 January.

The Cecil draft, again, said nothing about guarantees, but it was far more forthright about enforcement action than the available American proposals. This was not surprising: Wilson had no option but to rely on the force of moral suasion for the implementation of the Covenant, the American people being new to intervention in world affairs and only the Congress, not the President, having the right to declare war. It is hard to see how any American leader could have accepted proposals like those of the Cecil draft, which flatly stated that all League members would be 'at war' with any state which failed to comply with the now widely accepted rules for the peaceful settlement of disputes: that is, no war before the reference of an issue in dispute to arbitration or an international conference, or before the issue of an arbitration award or conference report on the dispute, or against any state which complied with the arbitration award or conference report.

This meant that, as in the Phillimore plan, war would still be legal in certain circumstances, but in virtually taking out of the hands of member-states the right to declare war, it made inroads into national sovereignty hardly likely to prove acceptable.

The Cecil draft went into more detail about structure and procedures in the new world organisation than any previous official British document on the subject. As in Wilson's first draft, there was provision for a permanent secretariat, which was to act as a 'channel of communication' with 'all International Bodies'. But the 'pivot of the League', as it was called, was to be 'regular conferences between responsible representatives of the Contracting Powers', and the conferences, at which all decisions would be based on unanimous voting, would take two forms: annual meetings of the five great Powers (the British Empire, France, Italy, Japan and the United States) and of such other states as the five recognised as great Powers; and four-yearly assemblies of all member-states. Thus, the basic twofold division of the organisation into a quasi-legislative organ and a smaller, high-powered executive was becoming established. Disputes between member- and non-member states, and between non-members themselves, were to be dealt with by non-members being invited to accept the obligations of the organisation for the purpose of settling disputes between them, though there was no question of their being in any way constrained to do so. Provision was also made, as in the House plan, for the establishment of a permanent court of international justice, which was to be in continuous session.[10]

While the Cecil draft was in preparation, an influential contribution to the debate on the future League was made by the veteran South African soldier, philosopher and statesman, Jan Christian Smuts, at that time a member of the Imperial War Cabinet. He published his ideas on 16 December under the title 'The League of Nations. A Practical Suggestion'. The Smuts memorandum was distinguished, as was to be expected, by its inspiring language, much of which has entered into the folk-memory of the League generation ('the tents have been struck and the caravan of humanity is once more on the march') and by its magisterial comprehensiveness: Smuts discussed all the central principles of international organisation for maintaining the peace, adding a few of his own and bestowing on each of them an original twist. Unlike most British and American outlines of the League system so far, he saw the new body as much more than an agency

for the settlement of international disputes. 'An attempt will be
made in this sketch', he began, 'to view (the League) not only as a
possible means for preventing future wars, but much more as a
great organ of the ordinary peaceful life of civilisation'. The
League must become 'part and parcel of the common international
life of states ... an ever visible, living, working organ of the polity
of civilisation'. No super-state was proposed: 'states will have to be
controlled, not by compulsion from above, but by consent from
below'. And yet, Smuts went on, the 'general conference, or
congress, of all constituent states' would 'partake of the character
of a Parliament, in which public debates of general international
interest will take place'. The Council, to consist of the five great
Powers, with Germany drawn in later, and four smaller states,
would 'take the initiative for the work of the conference' and
would 'manage and control' international administrative bodies
'now performing international functions in accordance with treaty
arrangements'. The most considerable new task assigned to the
League in the Smuts scheme of things, however, was to serve as
the 'reversionary' for peoples and territories formerly belonging to
Russia, Austria-Hungary and Turkey.

These, according to Smuts, were now 'bankrupt estates' and the
League was best qualified to become the 'liquidator or trustee' for
them which Europe needed. The League would have to delegate
'authority, control or administration' to another state to act as its
agent or mandatory for the independent states now emerging with
the break-up of the old European system. This proposal, so
strangely out of touch with the fervent nationalism rampant at the
end of the war among the peoples released from the Austro-
Hungarian, German, Russian and Turkish empires, was the
embryo of the later mandates system of the League, though this
was limited to the former German colonies in Africa and the Pacific
and the non-Turkish parts of the old Ottoman empire. Smuts
regarded Germany's former colonies as inhabited by 'barbarians'
for whom statehood was not in sight and perhaps never would be.
They would have to be dealt with, he thought, in accordance with
the fifth of President Wilson's Fourteen points, which called for an
'open, fair-minded and just settlement of colonial claims': in other
words, re-distributed through the ordinary bargaining process.

The Smuts plan included the now standard recommendations
for pacific settlement: arbitration and conciliation, the distinction
between justiciable and non-justiciable disputes, and the principle
of the Cecil draft that states resorting to war without complying

with the procedures for peaceful settlement would be *ipso facto* 'at war' with other members of the League. According to Smuts, the sanctions system was 'the most important question of all'. Smuts also attached great importance to disarmament: he would arm the Council with powers to inspect all national arms factories; the private manufacture of armaments would be abolished; Smuts also said he would 'plead most earnestly' for the abolition of conscription at the peace conference. Conscription was the 'taproot of militarism', and unless it is abolished, he warned, 'all our labours will eventually be in vain'.[11]

Wilson admired the Smuts plan and evidence of his admiration is to be found in his second draft of the Covenant, also known as the first Paris draft since it was compiled after his arrival in the French capital for the peace conference. It was dated 10 January, a week before the conference opened in plenary session. This draft spelled out the make-up of the Executive Council on much the same lines as the Smuts memorandum: the five great Powers, together with four smaller states to be selected from two panels which would be designed to distinguish between second-rank Powers and the general body of member-states. Three votes on the Council would count as a veto. Conscription was to be abolished, as in the Smuts plan, though there was no insistence on the abolition of the private manufacture of armaments. States violating the provisions for peaceful settlement would, as in the Cecil and Smuts plans, be '*ipso facto* at war with other members', though the latter, it was said, could not be expected to go beyond the use of economic sanctions against offending members. The Executive Council nevertheless would recommend military sanctions if the economic measures proved insufficient. Rather harshly, a state which had once broken the Covenant was to be disarmed in perpetuity. But, whereas the Smuts proposals made no reference to guarantees, Wilson in his second draft continued to give them the fullest prominence. The President conceded, however, that occasional territorial readjustments must be allowed to temper the rigidity of the guarantee system, if three-quarters of the 'Body of Delegates' – that is, the general assembly of national delegates – agreed in a given instance. The territorial re-adjustments Wilson considered likely were of two kinds: those rendered necessary 'by reason of changes in racial conditions and aspirations, or in social and political relationships pursuant to the principle of self-determination', and those that, in the opinion of three-quarters of the delegates, 'may be demanded by the welfare and manifest interest of the peoples concerned, if agreeable to those peoples'. It was clear that this provision, which in a modified form was to become known under the heading 'peaceful change', would remain a lasting thorn in the side of Anglo-American relations.

Smuts' proposals for a mandates system, however, were adopted, in a modified form, by Wilson. They chimed in with enlightened thinking in the United States about responsibilities for the welfare of American Indians and might be used to head off annexation designs of the European allies towards territory available for re-distribution at the peace conference. But the President, in the first of what he called 'supplementary agreements' attached to his second draft, included Germany's colonies, which Smuts omitted, in the scheme, and followed Smuts' suggestion for extending the mandatory system to former Austro-Hungarian territory in Europe. To this, his legal adviser, Hunter Miller, raised the natural objection that the latter was inhabited by developed historical communities such as the Czechs, the Slovenes and Croats, who would brook no supervision from the League of the independent states they were already in process of creating. They were to come under a form of League control, however, in the shape of treaties later negotiated between the new successor states and the League for the protection of national minorities incorporated within the former. To some extent this was anticipated in another 'supplementary agreement' in the second Wilson draft, which called for the equal treatment of racial and national minorities within all member-states.[12]

The mandatory system for Germany's former colonies and the non-Turkish portions of the Ottoman empire was eventually spelled out in Article 22 of the Covenant, which we will discuss in the next chapter. Its roots in the Smuts plan are evident enough, though they could equally be regarded as implicit in the logic of the international situation in 1919. On 30 January, twelve days after the formal opening of the peace conference, the Council of Ten, which at first acted as the executive committee of the conference, was forced to come to some decision about the German colonies (the fate of the non-Turkish portions of the Ottoman empire was not decided until the following year) as a result of the strident claims of Messrs Botha, Hughes and Massey, of South Africa, Australia and New Zealand respectively, for the outright annexation of South West Africa (by South Africa), German Samoa (by New Zealand) and German Guinea (by Australia). The chief British delegate, Lloyd George, though having little interest himself in Germany's African dependencies, felt bound to sympathise with the views of colleagues within the British Empire delegation, though not to the extent of embarrassing the American President. In a dramatic incident at the Council of Ten on 30 January Wilson asked Hughes bluntly whether he was threatening to quit the conference unless the principle of annexation were conceded. Hughes climbed down, and this meant that, once it had been decided that the colonies should not return to Germany, and no-one proposed that, annexation by the allies was ruled out as well in view of Wilson's veto and perhaps the prevailing state of world public opinion. The mandatory regime within the League system therefore became a kind of residual alternative.[13] It remained to settle the details and work out the famous three-pronged division of the mandated territories. The distribution of the mandates among the expectant delegations took place at a meeting of the Council of Ten on 7 May.

III

President Wilson rewrote his League plan twice more, the resulting documents being known as the third and fourth drafts, or the second and third Paris drafts respectively, with the prudent assistance of Hunter Miller. The final draft was completed on 2 February, and by that time the plenary conference had appointed its committee to draw up a League of Nations plan.[14] This it did in the form of a resolution drafted by the British delegation, which ran as follows:

The Conference, having considered the proposals for a League of Nations, resolves that
1. It is essential to the maintenance of the world settlement which the Associated Nations are now met to establish, that a League of Nations be created to promote international co-operation, to insure the fulfilment of accepted international obligations and to promote safeguards against war.
2. This League should be created as an integral part of the General Treaty of Peace and should be open to every civilised nation which can be relied upon to promote its objects.
3. The members of the League should periodically meet in international conference and should have a permanent organisation and secretariat to carry on the business of the League in the intervals between the conferences. The

Conference therefore appoints a Committee representative of the Associated Governments to work out the details of the constitution and functions of the League.[15]

The resolution represented a major victory for the American President. It stated in the most affirmative terms that the 'associated nations' (it was Wilson himself who objected to the expression 'allied') were committed to establish the League, that it was to be an integral part of the peace treaty, one of Wilson's most cherished ideas, and that the League was essential to the maintenance of the peace settlement, or in other words that the peace-making states should not expect to enforce the peace unilaterally. This meant that neither the Europeans nor the Americans could have the peace treaty without the League or the League without the peace treaty; both would stand or fall together, and that was exactly what they were to do. The resolution also touched on the general principles and structure of the new world organisation, showing how the schemes we have already referred to had influenced the conference's thinking. On the whole, this outline was fully in the spirit of the different British plans. In particular, the resolution made no reference to the sacred Wilsonian philosophy of guarantees.

The Committee, or Commission, as it was also called, was thereupon appointed. It consisted of the five great Powers, with Wilson, as chairman, and Colonel House acting for the United States, Cecil and Hurst for Britain, Bourgeois and F. Larnaude, a distinguished international lawyer, for France, Prime Minister Orlando and Vittorio Scialoga, another international lawyer, for Italy, and Baron Makino, the Japanese Foreign Minister, and Viscount Chinda, the Japanese ambassador to London, for Japan. There were also representatives from five of the smaller states: Hymans, the Belgian Foreign Minister, V. K. Wellington Koo, the Chinese ambassador to Washington, the Portuguese Minister to Russia, Jayme Batalha Reis, and the Serbian Minister to Paris, Vesnitch.

The total Committee membership thus numbered fifteen. At the first meeting of the Committee on 4 February, however, a sharp dispute sprang up, the first of many characterising both the Committee and the conference as a whole, between the great-Power representatives and those of the smaller states, led, among others, by Hymans, arising from the demands of the latter for greater representation. Britain and the United States opposed these demands, chiefly on the ground that the larger the Committee, the slower would its work get done. They were outvoted, however, and at the Committee's fourth meeting representatives of four more states took their places around the table in Colonel House's room in the Hotel Crillon, the headquarters of the American mission at the peace conference, where the Committee held its meetings. These new members were Czechoslovakia, Greece, Poland and Rumania. They brought the Committee's membership to nineteen and that remained its size until the end.

The Committee met on ten occasions from 3 February until the 13th at times when its members were not attending the general conference, the meetings generally being of three hours' duration: so that, by the time its work was substantially completed and its first version of the Covenant was ready for presentation to the plenary conference on 14 February (when President Wilson left for a visit to the United States), its deliberations had occupied no more than thirty hours in all. The result of its labours was in effect the Covenant in the final form in which it appeared in the peace treaties signed in June. After Wilson's return on 14 March, the Committee held five further meetings and met for the last time on 11 April. Its work was done.

The speed with which the Committee completed its task was partly due to the simplicity and informality of its proceedings: translating, for instance, was invariably done simultaneously, the working languages being only English and French, and time did not have to be spent in circulating translations of a member's interventions. Another factor was the personality and the immense authority of Wilson himself: the League he regarded as his personal creation and he treated it as a child of his own; he insisted on being chairman of the Committee and discharged that role in an admirably businesslike way. Other members of the Committee deferred to the President's authority, readily withdrew proposals which he disliked and accepted his assurances when their suggestions were not acceded to. But by far the most important reason for the efficiency of the Committee as a piece of international machinery was the fact that it worked systematically and uninterruptedly during its first vital ten or eleven days through a carefully prepared draft of twenty-two articles. This was the so-called Hurst-Miller draft of the Covenant, an Anglo-American version of the League's constitution and working rules, which the Committee amended but did not radically change, and which was the only draft to come before the Committee. 'Day after day', it was written afterwards, 'the draft was held up to the light and criticised and amplified'. There was never any suggestion that anything but the Hurst-Miller draft should furnish the basis of the Committee's work. When the Committee met for the first time on 3 February, there was some doubt in Wilson's mind whether it should work on the Hurst-Miller draft or on his own fourth and final draft Covenant (the third Paris draft), and he decided only at the last moment in favour of the former. The result was that when the Committee sat down on 3 February to examine the draft presented to them, it was the first time that most of them had seen it. It had in fact been printed only the previous day. It is a curious fact that no French text of the whole draft was ever made; when amendments to the Hurst-Miller draft in the French language were put forward, which was rarely enough, they were simply worked as translations into the English text if accepted. The entire management of the Committee was a triumph for Anglo-American diplomacy, though in the end this was not without unfortunate consequences.

The Hurst-Miller draft had resulted from talks which Lord Robert Cecil and David Hunter Miller held in Paris on 21, 25 and 27 January in order to reconcile President Wilson's third draft of the Covenant (his second Paris draft) with a final draft which British officials had made on the basis of the Cecil plan. A number of further British desiderata were discussed, such as separate representation in the League for the self-governing Dominions, Australia, Canada, New Zealand and South Africa, and for India, the limitation of the proposed Executive Council to the great Powers and such other states as the great Powers were willing to admit into their circle, and an increase in the importance to be attached to the Chancellor, as he was then called, the permanent head of the League's secretariat. On 1 February, these talks were continued, with Cecil Hurst now acting in Lord Cecil's place, and from them issued the Hurst-Miller draft, the basis of the Committee's work. When Wilson saw this draft on the following day, Sunday, 2 February, he did not like it and promptly set to work amending it into his fourth draft. Then he changed his mind and on the next day it was the Hurst-Miller draft which came before the Committee's first meeting.[16]

The Hurst-Miller draft, which, after further amendment in the Committee and re-drafting and approval by the plenary conference, finally became the League Covenant, incorporated almost all the thinking which had gone on on both sides of the Atlantic during the preceding six months. The machinery of the League was dealt with first: there was to be a Body of Delegates, made up of two representatives from each of the High Contracting Parties, which would vote by majority on procedural questions and unanimously on other matters; an Executive Council, which would meet more frequently and be limited in membership to Britain, France, Italy, Japan and the United States, who would invite other states to join the Council when their interests were directly affected; and a permanent secretariat with a Chancellor as its head. New states could be admitted into the organisation on a two-thirds vote of the delegates, but their armaments would have to conform to the League's requirements. Then came the guarantee article under which the contracting parties were to 'respect and preserve as against external aggression' (the last four words originated with the American Commander-in-Chief, Tasker Bliss) the territorial integrity and existing political independence of all other member states: there was no provision in the draft, however, for the sort of changes in the *status quo* which had formerly been agreed between Cecil and Miller. As for disarmament, the requirement that members must reduce their arms to the lowest point consistent with domestic safety and the enforcement by common action of international obligations was repeated. The Executive Council was charged to formulate a general disarmament plan. An inquiry was to be instituted into the possibility of abolishing conscription and provision was to be made for giving 'full and frank' publicity to the state of world armaments.

Any war or threat of war was declared a matter of concern to the League as a whole, and in the event of either the contracting parties were accorded the right 'to take action deemed to be wise and effectual' to safeguard peace. It was further stated to be the 'friendly right' of the contracting parties to draw the attention of the Body of Delegates or the Executive Council to 'circumstances threatening to disturb international peace'. The familiar references to the peaceful settlement of disputes followed: no war before submission of the dispute to arbitration or inquiry by the Council, or until three months (a new idea) after the issue of an award or report, or against another state which complied with the award or report. The Executive Council was to formulate plans for a permanent court of international justice to which legal disputes could be referred. Then, in a phrase designed to meet Hunter

Miller's objection that in the United States only Congress could declare war, states disregarding their covenants concerning the peaceful settlement of disputes were described as 'deemed to have committed an act of war' against all other members, which were to submit the offending countries to an interruption of trade relations, offering themselves mutual support against the ensuing financial losses as they did so. The Executive Council would then advise on suitable military sanctions should it prove necessary to go that far.

The remaining articles dealt with procedures for disputes with and between non-member-states, the supervision by the League of the trade in arms, the mandatory regime for territories formerly belonging to the German and Turkish empires, now described as a 'sacred trust for civilisation', the ensuring of 'fair hours and humane conditions of labour', freedom of religion and the ending of discrimination on religious grounds, and freedom of transit and the just treatment of the commerce of all member states. All treaties between member states were to be registered with the League and published, and any inconsistencies between a state's obligations under the League Covenant and its obligations under other international engagements were to be ironed out in such a way as to give precedence to the Covenant.

IV

Such was the Hurst-Miller draft on which the Committee of the conference began and completed its work in February 1919. By and large, the draft survived practically all the criticism levelled against it, and that was invariably expressed in the most friendly terms. There were in fact three types of conflict in the Committee: between the British and American viewpoints; between the big states and the small; and between France and the rest, and between Japan and the rest. The first of these, the old Anglo-American controversy over guarantees, came out into the open, Cecil wanting the guarantee article struck out (it was Article 7 in the Hurst-Miller draft, Article 10 in the final Covenant), Wilson and Orlando being in favour of retaining it, and Larnaude, for France, holding a position somewhere in the middle. In the course of this debate, the idea was mooted of going back to Colonel House's idea of making the guarantee system dependent upon the occasional modification of the *status quo*, and this eventually won the day in the form of Article 19 of the eventual Covenant.

The conflict between the bigger states and the smaller made a more important impact on the drafting of the Covenant since Hymans of Belgium and those supporting him won their battle for the enlargement of the Executive Council by the addition of states chosen by the Body of Delegates, though the number of these was left undecided: it could be two or four. This was in effect a reversion to the idea of small Power representation in Wilson's drafts, in which four small countries, one less than the number of great Powers, were to be represented on the Council. Hymans, however, lost his campaign to have Brussels named as the seat of the organisation. Moreover, the Hurst-Miller draft survived two of the strongest assaults against it in the Committee, one from Bourgeois and Larnaude, the other from the Japanese members, Makino and Chinda.

The French, true to their belief that 'covenants without swords' are futile and their lack of confidence in the sanctions of public opinion, called for the formation of an international army, to be commanded by an international general staff, to enforce the Covenant and deter potential violations of it.[17] This the British and Americans firmly set their face against, the British convinced that any such force would be bound to be dominated by the French and to serve French political ends, the Americans owing to their old concern about constitutional impediments to their executive's use of armed force in international relations. France lost the battle, and all that was offered by way of compensation was a new article (Article 9 of the eventual Covenant) which made provision for a permanent commission to advise the Council on the armaments of new members, the disarmament plans of the organisation, and 'military, naval and air questions generally'. It was a serious setback for the French which they and others remembered in later years, when the League was condemned as 'the Geneva talking shop', the words of which no-one respected.

A similar setback, and with similar consequences for the future of the League, was suffered by the Japanese pair, Baron Makino and Viscount Chinda, when they sought the insertion into the Covenant of a clause upholding the principle of racial equality. They argued that this would serve as a useful parallel to Wilson's principle of religious equality, which had found a place in the Hurst-Miller draft. The emotions which surged round the table and even outside the Committee room when the quiet-spoken Japanese adumbrated their wishes can be felt today. What would become of the time-honoured principle (though it was not yet alluded to in any of the drafts) of the exclusivity of domestic jurisdiction if a member state could be arraigned before the League for discriminating against immigrants on grounds of race? The United States and Australia were already well known for doing so. And where would such states stand in the future if an arbitral tribunal, or even the League Council itself, were to declare them in the wrong in a dispute about immigration with a negroid or oriental country? President Wilson dealt with the problem by simply ignoring it. But on 14 February, the last day of the Committee's first series of sessions, he left to go back home and Cecil was in the chair. In not inconsiderable shame, Cecil moved on to the next business and said that discussion on that particular item would be resumed. It was resumed at the last meeting of the second series of sessions on 11 April. The Japanese kept up their pressure, but now merely asked for a phrase in the preamble to the Covenant endorsing the principle of the 'equality of nations and the just treatment of their nationals'. In the ensuing debate, eleven of the nineteen Committee members voted in favour of the Japanese amendment, but Wilson declared that 'in view of the serious objections on the part of some of us' the amendment was not carried.[18] It is perhaps no coincidence that the first serious challenge to the League Covenant and the peace system was to come from Japan.

3   The Covenant reviewed

I

The Covenant of the League of Nations which emerged from the commission chaired by Wilson was approved by the conference of Allied and Associated Powers in Paris on 28 April 1919.[1] It was signed by those states and by the Central Powers as an integral part (Part I) of the treaties of Versailles (on 28 June), St Germain-en-Laye (10 September), Neuilly-sur-Seine (27 November) and Trianon (4 June 1920).[2] The Covenant was also embodied in the abortive treaty of Sèvres between the Allies and Turkey of 10 August 1920, but not in the final treaty signed with Turkey at Lausanne on 24 July 1923. The League itself came into existence on 10 January 1920 with the coming into force of the treaty of Versailles.

The original members of the League were therefore the thirty-two Allied and Associated Powers which signed the treaties. In addition, thirteen states which had been neutral during the war were invited to join and twelve of these did, though one, Salvador, gave notice of withdrawal in August 1937.[3] Austria, Bulgaria, Germany and Hungary accepted the League Covenant by their act of signing the treaties, but did not thereby become League members. Austria and Bulgaria joined the organisation in 1920, Hungary in 1922 and Germany in 1926. Germany also became a permanent member of the League Council, the organisation's executive body.

Among the original members, Britain's position was unique. Beneath the heading 'Original Members of the League of Nations' in the Annex to the Covenant, Britain appeared as 'British Empire' and underneath and inset from the margin were the names of the so-called Dominions, Canada, Australia, South Africa, New Zealand, and India. In theory the policies of all five countries were still decided in London, though the first four were to all intents self-governing: it was not until 1926 that the Imperial Conference approved the so-called Balfour Resolutions which recognised the independence of the four from Britain, not until 1931 that an Act of the British Parliament, the Statute of Westminster, accorded them formal authority to make their own law, and not until 1947 that India became a fully independent state. When the League was created therefore, Britain disposed of at least two votes, and effectively rather more, in its principal organs. This came about partly because of the influence of Britain in the making of the League, partly because of the self-assertion of the white Dominions, especially Australia and New Zealand, at the peace conference.

The first Article of the Covenant provided that, in addition to the thirty-two original members and the thirteen neutral states named in the Annex, 'any fully self-governing State, Dominion or Colony' could be admitted to membership by a two-thirds vote of the Assembly, in which all member-states were represented.[4] This was made conditional on any new member giving 'effective guarantees of its sincere intention to observe its international obligations' and its acceptance of 'such regulations as may be prescribed by the League in regard to its military, naval and air forces and armaments'. In practice, these conditions were never very seriously insisted upon: the principle came to be accepted, as it has in the United Nations regime since 1945, that an organisation for the maintenance of peace cannot be too discriminatory in its attitude to potential new members. Nor was the rather loose designation 'any fully self-governing State, Dominion or Colony' rigorously applied, it being in any case hard to see how a colony could be fully self-governing. The phrase made provision for the separate membership of India, but no other country was ever admitted to League membership which was constitutionally subject to another state.

In accordance with the spirit of voluntarism permeating the Covenant, no obstacles were placed in the way of a country wishing to leave the organisation, though Article 1 of the Covenant required two years' notice of a state's intention to do so, and that 'all its obligations under this Covenant shall have been fulfilled' at the time of withdrawal. In practice, the observance of these conditions was bound to be perfunctory. When Germany, Italy and Japan withdrew from the League in the 1930s, most of the other members were so keen to see them return that there was no thought of alienating them still further by inquiring whether all their Covenant obligations had been fulfilled.

Besides voluntary withdrawal, a member-state could be expelled from the organisation under Article 16 for violating 'any covenant of the League', and this had to be done 'by a vote of the Council concurred in by the Representatives of all the other Members of the League represented thereon'. This was another way of saying that a member being considered for expulsion would have a right to sit on the Council when its case was examined, but not to veto a unanimous vote to expel it. The fact that this reference to expulsion comes at the end of Article 16, which deals with sanctions in the event of an illegal resort to war, suggests that expulsion was envisaged as a form of penalty for that offence: in the UN Charter, too, a member-state against which enforcement action has been taken may be suspended from the rights and privileges of membership and may be expelled if it has 'persistently violated the Principles contained in the present Charter' of the organisation.[5] These were the circumstances in which the Soviet Union, the only country to be expelled from the League, suffered that experience in December 1940, when it was arraigned before the Council for its invasion of Finland. Nevertheless, Article 16 expressly states that expulsion may be the penalty for the violation of *any* covenant of the League, and theoretically that must be regarded as the legal position.

II

The Covenant then proceeded to describe the League's organisational structure (Articles 2 to 7 inclusive), which consisted of three principal organs, the Assembly, the Council and the Secretariat. In September 1921, a fourth was added when its statute, drawn up by a committee of ten jurists, came into force. This was the Permanent Court of International Justice (PCIJ), a tribunal of nine highly qualified judges from a wide geographical and cultural spectrum, with its seat in the traditional home of international law, The Hague.[6] The Covenant was accordingly amended to make room for the Court. Even during the sessions of Wilson's commission on the League in Paris, the Court had always been regarded as a vital part of the League system.

The Assembly, representing all member-states in a deliberative conclave, and the Council, being a kind of executive to give shape and form to the Assembly's business, had been elements in practically all the different plans for the League, as we saw in the last chapter. The bicameral arrangement represented a fusion of the old, exclusive Concert of Europe with the post-1918 theory that every nation-state, no matter how small, has a right to a say in world affairs. The same pattern has been preserved in the UN, with the important difference that in the latter body the Council has become the Security Council, charged with primary responsibility for the maintenance of peace and security; it includes the five major Powers (as they were in 1945) – Britain, China, France, the Soviet Union and the United States – and is endowed with powers under Chapter VII of the Charter, dealing with the enforcement of peace, to decide upon practically any form of action (provided the Big Five all agree) and, by Article 25 of the Charter, to make its decisions law for all other member-states. The League Council was an entirely different body. It was not specifically designed for the maintenance of peace, though, like the UN Security Council, it included the great Powers (that is, the Principal Allied and Associated Powers) as permanent members, which were not named: four non-permanent members were to be selected 'from time to time in its discretion' by the Assembly.[7] The Council was authorised by Article 4 to deal with 'any matter within the sphere of action of the League or affecting the peace of the world', in other words, with any subject. Its jurisdiction was concurrent with that of the Assembly, the province of which was defined in Article 3 in the same words.

Moreover, the League Council was not intended, in theory at least, to take any initiative in the enforcement of peace or the punishment of aggressors, and there was no suggestion, as there is in Article 43 of the UN Charter, of member-states putting armed forces at its disposal. The League Council was designed as an essentially deliberative body, hearing arguments from interested parties about international disputes, then issuing a report on the merits of the case and leaving the rest to member-states. The Council was not even intended to initiate studies of international conflicts of its own accord. Unlike the UN Security Council, which is supposed to range around the world looking for trouble, the League Council was there simply to help if member-states were unable to settle their disputes by other means and referred them to the Council (Article 15). To underline the deliberative character of the Council, by Article 4 a member-state not represented on the Council could be invited to join it *as a member* – that is, with the right to speak and vote – 'during the consideration of matters specially affecting the interests of that Member'. The same right has been conceded to UN members if party to a dispute under consideration by the Security Council, though without the right to vote.[8]

If it be asked how any body as passive, one might almost say as contemplative, as the League Council could have been designed as the 'Cabinet of the League', it must be remembered that in the early years League supporters attached immense importance to the force of public rebuke from a tribunal like the Council when a state is caught out on the wrong side of an argument. When a state was in the dock and the Council had pronounced an adverse verdict, that state's own people (it was thought) would turn against it and force its government back into the paths of righteousness. This was, of course, a highly optimistic assumption; it was belied, too, by the fact that in reality the Council played a much less passive role than that doled out to it in the Covenant. The permanent presence on the Council of the great Powers, or such of them as joined and remained in the League, ensured that it would: the smaller states which made up most of the League's membership were bound to take their cues from the great Powers, and hence from the Council.

The periodicity of meetings of Council and Assembly was not stated in detail in the Covenant, except that Article 4 required that the Council should meet at least once a year and otherwise 'as occasion may require'. The Assembly, which, with about fifty states in the League at any one time, and each of them having three representatives, was to form a sizeable body, was simply to meet 'at stated intervals and from time to time, as occasion may require'. This suggests that the Assembly tended to be regarded, in the smaller world of those days, as potentially a rather cumbrous body, especially as its jurisdiction was so vast, and hence that it should not be encouraged to meet too often. Some degree of precision was, however, given to the Assembly's sphere of work by the stipulation of certain specialised functions, and since these concerned the day-by-day running of the organisation, some definite provision for regular Assembly meetings was essential. These tasks included the selection of the minor states to be represented for short periods on the Council, the approval of the appointment of the League Secretary-General, the head of the Secretariat, and the admission of new members.[9]

The third principal component in the League's structure was the permanent Secretariat to be established at the seat of the League, Geneva, and recruited and controlled by the Secretary-General with the Council's approval. It was laid down in Article 7 that posts in the Secretariat should be open equally to men and women, and that Secretariat officials, together with the representatives of the different member-states, should always enjoy diplomatic immunities and privileges. The first Secretary-General, Sir James Eric Drummond, a British career diplomat, was chosen before the League came into existence and was named in an annex to the Covenant.[10] Drummond, who served as head of the Secretariat until June 1933, when he was succeeded by Joseph Avenol,[11] was strictly cast in the mould of the British higher civil servant, discreet, retiring, cautious about change and innovation, and bent on keeping the administrative machine turning, rather than propelling it into new courses. That was the attitude of mind most called for when the League and its Secretariat were new and suspected in many quarters. Fears abounded that the League's permanent staff might become a horde of overpaid busybodies. Drummond, not well endowed with the power to set men's hearts aflame, nurtured the image of the League as a modest addition to the machinery for managing human affairs rather than the symbol of a new order.

III

That is the image of the League which is projected by the administrative system provided by the Covenant; tentative and modest, rather than innovatory or radical. The League was decidedly not a super-state, and it was for this reason that, in 1944, when the United Nations forces allied in defeating the Axis powers met in conference at Dumbarton Oaks, Washington, D.C., to plan a successor to the League, the idea which inspired them was that the League had failed *because* it was not a super-state, and that something like a super-state would have to be created if aggressor states as strong as Nazi Germany were going to be halted in their tracks in future. The Dumbarton Oaks scheme was *almost* a plan for a super-state, with power to overawe aggressors concentrated in the Security Council.[12] The question left unanswered was whether any great Power in the Security Council would ever allow sanctions of this magnitude to be enforced against itself: that element – the voting formula in the case of enforcement action by the Security Council – had to be omitted, for the time being, from a security system which looked in other respects like a recipe for a world state. The Big Three – Britain, Russia and the United States – took up the missing part of the jig-saw puzzle at their summit meeting in Yalta in February 1945, and almost at once realised that the great-Power veto was unavoidable. Otherwise, Security Council enforcement action would be resisted by a dissenting great Power in the field of battle rather than at the conference table, and that would be a sad end for a world organisation created 'to save succeeding generations from the scourge of war'.

The League system never found itself in that kind of dilemma because the super-state idea was never in prospect. The new organisation was unhesitatingly based on national sovereignty: it existed merely to help states do together what they could not so easily do alone. It never sought to do more. The watch-word was voluntarism through and through.

States were free to join the League, if they wished, on the basis of minimum qualifications. They were free to leave without having to satisfy any very searching conditions. The decisions of League bodies were recommendations only and carried no binding force, except that member-states at war in defiance of a report on their disputes by the Assembly or Council were deemed to be in default under the Covenant and could be subjected to sanctions. The greatest precautions were taken to ensure respect for sovereignty. Article 10, which contained the famous guarantee of the territorial integrity and political independence of all members, stated that these were to be respected and preserved as against *external* aggression, there being no suggestion that a state had a right to intervene to protect the territory or independence of another state against internal attack, that is, against revolutionary forces *within* that state. Again, Article 21 contained a reference to the Monroe Doctrine and other such 'regional understandings', the validity of which was said not to be affected by the Covenant, and the Monroe Doctrine was a warning by a great Power, the United States, not only against external interference in its own affairs, but in those of the whole hemisphere in which it was situated.

The internal jurisdiction of member-states was further safeguarded by the clause in Article 15 which stated that if a party to a dispute claimed that the dispute arose from a matter which 'by international law is solely within the domestic jurisdiction of that party', and if the Council accepted that claim, the League's efforts to resolve the dispute came to an end. The Council simply reported the matter to be one of domestic jurisdiction and made no recommendation about it. Of course, the matter in question had to be *solely* within the domestic jurisdiction of the party making the claim, which meant that if it was only partially so, the clause could not be cited. Nevertheless, it did open up a substantial breach in the accountability of states to international tribunals of inquiry.

Above all, the Covenant reaffirmed the principle that a state cannot be legally bound without its consent, and that was implicit in the provision that the Assembly and Council should generally act on the basis of unanimous voting: in the League system every state had a veto, not merely the great Powers, as in the United Nations. The rule was by no means absolute. The admission of new members was to be effected on a two-thirds vote in the Assembly (Article 1). By Article 4, the Assembly might, on the basis of a simple majority vote, join with the Council in nominating additional permanent members of the Council. As a result of an amendment to the Covenant adopted in July 1926, the Assembly could determine by a two-thirds vote the rules dealing with the election of non-permanent members of the Council. All matters of procedure in the Council and Assembly were to be decided by a majority (presumably a simple majority) of members' representatives present at the meeting (Article 5). Secretaries-General, after the first one, had to be approved, on appointment by the Council, by a majority, again a simple majority, of the Assembly (Article 6). Most importantly, by Article 15 (4), members agreed that a dispute 'likely to lead to a rupture' should be submitted to the Council if it was not regarded as suitable for arbitral or judicial settlement, and the Council could then make a report on it *either unanimously or by a majority vote*, though the report could not form the basis of any state's obligation not to go to war with another state which complied with the report unless the report was accepted by all the Council's members except those actually party to the dispute.

Apart from these exceptions – which mainly concerned matters of internal organisation and procedure – the rule of unanimity was general, though, of course, a veto applied by a more powerful state was always of greater importance than the veto of a lesser state. The votes of smaller and poorer states which stand out against a majority which includes bigger and richer states can often be purchased, if not always by money, at least through various sorts of pressure. All this reflects the fact that, within the League, states played much the same kind of diplomatic game as they had done before the League was born, only now there were rather more rules and the resort to force by states was hedged about by rather more restraints. But, in the last resort, it rested with states whether they would make much or little of the new arrangements. The ultimate and most effective sanction, wrote the official British commentary on the Covenant, published in 1919, 'must be the public opinion of the civilised world'.

> If the nations of the future [the commentary went on] are in the main selfish, grasping and warlike, no instrument or machinery will restrain them. It is only possible to establish an organisation which may make peaceful co-operation easy and hence customary, and to trust in the influence of custom to mould opinion.[13]

IV

The voluntarist character of the Covenant also colours its central sections (Articles 8 to 17 inclusive), dealing with the preservation of peace and the prevention of war, the League's most important task. The notion of the enforcement of a peaceful world society was there, but in the final resort it was left to the individual member-state to see that the job was done.

The war-prevention strategy of the Covenant can be understood under four headings: reducing the means to fight wars with; enforcing the reference of unsettled disputes to third-party settlement and taking measures against states which refuse to use such means or ignore the verdicts of third parties when they are given; the exchange of guarantees of the *status quo*, together with arrangements to modify it from time to time; and defusing international conflicts *before* they become a danger to peace.

The reduction of the means to fight wars which was supposed to be the function of multilateral disarmament, which it was fervently believed the League would bring about. In contrast with the almost perfunctory dismissal of disarmament in the UN Charter as merely one of a list of subjects the General Assembly might take up (Article 14), the League Covenant was framed by Anglo-Saxons (with some grudging acquiescence on the part of the French) who believed that the First World War had sprung from great armaments, and that the most hopeful road to peace lay through general and complete disarmament. Accordingly, Article 8 of the Covenant, after stating the basic creed that the maintenance of peace 'requires the reduction of national armaments to the lowest point consistent with national safety and the enforcement by common action of international obligations', charged the Council with formulating plans 'for the consideration

and action of the several governments': these plans were to be
reconsidered and revised at least every ten years, no doubt to take
account of technological innovation in armaments which always
plays havoc with attempts to stabilise ratios of armed strength
between different states.

The initiative in disarmament therefore lay with the Council,
though ultimately the individual state would have to determine
whether the Council's proposals were acceptable. Once having
adopted the Council's plan, however, member-states were bound
not to exceed the force-levels stipulated without the Council's
agreement. Furthermore, as had been foreshadowed in many of
the pre-armistice outlines of the League's constitution, the private
manufacture of armaments was condemned as 'open to grave
objections' and the Council was authorised to advise on ways of
reducing its evils without handicapping too much states unable to
manufacture munitions for themselves. Lastly, member-states
were enjoined by Article 8 to exchange 'full and frank information'
about the scale of their armaments, their military policies and the
state of their war industries. Some of this information appeared in
the *Armaments Year Book*, later compiled and published by the
League Secretariat, though how convinced the League staff were
that this was a complete disclosure of the weapons situation is
another story. Partly to organise the material which it was hoped
would become available through these arrangements, Article 9 of
the Covenant created a permanent commission to advise the
Council about military affairs, including the drawing up and
negotiation of the disarmament plans called for by Article 8.

Like so many other things in the League's history,
developments in the disarmament field did not go precisely
according to plan. The Council was not left quietly to assess the
arms requirements of each member-state and then to get
agreement with that state on maintaining a ceiling on armaments at
that level. The occurrence of a strange race in naval armaments
between Britain and the United States immediately after the war
ensured that the most substantive arms negotiations in the inter-
war years took place in the naval field outside the League system,
as for instance at the Washington naval conference in 1922.[14]
Moreover, the protracted dispute between Germany and her
former enemies in the First World War about the legality of the
unilateral disarmament imposed on her by the Treaty of Versailles
necessitated arms negotiations on a world-wide scale rather than
bilateral transactions between the League Council and individual

League members. The general conference on the reduction and limitation of armaments which finally met at Geneva in February 1932 was deeply entangled with the whole European diplomatic situation.[15]

It became clear in the early 1920s, too, that states were disinclined to disarm unless they felt secure, and hence disarmament became part and parcel of all the efforts to increase security by international action. This in its turn involved the peaceful settlement of international disputes since unsettled disputes poisoned the atmosphere between the parties and encouraged them to rearm in order to be able to impose their point of view on their rivals. If states undertook to refer their disputes to impartial third parties – that is, the second stage in the prevention-of-war strategy – there was some hope that the security dilemma could be overcome.

Articles 12 to 17 of the Covenant inclusive therefore spelled out the rules for the settlement of disputes: these had formed part of Anglo-American plans for a League of Nations since the Phillimore report. Disputes likely to lead to a rupture were to be submitted to arbitration, judicial settlement (after the formation of the PCIJ) or inquiry by the Council, and states were bound not to resort to war until three months after one or other of these three bodies had reported (Article 12). If the dispute was considered more suitable for arbitral or judicial settlement than for settlement by diplomacy, that method was to be preferred, such disputes being defined as differences as to 'the interpretation of a treaty, as to the existence of any fact which, if established, would constitute a breach of any international obligation, or as to the extent and nature of the reparation to be made for any such breach'. These were legal disputes properly so called. Members agreed that they would carry out any award resulting from such an arbitral or judicial process, and would not resort to war against any state which did the same (Article 13). There is some contradiction between these two articles in that Article 12 seems to recognise that making war would be legal three months after the arbitrators or the world court have issued their award, whereas Article 13 sets no time limit for the illegality of war waged against a state complying with such an award.

Article 15 took into account the opposite situation, that is, when a dispute likely to lead to a rupture was *not* submitted to arbitration or judicial settlement. The appropriate organ in this case was the Council, and the article spells out the procedure for the conduct of an inquiry by that body. If the Council reached a report unanimously agreed to by its members, states undertook not to go to war with other states which complied with the report. If, however, the Council was unable to agree on a unanimous report (not counting the votes of parties to the dispute), the melancholy conclusion was reached that there was nothing for it but for League members to take such action 'as they shall consider necessary for the maintenance of right and justice'.

Such were the procedures and machinery for peaceful settlement. The hope was that states would make use of them and so render war unnecessary. But suppose they did not? Suppose they made war either without having recourse to the machinery for third-party settlement, or without waiting for arbitrators, court or Council to deliver their verdict, or without regard to whether the other state had or had not complied with the third-party verdict? In that case, under the following Article 16 the war-making state was deemed to have committed an act of war against all other League members, and by this Article they undertook to sever all commercial, financial and personal relations with it, and not merely their relations, but the relations of all other states as well, whether they were members of the League or not. League members also undertook to support each other in bearing the financial burdens resulting from this Article and against any reprisals instituted by the Covenant-breaking state. This, then, is the famous sanctions Article of the Covenant, and it is important to note that the initiative which set it in motion was the realisation by member-states individually that an illegal act of war was being committed. It was not the Council, as in the United Nations system, which had to make the first move. The Council only came into the picture to *recommend* (this permissive word is important) what contributions members should make to the armed forces to be used to protect the covenants of the League. The vagueness of this last phrase suggests that, at the outset of the League's life, it was thought by League supporters that economic and financial boycotts alone would be sufficient to bring an offending state to heel. This view stemmed from the assumption on the Allied side after 1918 that the wartime blockade of Germany had been instrumental in bringing about her defeat.

A significant extension of the League's authority was contemplated in Article 17, the last in the section having to do with the safeguarding of peace. This dealt with disputes between members and non-members and between states neither of which

58

belonged to the organisation. In such cases, non-members were invited to accept the rules of peaceful settlement laid down in Articles 12 to 16 for the purpose of settling the dispute, but if they were unwilling, and if they committed an act of illegal war, as the Covenant defined it, League members were authorised to bring the illegal act to an end by putting into effect the sanctions system. This represents, of course, a considerable departure from the traditional rule of international law that states have no right to impose on third states arrangements they find convenient between themselves: *pacta tertiis nec prosunt nec nocent.* The basis of it, however, was the transfer to international society of the institution known in England as the King's Peace (yet another Anglo-Saxon element in the League structure): the traditional assumption that a sovereign had a right to maintain law and order even in areas outside his jurisdiction. The idea of the King's Peace was also reflected in the famous Article 11 of the Covenant, which authorised the League 'to take any action that may be deemed wise and effectual to safeguard the peace of nations' in the event of any war or threat of war, 'whether immediately affecting any of the Members of the League or not', since such events are declared 'a matter of concern to the whole League'. Article 11 also declares it to be the 'friendly right' of members to bring to the attention of Assembly or Council 'any circumstance whatever affecting international relations or the good understanding between nations upon which peace depends'.

The Anglo-Saxon world tended to compare the spirit behind Article 11 with that of the venerable English practice of the 'hue and cry', the flocking of ordinary people to defend the law when the cry 'Stop thief!' goes up. Some rather rough justice might be done when the crowd takes the law into its own hands in this way, but the idea that everyone has an interest in the public peace at a time when violence takes on the appearance of a forest fire in a high wind was sensible enough.

These arrangements to make peace somewhat more secure were a modest step forward, but that they were tentative, vague and contingent there can be no doubt. Disturbing questions surged in the minds of those who appreciated how near to extinction civilised life had come during the Great War. First, the Covenant system revolved around the idea that international conflicts spring from disputes, that is, formulated differences of opinion between states about matters of law or fact, which can be stated in a fairly precise form, with the rights and wrongs of the case arranged on opposite sides. It was a legal, or rather legalistic, conception of international conflict and reflected the fact that the legal profession was well represented among the founding fathers of the League. Later events were to show that some of the most dangerous conflicts between nations are often in the form of 'situations likely to endanger the maintenance of international peace and security', in which the formulated dispute is merely the spark which touches off the explosion, the symbol of the conflict, rather than its cause.[16]

Secondly, the Covenant provisions for peaceful settlement presupposed the notion of a legal state of war, which came into existence at a determinate moment by a declaration by one or other of the parties. The state of war was highly visible: ambassadors were withdrawn, embassies closed for the duration, troops called to the colours. It *had* to be visible, if League members were to act together in the imposition of effective sanctions. But force between states may take many forms, from a 'war of nerves' accompanied by sporadic acts of violence, raids by irregular forces, the blowing up of the other state's dams or factories by secretive guerrillas, to the crossing of frontiers by regular troops. It is not always easy to say when a 'resort to war' has occurred. In one notorious instance, the Japanese always spoke of their war with China which broke out in July 1937 as an 'incident', and people who wished to think of it as such were free to do so. But this is the difficulty about all attempts to define in a document an international offence which incurs certain stated penalties. To avoid the penalties, or to make it more difficult for states applying the penalties to agree about them, the offence may be disguised, and force in the form of war is not too difficult to disguise as force in some other form, or even as though it were not force at all.

But suppose the issues in dispute were clear, and suppose the 'resort to war' were quite unambiguous, the Covenant still did not condemn *all* war as illegal. The UN Charter of 1945 puts all, or almost all, force or threat of force, and not war only, under a ban, though it exempts certain sorts of self-defensive force. The Covenant, however, still left gaping holes in its war-prevention system, and states were free to conduct quite a lot of war without placing themselves on the wrong side of the law. For instance, the arbitrators, court or Council to which a dispute had been submitted might be unable to agree on a verdict, and in that event League members were free to 'take such action' – which might include making war – 'as they shall consider necessary for the maintenance of right and justice'. It need hardly be said that disagreement about a contentious matter like an international dispute in a political body such as the League Council is such a regular occurrence as almost to be the norm. Of course, one way of ensuring agreement – or, in other words, of winning over an obstructive minority if the vote needed to be unanimous – is to continue watering down the draft resolution until it is entirely innocuous, and this was a practice often resorted to in the League system. These 'gaps' in the League Covenant, or circumstances in which a war might be perfectly legal and no sanctions could be mounted against it, terrified those, especially France and her successor-state allies in eastern Europe, who thought that Germany's defeat in 1918 was a close-run thing, and feared that the Germans would try their luck again. A security system as full of holes as the Covenant, they considered, would not do much to restrain them. Hence it came about that much of the early life of the League was spent in a fruitless effort, by some to plug the gaps in the Covenant, by others to win time in which the all-important confidence between nations might grow, thus making it unnecessary to fill the gaps.

These deficiencies in the Covenant placed a question mark over its operation even if member-states had had all the goodwill in the world. The fact was, however, that all of them, and their peoples, too, had their fair share of human weakness: laziness, complacency, the wish to paper over problems for the time being, fear of entering into unfathomable commitments, of taking stands against powerful trouble-makers – at the other end of the spectrum – impatience, perfectionism, the demand to have all or nothing, vindictiveness, the inability to forget old feuds. It cannot be argued that the Covenant was so loosely drafted that it gave positive encouragement to such failings in its human instruments. But the fact was that the international delinquent who sought to exploit the imperfections of the Covenant to his own advantage could find plenty of material in these articles to work on.

Moreover, in the process of securing agreement on the Covenant at the peace conference hostages were given to fortune in the form of compromises which could not fail to come apart later. One notorious example was the guarantees Article 10, so-called even though the word 'guarantees' did not appear in it. By this extraordinary provision League members undertook 'to respect and preserve, as against external aggression, the territorial integrity and existing political independence' of all other members. If such aggression occurred or was threatened, the

Council was to 'advise upon the means by which this obligation shall be fulfilled'. There could not be a more Herculean task.

Article 10 was, as we saw in the last chapter, President Wilson's personal bequest to the League. Not the least of that organisation's many tragedies was that it was thus saddled with a commitment which stood not the slightest chance of being implemented without the United States, the Power which rejected the League and was never to join it. With America's defection from the League, the burden of Article 10, if it was ever to be fulfilled, must fall on the shoulders of Britain. Only Britain, using her fleet for the transport of troops to any part of the world where some state or other was threatened, could have injected any meaning into the guarantee system. And clearly, the task of underwriting the *status quo* throughout the globe must have far exceeded Britain's resources, even had they all been devoted to it. But it was quite impossible that the British, in the frame of mind in which they were for most of the inter-war period, would have agreed to shoulder such a labour. A substantial part of the 1919 peace settlement itself was distasteful to the British, and had been railroaded through the Paris conference in the teeth of the gravest warnings from some of Britain's leading statesmen, not least her Prime Minister, Lloyd George. In other parts of the world, too, beyond the scope of the peace treaties, British opinion was appalled at the prospect of having to stand for all time, like King Canute, in opposition to the tides of change.

The British had no stomach for Article 10 and would not agree to it without the addition of another article providing for occasional adjustments in the *status quo*. But two disasters overcame that endeavour. One was the physical separation of the new article, which became Article 19, from the Article 10 it was supposed to qualify. The ironical outcome of this was that Article 10, standing alone, acquired an even more inflexible appearance than even Wilson ever wanted to give it. And because it seemed so inflexible, it became totally ineffective since the British and others, especially the British Dominions, refused to pay any serious attention to it. And precisely for that reason, Article 19 lost most of its significance, too, since, if Article 10 was not taken seriously, there could not be much case in taking Article 19, which only had meaning by reference to Article 10, seriously either.

The second disaster which overtook Article 19 was that, in order that it should not seem to threaten the *status quo* too much, it was watered down to such an extent as to lose most of the force it ever had. In the end, the article simply invited the Assembly to advise member-states (the article did not expressly say that the Assembly should be unanimous when it did so, though the implication was that it should) to reconsider 'treaties which have become inapplicable', and to consider 'international conditions whose continuance might endanger the peace of the world'. The intention was that, from time to time, states should be encouraged to revise their political and territorial arrangements so that they are not obliged to 'respect' and 'preserve' (in the language of Article 10) states of affairs which have become obsolete. But reconsidering 'treaties which have become inapplicable' (even if the Assembly could agree to advise it in particular cases) seems a superfluous kind of activity: if a treaty really is inapplicable, there is not much point in reconsidering it. On the other hand, inviting states to consider conditions which might endanger the peace of the world, as Article 19 says, could become a way of provoking states which wanted to change those conditions to endanger the peace of the world in order to draw attention to their grievances. And this is what the later history of Article 19 showed. The article was anxiously pondered by *status quo* states in the 1930s, when the international legal order came under threat and people wondered if the sort of changes in the map that the revisionist states wanted could be effected without force. The strange outcome was that the revisionists became rather more warlike, not less, since they realised that threatening war produced results, and the sort of results they wanted. This might not have occurred had Article 10 not been lodged in the Covenant, largely through Wilson's influence, forcing member-states to find some means of mitigating its absurdities.

We have seen how in Articles 16 and 17 the Covenant took on the image of a form of higher law, in so far as those articles assumed for the League the right to ensure that non-members conformed to the procedures for pacific settlement accepted by League members and suffered the same kind of economic and military sanctions as League members if they resorted to war (even war between themselves) without complying with the procedures for peaceful settlement. This conception of the Covenant as a kind of higher law is also implicit in Article 18, which provided that all treaties entered into by members should be registered with the Secretariat and published by it as soon as possible, thus complying with part at least of the first of President Wilson's Fourteen Points of January 1918 – 'open covenants, openly arrived at'. Article 18 ruled that treaties between members are not binding unless so registered and published, which was interpreted in practice as meaning that they could not be cited before the PCIJ. The 'higher law' conception was implicit, too, in Article 20, which laid down that agreements between member-states which were inconsistent with the terms of the Covenant were automatically abrogated; that members would not in future enter into such agreements; and that they would seek release from agreements of this kind into which they had already entered.

These articles appear to make the Covenant the criterion of legitimacy for all legal engagements between members, though this is somewhat offset by the statement in Article 21 that the Covenant did not affect the validity of 'international engagements such as treaties of arbitration or regional understandings like the Monroe Doctrine' for the maintenance of peace. If any such engagements are inconsistent with the Covenant, their validity *would* seem to be affected by reason of the preceding Article (20). We must assume that the Monroe Doctrine, at least, would have to remain sacrosanct, and publicly declared to be such, if the United States was expected to join the organisation. Article 21 was that declaration.

Like the exchange of guarantees in Article 10, Article 21 is the mark the United States left on the Covenant. Once it became clear that that country was unlikely to join the organisation, the two articles fell into disuse. Logically, there was a case for eliminating them: one was impractical, the other at odds with the rest of the Covenant. But no doubt the United States was considered more likely to resume its seat in the organisation if the two articles were left in the Covenant, and hence the case for removing them was never seriously argued.

V

There remain three more important functions of the League, as set forth in the Covenant, to be discussed. One was the system, alluded to in the previous chapter, by which colonies and other territories formerly under the sovereignty of the Central Powers were defined as a 'sacred trust of civilisation', with securities for the performance of this trust embodied in the Covenant (Article 22). The idea was that the tutelage of the inhabitants of these territories should be entrusted to 'advanced nations' best fitted to exercise it by reason of their resources, experience or geographical situation, and these would discharge their tasks as 'Mandatories of the League'. The mandatories would submit annual reports on the discharge of their responsibilities, and these reports would be examined by a permanent commission composed, not of representatives of states, like the UN Trusteeship Council, but of experts in colonial administration chosen in their personal capacity. The commission was to advise the Council on all matters relating to the mandates system.[17]

The character of the mandate was to vary according to the territory and its people, and distinctions were drawn in Article 22 between three different kinds of mandate. First, the so-called 'A' mandates (though this designation is not used in the article) included 'certain communities formerly belonging to the Turkish empire', which were so highly developed that their independence could be provisionally recognised, subject to a limited period of 'administrative advice and assistance' until they were able to stand on their own feet. 'B' mandates comprised former German colonies in Central Africa (Cameroons, Ruanda-Urundi, Tanganyika, Togoland) for which no definite future was envisaged and which would be administered indefinitely by the mandatory Power with certain safeguards for the population against abuses, such as the slave trade and the traffic in liquor, and for equal opportunities for trade for League members. Lastly, South West Africa and former German islands in the Pacific, known as 'C' mandates, were regarded as so small, scattered and remote that they were best administered as 'integral portions' of the mandatory's territory, though with all the safeguards for the local population provided in the case of 'B' mandates.

The three sorts of territory were allocated to the mandatory Powers (Australia, Belgium, Britain, France, Japan, New Zealand, South Africa), not by the League, but by the Supreme Allied Council at its meeting in San Remo in April 1920.[18] This share-out naturally took on the appearance of a division of spoils of war: the assignment of Syria and Lebanon (much against the will of the local population) as mandates to France, and of Iraq, Transjordan and the ill-fated Palestine to Britain echoed the secret Sykes-Picot agreement of May 1916, which was fully in the spirit of the imperialist European diplomacy of pre-1914. In these cases, the principle laid down in Article 22 of the Covenant that, for 'A' mandates, 'the wishes of these communities must be a principal consideration in the selection of the Mandatory' was hardly respected.

Nevertheless, for all its faults the mandates system (we will consider its history in a later chapter) was a half-way house between outright annexation of former enemy colonial territory and the grant of immediate independence.[19] The latter, in those days of assured white supremacy, was deemed out of the question because the peoples concerned were 'not yet able to stand by themselves under the strenuous conditions of the modern world'. The mandates system went far to establish the international accountability of dependent territories and helped shape (for better or for worse) that mental climate which resulted in the United Nations era in the almost total abolition of the status of dependent territory, at least in the formal sense.

In the process of doing so, the mandatory regime helped to raise the level of colonial administration generally. The fact that the mandatory could be called to book (though in the most gentlemanly way) for the discharge of responsibilities assumed under Article 22 meant that the administration of its colonial territories proper would sooner or later be answerable to world opinion. This would be even more likely to occur if a strong and watchful parliamentary democracy existed in the mandatory's own state. It is interesting to see that Article 23, which follows the mandates article in the Covenant, included an obligation on member-states 'to secure just treatment of the native inhabitants of territories under their control', a faint harbinger of the arrangements relating to non-self-governing territories in Chapter XI of the UN Charter. From the League commitment, among other sources, sprang the process of decolonisation which has transformed the world since the Second World War.

The undertaking in respect of colonial dependencies in Article 23 formed part of a battery of obligations in the social and economic field which was lodged in the Covenant and was to become yet another link between the world of the League and that of its present-day successor, the UN. None of this could have been familiar to President Wilson or the other leading figures at the Paris peace conference. They belonged to the system of almost unmodified nineteenth-century capitalism which drew a sharp distinction between the realms of government and business, the latter involving the working and living conditions of the mass of ordinary people. But in the making of the Covenant a great many organisations which strove for the improvement of these conditions had a hand, or at least sought to play one. These argued the perhaps rather questionable but increasingly fashionable thesis that world peace depends, not only on political and diplomatic arrangements, but on social and economic justice as well. The latter, like everything else, needs to be organised. Trade union leaders, social reformers, women's rights advocates, the promoters of betterment of every kind and description, felt that they could leave nothing to chance.

The social engineering mentality of the Fabian Society had invaded the Covenant. The first item in Article 23 is aimed at securing and maintaining 'fair and humane conditions of labour for men, women and children, both in their own countries and in all countries to which their commercial and industrial relations extend'. International organisations were to be created to achieve this, though in practice only one, the still-surviving International Labour Organisation (ILO), was formed, and this in the same year as the League. The ILO was never to bring about those world-wide conditions of labour which, say, the most optimistic British trade union leader would desire; bargaining between employers and trade unions within the national state was to remain the chief means by which those conditions were improved. But the ILO, like the League itself, helped to make international co-operation in yet another field normal and natural, part of the established landscape, and that was an achievement.[20]

Next (after the commitment to the just treatment of colonial peoples) came the entrusting to the League of supervision of agreements relating to the traffic in women and children, and in opium and other dangerous drugs; supervision of the trade in arms and ammunition (a vain hope, if there ever was one); the maintenance of freedom of communications and transit, and of equitable treatment for the commerce of all League members (a residue of an Italian campaign at the peace conference in favour of a Covenant article guaranteeing freedom of access to raw materials); and a commitment 'to take steps in the matter of international concern for the prevention and control of disease' (to issue, twenty-five years later, in the mammoth UN specialised agency, the World Health Organisation, or WHO).

An agenda for the social and economic work of the League was thus sketched in the Covenant, and a small committee for intellectual co-operation, the forerunner of Unesco, was created in 1922. It was new, almost entirely new, territory for inter-governmental organisations like the League to work in, and therefore had to be approached with caution. Some governments, like the British and those of the British Dominions, had visions of gigantic bureaucracies in Geneva, swallowing up the taxpayer's money. Practically all of them suspected inroads into the private domains of national sovereignty. The League nevertheless managed to acquire, through its network of committees to discuss what to do in these various fields, the rudiments of machinery for world co-operation with a writ as broad as that of any government, though far less cumbrous and elephantine than that of its UN successor.[21] Later, as the League's life drew to its close, many thought that this work in the economic and social fields was the best it ever did. In 1939, the Bruce report on the League's future recommended that the world organisation should be truncated and only its economic and social work preserved.[22]

Lastly, the Covenant established, or sought to establish, the League of Nations as the general manager and overseer of all the international organisations which had sprung into life with the growing interdependence of nations in the previous hundred years. By Article 24, 'all international bureaux already established by general treaties' (the UPU described in the first chapter of this book was the best known example) were to be 'placed under the direction of the League', if that was the will of the parties to them. All such bureaux and 'all commissions for the regulation of matters of international interest' as were formed subsequently would also be placed 'under the direction of the League'. As a possibly formidable addition to the League's commitments, the article further stated that the expenses of bureaux and commissions placed under the League's direction might be included among the expenses of the League Secretariat, with the plain implication that they might, on the other hand, be invited to pay their own way. In the next Article (25), the League was authorised to 'encourage and promote' Red Cross organisations for the improvement of health and the mitigation of suffering.[23]

This supervisory work of the League naturally lent itself to much later rhetoric about the building of a world community to 'underpin' the world organisation's efforts to prevent war between nations. How much of such a world community would actually be built only time would tell. But there was good sense in the advice that the new body, with its tasks so enormous and suspicions about it still so prevalent, should move in a cautious and modest way, avoiding the temptation to take on more commitments than it had any reasonable expectation of being able to fulfil. Since the League would always depend from first to last on the goodwill of governments and peoples, it would have to do all it could to avoid making enemies, either by taking on work better left to others or failing to complete commitments owing to lack of resources or the knowledge necessary to carry them through.

VI

The rules for the League which the Covenant comprised were, of course, more than merely rules: they were also hopes as to how this contraption, the like of which the world had never seen before, would work. The different people who were involved in the League experiment entertained different sorts of hopes. Some considered that the League would consolidate and enforce the treaty system imposed on the defeated Powers; some that it would make possible a revision of those treaties; some that, by means of it, public opinion throughout the world would compel governments to be law-abiding and co-operative; and some that it would be the non-political, non-diplomatic part of the League's work that would develop and form the real basis of a world community.

The Covenant, too, had come into existence as a matter of bargaining and compromise, and that process would continue as long as the League existed. The outcome of bargaining and compromise was a League rule-book vague in many of its clauses, where agreement could not be reached to make greater precision possible. Some of its provisions lacked the automaticity which certain governments desired in order to make their national security doubly sure, while others positively favoured loopholes and provisos because, without them, the League might become an engine of enforcement rather than reconciliation. Men would have to wait and see how these forces shaping the League's nature and personality would develop.

The League Covenant, as so many so often said, was not a prescription for a world state. To be sure, the matters the League was charged by its Covenant to take into its grasp were comprehensive enough by any test, from the settlement of international disputes to the prevention of epidemic diseases, from sanctions against war-making states to eliminating white slave traffic. Potentially, and by reason of its scope, the League could become a world state, though certainly at the moment of its birth the emphasis from first to last was on voluntary co-operation. The Covenant provided member-states with as much international regulation of their affairs as they wanted at any given moment. And the regulation would have to be done by themselves, through their diplomatic representatives in the Council or Assembly, or their robed judges in the world court at The Hague, or their departments of commerce, finance, transport or health represented in the network of League committees. The League was not going to impose order from above – there was no-one in the world to do that; order would have to come from below, from the recognition by states that, whatever objectives they set themselves, they were more likely to achieve those objectives by co-operation with other states than by ignoring or using force against them. The Covenant provided the framework for that co-operation between states. It would depend on them whether and to what extent they would use it.

4 Beginnings and setbacks

I

By 1945, when the United Nations Organisation first saw daylight, international organisations were part of the established landscape. The case for them hardly needed to be argued. True, the League had failed, but that, it was said, was because it never had the power to enforce peace, and this time the UN would have that power. By contrast, when the League came into existence on 10 January 1920, it faced a sceptical world and the case for it was far from universally accepted. Even in the Anglo- Saxon countries and Scandinavia, where support for the League was strongest, powerful sections of opinion were indifferent, even contemptuous. By and large, French opinion did not believe the League could prevent renewed German aggression and France's strongest allies, the new states of Eastern Europe, looked, like her, to their own armies rather than the League for their security. The Germans regarded the League as a tool for enforcing the hated treaty they had been forced to sign in 1919; in any case, the French veto prevented them joining the new body. The Bolsheviks in Russia spoke of the League as a 'band of robber nations'. Their view was reinforced in 1926, when, to the horror of the Russians, Weimar Germany was at length allowed to join the League.

Symptomatic of the hostility which faced the League all its life, and especially in its earliest years, was the stream of complaints about its alleged financial extravagance, none being more sustained than those of Britain and the British Dominions, as they were then known. From the first session of the Assembly in November-December 1920 until the League's demise, the Secretariat worked in an atmosphere of continuous carping about money, even though regular inquiries into the management of League finances invariably resulted in a clean bill of health. The parsimony the League's officers were compelled to practise had hardly any parallel within the administration of its member-states. In one of the League's bodies, the Committee for Intellectual Co-operation (an ancestor of the present-day Unesco), the learned men and women making up its membership paid their own fares to and from Geneva and occasionally clubbed together to finance the Committee's correspondence.

The average annual cost of the League, the ILO and the Permanent Court at The Hague during the whole of their lives (1920-1946) was $5.5 million, when the dollar stood at somewhat below five to the pound sterling. Britain, the largest single contributor, paid on the average 11 per cent of the League's budget, a sum amounting to £150,000 a year, or slightly more than one half-penny per head. The spending of tax-payers' money needs always to be carefully controlled, especially when those doing the spending are geographically, and perhaps culturally, remote from the source of the funds. But it is hard to avoid the impression that the grudging watchfulness surrounding the League's finances concealed a basic distaste for the whole enterprise.[1]

The climate in which the League was born being so chilling, the setbacks it suffered needed to be few and far between if confidence in it was to grow; yet confidence was only likely to grow if the new body was seen to be making a real contribution to the welter of problems which oppressed the world when the war ended in 1918. In its first two or three years therefore, the League had to choose between doing little or nothing and risking failures, and the tendency was to lean towards the former. During 1920, 1921 and 1922, the League, which, in the opinion of its supporters, was going to be the saviour of mankind, sat in the sidelines while world politics were filled with tumult. In Eastern Europe was chaos and seemingly endless war, within the Soviet state and between it and its neighbours. In the Near East, as it was still called, a revolution raged in Turkey which led to war with Greece, ending disastrously for the latter and almost embroiling Britain, too. In Central Europe, Germany teetered on the brink of revolution and intermittent fighting raged on her eastern borders with the reborn Poland until well into the 1920s. In Western Europe, Britain and France quarrelled over enforcement of the treaty they had made with Germany and seemed at times not far short of resorting to arms to settle the question.[2] The aftermath of war was hard, yet at Geneva the League was all dressed up and nowhere to go.

One reason for this was that the Allied Powers, Britain, France, Italy and, to a lesser extent, Japan, had no intention of letting the League interfere with the way in which they handled problems left behind by the war, unless they should prove completely insoluble or some technical issue could be passed on to the League, as happened, for instance, at the inter-Allied conference on reparations at Genoa in April 1922.[3] The war, after all, had cost the Allies dear and the rewards they had won by fighting to the end already seemed to be slipping from their grasp. They had no wish to see the profits shared out in the company of little states in the League which had not borne the burden of the war. The Allies had their own agencies for handling such questions and contended that they did not come within the League's purview. One such body was the Allied Supreme Council, representing the Big Four and the United States, so long as America chose to be represented, a continuation of the Supreme War Council for co-ordinating policies during the struggle with the Central Powers. Another was the Conference of Ambassadors, meeting in different capitals and representing the same four or five leading states. A third body was the Inter-Allied Reparations Commission established by the peace conference in 1919 to determine, then to exact, the compensation to be paid by the defeated for the loss and damage they had allegedly caused.

The League thus tended to be left with the small change of diplomacy, questions which, for one reason or another, the Allies did not wish to keep in their own hands. The League Council, consisting of the same four Allies, Britain, France, Italy and Japan (the American government still had no authority to attend its meetings), together with representatives of four other states, at its first meeting in Paris on 16 January 1920, and the Assembly, at its first plenary session in Geneva in October and November of the same year, thus found themselves concerned with three kinds of assorted questions, which were to dominate their agenda for the next few years: matters the League was charged to attend to by the 1919 peace treaties; matters referred to it by individual countries or by such bodies as the Supreme Council; and matters of internal organisation, most of which arose from the Covenant itself.[4]

II

Among the first of these three groups of questions, the disposition of the Saar Territory was dealt with expeditiously, considering the intense emotions it stirred between France and Germany. Lying to the south-west of Luxembourg, the Saar basin was an 800-square mile area rich in coal and populated by 650,000 German-speaking people and a small French minority. In 1815 it had fallen under Prussian control and formed part of the united Germany of 1871. In 1919, its coal mines were ceded to France in full and absolute possession as compensation for the destruction of mines in the Nord and Pas-de-Calais area of France during the war. The government of the territory, however, was assigned by the Versailles Treaty to the League as a trustee, and after fifteen years the League was to hold a plebiscite to determine the future of the territory.[5] The League Council's task was twofold: to set up a five-member commission, one to be appointed by France, another by Germany and the other three by the Council, to trace on the spot the Saar's frontiers as laid down by Article 48 of the treaty, and to establish another five-member Commission, which would reside in the Saar Territory and administer it until the plebiscite in 1935.

At its first sessions the Council settled down to creating the two bodies, the more important Governing Commission eventually consisting of a French chairman, Victor Raulte, a Saarlander, and Belgian, Danish and Canadian members.[6] No sooner had the Commission taken up its residence in the capital, Saarbrucken, however, than friction sprang up between it and the local population. Disputes raged about the powers of the Advisory Council of thirty Saarlanders which the Governing Commission established in March 1922, the Saarlanders insisting that it should be regarded as a Parliament, the French disagreeing. In February 1923, during the height of the crisis arising from the French occupation of the Ruhr, a miners' strike broke out and the League Council had to consider Raulte's plea for doubling the French garrison of 2,000 men. With the improvement of Franco-German relations in the mid-1920s, however, the situation improved and in April 1927 the French garrison was withdrawn.[7] Eight years later, the Saarlanders voted overwhelmingly to return to the Motherland and the League's responsibilities in the territory came to an end.[8]

A similar chore assigned to the League by the Versailles treaty, which also reflected its role as a tool of the Allied peacemakers, was the disposition of the districts of Eupen and Malmédy, which in August 1914 lay to the east of Germany's border with Belgium. Article 34 of the Versailles Treaty assigned to Belgium all rights and title over the two districts and Belgium was charged with opening registers in which the inhabitants would indicate whether they wished to remain under German sovereignty or be included in Belgium. The outcome of this 'public expression of opinion' was to be communicated to the League and Belgium was bound to accept the League's decision in the matter. The Germans pressed the League Council to appoint a commission to supervise Belgium's arrangements for testing opinion in Eupen and Malmédy, but at its session in San Sebastian in July 1920 the Council refused to take action until Belgium had done her part.[9] Shortly afterwards the Belgians held the plebiscite, which they reported as confirming the transfer of the districts to themselves. Germany protested, but the Council was unmoved.

The third item under this head was the tangled question of Danzig. Danzig, the great German port on the Baltic, was excluded from the German territory, later called the Polish Corridor, which was handed to the reconstituted Poland by the 1919 peace conference in order that it should have an outlet to the sea. By Article 101 of the Versailles Treaty, the port and its hinterland were established as a Free City under the League's protection. The League was to appoint a High Commissioner, who would live in Danzig and co-operate with the duly appointed representatives of the Free City in drawing up a constitution for Danzig, and this would be guaranteed by the League. The League was thus firmly locked into the Polish-German settlement of 1919, although important questions affecting the city were still left to the Allied Powers, and the way in which these were settled could not but affect political stability in the area on which the constitutional arrangements which the League was supposed to guarantee would depend. By Article 104 of the treaty, for example, the Allies were charged with negotiating an agreement between the new Poland and Danzig for the regulation of such matters as Danzig's foreign relations, which Poland was to conduct. The Allies, too, were given charge by Article 107 of the Versailles Treaty of all properties in the city formerly belonging to the German Empire, which they were free to dispose of as they liked. It looked as though the Allies and Poland were going to take the big decisions in Danzig and the League was expected to take care of the consequences.

Danzig was on the League Council's agenda at its first meeting in Paris on 16 January 1920, and when it met on 13 February in London it appointed the first High Commissioner for the Free City in the person of Sir Reginald Tower, who was already acting as the

Temporary Administrator appointed by the Allies.[10] Tower's term came to an end in November, when the Free City was formally established and in December Sir Richard Haking was appointed by the Council for one year as from 20 January 1921.[11] In February 1923 Haking was succeeded by M.S. MacDonnell, Governor of the Western Province of India.[12] Disputes between Poland and the Free City continued throughout the inter-war years, forming the bulk of the questions affecting Danzig which were brought before the League Council, until they were swallowed up in the general tensions between Poland and the Third Reich which preceded the outbreak of war in September 1939. The League, through its involvement in the Danzig question by the peace treaties, was thus caught up in the cross-fire between Germany and the democratic states as a guardian of the *status quo* ordained by the latter at the end of the war.

The League was also tied into the peace settlement through the minorities treaties signed between the Allied Powers and the successor states which came into existence as a result of the collapse of the Central Powers in the closing stages of the war. Theoretically, the overriding principle of the peace settlement was national self-determination, which was supposed to mean that everyone had a right to live in a state of his or her own nationality. The ethnographic map of Europe, especially in the east and south-east, however, was highly irregular and national minorities were inevitably left within the new states emerging from the peace settlement, no matter how carefully their borders were drawn. Since so much stress had been laid by Woodrow Wilson and other Allied leaders on the rights of nationality, measures had to be taken to ensure that national enclaves within states of predominantly different nationality enjoyed human rights, especially the use of their own language, to the full. It was natural that these arrangements for the protection of minorities should be placed under the League's guarantee, and equally natural that not a little of the rancour engendered by the minorities treaties, both on the side of the states concerned and that of the minorities and the external states to which they looked for protection, should rub off on the League.

By Article 12 of the minorities treaty between the Allies and Poland, signed in 1919, for instance, it was agreed that the arrangements should be placed under the League's guarantee. A more difficult case was that of the non-Islamic enclaves in Turkey, a familiar concern of the European Powers in the nineteenth century. At its fourth session in Paris in April 1920, the Council had before it an inquiry from Lord Curzon, the British delegate to the Supreme Council, whether it would agree to the protection of these two million people: the Council did agree, but since peace with Turkey had not yet been made and that country was in a state of revolutionary turmoil, the Council's agreement could not mean much.[13] The humiliating treaty of Sèvres was signed on the Sultan's behalf on 10 April 1920, but it was repudiated by the Turkish Parliament, and the Council, though it agreed to nominate members of a commission to supervise minority rights in Turkey, wisely insisted that the commission could only act under the control of the parties to the treaty, which was another way of saying that the Allies must create the conditions under which the commission could work.

A somewhat different form of activity of the League in the human rights field was the Council's agreement to nominate two members of a commission to execute a treaty of 27 November 1919 between Bulgaria and Greece for the reciprocal emigration of minorities in the two countries. By 1922 the Council was reporting through the Secretary-General to the Third League Assembly that the organisation had undertaken guarantees of minority rights in Austria, Bulgaria, Czechoslovakia, Hungary, Poland, Rumania and the Serbo-Croat-Slovene state (later Yugoslavia).[14] The list was soon extended to include Albania, Estonia, Finland, Latvia and Lithuania. The procedure of inquiry into allegations of violations of these minorities treaties was that any Council member was free to draw the Council's attention to 'any infraction, or danger of infraction, of obligations resulting from the stipulations in question'. The Council was charged, after being so notified, 'to take such action and give such directions as may seem proper in the circumstances'.

III

When we consider the second group of questions coming before the League in its first years, those referred to it by outside bodies, the impressive feature, again, is their range and variety, and their miscellaneous character. They formed the small change of world affairs and the people who instigated the League to act could presumably think of no better destination for them. The League authorities did the best they could, on the basis of ridiculously small resources.

One such question, the result of appeals from many quarters, brought on to the League stage one of its mightiest personalities, the Norwegian explorer, Fridjof Nansen, whom the Council at its fourth session in Paris on 11 April 1920 summoned to its aid for the repatriation of the two to three million prisoners taken on the Eastern front during the war and then scattered through Russia by revolution and civil war.[15] The organisation which the indefatigable Nansen built up within the League's framework almost single-handedly formed the foundation stone for all the later international relief work for refugees. The Council's other intervention in Russian affairs in these early years, however, was attended with less success. At its third session in Paris in March 1920, the Council had before it a letter from the British Prime Minister, Lloyd George, asking for a study to be made for the Supreme Council of the state of affairs in Russia, especially the conditions of labour. One of Lloyd George's most persistent notions was that European recovery was impossible without co-operation with the Russians. The Council duly decided to send a team of inquiry to Russia, but the Bolshevik authorities retorted that visitors would not be welcome who had been 'associated with plots against the Russian government' or who had helped the country with which Russia was then at war, Poland. The Council read this reply as tantamount to a refusal and abandoned the project.[16]

The League Council was also embarrassed by yet another attempt to embroil it in Soviet affairs when in May 1920 the Persian government appealed to the League under Article 11 of the Covenant, which referred to action in the event of war or threat of war, when Persia was invaded by Soviet forces across its northern borders with Russia. It was the first issue submitted to the League by a member-state. Fortunately, the Council was able, with some show of relief, to argue that Persia and Russia were already involved in negotiations over the matter. The League's intervention was therefore not called for.[17]

A more successful enterprise involving the League at this time was the settlement of the troublesome, though not dangerous, dispute between Finland and Sweden concerning sovereignty over the Aaland islands, a group straddling the exit from the Gulf of Bothnia into the Baltic Sea. The case was referred to the Council under Article 11 of the Covenant by Britain, who called for a special meeting of the Council to deal with it.[18] This was opposed by the Finnish authorities, who claimed that it was a matter of domestic jurisdiction, and therefore outside the League's purview, while Sweden wanted a plebiscite. The issue of domestic jurisdiction was dealt with by a committee of three jurists appointed by the Council (the world court at The Hague was not yet constituted), which declared against Finland and authorised the Council's intervention. The Council then took up the matter again at its eighth session in Paris in September 1920 and appointed a three-man group of rapporteurs.[19] When the Council met on 24 June 1921, it accepted the rapporteurs' recommendation that the islands should belong to Finland but with guarantees for the protection of the islanders. The Swedes reluctantly agreed.[20] Negotiations then began on the neutralisation and demilitarisation of the islands and on 20 October 1921 a convention to achieve these ends was signed at Geneva by ten states. It was the first European international agreement to be concluded under the direct auspices of the League.[21]

Settlement of the Aaland islands question could be counted a success. The same could not be said for the League's involvement in the long-drawn-out Lithuanian-Polish question, yet another East European controversy. Lithuania and Poland were two countries resurrected by the peace settlement which immediately proceeded to quarrel with each other (and with their neighbours) about land. On 5 September 1920, the Polish Foreign Minister, Prince Sapieha, wired the League Council about his fears of imminent war between the two countries as a result of frontier disagreements. On 7 October, a commission appointed by the Council had negotiated an armistice, though Lithuania still complained about Polish advances into territory assigned to herself by the Supreme Council. Two days later, on 9 October, however, General Zeligowski, with a Polish force for which the Warsaw authorities assumed no responsibility, seized the city of Vilna and proclaimed a Government of Central Lithuania under his own protection.[22]

The League Council called for a plebiscite in the disputed territory and referred the question to a committee chaired by the Belgian Foreign Minister, Paul Hymans, the report of which both Lithuania and Poland refused to accept. On 24 September 1921 the Second League Assembly heard Hymans relate the deadlock and once again appealed to the two countries to reach agreement. But their relations worsened further and in March 1922 the Poles formally announced the annexation to themselves of the Vilna province to the tune of complaints from Lithuania of the arrest of Lithuanians and White Russians in the territory and of prisoners held in insanitary conditions in Kovno. The situation remained tense until, on 14 March 1923, the Allied Conference of Ambassadors, acting in accordance with Article 87 of the Versailles Treaty, which authorised the Allies to determine frontiers not settled by the treaty, fixed the frontier along the lines broadly laid down by the Hymans committee.[23] Vilna was left inside Poland, and thus the Allies, with the assistance of the League Council, in the end endorsed Zeligowski's original act of force.

The same tendency for events to be decided by armed force while the League could do little but sit and observe was witnessed in the tragic case of Armenia. The sufferings of the Armenian Christians at the hands of the Turks and their aspirations for a state of their own had been a theme of European diplomacy throughout most of the nineteenth century: it received passionate expression by speaker after speaker at the First League Assembly in November-December 1920.[24] The Allies had proposed to form an autonomous Armenian state when Turkey capitulated in 1918, but how was that to be enforced against the new Turkey forged from defeat by Kemal Ataturk, which renounced the Arab portions of the old Ottoman empire but would allow no dismemberment of Anatolia, along the eastern borders of which with Russia the Armenians lived? The Supreme Council hopefully inquired of the League, through its Council, if it would accept a mandate for Armenia, and when A.J. Balfour, speaking for the Council on 11 April 1920, pointed out that the League had no authority to accept mandates, but only to supervise them, the Supreme Council approached the United States with the same request.[25] The American Congress rejected the idea in June with large majorities in both Houses.[26]

mandate which meant fighting the Turks, and doubtless the Russians, too, to establish it. René Viviani, a former French Prime Minister, let the truth slip about the League in this and so many other questions when he said in the First Assembly that we are 'in the ridiculous position of an Assembly which considers what steps shall be taken, though it is perfectly aware that it is impossible for them to be carried out'.[27] But more than authority was lacking: there was also the money and the armed force to put glowing words about Armenia into effect.

The point was underlined again in March 1921. The Allies had occupied certain towns in the Ruhr, including Duisburg, Düsseldorf and Ruhrort, as a form of sanction against alleged non-payment of reparations by Germany. The German government complained to the League Council and the Secretary-General circulated the complaint to member-states.[28] There was no response. The Council could not put such an item on its agenda unless a member-state took the initiative and no initiative was taken.

The delimitation of the boundary between Germany and Poland in Upper Silesia, however, proved to be a happier example of how the League could help damp down the residual fires of war. The League's plan for the boundary became the basis for a transitional regime in the area destined to last for 15 years; when it lapsed in 1937, Poland had long been enrolled in Nazi Germany's list for destruction. The Upper Silesian settlement in 1922 bought valuable time and provided the basis for a peace in Eastern Europe that might have endured had the wider political forces been favourable. The issue was referred to the League Council by Aristide Briand on 12 August 1921, after a plebiscite had awarded the bulk of the disputed territory to Poland, with a request that the Council should relieve the Allies of the task of demarcating the frontier. The Council agreed and set up a four-man commission, representing Belgium, Brazil, China and Spain, to make a preliminary study.[29] The commission recommended the negotiation of a convention between the two countries and a conference with this object in view met in Geneva in November 1921 under the chairmanship of Felix Calonder, a former president of the Swiss Confederation. After only five meetings the conference reached final agreement on 13 April 1922. The text of the convention was published in Geneva on 15 May.[30] While indignation surged in Germany against it – the convention awarded the bulk of the territory to Germany, but most of its mineral wealth and many of its industries were left in the residue which went to Poland – both states nevertheless ratified the agreement and on 22 June Allied forces left Upper Silesia, which they had been occupying since the war. Tension remained high between Germany and Poland throughout the inter-war period, but, in an unspectacular way, the League had played a useful part.

Another instance of timely League assistance in the solution of early problems of the peace years, helping the Allies to make tolerable the world they had made, was its contribution to the reconstruction of the two ex-enemy states, Austria and Hungary.

The plight of Austria was tragic after the war, its brilliant capital city, Vienna, once the centre of a vast Central European empire, now shorn of the provinces from which it drew its wealth, like an overgrown head crowning a shrunken torso. By February 1922, economic collapse was feared, emergency advances being tendered by Britain, Czechoslovakia, France and Italy. In August the Allied Supreme Council referred the Austrian situation to the League Council and that body, on the basis of a report from its Financial Committee, formed an Austrian Committee consisting of three Council member-states (Britain, France, Italy), a Czech delegate invited to join the Council for this item and Chancellor Seipel of Austria. The Committee produced a scheme of reform which reflected orthodox economic theory – 'Austria has been consuming much more than she has produced' was the main theme – and measures were proposed for the more efficient running of state enterprises and balancing the budget.[31]

On 4 October 1922 three protocols were signed. The first confirmed Austria's independence and thus ruled out what many, especially in France, feared, namely a German take-over designed to avert a complete collapse of Austria. The second protocol detailed the guarantees to be given by the British, French and Italian governments of loans for Austrian reconstruction to be raised in the world's money markets. The third spelled out Austria's obligations – the country was, in short, expected to put its house in order and balance its budget by 1924 – and the role of a Commissioner-General, who was to reside in Vienna and report monthly to the Council on the implementation of the programme. As Commissioner-General the Council appointed Dr Zimmerman, the Burgomaster of Rotterdam. As for the foreign loans envisaged in the scheme, these were of two types: a short-term loan of £3 million to be placed in the Amsterdam, Brussels, London, Paris, Stockholm and Swiss stock markets, and a twenty-year loan amounting to 585 gold crowns or £26 million. The essential features of the agreement were thus a programme of financial reform extending over two years; provision to meet deficits during these years by guaranteed loans; an arrest of the collapse of the Austrian crown; and strict supervision of the Austrian government's implementation of the scheme.[32]

The plan of assistance for Austria was one of the League's most notable achievements. The two loans were floated in the money markets in the summer of 1923, but so successful were the financial measures recommended by the League Council's committee that by 1924 the Austrian budget was balanced without the loans needing to be called upon. In 1926 the League Commission was withdrawn from Vienna.[33] True, the later history of Austria, up to and including its absorption by Nazi Germany in March 1938, was far from happy, and this was due to deep-seated economic problems and the accompanying social conflicts which the war had left in its wake. Nevertheless, the immediate post-war reconstruction effected under the League's auspices was a resounding success.

The scheme for Austrian reconstruction served as a model for a similar arrangement, though on a smaller scale, for Hungary, which had become a separate state with the dissolution of Austria-Hungary, or the Dual Monarchy, in November 1918. Hungary was unanimously admitted into League membership in 1922 at the Third Assembly. The economic and financial restoration in 1922 of that country was based on two protocols, similar to the arrangements for Austria, which were signed at the League's headquarters on 14 March 1924.[34] Naturally, if Germany's allies could be admitted into the League, and helped to return to financial health by the League, the question was bound to be asked: how long would it be before Germany returned to favour?

IV

The third and final group of questions coming before the League in the early years were matters of internal organisation: they arose from the Covenant itself and took the form of commitments laid down for the League by its constitution. Of dominant and persistent importance under this head was disarmament, or, as it was generally known in the inter-war period, the reduction and limitation of armaments. The Council's first task in this field was to appoint on 19 May 1920 a body, called the Permanent Advisory Committee, or Commission (PAC), to advise on the drawing up of the general scheme of disarmament referred to in Article 8 of the Covenant and on the armaments position of new member-states, as required by Article 1. The Committee was to consist of naval, military and air warfare experts nominated by each of the states represented in it.[35]

The PAC met for the first time in December 1920 and recommended that to draw up a scheme of arms reduction would be 'premature'. The Assembly, however, at its first general session in 1920 clamoured for action and this pressure led to the formation of another body, called the Temporary Mixed Commission (TMC), consisting of sixteen unofficial members, which was charged with preparing an arms reduction plan for the Council. Such a plan was drawn up by the British member, Lord Esher, which took the form of a simple percentage cut in armed forces, rather like that applied to battleships in the five-Power Washington naval treaty in 1922.[36] Objection was raised to the proposal on the ground that it would favour countries with large land armies since their equipment would be unaffected. Moreover, the Esher plan demonstrated the impracticability of the direct approach to disarmament – that is, the reduction of armed forces without political devices for security, since few countries were likely to abandon their armaments without some alternative system of security being provided. According to Resolution XIV, unanimously adopted by the Third Assembly in 1922, 'in the present state of the world, many Governments would be unable to accept the responsibility for a serious reduction of armaments unless they received in exchange a satisfactory guarantee of the safety of their country'.[37] Disarmament postulated foolproof collective security, and the quest for this was touched off by the TMC's first venture into the field. The question, however, merges with the larger issue of the development of the Covenant during these early years and will be taken up again later in the present chapter.

Next among the matters arising from the Covenant came the finalising of arrangements for the mandatory regime, outlined in Article 22. When all the rhetoric was stripped away, the mandates were in effect the rewards for the Allied victory in the late war. They were not annexations; nevertheless, the Allies were determined that they themselves should administer former German and Turkish territories which they had liberated and which were adjacent to their own lands. This meant that the Allied Supreme Council was inevitably the body to allocate the mandates: it did so during sessions of the Paris peace conference in May 1919 and at a session of the Supreme Council held in San Remo in April 1920. The 'A' mandates, consisting mainly of Arab-inhabited territories in the Middle East, went to Britain and France: Palestine, Mesopotamia and Transjordan to Britain, Syria and Lebanon to France. Germany's former African territories went as 'B' mandates to Britain (Tanganyika, a half of Cameroons, a half of

Togoland), France (the other halves of the Cameroons and Togoland), Belgium (Ruanda-Urundi), and South Africa (South West Africa), though the last was designated a 'C', not a 'B', mandate. Germany's former dependencies in the Pacific north of the equator were assigned to Japan as 'C' mandates (with American complaints about Japan taking over the naval base and communications centre of Yap), while those south of the equator went to Australia, except for Samoa, which became a New Zealand mandate, and Nauru, which came under British administration. The League Council had little to do in the early days except to 'define the terms of the mandate' with the administering authority. These negotiations were strictly confidential. The Wilsonian axiom of open diplomacy was limited in its application.[38]

Finally, and again arising mainly from the Covenant itself, came a congeries of miscellaneous technical questions, chiefly derivative from Article 23 of the Covenant, which gave the League a footing in the whole range of non-political international relations widely regarded at that time as the truly novel feature of the modern world. Under this heading came the establishment of a Transit Organisation intended, in the words of Article 23, 'to secure and maintain freedom of communications and of transit and equitable treatment for the commerce of all Members of the League'. The first conference of the Organisation, attended by forty-four states, met in Barcelona in March 1921 and drew up two conventions on communications and transit which remained in force until 1939; it agreed to meet in future at intervals of four years.[39] In the previous May the Council had set up a temporary Epidemics Committee to combat the outbreak of infectious diseases, including typhus, in Central Europe. This became the embryo of the League's Health Organisation; its appeal for funds, however, to deal with the typhus outbreak in Europe met with a poor response.[40]

On 13 February 1920, the Council resolved to call an international financial conference, which at length met in Brussels in September, to deal with the prevailing world-wide financial and exchange crisis.[41] A notable feature of this was the attendance of an American observer, Roland W. Boyden, despite the general boycott of the League being practised by the American authorities. Meanwhile, the first paragraph of Article 23 of the Covenant, referring to 'fair and humane conditions of labour for men, women and children', had already been implemented by a conference which met in Washington from 29 October to 29 November 1919 and brought into existence the still surviving

International Labour Organisation (ILO), with its unique threefold system for the representation of governments, employers and workers and its annual conference for the adoption of recommendations meant to provide, in the course of time, a world-wide body of labour law.[42]

The work of the new League in the technical field continued to grow throughout the Geneva organisation's life, taking in its province the traffic in opium and other dangerous drugs, the trade in women and children, the protection of minorities and refugees, the sale of arms and ammunition to countries in which it might have adverse effects. The field of work was virtually unlimited. The danger was that, in their enthusiasm, League bodies might take on more commitments than they could ever hope to command the resources to fulfil. An important rule must be that it was just as vital to find other agencies to do such work and to encourage them as much as possible, as to involve the League itself in such undertakings.

V

Thus the League's efforts to overcome its first disappointment, that of being elbowed out of some of the most burning questions, were partially successful. Other setbacks, however, crowded in during the organisation's infancy, by far the most damaging being the decision of the United States not to ratify the 1919 peace treaties and hence to abstain from League membership. The irony that the American President, Woodrow Wilson, had been the chief driving force behind the League's creation was matched by the catastrophic effects for the League and world peace of his failure to secure for the peace settlement the support of his people, or rather, of the American Senate, the consent of two-thirds of the members of which is necessary for the ratification of treaties.

As historians have almost unanimously agreed, some responsibility for this failure lay with Wilson himself. Utterly dedicated to the League idea, utterly hostile to the 'power politics' of Europe which the League was intended to supplant, Wilson brooked no opposition to his ideals, or suggestions that he should dilute them in order to secure the assent necessary to action. His first mistake was to make the system of universal guarantees the heart of the Covenant, a proposal which no other founding father of the League could accept, and which ultimately fell foul of the Senate. His second was to refuse to associate the Republican party, in which isolationist forces were strongly represented, with this radical venture in American intervention, which ran against all the traditions of foreign policy reaching back to George Washington. Even after the victories of the Republicans in the mid-term elections in November 1918, which gave the Republicans a majority of forty-five in the House of Representatives and resulted in a Senate Foreign Relations Committee 'packed with irreconcilable foes of the President', Wilson declined to take Republican leaders (or even Democratic leaders) to Paris with him to make the peace.[43] It was a mistake no interventionist American President has been foolhardy enough to repeat since.

The effect of this blunder was not merely the loss of an opportunity for Congressmen to modify the treaties before they were called upon to approve them. It was also to drive even the more sympathetic American politicians into the arms of the more intransigent isolationists: the supporters of extremists like Senator Lodge, who led the fight against the treaties, grew, while those of Taft and other moderates shrank. Yet even Lodge was not an unqualified opponent of the League. The fourteen reservations which he and his followers introduced into the Senate debate on the treaties (they were not called amendments and hence were regarded as less than definite attempts to change the treaties) were not unreasonable. Two of the most important, the strengthening of the reference to the Monroe Doctrine in Article 21 of the Covenant and the modification of the guarantee system in Article 10 so that Congressional agreement would be required whenever a call was made to implement the guarantees, concerned issues on which the European Allies shared many of the American doubts. The Allies had gone a long way to meet American fears about the effects of the collective security system on the Monroe Doctrine and were no doubt prepared to go even further. As for Article 10, it was the one about which European statesmen always strongly dissented from Wilson.[44]

It is conceivable that, with more flexibility, the President could have secured the passage of the treaties through the Senate. In the final Senate vote on 19 March 1920 (the first was on 19 November 1919) there was actually a numerical majority in favour of ratification (49 to 35), but this fell short of the required two-thirds. Had the President's supporters not been persuaded to join an unholy combination with the diehards against the treaties, instead of negotiating some compromise with Wilson's opponents, the situation might have been saved. On the other hand, it is questionable whether, even had the vote gone the other way and the United States had joined the League, its commitment to the world organisation would have been firm. The revulsion in the United States against the world diplomatic system in the 1920s was strong. It was reminiscent of similar feelings in Britain. Just as many British people considered after 1918 that their involvement in the Great War was due to French intrigue, so Americans blamed the wily Europeans, or their own financiers or private armaments manufacturers, for their entanglement in a struggle from which they had gained few apparent benefits. Wilson, as an ex-academic, might have some theoretical basis for the new world system at Geneva. The ordinary American saw only the terrible price which he had paid, and, if he was not careful, would have to pay again, to rescue Europeans from their self-destructive nationalism.

Wilson went down to defeat in the elections in November 1920, despite a desperate attempt to rally support for the League in the form of a nation-wide tour which ended in a paralytic stroke in October 1919. He died on 3 February 1924. His successor, Warren Gamaliel Harding, entering the White House on 4 March 1921, wasted no time in declaring his opposition to the League, though his Secretary of State, Charles Evans Hughes, enjoyed some reputation as an interventionist. Harding even toyed with the idea of forming a rival organisation to the League, leading some European governments to reduce their contribution to the League's work in case it should be superseded by the new American body. American officials, too, took no trouble to make things easier for the League: often they neglected to answer, or took excessive time to answer, inquiries from the League, delayed the settlement of questions affecting Americans in the new mandated territories, and corresponded with the League through intermediaries rather than directly. The American habit of turning against defeated Presidents had the effect of making the League the recipient of revulsion directed against Wilson himself.

But whether American objections to the League system in the early 1920s were insurmountable, or whether they could have been overcome by better presentation of the League's case by American supporters, the fact remains that the absence of the United States from the League was by far the most serious blow during its lifetime. It is no exaggeration to say that the failure of the League to prevent the Second World War after only two decades of peace was more due to the absence of the United States from its peace-keeping arrangements than to any other cause. The peace which the United States had signally helped to win in 1918 and the content of which she importantly contributed towards shaping she did not stay to enforce.

There are also the more immediate effects of the American disaster on the League's prospects. First, the world-wide network of social and economic co-operation, which the League began to build up in its early years, while its burden of political work, as we have seen, remained light, could hardly be comprehensive while a country the size and importance of the United States remained outside.[45] Again, and even more importantly, the effects of American non-membership of the League were almost fatal for its peace-enforcement procedures and machinery. The essence of the Covenant was the obligation laid on member-states to sever all links with countries resorting to illegal forms of war, and, if that was not effective, to bring the offending state into line by more forcible restraints. There were the famous principles of collective security. But if a giant state like America was not a party to such world-wide ostracism, the prospects of it succeeding might almost be written off. Blockades of aggressive states necessitated American participation. The loopholes would be too big without it.

Since the United States would not participate in the League's enforcement of peace, it followed that other member-states would have to do more. But the wholly undefined commitments of collective security were already frightening; when it was known that the United States would not be a participant on the same terms as everyone else, the effect was stunning. The Senate's action in refusing to ratify the treaties thus played a major role in the whittling down of the League's requirements from member-states which began almost with its birth.

Possibly the most serious consequence of the American defection from the League, however, was to widen the gulf between British and French attitudes towards the peace, and thus to contribute to their fatal inability to act together when the great challenges to the League came in the 1930s. On almost every major issue of international affairs during the inter-war period the British and French failed to see eye to eye; about the only occasion on which they did was in the last months of the peace, when they decided, far too late, that they must take up the challenge posed by Hitler's Germany. These differences took the sharpest form over the question of sanctions against aggression.

British politicians believed that the Senate's refusal to ratify the treaties could not be its last word: that that body might have second thoughts and America might join the League after all. That possibility must be allowed for, otherwise the League experiment might as well be wound up. But this seemed more likely if Covenant obligations were made as light as possible. What the British in effect tried to do was to reintroduce the Lodge reservations back into the Senate debate, and thus secure the two-thirds vote for them which Wilson's supporters had prevented by refusing to give way. These tactics were consistent with a whole range of British attitudes to the Covenant: the British discouraged 'legalistic' arrangements for collective security, as distinct from more spontaneous commitments; they preferred to allow a League member to contribute to collective defence as and when it wished; and they were not averse to those parts of the treaty settlement to which Britain objected falling quietly into disuse because collective action could not be mustered to support them. It was almost as though British opinion actually welcomed American non-participation in the League because it had the effect of making more attractive the looser, less hidebound organisation which the British wanted anyway.

The French, on the other hand, with greater realism, perhaps pessimism, were less hopeful that the Americans would change their minds and join the League if the Covenant were sufficiently diluted. The French had already, during the Paris peace negotiations in 1919, abandoned important demands in order to please the Americans, when they gave up their proposal for the separation of the west bank of the Rhine from Germany in return for an American pledge, in which the British joined, to come to their assistance if attacked. That pledge had fallen to the ground when the Senate rejected the treaties, and the French did not want to trust in American promises a second time, sacrificing hard-won national interests in the process. But if France had to reconcile herself to the fact that the United States never would join the League, then the League needed strengthening to compensate for the American defection. Hence the French did not agree with the British that American non-membership made a strong League less desirable. Quite the contrary.

VI

In the debate that now opened between Britain and France over security arrangements in the League Covenant, the French wanted to 'fill the gaps' in the Covenant, the most important being that which allowed wars to be legally waged if the peaceful settlement of disputes for one reason or another broke down, as, for instance, if the League Council was unable to reach a unanimous report on a dispute. Two years – 1923-24 – were spent in unavailing efforts to fill these gaps. The Covenant remained – unfortunately for the French, fortunately for the British – the hit-and-miss contrivance it had always been. Moreover, at the end of the two years, Article 10, with its system of guarantees, had been the subject of so many 'interpretative resolutions' that hardly anyone could take it seriously. A Canadian resolution at the Fourth Assembly in 1923, for instance, sought to dilute Article 10 by leaving it to member-states whether to use armed force to defend victims of aggression. This was vetoed by Iran, but the Canadian purpose was achieved: henceforward a question mark hung over the automaticity of the guarantee system, and states must feel that they could not but look to themselves and their allies for security.[46]

The destruction of the League system of automatic collective action against aggression came, strangely enough, with the first attempts in 1920 to make progress with the League's far-reaching disarmament programme. We have seen earlier in this chapter (p.83) that the League's first discussion on disarmament had ended in the almost universal conviction that states were unlikely to disarm without the provision of some alternative system of security. This conclusion was embodied in Resolution XIV of the Third Assembly in 1922 and the Assembly then gave instructions for a draft treaty embodying the principle to be drawn up. It should be noted that the system of guarantees contemplated in the resulting Draft Treaty of Mutual Assistance, framed by the Assembly's Political Committee in co-operation with the Temporary Mixed Commission, was meant to be less comprehensive than that of Article 10 of the Covenant, thus showing that the whittling down of Article 10 was already in process. Thus, the states were expected to come to the assistance of a victim of aggression only if situated in the same continent. Moreover, the victim state appeared only to qualify for assistance if it had reduced its armaments to some agreed extent. There was no suggestion, as there is in the original Covenant Article, of a universal guarantee of all states, wherever situated and whatever the state of their armaments.[47]

The 1923, or Fourth, Assembly was unable to agree about the

Draft Treaty and therefore submitted it to member-governments for their comments. The treaty embodied the now accepted principle that member-states would qualify for assistance against aggression only if they had co-operated with the Council in its general disarmament plan. It also much strengthened the Council's powers by authorising it to decide within four days which of the signatory states was the victim of aggression, if aggression occurred; the economic sanctions to be applied against the aggressor; and the states expected to co-operate in the application of sanctions. The Council was also to decide, and not merely, as in the Covenant, to recommend, the armed forces to be placed at the disposal of the League by member-states. In some respects therefore, the Draft Treaty represented a strengthening of the Covenant and accordingly pleased the French. In so far, however, as it limited the circumstances in which a state was entitled to receive assistance, it reflected a tendency to restrict the League's operations. The important thing, however, was that the Draft Treaty was unfavourably received by enough states, led by Britain, to destroy its prospects, and the effect was to raise still further question marks about the automaticity of the League's guarantee to member-states against aggression.

British objections to the Draft Treaty, voiced at Geneva by James Ramsay MacDonald, Prime Minister in the first British Labour government, formed in January 1924, could not have stemmed from any ill-will towards the League as such. The most positive belief uniting the British Labour party (and the same was true for the contingent of Liberal M.P.s whose support made the MacDonald government possible) was that world peace could only be secured by means of the collective security arrangements of the League, not through the balance of power, arms races and other devices of traditional diplomacy. Moreover, the time was ripe for putting the finishing touches to the League Covenant. The angry rift between France and Germany arising from French doubts about German good faith in implementing the Versailles Treaty and culminating in the Franco-Belgian invasion of the Ruhr in 1923 had been resolved at a conference in London in August 1924, the greatest triumph of MacDonald's ministry, which launched the Dawes plan for German reconstruction. The plan paved the way to the golden years of 1925 to 1930, the years of Franco-German reconciliation and relative European prosperity.[48] By 1924, too, the turmoil of the communist revolution in Russia was subsiding; fear of a spread of Bolshevism to central and western

Europe had faded, and, beginning with Britain and Mussolini's Italy in 1924, the Soviet state was gradually being accorded diplomatic recognition, though still kept at arm's length. 1922 had seen the widely acclaimed naval disarmament conference in Washington, and, at the same conference, the United States had taken some small steps towards resuming its world responsibilities by signing a nine-Power treaty to respect the *status quo* in China and a four-Power treaty to do the same for the Pacific.

The Foreign Office in London, however, looked at it differently, Villiers minuting on the Draft Treaty on 3 August that 'at Geneva our attitude should be one of mild approval and benevolence, coupled with a determination to shelve any such proposals *sine die*'.[49] The Treaty was accordingly rejected by the British delegation to the League, by the so-called British Dominions, and by the Scandinavian states which tended to follow the British lead. Their objections were reportedly to the form, not the principle, of the Treaty. There could be no suggestion that democratic socialists like MacDonald objected in principle to disarmament and mutual assistance against aggression. But when the Fifth Assembly in 1924 looked at the British objections, it became clear that the objections *were*, at least in some sense, matters of principle, and not only of method and technique.

The chief British doubts about the Draft Treaty concerned the extraordinary powers it assigned to the Council. The Council's duty under the revised Covenant would be to decide almost at once (within four days) whether an act of aggression had been committed, to allocate responsibility for it, to call upon League members to assist the victim, and to restore the situation to what it was before the peace was disturbed. The intention was, of course, to prevent *faits accomplis* which might become entrenched while talk at Geneva still continued. Nevertheless, this was a radical departure from the investigatory role of the Council contemplated in the Covenant. It would have made the Council into the sort of all-powerful body (albeit with an Achilles heel in the shape of the great-Power veto) which the United Nations Security Council was to be in the 1945 Charter. In the 1920s the European states were too jealous of their sovereignty to allow for a Leviathan of that kind.

Yet when the Assembly and its Political Committee went to work in autumn 1924, carefully heeding the advice of MacDonald and the Dominions Prime Ministers, the result of their labours, called the Geneva Protocol for the Pacific Settlement of

International Disputes (the name 'Protocol' was intended to imply that it was a gloss on the Covenant rather than a departure from it), was no more agreeable to Britain and her friends, and without British backing no scheme for improving or reforming the Covenant stood a chance. It is true that, by the time Britain gave its official negative to the Protocol, that is, in March 1925, MacDonald's government had fallen and a Conservative team under Stanley Baldwin, with Austen Chamberlain as its Foreign Secretary, now ruled the roost in London. But there is evidence that, even if the Labour party had won the elections in October 1924, MacDonald would still have rejected the Protocol, though perhaps not quite on the same grounds as Chamberlain. At the Fifth League Assembly which recommended the Protocol to member-states in September 1924, the French Prime Minister, Herriot, invited the British delegation, led by Arthur Ponsonby, to sign the Protocol there and then. But Ponsonby had no such instruction from his government.[50]

Even if MacDonald had remained in office and accepted the Protocol, it is doubtful whether he could have taken it with much seriousness. For him, as for most British politicians and officials who wished to go along to the uttermost with the mid-1920s movement to strengthen the Covenant, the aim was to placate the French, to allay their fears. Later MacDonald spoke of the Protocol as a 'harmless drug to soothe nerves'.[51] It was not really credible that, even if Britain had accepted the Protocol, the occasion would ever arise in which she had to make good her word and go into action to defend the peace. For the British, it seemed as though the First World War had been such an appalling blunder that it was inconceivable that any government would ever want to run the risk of repeating it by challenging the *status quo*. It continued to be inconceivable until the eve of war in 1939.

Austen Chamberlain, however, when he faced the expectant Council on 12 March 1925 to give Britain's reactions to the Protocol, was not so sure that, if Britain gave her pledge under the Protocol, she would never be called upon to redeem it. True, he did advise the Council, or rather the French and the allies, not to be always dwelling on the possibility of war, like a man 'always brooding over the possibility of some severe surgical operation'.[52] But he knew that threats to the peace, even forceful ones, were all too likely, even in the relative tranquillity of the mid-1920s, and that there was no mandate from Parliament or public opinion at large for pledging the country to take up arms against all and sundry threats to the peace, whatever their seriousness and however remote from the British Isles. Nor was there such a mandate in any of the Dominions.[53]

The essence of the Geneva Protocol was the proposal that all international disputes, if legal in character, must be submitted to the world court at The Hague, the ultimate award of which would be binding on the parties. Their willingness to comply with the court's judgment would be the test of their guilt or innocence should the dispute end in the use of armed force, and the court would decide whether they would be at the target or the beneficiary end of any sanctions the League applied. This would mean, that Britain, then the *primus inter pares* of the international system, was marked out for the role of law enforcement in every quarter of the globe. Whenever a country refused to take its disputes with another state to court, Britain, more than any other League member, would be expected to ensure that it did. Whenever a state, having referred its disputes to the court, failed to carry out the court's award, the British fleet, with British soldiers on board, would have to set sail to see that the court's directives were carried out. A Naval Staff memorandum on the Protocol stated that they were 'opposed to portions of the Navy being practically at the disposal of the League for a series of campaigns of indefinite duration and magnitude'.[54] The First Lord of the Admiralty, L.S. Amery, writing on the same subject in 1925, declared that 'such a treaty, whatever its shape, could only add unnecessarily to our military commitments and increase the danger of dragging us into wars in which we have no real interest, without in the slightest degree promoting either our own peace and security or those of other nations or leading to any reduction of armaments'.[55]

This was not at all what British people (and even more people in the Dominions) were in the mood for in the 1920s. For the present, they had seen enough of service in foreign wars. They had thrown out of office one of their greatest leaders, Lloyd George ('the man who won the war'), in October 1922 because they thought he was too fond of leading Britain into foreign wars. Lloyd George's Conservative successor, the colourless Bonar Law, won the election on the basis of the slogan 'tranquillity'. Besides, compulsory jurisdiction by the world court, or arbitration, as the Labour party preferred to call it, might make a fair-sounding trinity in MacDonald's mouth with disarmament and security, but what did judges in courts actually protect? The *status quo*. But the *status quo* in Europe, or much of it, was abhorred by the British. It was sanctified by the 'Carthaginian peace' of 1919, which the French and their friends admired, but which the British saw as containing the seeds of future wars. Seen from London, the League ought to be a means of revising the 1919 settlement, not of standing guard over it for ever.

VII

Austen Chamberlain's celebrated formula – 'special arrangements in order to meet special needs' – which he proposed in his League Council speech in March 1925 as an alternative to the general security formula of the Protocol and the Draft Treaty (and, it must be said, of the Covenant itself) was, of course, framed in the knowledge of the offer of the German Foreign Minister, Gustav Stresemann, of precisely such an arrangement to cover the Rhine. The idea, later incorporated in the Locarno agreements signed in October of that year by Belgium, Britain, France, Germany and Italy, was that Germany should freely accept her frontier with Belgium and France, which had been imposed on her by the Allies in 1919, together with the permanent demilitarisation of the west bank of the Rhine, also laid down at Versailles, and that the settlement should be guaranteed by Britain and Italy against disturbance either by Belgium, France or Germany.

The Locarno agreements were highly satisfactory to the British people and their politicians, marking, as Austen Chamberlain said, 'the dividing line between the years of war and peace'. They brought France and Germany together after the angry conflicts of the past. They won over the Weimar Republic in Germany for the time being to the West and broke the dangerous links it had formed with Soviet Russia since the Rapallo agreement between the two countries of April 1922. True, Locarno to some extent tied Britain's hands, but it was a strictly limited commitment: few seemed to note that, in undertaking the Rhine guarantee and refusing similar guarantees for Germany's Eastern borders, Britain advertised to the world, and to German nationalists, that the East European settlement of 1919 was no longer a firm commitment as far as Britain was concerned, if it ever had been.

The Locarno agreements were limited in another sense, namely that British politicians never seemed really to believe they would have to be implemented. Like the Geneva Protocol, as Ramsay MacDonald conceived it, Locarno was a sort of confidence trick, an arrangement for giving the French a sense of security, rather than the reality. It was not exactly an illusion, because few British people really thought that France was in danger from another round of German aggression. But the French did. That was *their* illusion, and the Locarno agreements formed part of the arrangements required to persuade them out of it. Hence the Locarno system was never followed up by military staff talks to prepare against the day when the system might be violated. Britain had burned her fingers with staff talks with France before 1914, or so most British people thought. They wanted no more of them. Besides, how could Britain hold staff talks with both France and Germany, and so become privy to the war plans of both? The idea was absurd and no attempt was made to implement it. Moreover, although Chamberlain in his League Council speech in March 1925 had spoken of 'special arrangements' and 'special needs', the Locarno system, splendid as the British thought it, was repeated nowhere else on the map. The British had done their duty by France, or as much of it as they decently could, and that was that.

This is not the place to evaluate the complicated system of Locarno treaties, though it could be said that their general effect, while at first sight confirming the 1919 peace settlement, was in reality gravely to jeopardise it. The treaties, by giving an Anglo-Italian pledge against violations of the Belgian-French-German frontier system, placed a barrier in the way of France using force against Germany in the future, as she had tried to do during the occupation of the Ruhr in 1923, or coming to the assistance of her East European allies – Czechoslovakia, Poland and Rumania – by entering Germany from the west if the allies, or any one of them, were to be involved in hostilities with Germany in future. Locarno in fact destroyed the security system France had painfully built since 1919, the object of which was to hem in Germany from two sides. And, by dissociating Britain from the *status quo* in Eastern Europe, the Locarno agreements gave the clearest possible indication to Germany that if ever she were to apply pressure against her Eastern borders as settled in 1919, she would stand a reasonable chance of altering them.

It is, however, the significance of the Locarno agreements for the League Covenant with which we are concerned. It has been stated that 'every line of the Locarno pacts was based upon the Protocol or the Covenant'.[56] Whatever may be said of particular lines or clauses of those pacts, there can be little doubt that, on the contrary, the general drift and purport of the Locarno accords were totally at variance with the League system, and went far to destroy it, even though the immediate consequence was to improve the international climate, certainly in Western Europe, and from this the League was to some extent a beneficiary.

In the first place, the Rhine pact represented a partial confirmation of the territorial *status quo* by some of the greatest Powers of the day. It did not signify a resolve by all the Powers, or by all member-states of the League, to come to the defence of any country, or League member, if it fell victim to aggression. The celebrated Soviet Foreign Minister, Maxim Litvinov, who, later in the 1920s, spoke of collective security as based upon the 'indivisibility of peace', could not have accepted Locarno as the collective defence of peace which the League was supposed to uphold. So far from Locarno being consistent with the universal guarantee system enshrined in Article 10 of the Covenant, it gave the world the clearest indication that some parts of the international system were open to revision, and not solely by peaceful means, as Article 19 of the Covenant contemplated, but, if need be, by force. Indeed, the Locarno system was fully in the old tradition of partial great-Power guarantees which the League system supposedly rejected.

This is not to say that the League system of universal collective security was a practicable one, or that the world took the wrong turning when it moved away from this system in 1925 and came down on the side of partial arrangements. The League Covenant had been offered to the world as a general collective security system, but country after country had rejected it when it counted up the open-ended commitments it was likely to be undertaking if it accepted the system. The Draft Treaty and the Geneva Protocol had been attempts to make the Covenant doubly sure, but they had failed because states, or enough of them to matter, shrank from the cost. The Locarno system was an attempt to deal with a severely local problem, but it was mounted on the ruins of the grand enterprise of making the security of each state the common concern of all, and to do this by giving each and every state a stake in the survival of all the others as vital as its stake in its own security. Henceforward, for the rest of its life, the League would act as a forum for the different countries to achieve as much co-operation in solving their common problems as they could. But collective security, in the strict sense of that term, must take second place.

5   The system takes shape

When the League opened its doors for business in January 1920, its members consisted of the original thirty-two states which had signed the peace treaties and were named in an annex to the Covenant. These were the Allied and Associated Powers of the First World War and their supporters throughout the world, including eleven Latin American countries. The United States, heading the list, dropped out of it in 1920 owing to its failure to ratify the peace treaties. In addition, thirteen states were invited to accede to the Covenant, six of them being Latin American, and twelve of them did. Their membership did not have to be approved under Article 1 (2) of the Covenant, unlike that of other states which wished to join the League later.

The First Assembly, meeting in November 1920, was faced with fourteen applications for membership, of which it approved six, those of Albania, Austria, Bulgaria, Costa Rica, Finland and Luxemburg.[1] Bulgaria's was a troublesome case because, as an ex-enemy state, its relations with its neighbour, Greece, were still unsettled; so was Albania, since, having existed only since 1913, its borders remained undecided. The other four called for little discussion; Austria evoked much sympathy owing to its shrunken state after the imperial days of the past, and Luxemburg won applause for its renunciation of neutrality in order to comply with Covenant obligations. The applications of the Baltic states, Estonia, Latvia and Lithuania, and also those of Georgia and Armenia, were deferred for a year owing to uncertainty about their relations with the new regime in Russia. The Baltic states were admitted at the Second Assembly in 1921, bringing total membership to fifty-one; but it was not long before Georgia and Armenia were brought under Bolshevik control and forced to abandon hopes of independence.[2] Two years later, at the Fourth Assembly, Ethiopia and the Irish Free State were admitted, the former on the basis of a pledge to abolish the slave trade.[3]

Austria and Bulgaria thus having recovered respectability as ex-enemy states – and the same was done for another such country, Hungary, two years later – the question inevitably arose as to how long it would be before a German delegation was seen at Geneva. For some years, the idea met with resistance in both camps which had recently fought each other in the war. Many Germans looked on the League as the guardian of the 1919 settlement which they hated; others considered there was more to be gained, for the moment, in maintaining the friendship with Soviet Russia which the two pariah states struck up at Rapallo in 1922, and Soviet Russia's views on the League were notorious. Within the League, Britain stood for reconciliation with Germany, all the more so after the failure of the economic conference at Genoa in 1922, which Lloyd George had tried to use to heal the wounds of war and to reunite the European family. Scandinavian countries sided with Britain, and so, more or less, did the British Dominions, as they were then known, Australia, Canada, New Zealand and South Africa, now members of the League in their own right.

The inevitable obstacle to Germany's joining the Geneva family was France and her East European allies. In the Assembly and outside in its corridors, the French Foreign Minister, Viviani, reminded all and sundry of the price France had paid time and again to stem German aggression. Besides, France (and Belgium, too) was becoming locked in its struggle with Britain to extract reparations from Germany. In 1921, the French had succeeded in engineering an Allied occupation of certain towns in the Ruhr as part of this strategy. The row in the inter-Allied Reparations dragged itself out through 1922, Lloyd George proposing in August that the issue be referred to the League and the steely-minded French leader, Poincaré, refusing. The break came in December over French allegations in the Commission of German non-payment of timber reparations – France's wooden horse for forcing an entrance into the German Troy – after which the French, with some half-hearted Belgian and Italian assistance, took the bull by the horns and invaded the Ruhr. The idea was to seize what Poincaré called 'productive guarantees' of Germany's willingness to pay her debts.[4]

Again, the British government, now led by the Conservative Bonar Law after Lloyd George's fall, attempted, with

Scandinavian backing, to bring the League into the argument. Branting, the Swedish delegate, initiated a move to place the Ruhr invasion on the League Council's agenda for 29 January, and unsurprisingly the French withheld consent. The same thing happened again, when, at a secret meeting of the Council, Branting produced a motion to have the affair on the agenda; it was a mildly worded resolution, but too strong for Viviani and his Belgian collaborator, Hymans.[5] The incident did nothing to strengthen the hands of those in Germany who wanted to see their country inside the League.

The Ruhr crisis, however, could not last. The vast inflation in Germany touched off by the Franco-Belgian invasion was too much a threat to the economy of Europe to be allowed to continue. Poincaré's notion of forcing Germany to pay was unworkable: the Germans would sooner pull down the European house around them than submit, and the French people soon realised it and took their leave of Poincaré. The Dawes Plan of 1924 and the Locarno agreements of October 1925, which set Germany (and France, too) on the road to recovery and laid the basis for the Franco-German reconciliation marking the second five years of the 1920s, also changed French thinking on the issue of Germany's League membership. Formerly, France fought against it; now she began to insist upon it. It was an unstated assumption of the Locarno negotiations by which the Weimar Republic voluntarily accepted the peace settlement in the West imposed at Versailles in June 1919 that Germany should join the League and thereby become a pillar of the *status quo*. Article 10 of the agreements signed at Locarno on 16 October 1925 stated that they would only come into force after Germany had entered the League.[6]

There was a further point. Rapallo had been a shock to the Entente states, Britain and France. Perhaps the Locarno treaties were not designed to break the links between Germany and Russia, but they undoubtedly weakened them. If Locarno could be coupled with German membership of the League, a body feared and denounced by the Russians, it would be a double victory for Western opponents of Bolshevism. And if Germany could in some way be integrated with the sanctions system of the League – who knows? – would that not be useful if some day the Western Powers had to deal with an aggressive Russia?

It was this element in British and French designs for Germany's entrance into the League which Stresemann, the German Foreign Minister, saw as a device for advertising to the world Germany's unequal position under the 1919 treaty system.[7] On 23 September 1925, when the air in Geneva was thick with talk of Germany's imminent entry into the League, the Cabinet in Berlin made known its intention to apply for League membership under Article 2 (1) of the Covenant, but insisted that this must mean the immediate grant of a permanent seat on the Council. There was little or no objection to this from the ten Council members, whom Stresemann then consulted individually, nor to the demand that there must be no reference to Germany's responsibility for war in 1914 in any engagements between the League and the German Republic. Another condition required by Germany, namely that they should participate in the League's Mandates system, caused more eyebrows to rise, but the idea could have been little more than a sop for Right-wing German objectors to League membership. The condition in Stresemann's statements which did cause difficulty, however, was that, owing to her disarmed state, Germany could take no part in the enforcement of economic or military sanctions by the League.

On the surface, this made a certain sense, but it raised questions. How could a League member, especially one so important that it could demand an immediate seat as a permanent member of the Council, be exempted from obligations falling upon others? Article 1 (2) stated that a country's application to join the League could only be accepted if, *inter alia*, 'it shall give effective guarantees of its sincere intention to observe its international obligations'. There could be reason for suspecting, too, that the German authorities were claiming this exemption mainly to draw attention to their country's enforced disarmament, and thus to be able more effectively to argue the case for release from that condition. In the end, the problem was circumvented by resort to a phrase used in the abortive Geneva Protocol which committed each signatory 'to co-operate loyally and effectively in support of the Covenant, and in resistance to any act of aggression, in the degree which its geographical position and its particular situation as regards armaments allow'. It was a phrase which could mean almost anything, and therefore served the purposes of different delegations with different views.

The admission of Germany was therefore proceeding without too much difficulty. But there then occurred a hitch which contained all the elements of farce and did little for the League's prestige. A special meeting of the Assembly was convened for 8 March 1926, and it was at this that Germany's long-awaited entrance into the League was to be effected. By this time, however, support was growing in France for a proposal that Poland, too, should be given a permanent seat on the Council, in defiance of the old idea that such seats should be reserved for the great Powers. French Foreign Minister Briand warmed to the proposal and even persuaded his British colleague, Austen Chamberlain, who happened to be passing through Paris at the end of January, to put it before his Cabinet. But why should not other states clamour for the same honour? If they did, at least it would show that high standing in the League was becoming a point of pride with member-states. Brazil and Spain promptly came forward with pleas to be considered, both threatening to hold up Assembly business if they did not get their way. Then Belgium and China let it be known that, if permanent seats on the Council were being given away, they had as good a title as anybody. In all the clamour, the Germans, who had turned up in force at the special Assembly session, were insisting that, no matter how many more permanent seats on the Council were created, their own claim must have priority. Those who had worked hard for Germany's admission now feared that, sooner than face humiliation, her delegation would pack their bags and leave.

All the Assembly could do for the present was to appoint two committees, one to report on the German application for membership, the other to consider its budgetary implications. But this the Assembly, which alone had the authority to admit Germany, could not do since the German delegation would not accept membership unless a permanent seat on the Council was assured for them. After an agonising week's delay, a formula was agreed to by which Germany's permanent seat was guaranteed, Sweden and Czechoslovakia would lose their temporary seats on the Council and the Assembly would be asked to vote for Holland and Poland in their place: this, it was hoped, would dispose of the Polish claim for a permanent seat.[8] The Germans and Poles, who were chiefly affected, accepted this, but, at an informal meeting of the Council which followed, the Brazilian and Spanish delegates insisted that their demands for permanent seats were not negotiable. Since their arguments could not be accepted (it would have been an infringement, if not of the Covenant, at least of the theory of the Covenant, to do so), the two countries gave notice of their intention to leave the organisation, though Spain in the end remained a member. They were the first two states to do so, although Costa Rica had withdrawn in January owing to inability to pay her membership contributions.

At the seventh ordinary session of the Assembly in September 1926, Germany's entrance into the League was finally completed and during the following three years the Council was reshaped so as to absorb that country's permanent membership without injuring too much the pride of other states. In accordance with the Assembly committee's recommendations, the Council was enlarged from ten to fourteen members divided into three classes: five permanent members (Britain, France, Germany, Italy and Japan: Japan resigned in 1933, so did Germany, and so, two years later, did Italy); two 'semi- permanent' members, namely Poland and Spain – this class came into being through the adoption of the committee's recommendation that not more than three of the states elected as non-permanent members should be eligible for re-election for a further three years if the Assembly so decided, and thus the desire of Poland and Spain for a more prestigious place on the Council was satisfied; and seven non-permanent members elected in the first days of each Assembly session to serve for three years each. These seven were chosen on a group basis as follows: three Latin American states, one Asian, one from the Little Entente, one European neutral, and one from the British Commonwealth, as it was then known.[9]

II

Thus far, as we have seen in the previous chapter, the League's business consisted to a large extent of putting its own house in order and dealing with matters left over from the peace settlement. Now its testing time began with the reference to it of an increasing number of disputes as confidence in the Geneva organisation gradually increased.

One of the earliest of these involved Albania. Albania had come into existence in 1913 as a break-away state from the Turkish empire. Its borders with the Austro-Hungarian empire in the north and Greece in the south were settled, though in a highly provisional way, by the Concert of Europe. This did not prevent Albanian territory becoming the focus of rivalry between Italy, Greece and the new state of Yugoslavia, formed from the old Habsburg empire, after the war. Albania was admitted into

League of Nations membership by the First Assembly in 1920, but the Assembly decided to leave to the inter-Allied Conference of Ambassadors the task of defining the Albanian frontiers.[10]

The Conference procrastinated. In June 1921, following an Albanian appeal to the League under Article 11 of the Covenant, it appointed a committee to help it reach a decision. But by the time the Second League Assembly met in September no conclusion had been reached, though the situation on Albania's borders worsened daily. Greek troops were conducting forays into the country from the south while Yugoslav forces were engaged deep in the northern part of the country. The League Council, pressed by the Albanian authorities to take action, could do little more than urge the Allied body to bring the matter to a close. Greece and Yugoslavia agreed that this was where responsibility lay.[11]

The matter was thrashed out in the League Assembly in September 1921, but to little further effect than the production of a resolution calling upon the Council to act, in particular by sending a commission of inquiry to Albania, which the Council did. It was not until 9 November that the Conference of Ambassadors finally came forward with the decision that Albania's frontiers should be those of 1913, with three minor changes which favoured the Yugoslav side of the argument. This show of vigour, after so many months' inactivity, no doubt reflected a telegram received the previous day, 8 November, by Drummond, the League Secretary-General, from Lloyd George, the British Prime Minister, demanding an immediate meeting of the League Council to deal with the matter and a warning to Yugoslavia that, if she did not at once comply with Covenant obligations, economic sanctions would be instituted against her. It still took ten days for this bombshell to have effect, but, after a little further delay, the Yugoslavs fell into line and withdrew their forces to the frontier laid down. This allowed the League Council to regard the incident as closed and to instruct its commission of inquiry to supervise the Yugoslav withdrawal and Albania's reoccupation of her territory. In a report dated 20 December 1921 the commission stated that the evacuation of Albania was complete.[12]

The Yugoslav-Albanian dispute did not exactly demonstrate the League's power to defend small countries against their more powerful neighbours, as it sometimes claimed. The British intervention probably played a far greater role in securing the Yugoslav evacuation. But it did give the League Assembly a chance to concentrate world attention on blatant pressure exercised by a greater state against a smaller, and thus to help bring it to an end. At the same time, the continued dominance of the Allied Powers was inevitable throughout the crisis, and everyone, within the League and outside it, had to take account of that fact. The central role of power, despite what the Covenant and Assembly resolutions might say to the contrary, is evident, too, in the sequel to the Albanian affair. The Conference of Ambassadors, in making known their decision about Albania's frontiers, also issued a statement on 9 November 1921 giving Italy the right to protect Albania's political and economic independence, a strange reversion to classical European forms of international over-lordship.[13] From 1926 onward the Italians acquired an increasing grip over Albania's economic resources. In April 1939 the process was complete when Italy finally annexed the country.

The sway of the European Powers was likewise illustrated in the successful British manoeuvres to acquire Mosul, a province lying along the Tigris river in northern Mesopotamia, as it was known until the 1920s, or Iraq, as it is known today. Mosul acquired importance during the First World War owing to its oil wealth. Its population was Kurdish, and towards the end of the war, the Kurds, like other minority nationalities all over Europe and the Middle East, were swept by aspirations for independence. This would have meant, not only the destruction of Turkish rule, but the cession of Kurdish-inhabited areas in Iran, Iraq and Russia.[14]

Under the vindictive treaty of Sèvres, signed by the Sultan's government in Istanbul in August 1920, but rendered abortive by the nationalist revolution led by Kemal Ataturk, Mosul was assigned to Mesopotamia, which was awarded to Britain as an 'A' mandate within the League system. Eventually, peace was concluded between the Allies and Turkey at Lausanne in July 1923, and while Mosul, by Article 3 (2) of that agreement, was temporarily accorded to Turkey, its future was to be the subject of negotiations between that country and Britain: if no agreement was reached within nine months, the question was to be referred to the League Council.[15]

The negotiations took place but without result, and on 6 August 1924 Ramsay MacDonald, the British Prime Minister, appealed to the League Council to make a decision about Mosul.[16] Britain and Turkey made their statements to the Council, the indefatigable Branting was appointed rapporteur, and the inevitable com-mission of inquiry was despatched by the Council to examine the matter on the spot. In October the crisis worsened, when on the 9th the British government issued an ultimatum to the Turks to withdraw their forces from Mosul within 48 hours.[17] At a meeting of the League Council in Geneva on 30 October 1924, however, a line of temporary demarcation between the forces of the two sides was fixed, and this they respected.[18] In the meantime, the commission of inquiry, with Belgian, Hungarian and Swedish members (it was the first time since the war that a national of one of the former Central Powers, in the form of the Hungarian, had taken part in such a body), was testing local opinion. It found that, while there was little enthusiasm for either claimant (the Kurds were adamant in wanting an independent state of their own), Iraq, or rather Britain as the mandatory in Iraq, was regarded as the less of two evils. The commission therefore recommended that Iraq should be awarded·a twenty-five-year mandate over Mosul.

Seemingly encouraged by this, the British then proposed that further Turkish territory inhabited by Assyrians should be assigned to Iraq as well. The Turks replied that no such territory was authorised as transferable to another state under the treaty of Lausanne. The commission of inquiry also rejected the British demand. A further dispute then sprang up between Britain and Turkey as to whether, after all, a decision of the Council about Mosul could be regarded as binding, in the sense of ending all further discussion of the subject. Britain, knowing that the balance of opinion in the Council was on her side, argued that it would be binding, while Turkey, hoping to reserve for herself a veto on any decision the Council reached on the matter, agreed, but only if the parties, that is, herself and Britain, accepted that it was binding. The issue was referred to the world court at The Hague for an advisory opinion and this came down on the British side, stating that a Council decision was binding, though only if unanimously agreed to.[19]

On 16 December 1925, the Council decided by a unanimous vote to endorse the commission's recommendations, the most important of which was that the Mosul mandate would last for twenty-five years, unless Iraq was admitted into the League as an independent state before that. In that case, the status of Mosul would have to be reconsidered. The Kurdish minority was to receive guarantees of its rights from the mandatory Power, that is, Britain. That was a long way from the independent statehood dreamed of by the Kurds, but it did promise a better future than the experience they had had under Turkish rule.[20] On 11 March

1926 the Council declared the definitive settlement of the frontier.[21]

On 5 June 1926 a treaty was signed by Britain, Iraq and Turkey which concluded the arguments about Mosul. The province was firmly included in Iraqi territory and the frontier declared final and inviolable.[22] This represented a considerable achievement for Britain and British prestige benefited from it. The League Council played on the whole a subsidiary role, but the fact that it served as the channel through which a settlement was eventually reached no doubt helped to make it acceptable to the Turks. Turkey moreover was in receipt of reconstruction loans managed by the League. Its rehabilitation after the war was achieved through the League's help. It is not surprising that in 1931 Kemal, the maker of the new Turkey, made it known that he could accept an offer on Turkey's behalf to join the League if one were made.

Memel, the German port on the Baltic coast, and its surrounding hinterland, with a population of about 7,000 Germans in all, had remained in Allied hands after the war. The intention was, as indicated in Article 99 of the Versailles treaty, that it should be awarded to the new state of Lithuania, but the French and their allies, the Poles, seemed more inclined to a form of internationalisation of Memel, like that adopted for Danzig. The Lithuanians were therefore left to wait for an Allied decision and, in their impatience, seized the port by force in January 1923, perhaps taking a leaf out of the notebooks of the Poles, who had done the same in regard to Vilna in 1921. This *coup* stimulated the Conference of Ambassadors into drawing up a convention for Memelland, in which, however, the Poles would have some share in the administration, an arrangement which the French government favoured. The Lithuanians would not hear of any such proposal, and in September the Conference of Ambassadors, following what was now the usual practice of dropping awkward questions into the Council's lap, referred the dispute to that body.

On 17 December 1923 the Council appointed one of its standard commissions of inquiry, consisting of a Dutchman, a Swiss and an American, Norman Davis, which then drew up statutes for Memel which decidedly followed the lines preferred by Lithuania.[23] The statutes were approved by the League Council on 14 March 1924 and then accepted by the Allied Powers and Lithuania. The Polish delegate, however, M. Skirmut, strongly objected, though this did not prevent the Council bringing the new arrangements into force on 25 August of the following year. Poland, however, was in fact too distant from the Memelland to have much of a sustained interest in its future; accordingly, the tensions surrounding the Memel question tended to be transferred from Lithuania and Poland to Lithuania and Germany, the East Prussian provinces of which adjoined Poland's southern border. As Germany recovered from the war, and especially when its revisionist designs grew under Hitler in the 1930s, pressure from Berlin for the revision of the statutes of Memel mounted. This was strongly supported by the Memellanders, who consider themselves to be superior to their Lithuanian masters. In March 1939, the Germans reoccupied Memel after many quarrels about the port with Lithuania.

III

The Corfu conflict of 1923 was the first direct challenge to the League's authority and showed in starkest contrast the two opposing faces of the old-world system of *Realpolitik*, on the one hand, and the new guide-lines for world order being cautiously drawn at Geneva, on the other. The crisis began with an ambush in Greek territory near Janina on 27 August 1923 of a car in which a party of Italians, members of an international delimitation commission appointed by the Inter-Allied Conference of Ambassadors to define the borders of Albania, were travelling. The head of the group, General Tellini, three of his assistants and an interpreter were killed. The Conference of Ambassadors, representing Britain, France, Italy and Japan, drew up a note of protest to Greece on 30 August, which was delivered on the following day. Meanwhile, the Italian dictator, Mussolini, had delivered an ultimatum to Athens on 29 August, demanding a humiliating apology. The Greeks accepted four of the seven demands contained in the ultimatum, but because they would not comply with the other three, the Italian leader despatched a powerful naval squadron to bomb and occupy the Greek island of Corfu on 31 August.[24]

A dispute then arose between Greece and Italy at the League Council on 1 September as to which international body should deal with the incident. The Greek Foreign Minister, M. Politis, asked for the conflict to be considered by the League Council under Articles 12 and 15 of the Covenant, while Salandra, speaking for Italy, argued that the Conference of Ambassadors, the authority of which had been flouted by the murderers of the Italian party, was the appropriate instrument for dealing with it.[25] Opinion at the Fourth League Assembly, meeting on 3 September, was decidedly pro-Greek and anti-Italian, mainly because of the bias generally shown by the Assembly towards the weaker of two contending states. The Assembly's anti-Italian feelings were strikingly shown in its refusal to vote for an Italian among the Assembly's twelve Vice-Presidents. In response, feelings ran high in Italy, too, with street demonstrations against the League and Mussolini insisting that the Conference of Ambassadors should settle the issue. The legal argument resorted to by Italian spokesmen was that the League was relevant where there was a question of war, but that no war was in sight in the present imbroglio.

Some relaxation of Greek opposition to the Conference of Ambassadors as an instrument of settlement then became evident, and when the League Council met on 4 September to discuss the crisis, it heard that Greece was willing that the Conference should at least decide the amount of compensation to be paid for the murders. Nevertheless, the Council decided two days later to throw its weight behind a plan drawn up by its rapporteur, Quiñones de León. The essence of this was that Greek apologies and explanations for the incident should be presented, not to Italy, but to the three-man Delimitation Commission, consisting of British, French and Italian officers, of which General Tellini had been chairman; that these three states should take part in investigating the murders; that the world court at The Hague should be asked to decide the amount of compensation which Greece should pay; and that, pending the court's decision, Greece should assign 50 million lire to a Swiss bank, to be drawn upon as the court decided.[26] This plan was accepted, with some modifications, by the Conference of Ambassadors on the following day. Unsurprisingly, since some of the items in the plan had been suggested by Politis himself, the Greek authorities hastened to declare their agreement. Italian agreement also seemed to be implicit, without being expressly stated, and the ultimatum to Greece was not proceeded with.

Italian forces in Corfu, however, were not withdrawn; instead, they seemed to be reinforced. This led the Conference of Ambassadors to issue a sharp statement of 13 September to the effect that the commission of inquiry into the Tellini murders was to report within five days after beginning its investigation, and that, if the report showed that the Greek authorities had not been sufficiently energetic in seeking out the murderers, the Conference might insist upon the 50 million lire being paid to Italy without waiting for the court's decision.[27] When the investigating commission did at length report, however, it appeared that only the Italian member considered that the Greek government were to blame for the murders; the British, French and Japanese members thought that police services in the area were inadequate for the job they had to do. Nevertheless, the Conference of Ambassadors considered that the report showed that enough responsibility attached to the Greek government to justify Greece being forced to pay the 50 million lire to Italy. With the announcement of this decision, Italian forces were withdrawn from Corfu, which did little, however, to allay the indignation felt in Athens or the dismay expressed in the League Assembly.[28]

Dismay in the League Assembly was partly a reaction to the way in which the Council seemed to have been brushed aside in the Corfu dispute by the great Powers in their privileged position in the Conference of Ambassadors; this had resulted from the Italian representative on the League Council, Salandra, having successfully raised objection to the Council handling the dispute under Article 15 of the Covenant. It was also due to a feeling of shock that Italy appeared to have got away with the argument that the seizure of another state's territory was a justifiable reprisal for injuries suffered at the hands of nationals of that state. There was also alarm at the implication of the decision of the Conference of Ambassadors that a government could be held responsible for illegal or criminal acts committed in its territory. The representatives of small countries in the Assembly were afraid that the outcome of the Corfu affair might be to signal to the great armed Powers that their right to use their strength at the expense of the weak was still the law of life in the international system despite the birth of the League.

These reflections of the smaller states had some influence on the sequel to the Corfu incident. The British and Swedish representatives on the Council, Cecil and Branting, succeeded in getting an inquiry going on five questions: three of them into the Council's powers under Article 15 of the Covenant when one party to a dispute claims, as Italy did in the Corfu dispute, that resort to that Article to settle the issue is not appropriate; another as to whether acts of force which fall short of actual war are consistent or not with the Covenant; and a fifth concerned with the responsibility of states for crimes committed on their territory. These questions were not submitted to the world court, as Cecil and Branting wished, but to a committee made up of the nominees of several Council members. The committee's replies to the questions submitted to it tended to reaffirm the primacy of the Covenant, except on the fourth question. The committee's answer to this did not satisfy League members who wanted a stronger assertion that all acts of force are impermissible under the Covenant, at least until procedures of peaceful settlement have been exhausted.[29]

When the Assembly discussed the Council's report on the final stages of the Corfu incident on 28 September, some delegates could not disguise their feelings that the League system had suffered a reverse, and that the naked realities of power had penetrated the veil of principles for restraining it which the League had tried to create. Others considered that the crisis might have had a far more sinister outcome had not the participants in it, especially Italy, shown some degree of self-control, which having to answer to League organs encouraged. This was confirmed to some extent by Italian behaviour during the conflict with Yugoslavia over the Italian claim to Fiume, a more dangerous threat to peace than the Corfu affair. At first, Mussolini refused to agree to a Yugoslav proposal to register with the League the treaties of Rapallo and Santa Margherita which embodied a previous agreement of the two countries about Fiume. He insisted on direct negotiations away from the League system. Then he changed his mind and on 12 September the two treaties were presented to the League Secretary-General by the Italian and Yugoslav governments, and from that moment the negotiations between the two states went smoothly.[30] It was perhaps in itself a minor episode, but it did seem to show that the League was becoming a factor in the thinking even of the more powerful states. They, or some of them, were evidently coming to believe that getting a rap over the knuckles in a League body for some breach of the rules could become a political liability and, if possible, should be avoided. This was not quite the same as taking care to act as positively to win League approval, but it was a step in that direction.

IV

The brief conflict between Bulgaria and Greece in October 1925 was expeditiously dealt with by the Council and showed how effective in such situations its intervention could be. On 19 October an affray took place between Bulgarian and Greek troops along the common border between the two countries. Three days later, when the Greeks seemed to be getting the better of the fighting, the Bulgarian government called on the League Secretariat for help and asked for an immediate special meeting of the Council under Articles 10 and 11 of the Covenant.

The Council meeting took place on 23 October, its President, Briand, sending a telegram to the two sides urging them to stop the fighting and withdraw their forces from the battle zone within sixty hours. The appeal was reiterated by the Council when it met three days later. It was complied with by the Bulgarian authorities on the following day and by the Greeks on 28 October. The Council also agreed to send a party consisting of the British, French and Italian military attachés to the scene of the fighting to observe what was happening and to report back to the Council. The observer party told of the beginnings of a withdrawal by Greek forces, and this was accelerated when the Council then agreed to send a more formal mission of inquiry.[31] This was now a well-established League technique and it served the purpose of reducing tension well. The League had no power to compel transgressors to behave better than they would have done when confronted with the facts of a conflict in which they were engaged, as distinct from their own versions of the facts. Nevertheless, the commission of inquiry method helped ensure that states involved in disputes would try to have a good case for the commissioners to examine, and this was best achieved by avoiding actions which might spoil their case.

On 7 December 1925, the Council met for its 37th session and heard that the commission of inquiry was calling for an indemnity of £45,000 from Greece to Bulgaria and the appointment of an officer from a neutral country to keep the border under surveillance for two years. These requirements were accepted by the two countries and the dispute passed from the League's agenda.

6 The lure of disarmament

On no enterprise did the League of Nations spend more time and energy than on the attempt, in the words of Article 8 of the Covenant, to reduce armaments 'to the lowest point consistent with national safety and the enforcement by common action of international obligations'. The Article echoed the fourth of President Wilson's Fourteen Points set forth in his speech in January 1918, which called for 'adequate guarantees given and taken that national armaments will be reduced to the lowest point consistent with domestic safety'. Article 8 of the Covenant stated that League Members recognised that peace 'required' disarmament, and this was certainly the belief of many millions of League supporters, at least in the first half of its life. The First World War was widely regarded as having been precipitated by the arms race which preceded it, though it is doubtful whether many governments in the inter-war period ever seriously believed that disarmament by international agreement, on the scale called for by Article 8, was either desirable or feasible. Nevertheless, they had no alternative but to make every effort to achieve it in view of the fervent wishes for a world without arms on the part of their supporters.

Moreover, the Allied victors in the war were obliged by the peace treaties they had imposed on the defeated, if not to disarm, at least to try to do so. When they prescribed drastic measures of disarmament for Germany in Part V of the Versailles Treaty, and in the corresponding clauses of the treaties with Austria, Bulgaria and Hungary, they explained that this was to be regarded as a prelude to disarmament on a world-wide scale. Part V of the Versailles Treaty was introduced by a Preamble which read,

> In order to render possible the initiation of a general limitation of the armaments of all nations, Germany undertakes strictly to observe the military, naval and air clauses which follow.[1]

In the reply handed by the French Prime Minister, Clemenceau, on 16 June 1919 to the German delegation's observations on the treaty the words were included that

> The Allied and Associated Powers wish to make it clear that their requirements in regard to German armaments were not made solely with the object of rendering it impossible for Germany to resume her policy of military aggression. They are also the first steps towards the general reduction and limitation of armaments which they seek to bring about as one of the most fruitful preventives of war, and which it will be one of the first duties of the League of Nations to promote.[2]

It was natural for German politicians to contend that such a statement constituted a definite undertaking by the Allies to cast away their weapons, and that, if they failed when they tried to do so, the obligation on Germany to remain disarmed would lose its validity.

The League's member-states wrestled with the disarmament problem from 1920 until the eventual world conference met in 1932 and dispersed in 1934, and the failure of their efforts opened the way to the surge of rearmament among the European Powers which signalled the approach of the Second World War. The enterprise was full of self-contradictions and strange ironies. Instead of the League Council itself settling down to formulate plans for arms reductions for each and every state, as provided for in Article 8 of the Covenant, the work was shunted off to a Preparatory Commission, intended to do the preliminary business for the world conference. The Commission dawdled for five years while the nations stamped their feet impatiently, and then produced a draft convention stuffed with blank spaces to be filled in by figures for arms reductions if ever they were agreed.[3] When the conference at last assembled in Geneva on 2 February 1932 (its first meeting had to be postponed for one hour to allow the League Council to discuss a Japanese air bombardment of Shanghai), the convention was ignored. Instead, the leading governments, starting with the French, produced and defended their own disarmament plans, and these were debated one after the other in no logical order.

Not even the election of the conference president went according to plan. At first, the smaller countries were keen to have the indefatigable Eduard Beneš, the Czech Foreign Minister, as president, but, symbolising as he did the successor states of eastern Europe, with their close ties with France and their predilections for the *status quo*, many thought he would lack the respect of Germany and her allies in the late war. The alternative who found favour in 1931, when the conference arrangements were well in hand, was the talented and highly respected British Foreign Secretary, Arthur Henderson, who was unanimously elected to the post on 22 May. Unfortunately, the second Labour government broke up in August as a result of the financial crisis; Henderson was one of those who refused to join his leader, Ramsay MacDonald, in forming the National Government which ruled Britain until the wartime crisis in the summer of 1940. Hence, when the disarmament conference began in February 1932, Henderson had not only lost the prestige of his former office in Britain; he had no sympathy for the titular leader of the British delegation, MacDonald, or for hardly any of the other British Ministers who came to Geneva to argue their country's case. On the other hand, the alteration in Henderson's position resulting from the change of government in Britain served to enhance impressions of him as essentially non-partisan. It is in any case doubtful whether even Henderson could have coped effectively with the presidency of the conference and one of the most important Ministries in Britain at the same time.

How and why the League's work for disarmament ended in failure is the subject of this chapter. The story has a tragic quality about it, but also a certain tediousness, with the main threads sometimes lost to sight amid the mass of details inseparable from arms control negotiations. The chief factors in this failure are obvious enough; the underlying conflict between French fears, swollen by those of her allies in eastern Europe, of Germany's resurgence, especially after Hitler's accession to the Chancellorship in January 1933, and the German determination to break away from the fetters of Versailles and organise the country's military forces on a footing of equality with other states; Britain's unwillingness to join in broad guarantees of security without which the French could not contemplate lowering their armed guard; American isolationism and refusal to share in the risks and burdens of collective security; the virtual impossibility of measuring the arms requirements of one country against those of

116

another, and one type of weapon against another; the all but
insoluble difficulties of verification to ensure that disarmament
treaties are observed, and of organising sanctions in the event of
violations; the powerful emotions, not least of mistrust and fear, in
which all matters connected with national defence are steeped.
Not without reason was it said by a French journalist of the
Preparatory Commission's draft convention when it eventually
saw the light of day in 1930 that 'ce document a une grande vertu
qui est d'exister'.

The failure of disarmament was a grave blow to the League's
prestige. Should it have embarked upon such a hazardous
undertaking in the first place? Perhaps the most damaging effect of
the League's involvement with the disarmament movement was
the resulting tendency of the world organisation to be identified
with the renunciation of all force in international affairs, and hence
with outright pacifism. The League system was indeed meant to
discourage states from settling their differences by force, and to
provide them with alternative means of settlement. At the same
time, the sanctions arrangements contained in the Covenant's
Article 16 were equally meant to bring armed force to bear, on a
collective basis, should all else fail to deter states which resorted to
arms in defiance of the procedures in the Covenant for peaceful
settlement. The League was dedicated to peace, but it was not a
pacifist organisation. This the advocates of disarmament, or many
of them, were apt to forget. When they realised in the 1930s that
the restraint of aggression meant that force might have to be used
through the League machinery, their ardour for the League
system often cooled.[4] By the same token, those who were sceptical
about the disarmament movement because they thought it might
weaken the will of member-states to oppose aggression did not
support the League as strongly as they might have done had they
realised that, in the face of aggression, the League Covenant did
not enjoin submission, but resistance. Thus, the cause of
disarmament and the cause of the League were not always at one
with each other.[5]

Nevertheless, the League and the campaign for multilateral
disarmament could not be divided. Both were inspired by the same
yearning for peace bequeathed to the world by the First World
War. The union between the two was consolidated by the belief
that arms are the root cause of wars which that holocaust had
planted in the minds of millions. Governments had to reflect that
belief whether they genuinely entertained it or not. The same

situation has prevailed after the Second World War, when the discredited word 'disarmament' has generally been dropped in favour of the more accurate term 'arms control'. The ritualistic exercise of endless negotiations about armaments has continued year after year, partly because the sheer momentum of international talks, once begun, is all but impossible to stop, partly because the public, in almost all countries, insists that the process goes on. So it was in the 1920s and early 1930s. In their innermost hearts, Ministers who unfolded plans for a disarmed world in reality feared such a world because they could not conceive how, if it were ever brought into existence, the political game which they knew so well could be carried on, and they preferred the devil they knew to any less familiar devil. But their masters, the voters, would not let them withdraw from the ritual, while insisting, through it all, that national systems of defence should in no way be weakened, but rather, if anything, be made even stronger than before.

II

Almost as soon as the League of Nations raised to its lips the poisoned chalice of world disarmament, the features of it which made it undrinkable became evident, and it remained, prepared for swallowing but never swallowed. First, the Permanent Armaments Commission, consisting of military, naval and air force experts and created by Article 9 of the Covenant to advise the Council on disarmament and military, naval and air questions generally, scented the deep political perils of the subject almost as soon as it got to work on it and came to the conclusion that discussion of it would be 'premature'. But the First League Assembly, meeting in September 1920, wanted to get on with the job. The outcome of its debate was the appointment of an awkwardly named body, the Temporary Mixed Commission (TMC), made up, again, of experts and military men, to formulate ideas. The first product of this group, the Esher plan, named after the British delegate, Lord Esher, who fathered it, envisaged the adoption of somewhat arbitrary ratios of land forces between the major states, rather on the lines of the ratios between capital ships and aircraft carriers then being worked out at the Washington naval conference. The Esher principles received short shrift from governments when it was realised that the smaller countries, if such rough-and-ready force reductions were to take place, would be faced with quite disproportionate cuts in army equipment.

The Esher plan was the first of innumerable disarmament plans drawn up within the League system, to be discarded at, or shortly after, their birth. But one effect of discussions about it in the TMC and later the Assembly was to bring to the surface the fundamental truth that any effective disarmament system – that is, one which the great armed Powers, at least, are likely to accept – presupposes an equally effective security system. No country could be expected to reduce the means for ensuring its security unless that security was provided for by some other device, as for instance a collective security system. All the more was this so in that the country with the largest land forces at that time, France, was dissatisfied with the security provided by the peace treaties. France had forgone one vital element in her security system at the peace conference in 1919, namely the separation of the west bank of the Rhine from Germany, in exchange for guarantees against unprovoked aggression by Germany offered by the British and American leaders, Lloyd George and Woodrow Wilson.[6] But this had fallen into abeyance with the non-ratification of the treaties by the United States, and, with the resulting failure of that country to join the League, France considered the Covenant too weak to defend her against the German revanche which practically every Frenchman knew was coming. When negotiations for an Anglo-French defence pact failed at the Cannes conference in January 1922, French opposition to any disarmament scheme without a foolproof security system was confirmed.[7]

Britain had disarmed drastically as far as her land forces were concerned after the war. France had not. Therefore, if any general disarmament were to take place, France would need to be persuaded to follow Britain's example, which meant that the French bargaining position when arms talks began in the early 1920s was stronger than the British. Hence, through French pressure, the Third League Assembly in September 1922 adopted its famous Resolution XIV, which declared the indissoluble connection between disarmament and security and invited the TMC to continue its inquiries into this question. In complying with this invitation the Commission embarked upon a quest which was never to end, certainly not in success. The TMC's first suggestion, the draft treaty of mutual assistance, considered by the Fourth League Assembly at its session in 1923, was an attempt to organise help for victims of aggression, provided they had complied with prevailing regulations as to their armaments. Its arrangements for enforcement action were regarded, especially by Britain, as too incompatible with national sovereignty to be acceptable. The draft treaty was followed by the Protocol for the Pacific Settlement of International Disputes, or the Geneva Protocol, which the Fifth League Assembly approved in 1924. But this, too, was nullified by a British refusal, echoed by many other states, to shoulder commitments to take action against aggression in any part of the world. It should be remembered, that Britain's naval forces were bound to play a prominent role in almost any collective action to enforce the peace against an aggressor.

We have seen in a previous chapter how these universal formulae for strengthening collective security under the League Covenant gave way in 1925 to the regional security system known as the Locarno agreements, by which Britain and Italy agreed to guarantee the Belgian-German and Franco-German frontiers against flagrant aggression from either side.[8] The Locarno accords were welcomed with the greatest relief in Britain as marking an end to the dangerous feuding between France and Germany, symbolised by, among other things, the invasion of the Ruhr by French forces in January 1923, supported for a time by Belgium, in order to enforce reparation payments by Germany. The feelings of optimism engendered by Locarno were enhanced by the signature, three years later, of the Briand-Kellogg Pact for the renunciation of war as an instrument of national policy, originally a Franco-American agreement which was eventually adhered to by sixty-odd other states. The Pact of Paris (to give the arrangement its other name) did little to make another war less likely, but it reflected the atmosphere of optimism about the continuance of peace in the second half of the 1920s.

In the mood of euphoria created by the Locarno agreements, their more unfortunate consequences, as previously pointed out, tended to be overlooked.[9] These included the feeling in Britain that enough had now been done to satisfy France's fears, and that further 'special arrangements to meet special needs', to use Sir Austen Chamberlain's phrase, would not be required; the inevitable conclusion drawn by revisionists, especially in Germany, that, since one part of the map of Europe had been guaranteed at Locarno, other parts had been left open to question; and the implicit warning to France in the Locarno agreements that any further efforts on her part to enforce the treaties by use of arms against Germany might incur penalties from Britain or Italy, or both. Nevertheless, Locarno, and the general improvement in European international relations which followed it, allowed the disarmament process within the League to take a step forward, now that the security problem was seemingly resolved, at least for the time being.

Accordingly, the Sixth League Assembly invited the Council in September to undertake the preparatory work for the holding of a world disarmament conference, and in response the Council set up on 12 December a Preparatory Commission for the conference, which remained the principal instrument of all the League's work on disarmament until the conference met in Geneva in 1932. The Commission included representatives of all the states on the Council and six others. Four non-members were also included: Germany, which joined the League and the Council a year later, Soviet Russia, the United States, and, as from March 1928, Turkey. The Commission met for the first time in May 1926.[10]

The five years of the Preparatory Commission's life were not happy, with repeated complaints in the Assembly about its procrastination in summoning the long-awaited conference. The chief reason for the delay was the conflict, first, between British and French disarmament plans, then between Britain and the United States over the principles of naval disarmament, especially the question whether, in calculating tonnage of naval vessels, the agreed figure should refer to total weight or to the tonnage of different types of ship by category. From time to time during the five years cheerfulness broke in, as with the signature of the Briand-Kellogg pact in May 1928, the accession of Herbert Hoover to the American Presidency in the same year and the resulting hopes of closer American co-operation with the League, though the Hoover administration's arms proposals, presented to the Commission by Hugh Gibson on 22 April 1929, met with a cool reception, and with the conclusion of the London Naval Treaty between Britain, the United States and Japan in April 1930, which extended the Washington agreement of 1921 to cover cruisers, destroyers and submarines.[11] A fresh wind, too, began to blow through the Preparatory Commission after 1927, the year in which the Soviet Foreign Minister, Maxim Litvinov, later to become one of the most respected Geneva figures, arrived with his proposal for the abolition of all weapons. A second draft of the Litvinov plan limited itself to a substantial reduction of offensive armaments.

Painfully, though spurred on by a clamorous Assembly, the Preparatory Commission, its meetings invariably interrupted by months of private talks between the leading states, put together its first draft disarmament convention at its third session, held from 21 March until 26 April 1927, then its second draft at its sixth session from 15 April until 6 May 1929. Finally, the Commission adopted the final draft to be presented to the Conference at meetings between 6 November and 9 December 1930. On 23 January of the following year the League Council convened the disarmament conference for 2 February 1932 and recommended for its consideration the Commission's draft agreement. The latter reflected some measure of consensus among the Commission's member-states, though the items on which agreement was not possible stood out prominently. As to the points of agreement, the principle of the budgetary limitation of expenditure on arms was accepted, though the juggling with figures by Finance and Defence Ministers was regarded as inevitable. It was agreed that the period of service for armed forces should be limited and some formula for placing a ceiling on land, sea and air force effectives should be devised. A Permanent Disarmament Commission was proposed to supervise the implementation of the convention and enforce it against backsliders. The method of limiting naval armaments agreed to at the London naval conference in 1930, that is, limitation by categories, should be adopted. Finally, chemical and bacteriological warfare should be renounced, though this had already been effected by conventions signed in Geneva in 1925.[12]

The most important areas of disagreement in the convention were three. There was no provision for the inclusion of trained reserves. This meant that a state with a short-service system of conscription might find itself with an army of fully trained servicemen several times the size of its forces in uniform, and yet this would not be covered by the disarmament agreement. Secondly, nothing was said in the convention about the limitation of material for armies or navies. Finally, by a strange omission, no restriction was placed on the cost of material for air forces. All that could be said of the outcome of the Commission's labours was that a document of a sort did emerge, and that this indicated possible lines of approach to the problem, while leaving no doubt about the horrendous divisions which were bound to loom between the principal states when the curtain rose on the main drama.

III

This it duly did in Geneva on 2 February 1932, after the Council's discussion on the bombing of Shanghai. Sixty-four states had been invited to the Conference; fifty-nine were actually represented. Four Latin American countries – Ecuador, Nicaragua, Paraguay and Salvador – were among the absentees. The tables were loaded with millions of petitions from people yearning for peace all over the world. The churches rang with prayers for the long-awaited talks. But, with the circulation of the French slate of proposals and the defence of them by War Minister André Tardieu on 5 February, the shadows anticipated by those who had followed the proceedings in the Preparatory Commission began to hang over the scene. The French Minister wanted all civil aviation internationalised, an inconceivable proposition, but logically sensible in view of the sheer impossibility of separating the use of the air for military purposes and its use for civilian ends. There followed the demand for banning weapons above a certain size, one which would still place all kinds beyond Germany's reach. The French then proposed an international police force to be placed at the disposal of the League for enforcement of the disarmament convention, the same idea they had put forward during the drafting of the Covenant, and no more likely to be adopted in 1932 than it had been in 1919. To make the system of enforcement complete, arbitration was to be made compulsory, and, to ensure its effectiveness when threats to peace came, this demand was coupled with a proposal for defining aggression. In short, Tardieu wanted the League to have 'teeth', as the French always had said. Until then, and afterwards, Germany would remain subject to the Treaty of Versailles.[13]

Sir John Simon, the British Foreign Secretary, and Hugh Gibson, the American ambassador in Brussels, had little sympathy for these notions, though both spoke well of the principle of qualitative disarmament, or the prohibition of 'aggressive' weapons. The trouble was, and always has been, that the weapon one nation considers aggressive is liable to seem essentially defensive to its neighbour, and the other way round. When Litvinov's turn came, he reiterated his old plea for the scrapping of all armaments of whatever kind. But the conference received its reminder of the real issues at stake from the German Chancellor Brüning, with his insistence that, without acceptance of the principle of equality, or the reduction of all arms and armed forces down to Germany's level, hopes were dim that the Germans would continue to co-operate.[14] After the Easter recess between 19 March and 11 April, Brüning returned to his theme by spelling out what he meant by equality. Service in the Reichswehr should be reduced from twelve to six years, which would have the effect of swelling the number of Germany's training reserves; at the same time, the size of the German army permitted by the peace treaty, that is, one hundred thousand, would be doubled. As for equipment, Germany would be allowed to have weapons retained by other states under the eventual disarmament convention, but they would only be in the form of 'samples' or 'prototypes' if they were forbidden by the Treaty of Versailles.[15]

Even during the work of the Preparatory Commission, the chief German spokesman, Count Bernstorff, had constantly warned of the growing dissatisfaction in his country with the delay in recognising its claims, even though Germany had achieved a considerable step forward at a conference at The Hague in August 1929, when the total evacuation of the Rhineland by Entente forces had been conceded, six years before the time laid down in the peace treaties. At the election campaign in Germany in September 1930 all twenty-four competing parties placed treaty revision in the forefront of their programmes. On polling day on 14 September, the National Socialists, who made their attack on the Versailles *Diktat* the core of their policy, increased their strength in the Reichstag from twelve seats to 107, becoming the second largest party in the Chamber.[16] Rising nationalism in Germany was not alleviated by a three-day debate in the French Chamber of Deputies in mid-November, in which Prime Minister Briand's policy of collaboration with the German Foreign Minister, Gustav Stresemann (who had died a month before) was attacked. In the debate one Opposition spokesman, Franklin Bouillon, managed to create a crisis in Franco-German relations by calling into question Germany's good faith in fulfilling her obligation to disarm. On 2 December, the Foreign Affairs committee of the Reichstag passed a resolution sponsored by the Nazis which asked for the recall of Bernstorff from Geneva. German opinion was appalled to discover that when the Preparatory Commission approved the final version of its disarmament convention for the 1932 conference, Article 53 of the document reaffirmed Germany's continuing obligations under the Treaty of Versailles, and then stated that it was on this condition that France, among other beneficiaries of the peace treaties, agreed to attend the disarmament conference.

The day before the Conference reassembled on 11 April after the Easter break, the second ballot in the Presidential elections in Germany was held, the first having taken place on 13 March. The result was that, although the old patriarch, Hindenburg, was returned as head of state once more, Hitler, the National Socialist leader, received 13 million votes, more than twice the total voting strength of his party in the 1930 elections.[17] The time was clearly running out for all voices of moderation in Germany. At Geneva, MacDonald and American Secretary of State Henry Stimson felt they could not be blind to these portents. After a conference with Brüning, they appealed to Tardieu, now the French Prime Minister, to return speedily to Geneva in the hope of securing some relaxation in the French refusal to consider reductions in military strength unless the organisation of peace was improved. Such a gesture, the Anglo-Saxon couple believed, might help shore up Brüning's shaky political position and perhaps save him from the wolves.[18]

At this point a mischance of tragic proportions occurred, such as often dogged the labours of the League. It took the form of hints dropped into the ear of the French Ambassador in Berlin by the scheming German Defence Minister, Lieutenant-General von Schleicher, that Chancellor Brüning's days were numbered, and that the French might find his successor easier to deal with.[19] The first part of this communication was true; on 30 May Hindenburg dismissed Brüning and appointed von Papen in his place. But von Papen's evident intention to try to turn the rising Nazi tide to his own advantage left him with little hope for being more amenable in foreign affairs.

The French were frightened by these events. They were shocked by the League's inability to provide help to China against Japanese aggression. Tardieu, taking his cue from von Schleicher, dallied in Paris on the excuse of an indisposition, and, when Herriot took his place as head of the French government in June, the moment of opportunity had passed. It would be an exaggeration to say that the failure of the Geneva conference to reward Brüning with anything with which to cut the ground from under the feet of his critics at home was the cause of his fall. But the French might have tried harder to understand the depths of humiliation over the Versailles Treaty in Germany; they might have done more to strengthen the hands of the kind of German politicians they wanted, rather than riveting the fetters of Versailles more firmly on their necks. It was surely more sensible to appease the Weimar republic voluntarily than to be forced to appease those who killed it.

There was a faint chance that the German demand for equal treatment might be headed off, or at least prevented from turning into full-scale rearmament, if the Conference could be brought to agree on the illegalisation of especially dangerous weapons or weapons above a certain size. But what were especially dangerous weapons and what should the maximum size be? Certain weapons met the needs of certain countries, and weapons which seemed especially dangerous to some might not to others. In the Naval Commission of the Conference British and American spokesmen contended that capital ships were not weapons of offence: the Germans said they were, and that this was the reason why they themselves were denied them in 1919. Again, Britain and the United States demanded the abolition of submarines, a menace to big battleships and the merchant ships of great trading nations. The smaller naval Powers replied that submarines were the poor man's protection against great navies. But alliances of this kind, formed between two or three states as the disarmament debate swung this way or that, were usually of limited duration: they would dissolve into new combinations as discussion moved to other types of arms control and other kinds of weapons. This happened in mid-June, when Herbert Hoover, meaning to prod the Europeans into some action after so much stalling, and conscious of his ability to use the prospect of a debt settlement as a means of doing so, instructed Gibson to offer a flat-rate reduction of one third in all armed forces, coupled with a ban on offensive weapons and bombing from the air. 'We should cut through the brush and adopt some broad and definite method of reducing the overwhelming burden of armaments', the Presidential message ran.[20]

The Hoover proposals had a revivalist effect, at least for the moment, on the Geneva proceedings. Grandi, the Italian Foreign Minister, made an agreeable reply. So did Litvinov. The Germans looked interested; here was some way of whittling down the French army. But, unsurprisingly, Paul-Boncour, speaking for France, returned to the old complaint that the American plan said nothing about security. The Japanese were totally opposed. Preparing as they were for their trial of strength with China, they had no wish to see their forces lose a third of their strength at one blow. States with smaller armed forces were indignant, too, since a proportionate cut in fewer numbers is more serious than in a larger force. It was on this ground that Stanley Baldwin, for Britain, after giving a cautious welcome to the Hoover proposals, came out against them in the Commons on 7 July on the ground that Britain's traditionally small standing army would be too small to fulfil its vast imperial tasks if reduced by one third.[21]

The curious effect of the American intervention was thus to bring Britain and France closer together after the long period in which the differences between them had done so much to hold up progress. After an accord between the two countries signed in Paris on 13 July, they co-operated in a resolution presented to the Conference ten days later, which aimed at summing up the meagre results of the discussions so far before the adjournment until the autumn. Forty-one states voted, though grudgingly, in favour. Russia voted against, Litvinov explaining that he voted for disarmament but against the resolution. Germany's vote, too, was negative, her chief delegate, Nadolny, explaining yet again that his country could not collaborate further with the Geneva proceedings unless the sacred principle of equality was recognised. The saddest victim of the Conference's poor record to date, however, was the well-respected Italian delegate, Count Grandi, who lost both his post at Geneva and his office as Foreign Minister.[22]

Mussolini himself assumed control of the Ministry and General Balbo succeeded Grandi at Geneva. A new, hostile tone became evident in Italian policy, which had so far sought to build bridges between the French and German positions. One of General Balbo's first utterances on taking up his new post was to describe the League of Nations as a 'limited liability company under the control of England, France and the United States'. He warned that Italy might take its leave of the Conference. Nadolny, too, in a speech at the Conference on 22 July repeated that equality of rights – Gleichberechtigung – must be conceded to Germany if she was to continue to collaborate.[23] The melancholy position the Geneva Conference had now reached was summed up by a British historian as follows: 'the seven years which had elapsed between the opening meeting of the first session of the Preparatory Disarmament Commission on 18 May 1926 and the closing of the first session of the Disarmament Conference had seen no progress towards meeting the German claims for equality of status, and Herr Nadolny found himself in the same position as Count Bernstorff when in December 1930 he rejected the Draft Convention on behalf of Germany'.[24]

As the autumn session of the Conference came round, there could be little doubt that the dominant question was that of keeping alive Germany's interest in the proceedings, and that meant making the level of her permitted armaments the central issue. On 14 September, the new German Foreign Minister, von Neurath, wrote to Henderson saying that his country could not take part when the Bureau, the managing committee of the Conference, resumed its work on the 21st. She would never accept discrimination against herself.[25] Mussolini indicated support for this viewpoint and, for a time, Britain and France joined forces in opposing it. A British statement of 19 September pointed out that Germany would not be relieved of her Versailles obligations if the Conference failed. A week later Herriot confirmed his country's long-standing position that France could only disarm in proportion as her security was assured: this could only mean the establishment of some kind of international force controlled by the League. Paul-Boncour spelled out French ideas on 4 November in a speech at the Bureau of the Conference heavy with insistence on adequate international controls and schemes of regional mutual assistance.[26]

The head-on collision between German demands for equality and French calls for security guarantees seemed inescapable. Germany threatened to rearm, if she had not already done so, unless France disarmed: France would not disarm in view of evident German threats to rearm. Sir John Simon's call at the Conference on 17 November for a general renunciation of force could hardly impress either side in the Franco-German argument.[27]

It did show enough British detachment from the unbending French line, however, to encourage von Neurath to return to Geneva, and there he co-operated with MacDonald and Simon, Paul-Boncour, Norman Davis (for the United States) and Baron Aloisi of Italy in framing a famous statement which emphasised once more the central issue while doing nothing to resolve it. This declared that 'one of the principles that should guide the Conference on disarmament should be the grant to Germany, and to other Powers disarmed by treaty, of equality of rights in a system which would provide security for all nations'. The statement went on to say that this principle should find itself embodied in the convention containing the conclusions of the disarmament Conference. It was agreed that on this basis Germany would take her place again at the Geneva talks.[28]

Everyone knew what equality of rights meant. Either the other great Powers would reduce their armaments to Germany's level; or she would be allowed to increase her armaments to theirs; or there would be some combination of both processes. No-one, however, was quite sure what France and her supporters meant by a 'system of security for all nations', except that it referred to something going beyond the Locarno arrangements. In any case, Britain and the United States made it quite clear that they were not prepared to travel along that road. For ten years at least British governments had refused to move an inch beyond their offer to defend only the soil of France against German aggression. This did not include France's allies in eastern Europe, and moreover German aggression would have to be 'flagrant', as the Locarno agreements put it, Britain herself being left to decide, if and when the time came, what sort of aggression was 'flagrant'. It was an almost standard assumption in Britain that she had allowed herself to become too mixed up with French defence against Germany before 1914 to want to take the same kind of risks again. Besides, what with the political crisis in Britain in 1931 and the still rampaging world economic depression, most British politicians wanted to keep the hatches down for the time being and limit themselves to avoiding being blown off course. Eden flatly told the General Committee of the Conference on 3 February that Britain could not undertake further guarantees of security as France wanted.[29]

As for the United States, the economic disasters of the times had drained away practically all interest in foreign affairs. Much as Secretary of State Henry Stimson might have wished to co-operate with League member-states in the Manchurian crisis at the end of 1931, there was not the slightest hope of doing so in the prevailing isolationist mood. President Hoover had told the Conference time and again that, while the United States would do nothing to hinder the application of sanctions by the European Powers against an aggressor, neither would she do anything to make them effective. Moreover, Hoover was nearing the end of his time of power. At the elections in November 1932, American voters had turned to a new man, Franklin Roosevelt, who began his long reign on a wintry day, 4 March 1933, when his people almost despaired of the future. No-one knew what Roosevelt's international policy would be, except that he would no more embrace entanglements abroad than his predecessors. On 7 February, with the Roosevelt era only one month away, Hugh Gibson told the General Commission of the Conference that United States support for French security schemes could not be expected.[30] On the following day, a discussion in the Commission on mutual assistance against aggression came to an end without agreement being reached. The French would not consider disarmament without security, and without British, to say nothing of American, co-operation, security was not to be had.[31]

The British delegation, however, could not shrug off all responsibility for the parlous state at which the disarmament talks had now arrived. Britain, perhaps more than any other country, had worked to bring about the Conference. If it failed and rearmament became the order of the day, economic recovery in Britain would receive a set-back, or so the pre-Keynesians advising the government forecast. Moreover, as the 1930s drew on, the immense vulnerability of Britain, especially London, in an age of aerial warfare impressed itself more and more on governments; the phrase of Stanley Baldwin, 'the bomber will always get through', hung darkly in British minds. Above all, an event occurred in Germany on 30 January 1933 which sounded a warning bell: the summoning to the Chancellorship of Adolf Hitler by the old war hero, President Hindenburg. Von Papen, who was largely responsible for this momentous happening, thought, like many others, that he could manipulate the Nazi revolution for his own ends. But Hitler, the consummate politician, turned the tables on all who sought to use him. After fire destroyed the Reichstag building on 27 February, symbolising the incineration of German democracy, the new Chancellor stood forth as Europe's champion against Bolshevism. The Nazis won an overwhelming election victory on 5 March, enabling Hitler to kick away the constitutional ladder by which he had sprung to power.[32]

Though Hitler's earliest utterances, such as his speech to the Reichstag on 5 March, were conciliatory in the extreme, no doubt in order to allay alarm while Germany was still weak, it was clear that he meant to turn the country into an armed camp. This would enable him to embark, first, on the destruction of the 1919 treaty system, and, secondly, on making the Third Reich the master of Europe. For the moment, the Nazi revolution was allowed to speak through Hitler's tools, not through the Chancellor himself. In a speech at Münster on 12 May, the deluded von Papen described Germany as having 'struck pacifism from its vocabulary' when it handed the reins of office to Hitler on 30 January. The speech was a reply to a complaint by Lord Hailsham in the House of Lords the previous day about an article by von Neurath in the *Leipziger Illustrierte Zeitung* announcing Germany's intention to rearm whatever happened at Geneva.[33]

The British Government, or rather the section of the Foreign Office under Eden's control (his post at this time was Minister of State for League of Nations Affairs), at last bestirred itself in an effort to rescue the disarmament Conference from freezing to death.[34] MacDonald, now in mental and bodily decline, went himself to Geneva in March and presented a new British plan to the Conference on the 16th. It made certain gestures to French wishes, recommending, for instance, a transitional period of two years, during which the *status quo* in respect of German armaments would remain; it provided for supervision and proposed a permanent disarmament commission to prepare for the next conference in two years' time. The plan recommended the computation of effectives in terms of the number of days served with the forces, laid down figures for the land armies of the chief states – 200,000 for France and a further 200,000 for the French empire, eventually 200,000 for Germany – and the maximum size of their armaments, proposed the inclusion in the Treaty of London (signed by Britain, Japan and the United States in 1930 for applying to cruisers and submarines the ratios agreed for capital ships and aircraft at Washington in 1922) of France and Italy, which had declined to attend the London conference, and reiterated the old demand to make aerial bombing illegal, though with some exceptions, justified as 'police measures in outlying regions'. On the security issue, however, the MacDonald proposals offered practically nothing, merely advocating that, in the event of a violation of the Pact of Paris, presumably in the form of a resort to war as an instrument of national policy, the signatories, or as many of them as could be got together, would consult and decide what to do.[35]

Then, having deposited the plan on the Conference table, rather like an unwanted foundling, the Prime Minister, together with Foreign Secretary Simon, to everybody's astonishment took himself off to Rome to talk to Mussolini about a four-Power pact which the Italian dictator wished to organise. The suspicion among several delegations at Geneva that the Mussolini pact was partly intended to replace the League Council by a consortium of the dominant European states did little to lessen the shock of the abrupt British departure. In reality, the four-Power pact, which was initialled by British, French, German and Italian representatives in Rome on 7 June and signed in the same city on

15 July, involved little more than co-operation to maintain peace and consider the revision of treaties.[36] It appealed to British Ministers because it was in the spirit of Article 19 of the League Covenant, which recommended that from time to time the Assembly should 'reconsider treaties which have become inapplicable and conditions the continuance of which is likely to endanger the peace of the world'. Since 1919 many British politicians had hoped that Germany, instead of being forced to rearm by the inflexibility of an unfavourable treaty system, might prove more amenable as a result of treaty revision in accordance with Article 19. The same ideas were less attractive to France. It was in deference to the French that the term 'revision' was not included in the Rome pact: Article 19 was mentioned, however, though, again in deference to France, it was coupled with Article 16, the sanctions article.

It is not entirely clear why France agreed to the four-Power pact. She had no interest in encouraging British hopes of peaceful change, as revision of treaties was coming euphemistically to be known. Moreover, the pact could not but drive a wedge between France and her ally, Poland, as well as undermine confidence in France among all the successor states of eastern Europe. It seemed as though France was leaving them to face Germany alone, while she sought to consolidate her position in Europe's ruling power elite. Eventually, on 26 January 1934, Poland herself came to terms of a sort with Germany by signing a declaration with that country which committed both to avoid the use of force in their mutual relations.[37]

As for France's interest in the Rome pact, this was no doubt based on her desire to have Britain on her side in the growing conflict with Germany. Attention actually shifted away from the disarmament talks in June, when the world economic conference assembled in London. Henderson, charged to visit the main European capitals to try to unfreeze the arms deadlock, sat in at the London economic talks for a few days, hoping that someone would broach the armaments question with him, though that was not to be. He then moved to Rome, Berlin, Munich and Paris.[38] But the French did receive some reward in August, when Britain stood at their side in protesting against the Nazi war of nerves against Austria. Austria and Germany had been forbidden to unite by the 1919 peace treaties, but Hitler would not have been the nationalist he was if he had not desired it. Tensions arising from the Austrian crisis were part of the general worsening of European international relations which was now beginning to make rearmament, rather than disarmament, the theme of the hour.

Another summer passed. Another warning came from von Neurath, this time on 15 September, that the Geneva Conference must either produce equality for Germany or the whole idea of disarmament would collapse.[39] In a mood close to desperation, Eden talked over the situation with Prime Minister Daladier and Paul-Boncour in mid-September, then they were joined by American and Italian representatives. The meetings showed, if anything, a stiffening in the French position, reflected in an agreement reached among the four on 22 September, based on the idea of a standstill on armaments for three or four years, followed by a period of three or four more years in which actual disarmament would take place. This was no concession at all to Germany, who would have to comply with strict supervision and control of its armed forces, like the other signatories. The agreement was hopefully presented to von Neurath at the resumed Conference on 24 September, together with a demand that the German army be placed on a short-term, instead of long-term basis, and a refusal to allow the Reich to have 'samples' of weapons forbidden by the Versailles Treaty. Within the next four days it became clear to all that the deadlock was complete. The four-Power proposals were then revised, but only by making them even more unacceptable to Germany, though they commanded the approval of the rest of the Conference.[40] In their revised form, presented to the Conference by Simon, the transition period was extended to eight years; during a preliminary period of four years, the Reichswehr would be reorganised on a short-service basis under the supervision of an international commission; general disarmament, with details unspecified, would only be put into effect during a second four-year period. Germany would thus be permitted no increase in its armaments or armed forces over the entire eight-year term.[41]

This meant that the French had had their way almost entirely. They had secured agreement to defer the practical implementation of the German demand for equality for almost a decade. True, they had received no reliable assurances of the security they had harped upon for so many years: on the other hand, there was nothing in the four-Power proposals to prevent them lengthening their massive arms lead over Germany during the first four years, if they wished, and then refusing to reduce it when the four years ended. The German delegate, Baron von Rheinbaben, gave an interim non-committal reply, but soon after the meeting closed on 14 October, the Conference President received a telegram from the German Foreign Minister announcing his country's withdrawal from the Conference. On the same day, Hitler stated in a broadcast from Berlin that Germany was withdrawing from the League.[42] The Chancellor, in the manner to which the world was to grow accustomed, attached to the announcement a vague assertion of interest in further negotiations, though only in a wholly different context. 'We shall not return to Geneva', he told the Comte de Brinon of *Le Matin* on 16 November, 'The League of Nations is an international Parliament in which the conflicting groups of Powers can only quarrel. The differences, instead of being settled, only grow worse'. 'But', he continued, 'I shall only be too glad to enter into negotiations with anyone who wants to talk to me'.[43]

The kind of proposals the world could now expect from Berlin was intimated in an *aide-memoire* sent to the French capital a month later. It began with the offer to France, Poland and Germany's other neighbours of a ten-year non-aggression pact. The demilitarisation of the Rhineland was to be ended, which hardly seemed to allay fears of aggression, at least from Germany. The Reichswehr, limited by the Versailles Treaty to 100,000 men, was to become a conscript army of 300,000. Weapons denied to Germany by the Treaty were to be permitted provided they were considered defensive by the Conference. Offensive weapons were to be denied to all nations. The Nazi paramilitary organisations, the SA, SS and Stahlhelm, were to be regarded as non-military and excluded from the disarmament convention. Finally, the Saar was to be returned to Germany at once without waiting for the results of the plebiscite in 1935.[44]

The long quest for disarmament was drawing to its close. Germany's withdrawal from the Conference did not bring it to an end, but all sense of reality departed from it. The United States sank deeper into isolation. The Italian delegates received instructions to act only as observers. The tedious argument passed back and forth between Paris and Berlin, with Britain, as always, seeking to act in a mediatory role, but fewer and fewer believed that anything could come of it. The French perforce grew accustomed to the growth in German armed strength, though they never relaxed their demand for more security guarantees. Eden began a tour of European capitals on 16 February 1934, hoping to arouse interest in new British proposals. But French dissatisfaction remained: the British, so the French authorities complained in a note received in London on 19 March, were trying to legitimise German rearmament while limiting French armaments, without, however, guaranteeing French security. On 17 April, in their final communication on the subject, French Ministers could think of nothing to say to Britain but words of alarm about the mounting dangers from Germany.

The Conference, which began with lofty hopes of turning swords (or rather much more destructive implements) into ploughshares, was ending with the sound of armourers at work in almost every country. The German air estimates, published in March, showed an increase from 44 million Reichsmarks for the year 1932-33 to 210 million. In the same month increased naval, military and air estimates were published in Britain. Much as it went against the whole grain of his personality, Stanley Baldwin told the House of Commons that in the event of no agreement being come to, and particularly no agreement in the air, 'in air strength and air power this country shall no longer be in a position inferior to any country within striking distance of our shores'.[45] At Geneva, little remained to be done except to give the Conference as decent a burial as delegates felt it deserved. When the general Conference reassembled on 29 May, seven months had elapsed since its previous meeting. The atmosphere was one of unmitigated gloom. There were few speeches, the irrepressible Litvinov providing some bizarre diversion in the form of a suggestion for a permanent disarmament conference, no doubt with a view to advertising for all time the paralysis of the capitalist world in face of the greatest threat to its existence. On 11 June the Conference adjourned *sine die*. Everyone knew it would never meet again.[46]

IV

What had gone wrong? It is easy to blame the French, and this is what most British politicians at the time, if not most British people, did. The French had their massive military superiority over their greatest adversary, Germany, and had no intention of losing it, if it could be helped. The notion that the Germans, once they had been treated as equals and recovered their weapons, would collaborate with others in peaceful pursuits struck them, not merely as naïve, but naïveté of a dangerous kind. At bottom, the French did not believe in the Geneva game, or rather most of their politicians did not, and, with that frame of mind in one of its leading participants, the Conference was doomed from the start.

But if the French never looked as though they wanted the disarmament exercise to succeed, the British were never willing to satisfy the one condition on which it was ever likely to enjoy success. It had been obvious from the first grapplings with the subject in the Temporary Mixed Commission that there was no prospect of any country casting away its means of self-defence, least of all a pathologically fearful country like France after 1918, without some alternative system of security, such as the League, properly managed, might have provided. British Ministers understood this, but at no time were they willing to go beyond the guarantees of security they had given at Locarno in 1925. A score of reasons prevented them doing so: the conviction that promises of assistance given to France before 1914 had dragged Britain into the pit in the First World War; the entrenched isolationism planted by that bloody shambles in the British people, and in the self-governing Dominions, too, without the backing of which British Ministers dreaded involvement in enforcement action; the refusal of the United States to give pledges to use its strength against breakers of the peace. Yet, without some sign from Britain of readiness to come to France's aid, and that of her allies, in the event of renewed German aggression, pleas to France to disarm were bound to be unavailing.

In order to justify their aversion to such advance commitments, British politicians played down the dangers that might result when Germany regained her strength. Overwhelmed with guilt about the 'Carthaginian' peace of 1919, sensitive to German appeals to the time-honoured British sense of fair play, British Ministers were more worried about doing justice to the defeated than protecting the peace against trouble-makers. To them, the French army was a massive provocation to a victimised German people; in the interests of fairness, they were ready, as Churchill pointed out before the disarmament Conference met, to

> Let the boundless deep
> Down upon far-off cities while they dance –
> Or dream.[47]

The Germans were glad to see Britain help them back to a position of equality in the international community, or, as they put it more frankly, to strike off the fetters of Versailles. They repeated *ad nauseam* their claim that in 1919 the Allies had made German disarmament conditional upon the achievement of disarmament in all countries. Eventually, through sheer repetition, the argument began to sink in, at least for the British. By pushing at a gradually opening door, Germany eventually got what she wanted. But the fact that, in this respect, the firebrands in Germany had been proved right and the moderates wrong had also the effect of fastening more securely the chains of slavery on the German neck. By making escape from the fetters of Versailles their main objective, the Germans achieved the rearmament they wanted, but the consequences were horrendous for themselves.

Responsibility for the disarmament fiasco was widely distributed among the leading states in the League. But we cannot help returning to the question whether the real cause of failure was the fact that these states were attempting (though some put little into the effort) to achieve something they considered impossible, and this because it *was* in truth impossible, or almost impossible. Just as President Wilson's towering prestige, added to the horror aroused by the First World War, ushered the European great Powers into a League system entirely foreign to the diplomatic game as they had always played it, so the commitment to disarm, or to make an effort to do so, had been placed round their necks like a halter by forces they could not control, public opinion being one of them. Perhaps the search for agreement on disarmament might have achieved more success had men been more like saints and the times more clement. But in those days, as at present, weapons represented some sort of assurance against the dangers they thought they saw around them. Alternative forms of assurance might have been found, but for these no-one knew where to look.

7 Manchuria: the Covenant defied

I

The League of Nations came into existence theoretically as a world-wide organisation. In reality it was a regional system, the region being Europe, despite the major role in its birth played by President Wilson. Once the American Congress rejected Wilson's brain-child, the League's European character became even more pronounced. It is true that the score of Latin American states were active in different sectors of the League's work, especially in cultural relations, but in the political field they were rarely prominent. As for Africa and the Middle and Far East, those areas still lay under European control. The big exception was Japan, which reformed its way of life with startling suddenness when faced with the impact of the West in the form of the American 'black ships' in the 1850s, and then signalled its entrance into the inner circle of the great Powers, first, by defeating China in 1895, then, to the astonishment of the world, Russia in 1905. Allied to Britain as from 1902, Japan fought on the Entente side in the First World War and took her place in Paris in 1919 as a leading maker of the peace and also of the League Covenant.

That Japan should have found an ally in Britain is not remarkable considering the insular character of both countries and the fact that (at least until 1907) both had a common enemy in Tsarist Russia. There was another similarity in that both states were anchored off a politically turbulent continent, which, if it were ever brought under the control of a single political centre, would make the independence of either hard to maintain. China, the potential unifier of the Asian mainland facing Japan, had undergone a revolution in 1911, a delayed reaction to its defeat by Japan in 1895, in much the same way as Russia suffered changes of vast proportions in 1917 after its defeat by Japan in 1905. China had been on the Allied side in the First World War, but refused to sign the peace treaties owing to the Paris peace conference's decision to assign to Japan German properties in Shantung province, sacred to the Chinese as the birthplace of Confucius. At the Washington conference on the Far East in 1921-22, China was more of an object of diplomacy than a participant. Nine Powers, including Britain, France, Japan and the United States, signed an agreement to guarantee her political and administrative integrity.[1]

The Japanese could not look upon the gradual establishment of control over China in the 1920s by the nationalist party, the Kuomintang, with anything but dismay. Once China was united under one central government, replacing the rival warlords who had divided the country between them since the fall of the Manchu dynasty, Japan's privileged position in China would be at risk. Through their victory over the Chinese in 1895, the Japanese had secured a grip over Korea, the mountainous peninsula lying between China and Japan: in 1910 they annexed it. From Korea, Japanese forces were well placed for an attack on the sprawling salient of Manchuria, consisting of 200,000 square miles and a mainly Chinese population of 30 million. Manchuria was formed from three provinces: Heilungkiang, with its capital at Tsitsihar, Kirin, having a capital city of the same name, and Shenking, with its centre at Mukden, where in the late 1920s the Chinese governor of Manchuria, Chang Hsueh-liang, had his headquarters.

By the Treaty of Portsmouth signed in 1905 Japan fell heir to Russia's lease of the South Manchuria Railway (SMR), which ran from its terminus at Port Arthur, standing guard over the Yellow Sea, north to the Chinese Eastern Railway (CER) at Harbin. The latter system then ran west across the border with Soviet Russia to join the Trans-Siberian line, and east to the Soviet port of Vladivostok, thus cutting off the northern salient of Heilungkiang, round which the Trans-Siberian railway to Vladivostok had to run. The SMR was not only a valuable commercial venture. Its lease gave Japan the right to maintain 15,000 troops in the railway zone to guard the line.[2]

By the 1930s time was running out for the Japanese to scotch the snake of Chinese nationalism and the threat of a united China if they were ever to do so. Already in 1915 the Japanese authorities had formulated their programme for the control of China in the form of the famous Twenty One Demands, the acceptance of which would have amounted to a virtual Japanese protectorate over both China and Manchuria.[3] At the Washington conference in 1922, Japan was compelled to disgorge the German possessions in Shantung which had been awarded to her in 1919. But she retained all the German islands in the Pacific north of the equator which had come to her as 'C' mandates under the League at the peace settlement, and that meant annexation in all but name. Moreover, the five-Power naval treaty signed at Washington in 1922 gave Japan a strength in battleships and aircraft carriers almost a third that of the combined British and American fleets. The accompanying agreement to freeze the *status quo* in naval bases in the Pacific, with some exceptions, made her for all practical purposes immune against any armed pressure which Britain and the United States might later wish to bring to bear upon her.[4] Moreover, by a curious twist of fate the Japanese discovered that, in their battles against xenophobic Chinese nationalism, they had an unexpected assistant in Britain. Britain, owing to pressure from the United States and Canada, was virtually compelled to abandon the Anglo-Japanese alliance when it came up for renewal in 1921: it was replaced by a four-Power treaty (Britain, France, Japan and the United States) to respect the *status quo* in the Far East.[5] Nevertheless, in the 1920s the Japanese looked on with sympathetic interest when Britain fought to protect her concessions, trading port regimes and extra-territorial rights in China as Kuomintang forces struggled northwards in their battles against the warlords. Similarly, when Japanese forces took up the struggle against Chinese nationalists in defence of *their* interests in Manchuria, British Ministers, businessmen and Foreign Office officials saw in them champions of the same cause.

In this way, Japan found herself to be the first great challenger to the League Covenant when she took over Manchuria as from September 1931 and established a puppet state there, called Manchukuo, on 9 March 1932, with Pu Yi, the last emperor of China, as its executive head. The Japanese government recognised Manchukuo as independent of China on 15 September.[6] There has been much debate whether this defiance of the League Covenant, which paved the way for the general attack on international order by the dictators in the 1930s, was foisted upon the civilian government in Tokyo by the army, or whether the civilians agreed to have the affair so represented in order to confuse world opinion. The grip of the military on Japanese life and politics was powerful. Under the Japanese constitution, adopted in 1882, the appointment of Service Ministers in the government required the agreement of the General Staff, thus giving service officers a virtual veto over all governments. The military tradition, too, had always been strong, Japan having been, for hundreds of years before the reforms of the 1860s, a military dictatorship, the Shogunate, which overshadowed the emperor. Violence, perpetrated or instigated by the army, was no uncommon feature in Japanese political life. In 1930, a Prime Minister, Hamaguchi, had been assassinated on returning from the naval conference in Geneva for having allegedly betrayed Japanese interests.

The army had a peculiar interest in Manchuria. That country had been both the chief battleground and the chief prize in Japan's struggle with Russia in the war of 1904-5. Together with Korea, it provided a base for larger schemes for the control of China never far from the minds of Japanese officers. Supposedly rich in minerals and with a flourishing population, it seemed to offer prospects of an economic future for young Japanese servicemen grander than life on impoverished farms at home. These had in any case been brought to ruin by the catastrophic fall of raw silk prices in the world depression which began in 1929, Japanese farming by that time having become largely dependent on silk exports to foreign markets, especially in the United States.[7] It is not surprising that Japan's professional soldiers should have seized the opportunity to secure their future by making Manchuria the base for the Greater East Asia Co-prosperity Sphere which in the later 1930s became the central theme of Japanese foreign policy. In this, they had little difficulty in twisting the civil government in Tokyo to their own ends.

If Japan's military leaders did mastermind the Manchurian affair, they showed, for servicemen, uncommon flair for timing. The world-wide economic depression, which seems to have triggered off the Japanese move into Manchuria in September 1931, also dissipated opposition to it among the great Powers. Britain, heavily committed to preserve the *status quo* in the Far East by the League Covenant, the Pact of Paris, or Briand-Kellogg Pact, of 1928, and the Washington treaties respecting the *status quo* in China and the Pacific signed in 1922, and possessing, in theory at least, the naval strength to form the core of opposition to Japanese imperialism, was battling with the economic storm. On Sunday, 20 September, two days after the Manchurian affair erupted, Britain went off the Gold Standard, at that time an earth-shaking symbol of distress. Two days later, when the Council met in Geneva to discuss the Manchurian crisis for the first time, Britain faced the unprecedented experience of a mutiny, albeit a minor one, of naval ratings at the Scottish naval base of Invergordon, staged in protest against proposed cuts in pay.[8]

The two major continental League Powers, France and Germany, wrestled with similar economic shocks and were in any case insignificant naval Powers. The position of the United States, however, was different. She was not only a signatory of the Washington treaties, which were supposed to throw a protective cloak around China: she had also played a leading role in promoting them. She was also a naval Power on a level of equality with Britain and had a long tradition of support for China against imperialist states, going back to the days of American missionary activity in the country in the last century. The United States was not, of course, a member of the League. But she had played a leading role in organising the Pact of Paris in 1928, and had, from her birth at the end of the eighteenth century, taken a stronger interest in Pacific affairs than in European. If the United States was ever likely to co-operate with the League in protecting the peace, it was in the Far East and Pacific that it would happen. In 1931, moreover, America had a Secretary of State in the person of Henry L. Stimson with a strong concern that America should take its share in peace-keeping.

Stimson was well-endowed with the American penchant for sonorous moralisms in the international sphere. His principal contribution to the world debate about Manchuria which opened in September 1931, namely the so-called 'doctrine' of non-recognition of situations, like the creation of Manchukuo, which had been brought about in defiance of the Pact of Paris, was a good example of the American preference for moral postures to restraints of a more practical kind. The weakness, too, of Mr Stimson's position in respect of American public opinion was obvious: it was fully admitted in his later account of the Manchurian affair, *The Far Eastern Crisis*.[9] For, close as East Asia and the Pacific were in the early 1930s to American thinking, they were still formidably remote. The non-recognition of disagreeable acts remained the limit, further than which the American people and Congress would not budge. Certainly the Japanese challenge to Manchuria was no stimulus to American youth to get up and fight there to repel the invader. Besides, in 1931 and for at least two more years, the United States was rocked by the economic earthquake which shook the capitalist system to its foundations in its own homeland. When Franklin Roosevelt finally faced inauguration as President on a bitterly cold 4 March 1933, the country was for all practical purposes prostrate, as it had been during the previous eighteen months when the Japanese were consolidating their grip on Manchuria.

This opportuneness of the moment for attack could not have been lost on Japan's leaders, civilian or military. But there was another degree of astuteness in the form they chose of bringing Manchuria to heel. This was the fact that the League Covenant, like all arrangements to preserve the peace, was designed in the light of the First World War, at the end of which it came into existence. That conflict, in the way in which it began and in its legal status, corresponded to the classic nineteenth-century pattern. It was a legal war, properly declared and opening with the crossing of frontiers by national armed forces. In 1919, the framers of the Covenant naturally had those events in mind in contemplating how the next war, if there was one, would begin and the shape it would take. When they used the phrase 'should any Member of the League resort to war', as in Article 16, they almost certainly thought in terms of a repeat performance of August 1914, just as in 1945 the United Nations Organisation was framed to deal with the kinds of threats to the international system with which the world had become familiar between the two wars.

The Manchurian crisis, however, was far from fitting into the 1914 pattern. According to the Japanese, what happened on the evening of 18 September was that about 10 o'clock an explosion occurred on the South Manchuria railway line just north of Mukden and a group of Japanese soldiers, who were patrolling the line, as they had every right to do in order to defend it and the ground it stood on, were fired upon. The action they took in response resulted in Japanese forces occupying the adjacent Peitaying Barracks, from which the Chinese withdrew almost without firing a shot. Next day the Japanese took over Mukden and several other towns in the region. According to the Chinese the attack on the barracks was entirely unprovoked. When the League commission of inquiry under the Earl of Lytton (see below, p.149) studied the evidence it came down on the Chinese side with its conclusion that,

> The Japanese ... had a carefully prepared plan to meet the case of possible hostilities between themselves and the Chinese. On the night of 18-19 September, this plan was put into operation with swiftness and precision. The Chinese ... had no plan of attacking the Japanese troops, or of endangering the lives or

property of Japanese nationals at this particular time and place. They made no concerted or authorised attack on the Japanese forces and were surprised by the Japanese attack and subsequent operations. An explosion undoubtedly occurred on or near the railroad between 10 and 10.30 p.m. on September 18 but the damage, if any, to the railroad did not in fact prevent the punctual arrival of the south-bound train from Changchun and was not in itself sufficient to justify military action. The military operations of the Japanese troops during this night cannot be regarded as measures of legitimate self-defence. In saying this, the Commission does not exclude the hypothesis that the officers on the spot may have thought they were acting in self-defence.[10]

Whatever the truth about the events on 18-19 September, it is hard to see how the resulting situation could be regarded as a 'war' within the meaning of Article 16, or of Article 11, under which China actually appealed to the League on 21 September 'to take immediate steps to prevent the further development of a situation endangering the peace of nations; to re-establish the *status quo ante*; and to determine the amounts and character of such reparations as may be found due to the Republic of China'.[11] There was never a declaration of war; there were hardly any hostilities, Chang Hsueh-liang ordering his troops in Mukden to offer no resistance. Moreover, no-one in Geneva, where the Council met on 22 September to consider the Chinese appeal, knew what exactly was happening in Manchuria, which in the 1930s was far less accessible from Europe than it has since become. British, French and German representatives on the Council, who in any case had the strongest reasons for not involving their countries too deeply in the affair, had plenty of excuses for keeping aloof. Compared with the flourish of the 1914 invasions, Manchuria was a 'darkling plain where ignorant armies clash by night'.[12]

The image of Japan doing legitimate police work in Manchuria was strengthened by the doubts, of which Japanese propaganda made the most, whether China was even a state within the ordinary meaning of the term, that is, a united people inhabiting a clearly demarcated territory with a central government able to maintain order and safeguard the rights of its subjects and foreigners. Since the revolution in 1911-12, China had looked to many people as if it had slipped back to an 'era of warring states', with local chieftains commanding armies made up, more often than not, of brigands rather than ordinary soldiers, and frustrating all efforts of the authorities to establish central control. If this was true of China proper, the Japanese argument ran, how much more true was it of outlying provinces like Manchuria? Further, as China decayed in the latter part of the nineteenth century, it had disintegrated into zones in which external great Powers took under their control all the functions of government, collecting taxes and customs, administering police forces and courts of law, punishing felons and ruling Chinese people by the million.

It was the aim of the Kuomintang, and of every good Chinese nationalist, to end all this and bring the country back into the ownership of the Chinese people. Hardly any Asian people, after nationalistic feelings had been fanned by the First World War and its accompanying rhetoric, did not dream of terminating the extra-territorial regimes established in their countries by foreign imperialism and repatriating their fatherlands. Not surprisingly, the movement released a great deal of self-righteous emotion, which often meant rough treatment for foreign interests. In China's case, a century or more of suppressed indignation at the suffering of a proud people with a distinguished past at the hands of hated foreigners welled forth after 1918. In their struggle against this revolutionary nationalism, the Japanese could be regarded from Europe, not as aggressors tearing up the League Covenant, as William II of Germany tore up the 1839 treaty guaranteeing Belgium's neutrality, but as champions of law and civilisation.

II

On 19 September 1931, when the first news of the Mukden incident reached Geneva, the twelfth ordinary session of the League Assembly was drawing to a close in no exhilarated mood. The Austro-German customs union proposal, which many who remembered the League's work for Austria's economic reconstruction in the 1920s had hoped might save that country from the worst effects of the slump, had been judged illegal by the world court at The Hague, largely as a result of French pressure. France's own proposal, put forward by Briand, for a form of European unification, had gone the same way to defeat. A convention to improve the means of preventing war, which would have enabled the League Council, when deliberating on a dispute, to disregard the votes of the parties, had been adopted by the

Assembly, but its prospects of ratification by League member-states, now numbering fifty-four, were remote; in fact, the convention never came into force. Possibly more serious had been the Assembly's abandonment of the attempt to harmonise the Pact of Paris, or Briand-Kellogg Pact, with the League Covenant. Had it been successful, it might have made it easier to improve co-operation between the United States and the League Powers, the lack of which was to prove so disastrous in the Manchurian crisis. In the event, the Assembly could not do more than take note of the Manchurian affair and then disperse, leaving the sixty-fifth session of the Council to take up the problem.[13] The Council was in any case involved by reason of the Chinese government's invocation of Article 11 of the Covenant (China had been unanimously elected a League member in the previous year and a non-permanent member of Council in September 1931). Article 11 was the clause which declared that 'any war or threat of war, whether immediately affecting any of the members of the League or not' was a matter of concern to the whole League and charged the Secretary-General, at the request of any Member, 'forthwith' to summon a Council meeting. The League was then authorised 'to take any action that may be deemed wise and effectual to safeguard the peace of nations'. The assumption, of course, in all this proceeding was that a war or threat of war existed, and this the Japanese never admitted.

At the Council's meetings on and after 22 September, both the Chinese delegate, Dr Sao-ke Alfred Sze, and the Japanese spokesman, Mr Kenkichi Yoshizawa, gave such information about the situation in Manchuria as they had and undertook to provide more as they received it. From the first, Dr Sze insisted that the League should act, and act quickly. He urged that a commission of inquiry be sent to the scene of action and promised that China would comply with any recommendations the League felt able to make. The Japanese delegate, adamant that his country had no territorial ambitions in Manchuria and had now withdrawn most of its troops to the railway zone, saw no case for League intervention. He opposed the proposal for a commission of inquiry and said the dispute could be settled by direct negotiations between China and Japan. Mr Yoshizawa also argued against the legality of a proposal to send the minutes of the Council to the American president. Oddly enough, in view of the tough attitude towards the Japanese taken later by Secretary Stimson, his first reaction was to support them in their opposition to a commission of inquiry. The discussion then turned to Japan's complaint about the lack of security for the million Korean and Japanese residents in Manchuria, to which the inevitable reply was that this was something the Chinese were willing to guarantee, but not while Japanese forces were in illegal occupation of their territory. Nevertheless, Council members felt encouraged by the assurances given by Chinese and Japanese delegates that their countries would do nothing to make the situation worse. On this basis the Council adjourned its discussion on 30 September with a resolution, to which both Chinese and Japanese delegates acceded, pleading for the withdrawal of forces and the avoidance of provocative actions. The resolution included the assurances and undertakings given by the two disputing parties, first, the Japanese Government's statement that it had 'no territorial designs on Manchuria' and that it would continue 'as rapidly as possible, the withdrawal of its troops ... into the railway zone in proportion as the safety of the lives and property of Japanese nationals is effectively assured', and, secondly, the Chinese Government's statement that it would 'assume responsibility for the safety of the lives and property of Japanese nationals outside the zone as the withdrawal of Japanese troops continues'. The Council decided to meet again on 14 October to consider the situation as it then stood, but nothing was done to remove the impression the Japanese must have formed from the discussion, namely that it was left to them to decide whether conditions in Manchuria would ever be satisfactory enough for their troops to be withdrawn.[14]

As so often happened during the dispute, no sooner had Japanese assurances been given that no more than a limited police action was intended than the situation in Manchuria deteriorated and Japanese military activity increased, whether as cause or consequence. In early October, the officer commanding Japanese forces in Manchuria, General Honjo, announced that he could no longer accept the authority of Chang Hsueh-liang, who by this time had removed himself to Chinchow, in the south-western corner of Shenkiang Province and situated on the railway to Peking. On 8 October came the ominous news that Japanese aircraft had bombed Chinchow, which seemed to imply that the Japanese authorities were bent on terminating Chinese administration in Manchuria. At the same time, the Japanese delegation to the League made it known that 'negotiations of wide scope', as the delegation called them, must precede any settlement of the dispute; this formula seemed to embrace matters far beyond the security of the South Manchuria Railway.[15]

When it met on 13 October at China's request to deal with the worsening situation symbolised by the Chinchow bombings, the Council – with the celebrated and vastly experienced Aristide Briand in the chair – was encouraged by replies received from Secretary Stimson on the same and the previous day to the effect that the American government 'would endeavour to reinforce what the League does'. It was the strongest statement of co-operation ever received by the League from Washington during the crisis and was accordingly viewed with alarm by Japan as tending to strengthen the League's hand. The Japanese delegate put up the strongest fight to prevent the Council voting to invite the American government to send a representative to sit with the Council on the dispute though without power to vote. This, Mr Yoshizawa said, would be unconstitutional since the United States had no official standing in the League. In any case, the Japanese delegate continued, such a vote, on such an important matter, required the consent of all the Council, an intimation that he himself would veto it. Nevertheless, the Japanese argument was voted down and, by thirteen votes to Japan's solitary negative, the invitation to the United States to join the Council was approved on 15 October.[16] For the moment, though the moment was short, it almost looked as if the course of history was being reversed and the rejection of Wilson by the American Congress in 1920 annulled.

But that was not to be. After taking his seat at the Council on 16 October, the American Consul-General to Switzerland, Mr Prentiss Gilbert, confined himself to making a brief statement reaffirming American moral support, but nothing more, for the League.[17] Debate then began on the conditions for a Japanese evacuation of territory occupied since 18 September. At first, the Japanese delegate mystified his colleagues by saying that evacuation could not be carried out until 'certain fundamental principles in relations with China' were settled, while refusing for some time to explain what these principles were. At length, his reserve gave way and he argued that China's total attitude towards Japan's position in Manchuria would have to change: China must guarantee the rights of Japanese to settle and live in Manchuria without harassment, and must order her people, police and armed forces to refrain from interfering with Japanese visitors and residents. There was no prospect of Japan withdrawing her forces unless and until these conditions were secured. This meant in effect that, even if the stated conditions were complied with, it would be left to Japanese forces to determine when it would be safe for them to retire to the railway zone. The Chinese could hardly accept such a demand unless they consented to the administration of Manchuria as a whole being made over to the Japanese. They therefore withheld all agreement to negotiate about the 'fundamental principles' before the Japanese showed willingness to evacuate the land they had taken.

The Council, struggling to maintain a neutral position (though there was no good reason, apart from its member-states' fear of war, why it should do so), decided that Japanese forces should be invited to withdraw, and even set a time-limit of three weeks for this to be done. Negotiations to settle all outstanding issues between the two countries were deferred until withdrawal was complete. On her side, China was enjoined to do all within her power to make life tolerable for Japanese living in China. No very specific machinery was decided for implementing this resolution, which the Council adopted against Japan's solitary dissenting vote on 24 October.[18] The most important feature of the resolution, however, was that it was coupled with the recognition by the Council that resolutions under Article 11 must be unanimous in order to be binding. There could be no more dramatic indication that, in the last resort, if Japan persisted in extending her military control over Manchuria (she was by this time so heavily committed that withdrawal must have seemed an intolerable loss of face) the League could do little more than deplore her action and warn of the consequences.

On 16 November the Council met to consider the situation again, this time in Paris owing to Briand's inability to leave the French capital because of the press of government business (he was Prime Minister). It was now clear beyond doubt that the whole of Manchuria was being drawn into the grip of the occupying forces. The Council's recommendation of 24 October on the withdrawal of Japanese troops had not only not been complied with; Japan's area of control had extended and was continuing to do so. As a result of a clash between Chinese and Japanese in the vicinity of the Chinese Eastern Railway, the Japanese had now occupied Tsitsihar, the capital of Heilungkiang Province, situated some 250 miles from the railway zone where the trouble originally began. It was impossible not to doubt whether Japan could be dislodged by resolutions emanating from Geneva. Moreover, possibly because Japan's hold over Manchuria was growing every

day, United States confidence in the prospects of co-operation
with the League Powers seemed to wane. President Hoover now
chose to send General Dawes, the American ambassador in
London, to carry on Prentiss Gilbert's liaison work, but to do so in
a more detached fashion. Instead of taking a seat at the Council
table, Dawes remained in his rooms at the Ritz Hotel, with which a
one-way correspondence was conducted by the Council's
chairman. As though to underline the fact that close co-operation
between Washington and Geneva was now a thing of the past, Mr
Stimson issued an extraordinary statement to the effect that the
Manchurian business could be settled without resort to force – that
is, force applied against Japan.

Reassured by this weakening of opposition, and perhaps
welcoming another opportunity for delay, the Japanese now
agreed to the despatch of a commission of inquiry, which they had
opposed when suggested by China at the beginning of the League's
deliberations, provided its investigations covered China as well as
Manchuria.[19] The United States backed the idea and Dr Sze still
favoured it. Three more weeks elapsed, however, in debating the
text of a resolution to create the commission, while the Japanese
army seemed to be preparing for a move against Tientsin, only to
be deterred by a warning from the Council. On 10 December the
long-prepared resolution was adopted; it created a commission of
five – four Europeans and an American – who chose the British
Earl of Lytton as chairman.[20] The Chinese and Japanese were
invited to appoint an assessor each, the former selecting Dr
Wellington Koo and the latter Mr Isabura Yoshida. The group was
charged 'to study and report to the Council on any circumstances
which, affecting international relations, threaten to disturb peace
between Japan and China or the good understanding between
them on which peace depends'. The echo there of the language of
Article 11 of the Covenant, under which China had appealed to the
League, was not calculated to endear the commission to the
Japanese. On the other hand, they were the party in possession (or
would be by the time the commission reported) and had little to
fear. Briand, the Council's president, in explaining the text of the
resolution of 10 December, said 'it should prepare the way for a
complete solution of the question at issue', though the five-man
team were given no specific instruction to recommend a form of
settlement.[21] This, however, did not prevent them doing so;
Chapter IX of their report, entitled 'Principles and Conditions of
Settlement', discussed the lines of a long-term solution.[22]

All in all, the project bore every appearance of being little more than an academic exercise and this was reflected in the leisurely way in which the commission went about its work. It was not fully constituted until January: its European members left for the Far East on 3 February and, after joining their American colleague, went first to Tokyo, then for two weeks to Shanghai, where they studied, to the impatience of the Chinese, the efforts to end the fighting there between Chinese and Japanese forces. After visits to Nanking, the seat of the Chinese government, and Peiping (as the city was now called), the commission finally reached Manchuria, where it spent six weeks, in April, six months after the crisis began and almost two months after the Japanese-organised state of Manchukuo declared its independence. The commission's report, later generally known as the Lytton report, was drafted in Peiping after a further visit to Tokyo in late June, and signed in the Chinese city on 4 September. The League Council did not consider the report until 21 November and the thirteenth League Assembly not until 6 December, that is, almost a year after the Council resolution creating the commission was adopted.

While this process was in motion, both the Japanese delegation at Geneva and the League Powers could afford to sit back and rest from their labours. Meanwhile, the Japanese army on the plains and hills of Manchuria was allowed to proceed with the annexation of the country, under the guise of an independent state, which deceived nobody. Sir John Simon, the British Foreign Secretary, depicted the state of suspended animation which fell on the League once the commission had ventured forth to the scene of action. 'It would be quite improper for anyone', he told the House of Commons on 22 February 1932, 'to attempt to pronounce a partial or interim judgment in a matter when everything depends on the report which will have to be made by the League recognised on both sides as proceeding from a complete sense of impartiality'.[23] Mr Stimson, on the other hand, with his strange tendency to turn hot when the League Powers turned cold and *vice versa*, made up his mind not to let matters rest. His next step, by showing how out of accord with each other the United States and Europe could be, must have convinced the Japanese, if they really needed it, that they had nothing to fear by way of measures of restraint from either the United States or Europe.

Mr Stimson's initiative, taken on 7 January 1932, was in the form of a famous note stating that no American recognition would be accorded to any *de facto* situation or agreement which impaired the rights of American citizens, the Open Door principle, or the Pact of Paris of 1928 for the renunciation of war as an instrument of national policy. Believing that the note's moral effect would be enhanced if a similar stand were adopted by a number of nations, the Secretary of State appealed to Britain and other League Members to do likewise. The Stimson note was intended to rely on moral force alone. Mr Stimson himself described it as a 'substitute for sanctions'.[24] Nevertheless, it was a blunder of the first magnitude for the British government to reply with a Foreign Office note drawn up by Sir Victor Wellesley and initialled by Simon, which was published in the press on 11 January, stating that, in view of repeated Japanese assurances regarding the Open Door in Manchuria, a British note on the same lines as the American was unnecessary.[25] Anthony Eden, speaking in the Commons a month later, deployed the same argument.[26]

The effect must have been gravely to embarrass Mr Stimson as he grappled with a strongly isolationist public opinion in the United States. The British response, too, could not fail to encourage the firebrands in Tokyo, who wrote off world reactions to the annexation of Manchuria as words without meaning. About all that could be said by way of exoneration of the British retort to Stimson (the French remained discreetly silent) was that it was tiresome to have to listen to American leaders blowing hot and cold over the crisis when everyone knew that their power to take any decisive action hardly existed.

III

Almost immediately events ensued which demonstrated, not only how the European League member-states and the United States leaped into action when their own national interests, rather than those of China, were involved, but what they could have achieved by way of restoring the *status quo* in Manchuria had they really wished to do so. Those events were the heavy fighting which broke out in January 1932 between Chinese and Japanese in Shanghai, China's most important port, standing at the estuary of the Yangtse river, which ended in devastating the thickly populated suburb of Chapei.[27]

Shanghai had been opened to foreign trade by the British, who established a settlement to the north of the native city by the Treaty of Nanking in 1842. The French created their settlement in

1849, the Americans thirteen years later, and the Japanese followed suit after the Treaty of Shimonoseki in 1895, which gave them extra-territorial rights in China after their victory in the Sino-Japanese war. By the 1930s Shanghai was more of an international than a Chinese city. Foreigners ran their own settlements, performing all the functions of government within them, from running the police to paving the streets, and collecting local rates to provide the money. They had their own courts of law, collected customs and provided their own armed forces. In January 1932, there were 2,306 British, 1,253 American, 1,050 French troops in Shanghai, and, at the height of the troubles in 1932, as many as 20,000 Japanese soldiers. Not surprisingly, the Chinese nationalists, backed by the communists, vented their full spleen on the foreign settlements in Shanghai. In 1927, the British authorities were heavily involved in defending their settlement, calling in reinforcements from Hong Kong to strengthen their position. Japan's turn to face the music came in 1932.

Tension rose between Chinese and Japanese in the city early in the New Year, 1932, with derogatory articles in the Chinese press about the Japanese emperor. On 18 January a street fight occurred in which five Japanese, including some Buddhist monks, were roughly handled. The upshot was that groups of resident Japanese, besides going on the rampage and attacking Chinese property, called on their consul to take action, and on 20 January he served on the Chinese mayor of Shanghai a group of demands ranging from the handing over of apologies and compensation for injuries inflicted on Japanese residents to calls for the suppression of all anti-Japanese activities. When the mayor hesitated over his reply, the commander of the Japanese fleet in Chinese waters, Rear-Admiral Koichi Shiozawa, decided to act. A Japanese cruiser, an aircraft carrier and four destroyers were ordered to Shanghai.

Although in the end the mayor accepted the Japanese demands and the Japanese consul confirmed to his government that this was so, events in the city acquired a momentum of their own, the arrangements made for the defence of the foreign settlements against the disturbances being instrumental in this development. It had as a general rule been agreed between all concerned, as for instance in the Sino-Japanese war of 1894-95, that the foreign settlements should be exempted from military operations in or around Shanghai. On 28 January 1932, however, the day on which the mayor accepted the Japanese demands, the Municipal

Council, which represented all the foreign Powers with interests in the port, declared a state of emergency, which meant that each foreign country with a settlement in Shanghai must take measures for the defence of its own people and their property. In Japan's case, the settlement extended some distance into the Chapei district of Shanghai, the lines of demarcation not being clear. Japanese forces, in reality too weak to overcome substantial Chinese resistance, found the order to clear the Chinese out of the zone allotted to them impossible to carry out, and Admiral Shiozawa felt obliged to call up bombing aircraft, the effect of which was to reduce Chapei to rubble. For five weeks a 'war in everything but name', as J.H. Thomas, the British delegate to a special meeting at the League Assembly on 3 March, called it, raged.[28] The world disarmament conference, which was to have opened in Geneva on 2 February, had to be postponed to allow the League Council to discuss the situation. Truces were arranged, only to be broken; reinforcements were called up on both sides. There was even a brief bombardment of Nanking, the headquarters of the Chinese government, 200 miles distant from Shanghai, by Japanese warships in the Yangtse river and the government had temporarily to retire to Loyang.

The events in Shanghai and Manchuria were connected in so far as both reflected Japanese anger about Chinese campaigns against foreigners, in particular the anti-Japanese boycott, which by this time had become almost a national institution in China. But, whereas the Japanese made clear that they intended to bite off Manchuria and swallow it whole, Shanghai was far too much a property of world commerce for them to contemplate any such treatment for it. The considerable force the Japanese used in defence of their settlement was meant to ensure that it remained theirs, but that was about the limit of their designs, at least for the moment. On their side, the Chinese hoped that the Shanghai affair would not distract attention from their main concern, Manchuria, which was now in distinct danger of passing entirely under Japanese control. The Chinese knew that Shanghai was too vital to Britain and other Powers for them to allow Japan to appropriate it, whereas the stake of external countries in Manchuria was not big enough for them to do much more than pass harmless resolutions about it in Geneva.

In Shanghai, the Powers meant business, and they lost no time in showing that they knew how to conduct it when they wanted to. Their aims were twofold: to make sure that the hostilities did not seriously affect foreign settlements, and to bring them to an end at the earliest moment. In pursuit of the former object, the American authorities took the initiative as soon as the trouble started in collaborating with Britain, France and Italy in seeking from Japan assurances that foreign interests in Shanghai would not be interfered with. When, on 28 January, the Japanese told Britain that 'some drastic measures might be necessary' in order to check anti-Japanese activities, the British Foreign Secretary sent immediate instructions to the ambassador in Tokyo on the subject and himself saw the Japanese envoy in London to express his 'grave concern' and to 'draw the attention of the Japanese government to the international issues and obligations involved'.[29] During the following weeks the authorities in Tokyo were repeatedly warned by the United States and the European powers against using the Shanghai settlement as a base for operations against Chinese troops.

The external Powers were no less active in seeking to end the trouble. The American and British consuls in Shanghai enjoyed only limited success in their efforts to arrange a truce on the evening of 29 January. But on 2 February the British and American ambassadors in Tokyo, with French and Italian support, jointly urged the Chinese and Japanese to stop the fighting, to withdraw their forces from all contact with each other, and to begin negotiations 'to settle all outstanding controversies between the two nations' (which would seem to include the Manchurian imbroglio as well) 'in the spirit of the Pact of Paris and the Resolution of the League of 10 December'. American, British and French Ministers to China all went to Shanghai in mid-February to try to get talks going between the two sides. The commander of the British naval squadron in the region, Admiral Sir Howard Kelly, organised a meeting between Chinese and Japanese leaders on board his flagship, the *Kent*, on 28 February to discuss a cease-fire and the withdrawal of troops by both sides under neutral supervision. Another such meeting was held on 3 March.[30]

When an armistice agreement was eventually signed on 5 May after hard bargaining, much of the credit went to the British Minister to China, Sir Miles Lampson, whose job it was to persuade the Japanese that if they withdrew to their own settlement and laid down their arms, they would not have to face the situation which had existed before. By the time the Japanese had withdrawn their last troops on 31 May, leaving a garrison of only 2,500 men, the Chinese had lost 4,274 soldiers killed, over 2,000 wounded and 10,040 missing. On 11 May it was announced in Tokyo that the Japanese had lost 634 soldiers killed and suffered casualties of 1,791 wounded in the fighting in and around Shanghai.

IV

The struggle for Manchuria continued, if in fact it had not now ended in a total Japanese victory. The great Powers resumed their talks without giving much indication that they wished to do more. On 16 February, the twelve neutral members of the League Council issued an appeal to Japan to bring an end to her campaign in Manchuria, without the slightest hope of their wishes being respected. Changes brought about by aggression, they asserted, could not be accepted.[31] But what was there to do but accept them? Secretary Stimson wrote a long letter to Senator Borah, chairman of the Senate Foreign Relations Committee, on 23 February, re-stating his non-recognition principle, but the prospects for joint action by America and the League Powers over Manchuria (as distinct from Shanghai) were more remote than ever.[32]

Accordingly the Chinese opted for a new tactic to arouse the Powers to action. Hitherto they had been appealing to the League under Article 11 of the Covenant, but, although the Council had on occasion excluded the votes of the two states involved in its discussions on the Manchurian question under this Article, it was doubtful whether this was legal. Article 15, however, which explicitly dealt with 'disputes likely to lead to a rupture', explicitly excluded the votes of the parties from resolutions adopted by the Council when it approved reports on disputes. The Article then laid down that member-states may not go to war with any party which complied with a report of the Council. If China could secure from the Council a favourable report on the Manchurian affair which Japan could not veto, the report in itself would not eject the Japanese from Manchuria, but it would probably go a long way towards making China look right and Japan wrong. In the absence of more tangible benefits, that would be something. The Chinese authorities were at the same time invoking Article 10, with its famous commitment to respect for every League state's territorial integrity and political independence, but it was on Article 15 that they now rested their chief hopes, notifying the Secretary-General of their change of strategy on 29 January.[33] Under Article 15 the Secretary-General was required to make 'all necessary arrangements for a full investigation and consideration thereof', and, in so doing, must receive from the parties a full statement of their arguments. This was duly done and the Chinese and Japanese delegates rehearsed their well-known arguments before the Council. Mr Yen, for China, based himself squarely on the point that Japan was threatening Chinese territory far outside the railway zone in which she had police and other rights as a lessee. Mr Sato, for Japan, insisted upon the self-defensive character of Japanese activities. He undertook that 'as soon as the territory is cleared of undesirable elements and the safety of the lives and property of Japanese nationals is adequately safeguarded, as soon as the railway is no longer exposed to Chinese attacks, we shall be able to withdraw our troops within the railway zone'.[34]

Article 15 provided that, if a settlement could be achieved on the basis of such statements, that would be the end of the story. If it could not, the Council's report on the dispute would then become the League's official pronouncement on the rights and wrongs of the question. At no time, however, did the Council subsequently issue any such report, apart from the appeals from time to time to the parties to settle their quarrel peaceably. This was partly because, in the early weeks following China's invocation of Article 15, both Council and Assembly were fully occupied with the crisis in Shanghai. It was partly due, too, to the fact that representatives of the great Powers on the Council found it easier to accept Japanese assurances of the police-like nature of their acts in Manchuria than to formulate strictures against Japan, with the implications of threats which they knew in their hearts that they had no intention of carrying out. Mr Sato had little difficulty at the twelfth meeting of the sixty-sixth session of the Council on 19 February in securing acquiescence in his explanation that Japan had undertaken 'to withdraw our forces within the railway zone as soon as the life and property of our nationals in Manchuria had been safeguarded, but that the abnormal situation had continued and we have so far been unable to withdraw our troops'.[35] Moreover, the Council had appointed the Lytton Commission on 10 December of the previous year; the commission was not to complete its report until September. What could the Council do until then but mark time? About the only thing it could do was to endorse the decision by Drummond, the Secretary-General, to ask the consuls of the twelve neutral Council members in Shanghai to report on the situation in the port, and this it did. The consuls submitted four useful reports which were instrumental in bringing an end to the Shanghai crisis in May.

The Chinese became impatient. On 12 February, just within the deadline of fourteen days after submission of the dispute under Article 15, they asked for the question to be referred to the Assembly. The Assembly, or rather the representatives of fifty of the League's fifty-five member-states, accordingly met in special session on 3 March, most of the delegates being conveniently present in Geneva to attend the world disarmament conference which had opened a month before. It was the only special session to have been held up to that time, apart from the one called in March 1926 to deal with the issue of Germany's entry into the League. The session lasted nine days, with hearings from the spokesmen of thirty-three member-states. The same pleas for the peaceful settlement of disputes were heard as were customary in the Council's debates on the Manchurian question. Eduard Beneš of Czechoslovakia, for instance, explained that his country 'believes it to be necessary that every signatory to the (Briand-Kellogg) Pact should be obliged in all circumstances to resort to the pacific measures laid down in Article 12 of the Covenant'. But if anyone supposed that the world 'obliged', as used by Dr Beneš, meant 'compelled', Sir John Simon, for Britain, was quick to correct him. 'We should be abandoning our first duty', Sir John said, 'if we did not persist in pursuing the procedure of conciliation by every means in our power'.[36]

The Assembly's final resolution, adopted on 11 March by all forty-seven delegations present, except for China and Japan, which abstained, was in three parts. Part I reaffirmed the principles of Article 10 concerning respect for the territorial integrity and political independence of member-states and the rules of peaceful settlement of disputes. The second part recalled the Council's resolutions on the subject of 30 September and 10 December and the Assembly resolution of 4 March concerning the settlement of the Shanghai question, all of which called for the ending of hostilities and the withdrawal of armed forces. Finally, Part III of the resolution set up a committee of nineteen, consisting of the President of the Assembly, Paul Hymans, the other twelve Council members other than the parties to the dispute and six other member-states to be elected by the Assembly by secret ballot. The task of this body, which in effect took over the Council's work in the Far Eastern conflict, was to report on the cessation of hostilities by the two sides, to follow the execution of the Council's resolutions of 30 September and 10 December, and to report back to the Assembly. On the day after the adoption of the resolution, the United States Minister at Berne wrote to the Secretary-General expressing satisfaction with the outcome and his government's special gratification that 'the nations of the world are united on a policy not to recognise the validity of results attained in violation of the Treaties in question'.[37]

All the world was waiting for the Lytton Report, though everyone knew that, whatever its conclusions, the Japanese were most unlikely to be dislodged from Manchuria. And what Japan had achieved in Manchuria by force, other states could achieve elsewhere, if they had the force: the implications for the disarmament conference were clear. There was one card, however, in the Covenant pack which the Chinese might have played, but chose not to do so. This was Article 16, or the sanctions article, which provided for the cutting off of an aggressor state from contacts with other member-states, to be followed, if necessary, by more forceful measures. Article 16, however, required League members to recognise that a 'resort to war' had taken place, and more than a few governments would have had difficulty in agreeing that the events in Manchuria constituted a state of war. The Japanese, of course, described them, in the national style of understatement, as an 'incident', and other such euphemisms. But even the Chinese demurred at the notion of calling the crisis 'war'. Had they done so (and in those days, when wars were actually 'declared', it required only one side in a dispute to bring a war into existence by so naming it), the rest of the world, at least most of it, would probably have declared itself neutral, and that might have meant no supplies or credits reaching China from outside. Japan, being an altogether richer country, would have had no difficulty in surviving.

So a summer was lost while Japan's grip on Manchuria, or, as she now called it, Manchukuo, tightened. When the Lytton Report, for which the world had waited so long, finally reached the League at the end of September, it turned out to be, not merely an erudite account of the Manchurian problem and the Sino-Japanese tensions out of which it arose, but a substantial endorsement of the Chinese argument. It was admitted that Japan had received provocation, that she had far-reaching economic and strategic interests in Manchuria, and that her position there was quite unique.

There is probably nowhere in the world [the Report explained] an exact parallel to this situation, no example of a country enjoying in the territory of a neighbouring State such extensive economic and administrative privileges. A situation of this kind can possibly be maintained without leading to incessant complications and disputes if it were freely desired or accepted on both sides and if there were the sign and embodiment of a well-considered and close collaboration in the economic and in the political sphere. But in the absence of these conditions, it could only lead to friction and conflict.

Nevertheless, the Report was clear that 'without a declaration of war, a large area of what was indisputably Chinese territory has been forcibly seized and occupied by the armed forces of Japan and has, in consequence of this operation, been separated from and declared independent of the rest of China'.

On the other hand, 'a mere restoration of the *status quo ante* would be no solution'. Nor could the Japanese-imposed regime in Manchuria be accepted as permanent since it disregarded the wishes of the majority of the population. The answer must be sought, the commission went on, logically no doubt but with great optimism, in a *rapprochement* between China and Japan since each was essential to the welfare of the other. Japan, it was explained, 'could facilitate this *rapprochement* by renouncing any attempt to solve the problem by isolating it from the problem of her relations with China as a whole'. But there the commission took a wrong turning. As events were to show, the Japanese had no intention of isolating Manchuria from their relations with China; on the contrary, they meant to master both Manchuria *and* China and weld the two together under their own control. Lacking this insight into the Japanese frame of mind (and the fact that such an outcome hardly seems to have been thought of by the Lytton commission shows how readily Japanese professions of innocence were taken at their face value), the Report's proposals for a settlement now seem little more than well-intentioned day-dreaming: an advisory conference between China and Japan to frame a 'special administration' for Manchuria, the chief feature of which was to be a local gendarmerie to keep the peace, with all other forces withdrawn; a Sino-Japanese treaty to guarantee Japan's rights in the three provinces and Jehol; a Sino-Japanese treaty of conciliation and arbitration, non-aggression and mutual assistance; and a Sino-Japanese treaty to promote trade.[38]

The question was how such a document, with such a

conclusion, could be accepted by the committee of nineteen, which had to report back to the Council and Assembly on the Lytton findings – and it is hard to see how it could have done anything but accept them – without virtually committing League members to some form of action which would bring Japan back to legality and, in doing so, vindicate China. Plainly, opinion must, and did, divide in the committee between representatives of the great Powers, on whom the onus for taking action would mainly fall, and representatives of the smaller states, which stood to gain from the League's voice being raised on behalf of the weak against the strong, without themselves being called upon to do much about it. The division of views meant that the committee's deliberations were protracted. Not until 21 November, at its sixty-ninth session, was the Council in a position to consider both the Lytton Report and the views of the committee of nineteen about it.[39] Not until 6 December, a year after the Lytton commission's appointment and three months after the completion of its Report, was the Assembly able to do the same.[40]

The special committee of nineteen found no fault with the Lytton Report. It, too, sided with China. It did not doubt that Manchuria was under Chinese sovereignty. It called upon the two contestants to work for a peaceful settlement of their differences. It insisted that League member-states should not recognise the new state of Manchukuo. But that was as far as it went. There was no suggestion of economic or military measures to expel the Japanese from the parts of Manchuria which their forces had illegally occupied, the reason being that none of the great Powers, perhaps least of all the United States, was prepared for drastic action of that kind, despite the challenge to the whole international order implicit in Japan's strategy in Manchuria. The smaller states, which would have been glad to see forceful action against Japan, did not enlarge upon the kind of support they themselves would give were such action taken.

An Assembly resolution, following on the lines of the special committee's Report, was adopted unanimously – except for Japan – on 24 February 1933.[41] Thailand alone abstained. China voted with the majority. The only immediate outcome was that the Japanese delegate, Mr Matsudaira, promptly walked out, though it took his government another month formally to withdraw from the League. Japan's departure was followed in October by Germany's. Mr Cordell Hull, however, the new American Secretary of State in the Roosevelt administration, signified agreement with the Assembly's resolution: he also expressed willingness to accept an invitation to join the special committee to help with the Sino-Japanese negotiations hopefully envisaged in the resolution.[42] A similar invitation was dispatched to Moscow, this being the first time that Soviet Russia, which was not to become a League member until two years later, was asked to join in the League's work in the conflict. The Russians did not accept, possibly through fear of giving offence to Japan.

The negotiations, as must have been obvious from the outset, came to nothing. By the end of the month, February 1933, in which the Assembly adopted its final resolution on Manchuria, the Japanese army had completed its occupation of Jehol, a border province lying between Manchuria and China proper. There could be little doubt that the Japanese were preparing for the advance on China itself. On 31 May they concluded the Tangku Truce with a Chinese government oppressed by feelings of betrayal at the hands of the world community. The committee of nineteen in Geneva disappeared beneath the waves, only to surface again with the outbreak of the Sino-Japanese war in July 1937.

V

The League's failure to halt Japan's annexation of Manchuria in 1931-33 and to restore to China what was hers by right was by every test a grave, almost fatal blow, not only to the League and Covenant, but to the whole idea of the enforcement of peace by collective action. Taken in conjunction with the simultaneous failure of the world disarmament conference, the shock to the League system was profound. This was a time, too, when, as a result of the great depression, which reached its nadir in 1932 and 1933, men's faith in any sort of future was shaken to its foundations. The League survived for almost another decade, but the aftermath of the events in the Far East could not but reinforce a reluctant acceptance of old methods of dealing with the world's problems which had proved so ineffective in the past.

The international climate for collective action could hardly have been more inclement, even if the will to organise such an action had been present. With the unprecedented collapse of almost all the world's major economies, the sole preoccupation of most governments was staving off total disaster and somehow surviving. The idea that, at such a time, and with prevailing orthodoxies in economic thinking which favoured cuts in government spending as a means of dealing with recession, states should band together to shut Japan out of the shrinking world economy and send forces half way round the world to do battle in Manchuria, must have seemed little more than a tasteless joke.

There were also the inclemencies of the international posture of affairs. For all Mr Stimson's zeal about the non-recognition doctrine, his attitude towards co-operation with the League states was spasmodic and vacillating. In any case, American opinion did not countenance co-operation with those states in any forceful or effective sense, and even if Mr Stimson did not seem always to realise this, the European Powers, especially Britain, could hardly fail to do so. There is no evidence of the Japanese being seriously discouraged by fear of the consequences for Japanese-American relations.

Of the other states which might have brought Japan to heel, only Britain is seriously worth considering. France, Germany and Italy were only minor weights in the balance of forces in the Pacific. But even if they had been able to contribute anything by way of material restraint on Japan, the economic strains of the times, combined with the daunting logistical problems of bringing military pressure to bear in an area so remote from Europe, made the prospect unlikely. Britain, or rather the National Government in Britain under Mr Ramsay MacDonald, having emerged from the political crisis which had wrecked the second Labour administration in August 1931 and received a 'doctor's mandate' to end the country's ills at an election in October, felt no disposition to do more than try to reconcile the two disputants in the Far East, and, if that failed, to stand aside and let events take their course.[43] Contrary to later allegations by critics of the National Government that they called for strong action against Japan and the government refused, the official Opposition in Parliament made no forthright demand for sanctions.[44] Their leader, Mr George Lansbury, went no further on 25 November 1931, when he raised the matter on the adjournment, than to press for a change 'in the long run' in British relations with countries failing to honour their international obligations.[45] A year later, on 31 October 1932, Clement Attlee, moving a Labour motion which called for 'immediate, universal and substantial reduction of armaments on the basis of equality for all nations and the maintenance of Covenant principles by support for the Lytton Commission report', made no specific proposals for sanctions against Japan, but merely suggested that Britain should 'give a bold lead to the League'. He then went on to urge a scaling down of armaments to the level imposed on Germany by the peace treaty. Mr Attlee considered, hopefully, that the 'masses of Japan' would respond favourably to such a British lead.[46]

Only one Liberal member, Mr Geoffrey Mander, pressed for sanctions against Japan, which he proposed in a speech on 11 November 1931 in the Commons, three weeks after the crisis began. These should be confined, he said, to economic, financial and moral pressures, which would be sufficient to force the Japanese to realise that 'war is not going to be permitted to break out again'.[47] Hence the government felt no strong incentive to move from its judicial impartiality, of which the Foreign Secretary, Simon, was the embodiment. As early as December 1931, Simon had minuted on a Foreign Office memorandum that 'no one proposes that we should pick a quarrel with Japan'.[48] While continually urging patience until the Lytton Report was available, the Foreign Secretary, once the Report came to hand, let the cat out of the bag in a Commons debate on the Report on 27 February 1933, when he said that,

> I think I am myself enough of a pacifist to take the view that, however we handle the matter, I do not intend my own country to get into trouble about it ... There is one great difference between 1914 and now and it is this: in no circumstances will this Government authorise this country to be party to this struggle.[49]

Since this seems to have been the Government's view from the outset, it is hard to know what purpose they considered was served by the Lytton Commission, except perhaps to allow time for the Japanese to become so thoroughly entrenched in Manchuria that the idea of Britain, with no effective support from allies, taking action to expel them would seem utterly outlandish.

The political and economic crises affecting Britain, the prevailing horror of war, the remoteness of the theatre of operations, Manchuria – all sufficiently accounted for Simon's unwillingness to act. But neither can we ignore the fact that, for British Ministers and Foreign Office officials, Japan was more of a friend than an enemy. The Second World War and British experience, especially that of prisoners-of-war, at the hands of the Japanese during that war have obscured the British sense of partnership with Japan in the 1920s. The two countries had been allies in the First World War, had been joined in a treaty of alliance going back to 1902, which many British politicians regretted had had to be broken in 1922. The Japanese were serious trade rivals and their competition damaged the export trade of Lancashire; nevertheless, in China Japan was doing the work of Western capitalism, or so many British traders, manufacturers and trade unionists believed. Moreover, if Japan could find markets in China, perhaps the pressure of her exports in other parts of Asia would be less. The old question was raised which time and again proved so damaging to the League: if collective security means effective action against aggression, what happens if the aggressor turns out to be an old friend?

Britain and the other great Powers did not worry overmuch about the implications of the Manchurian affair for collective security. As always, they had more immediate questions to think about. In the result, collective security was dealt a blow from which it never fully recovered. The smaller countries were left to conclude that, if the League was to protect them, it would have to be when the great Powers were united against a common enemy, which happened to be victimising a small country. But it was as likely as not that the great Powers, so far from joining together to defend the small country, would join together to attack it, or to shut their eyes if one of them attacked it. Something like that had happened in the Corfu crisis in 1923, when Italy was sheltered by her status within the Allied consortium. Japan profited in the same way in the Manchurian affair. Later in the 1930s the European dictators were shielded by sympathisers in the form of states which were supposed to be the very pillars of the League system. And what were the smaller states to do in such a situation? They could make their peace with one or other of the great Powers in good time, perhaps losing part of their territory in the process of accommodation. Or they could relax their links with the collective system in the hope of diverting from themselves the predatory attentions of great Powers. In either case, the solidity of the League system was bound to be affected as it prepared for the next great challenge. That challenge was not long in coming.

8 The betterment of life

When, after the Second World War, people looked back on the history of the League and tried to form a judgment about it, one conclusion often reached was that its work for the maintenance of peace – that is, the collective security system – had failed, but that its contribution to international economic and social co-operation had been outstandingly successful. This success was not visible in any very specific form: men and women the world over were no doubt more comfortably off in 1939 than they were in 1919, but it was difficult to attribute much responsibility for this to the League. However, whereas the League's political history was studded with momentous failures, such as Manchuria and Abyssinia, its record in non-political co-operation was no worse than patchy. One of its major non-political organs, the International Labour Organisation (ILO), survived the war and still flourishes. All the economic and social activities of the League – from the liberalisation of world trade to the campaign against opium and the prostitution of women and children – have been taken over by the United Nations and received recognition in the form of a principal organ of the UN, the Economic and Social Council.

Moreover, whereas the idea of the collective enforcement of peace was new in 1919 and it remained to be seen whether or not it would succeed, social and economic co-operation between the different states was an established practice long before the League existed. It was so inherent in the modern world that it would be carried on if and when the League ceased to exist. What the League did was to bring together under one roof all or most of the innumerable public and private bodies at work in this field. Article 24 of the Covenant established the League as the universal umbrella under which they were to be accommodated. Article 23 committed League members to a list of social and economic objectives, such as the maintenance of 'fair and humane conditions of labour' for their people and (rather strangely) for people 'in all countries to which their commercial and industrial relations extend', the securing of just treatment for the inhabitants of their dependent territories, the control of the traffic in women and children and of dangerous drugs, the maintenance of freedom of communications and transit, and equitable treatment for the commerce of all League members, and the prevention of disease. A recent British study argues that the League 'undoubtedly achieved its greatest success in the field of social and humanitarian activities.[1]

The novel aspect of the League's entrance into these old-established fields was that it was linked with the maintenance of peace. International economic and social co-operation was not merely desirable in itself, but contributed to a peaceful world. In the field of labour, for example, it was laid down in Part XIII of the Versailles Treaty, which created the ILO, that 'universal peace', the League's object, 'can be established only if it is based upon social justice'. Equally, a more prosperous, better fed and educated, healthier world, free from prostitution and drug taking, would be one less riddled with war.

The peace theme served to justify efforts to create a global community by such co-operation; it supplied much of the incentive for it and stimulated public and private bodies to provide funds for conferences and expert reports on malaria, white slavery, the unification of customs nomenclature, the dredging of navigable rivers. Service on League committees being niggardly recompensed, if recompensed at all, the thought of working for the great cause of peace kept the system going. The linkage, however, had its dangers. If social and economic reform was in part justified by the contribution it made to peace, support for it was likely to decline as the prospects for peace declined, which happened in the late 1930s. There was a risk that all the international social and economic collaboration which the modern interdependent world demanded might wither through being shackled to the moribund carcass of collective security.

There was another problem which arose from the association of the cause of peace with the cause of social reform in the League system. The League idea sprang from the social philosophy of mid-nineteenth-century liberalism. It idealised a peaceful world, with few if any armaments, with restrictions on the free movement of people, goods and capital from one country to another reduced to a minimum. The state and state machinery, if they did not exactly disappear, would lose much of their importance in an ever-thickening web of relations between the world's peoples. It was the world which captains of industry in Victorian England dreamed about, humanised by legislation to temper excesses of capitalism, and confident that the pursuit of self-interest by entrepreneur, worker, trader, would at length ensure for all fair conditions of life almost of its own accord. Such was the spirit of Article 23 of the Covenant, closer to the 'night-watchman' conception of the state than to Fabian socialism.

Hence, the thinking pervading the League Secretariat and the experts convened by the League to give advice was over-whelmingly multilateralist, anti-nationalistic, libertarian. It deified free trade, the abolition of government controls, freely moving exchange rates under the Gold Standard, balanced budgets, the established axioms of classical economics. In conference after conference, the world was invited to lay aside the follies of government intervention and return to the free-trading system of before 1914. But the tides of history moved in the opposite direction and pulled the League down beneath the waters. In the first place, the 'conventional wisdom' of economists changed: orthodoxies of the 1920s became the heresies of the 1930s. Governments, especially in Nazi Germany and New Deal America, used the state machinery to move out of economic depression, leaving Keynes to explain later how this was possible. No government, faced in the early 1930s by shrinking trade, collapsing prices and mass unemployment, could live by the old rules when their electorates demanded action. They might still reiterate the old rules on the rostrum in Geneva, but when they returned home they behaved differently.

All this was in any case implicit in some of the very commitments assumed by the League at its birth, especially in regard to standards and conditions of labour, the province of the ILO. The trade union leaders who pressed the 1919 peace conference to set up a body like the ILO no doubt belonged to the same liberal school as Woodrow Wilson, Lloyd George, Viscount Cecil and the rest. At the same time, they strove for state intervention to do more of the sort of things the state in Britain and Germany had already been doing before 1914, that is, to regulate industry, agriculture and commerce so that, if 'social justice' did not emerge naturally, it would be made to emerge. Section I of Part XIII of the Versailles Treaty is headed, significantly, 'the *organisation* of labour' and begins with a schedule of 'improvements' in labour conditions which are 'urgently required', and include such positive acts of state intervention as the establishment, presumably by law, of a maximum working week, the prevention of unemployment, the protection of the worker against sickness, disease and injury arising out of his employment, provision for old age and injury, and so on: in other words, the agenda of the welfare state. It was the supreme irony of the League system that, while its moral philosophy renounced the national sovereign state, which it held accountable for the evil of war, its social and economic programme anticipated the age of government control which found its most advanced expression in the fascist dictatorships that were ultimately to destroy the League and all its works. On the ability of the League and its supporters to invent a form of state-guided economy which would answer the universal demand for welfare and social security without jeopardising the prospects for a politically more united world depended the prospects of mastering that dilemma.

The logic of national advantage and the logic of the world community thus clashed in the League's social and economic work. The former triumphed, though the nations were still left to grapple with the paradox that their own well-being still depended, in many important respects, on the well-being of all. The old adage, quoted so often by Gilbert Murray, one of the League's staunchest champions in Britain, claimed that 'no man can prosper in another's ruin'. There was an uncanny similarity in this respect, and many others, between the League's social and economic work and its other heroic undertaking, the struggle for disarmament, with which we dealt in an earlier chapter.

Both endeavours failed in that, after twenty years, League member-states were more busily rearming than they had been when the League was born, despite the millions of words poured out under the League's roof against the folly of armaments, and those same states were more actively using economic weapons against each other in the 1930s than they were in the 1920s, despite the warnings of countless League meetings. Likewise, delegates of member-states used one language in favour of disarmament and free trade at Geneva, and another language in support of armaments and trade controls when they returned home, like dipsomaniacs vowing that the previous evening's orgy was their last, and then opening another bottle to solemnise their conversion. The terminology of war crept into talk about trade. The economic conference at Lausanne in 1932 was spoken of as an 'armistice', while the economic conference held in London in 1933 was known as a 'peace conference', though it might more accurately have been called a declaration of war. 'Economic disarmament' and 'economic aggression' were familiar terms, so were 'tariff truces' and 'trade wars'. The word 'sacrifice' was used, both when a country was asked to lower its tariffs and when called on to reduce its weapons.

Perhaps the truth was that, in theory and the long term, the whole world *would* be better off if the nations lowered their economic and military guards, scrapped their tariffs *and* their tanks. But the voters who put the governments who make these decisions into office (and this was mostly how governments got into office in the League period) are generally not much interested in theory or the long term. They want practical action – to keep out foreign imports and foreign troops – and they want it here and now. The Genevan language of economic and military disarmament, so far from making Ministers and voters feel guilty about their own double standards, served rather to justify them by making it seem that the whole trouble arose from the foreigner's, not their own, failure to live up to those high standards.

II

Certain important questions arising from the war and the peace settlement were excluded from the League's work for international economic and financial co-operation. The extraction of reparations from the defeated Powers and the repayment of war debts, for instance, both of which were widely regarded as hindering post-war economic revival, were kept firmly in Allied hands, the former largely on French insistence, the latter on American. Nevertheless, the Covenant provided the League with more than enough to do. Its preamble prescribed 'open, just and honourable relations between nations', and those words were used to placate countries short of raw materials, like Italy, which feared discrimination against them in post-war trade policies. Article 23 included the famous principle of 'equitable treatment for the commerce' of all League member-states. The sanctions clause, Article 16, obliged members to subject states which waged illegal wars to the severance of trade and financial relations and the prevention of financial, commercial and personal intercourse with other states and to support one another in the financial and economic measures taken under this article. To advise it on these and other such questions, the League needed its own economic and financial organisation.

Hence, in October 1920 the League Council adopted a report drawn up by Leon Bourgeois which proposed the creation of a provisional committee, to be divided into two sections, each consisting of ten members, one for economic, the other for financial, questions. The membership was subsequently raised to twelve, and then, in 1927, to fifteen. Some such body had been called for by an international financial conference convened in Brussels by the Council earlier the same month. The first League Assembly approved the proposal at its session in December, although by that time the provisional committee had already had its first meeting a month earlier. In 1923 the Council dropped the word 'provisional' from its title. The committee usually met three or four times a year for between two and ten days each time. Its members, appointed by the Council, were regarded as experts acting in their personal capacity, rather than state representatives, and this was in accordance with the prevailing League philosophy that international problems (the most important of which were considered to be technical) were best left to technical experts. The idea, however, had the drawback of experts persisting in often outmoded theoretical prescriptions while governments strove to cope with economic and financial storms on the basis of crude calculations of national interest.

The financial committee, being made up for the most part of distinguished bankers and officials from Finance Ministries, was somewhat more independent of governments than the economic committee. The political implications of its business were not quite so obvious or near the surface. The financial committee, too, scored a considerable success early in its career with the management of the League loans to Austria and Hungary in 1922 for post-war reconstruction, which we discussed in an earlier chapter.[2] During the depression in the 1930s, the committee continued providing advice to these two countries and also to Bulgaria. Its sessions in 1933 and 1934 were also entirely taken up with these questions.[3] The economic committee had a more chequered constitutional career. Following a world economic conference in Geneva in May 1927 at which the slow progress of the committee's work came in for criticism, the Eighth League

Assembly decided to create the Economic Consultative Committee, consisting of thirty-five members, increased in 1931 to fifty-six, intended both to diversify the economic committee's work and inspire it with more thrust and vigour. It was a mistake, however, to believe that the basic conflict between the different governments' economic and financial policies and the liberal ideals of the League's expert advisers could be overcome by creating yet another advisory committee. A sympathetic student of the League's committee system, writing in 1931, contended that the Consultative Committee had done no work which could not have been done by one or other of its members acting as an expert at the request of the Economic Committee.[4]

The League's first major initiative in the field of economics, the world economic conference held in Geneva in May 1927, was hardly a success. It was attended by 194 delegates and 226 experts from fifty League member and non-member states, the latter including Soviet Russia, Turkey and the United States. Turkey and Russia, however, abstained from voting on the final report of the conference drawn up by a co-ordinating committee. The principal object of the three committees appointed by the conference – on commerce, industry and agriculture, the first being the most important – was to spell out the finding that 'the main obstacles to economic revival have been the hindrances opposed to the free flow of labour, capital and goods'. As the committee on commerce put it, 'the fundamental idea ... which has appeared with increasing force in the course of the discussions is the necessity of restoring greater freedom to a world hitherto hampered by many obstacles due to the war and its consequences and to erroneous economic ideas'. 'The time has come', the committee concluded, 'to put an end to the increase in tariffs and to move in the opposite direction'.

Sadly, according to one observer, 'the governments represented at this conference did not comply with this proposal but continued to place obstacles in the way of international trade'.[5] A draft convention for the Abolition of Import and Export Prohibitions, which was to have been the supreme achievement of the 1927 conference was ratified by only seventeen states and needed eighteen ratifications to come into force. Yet the climate of the times could hardly have been more favourable for reform. Britain was labouring with a hard core of one million unemployed and commodity prices were depressed the world over, but central and western Europe and the United States were enjoying a short-lived boom. By the time the next League-sponsored meeting was held, the world monetary and economic conference, a six-week affair which met in London on 12 June 1933, the world-wide economic depression was at its worst. Since 1929, raw material production throughout the world had fallen by 30 per cent. In some countries incomes had declined between 40 and 50 per cent in the same period. World trade in 1932 was only one third of what it had been in 1929; it changed hands at one half of the 1929 prices. Thirty million people were reported as unemployed, almost certainly an understatement.

The 1933 conference had its origins in a proposal included in the Final Act of an international conference at Lausanne, adopted on 9 July 1932, which dealt mainly with the reparations problem and which called on the League to convoke a world conference 'to decide upon the measures to solve the other economic and financial difficulties which were responsible for, and may prolong, the present world crisis'. Representatives of sixty-four states came to London, the meeting, unlike the 1927 conference, being a fully diplomatic assembly and consisting of heads of government and other Ministers with authority to commit their countries. A preparatory commission had prepared an extensive agenda, split into financial and economic sections, which defined the main tasks of the conference as: (1) the restoration of an effective international monetary standard; (2) some increase in the level of world prices; (3) the abolition of exchange restrictions and the stabilisation of budgets and economic systems; (4) the achievement of greater freedom of international trade.[6] The conference scored a modest preliminary success in the form of a tariff truce to cover the duration of the meeting: no new tariff measures were to be introduced 'which might adversely affect international trade'. Fourteen states signed the agreement before the conference assembled and forty-seven later adhered, making sixty-seven states in all and representing 90 per cent of world trade. That apart, however, there was little to show.

The conflict which destroyed the prospects of serious agreement was between the 'gold group', consisting of Belgium, France, Italy, the Netherlands and Switzerland, which were still on the Gold Standard and insisted on some minimum monetary stability before they would discuss tariff reductions, and the United States, which had abandoned the Gold Standard on 17 April and was implementing the reflationary policies of the New Deal and therefore opposed fixed exchange rates. After preliminary retorts on 17 and 22 June to calls for monetary stability from the gold group, President Roosevelt issued through his representative at the conference, Secretary of State Cordell Hull, an acid *non possumus* on 3 July which stated that he would

> regard it as a catastrophe amounting to a world tragedy if the great conference of nations, called to bring about a more real and permanent financial stability and a greater prosperity to the masses of nations, should, in advance of any serious effort to consider these broad problems, allow itself to be diverted by the proposal of a purely artificial and temporary experiment affecting the monetary exchange of a few nations only.[7]

Mr Roosevelt also said that the United States could take no part in discussions about international public works, another idea which enjoyed support at the conference as a means of relieving unemployment: this was a matter for each country to decide for itself, he declared. The monetary stability group replied to these American statements that they saw no further point in the discussions.

The irony was that, within a month after the break-up of the conference on 27 July, the United States reversed its position and returned to the Gold Standard, leaving the world to wonder whether the only trouble with the conference was that it was convened at the wrong time. But it is doubtful whether, in the economic climate of the early 1930s, when the only rule governments believed they could follow was that of *sauve qui peut*, the free trade arguments of the Preparatory Commission ever stood any chance of acceptance. 'The practical results of the Conference', was the summing up of one observer, 'were thus negligible. Even the agreements on wheat and silver were initiated by self-constituted groups of interested countries and were arranged for the most part in the course of private conversations. The Conference as a whole met only to inaugurate itself and to wind itself up. While the rather half-hearted debate was proceeding in committee, the attention of the delegates was distracted by the currency squabble, in which few of them had any part and concerning the course of which most of them knew as little as any newspaper reader. Many representatives of smaller states therefore returned home not only disillusioned but completely bewildered'. It was not much consolation that the conference was adjourned rather than ended, or that, like all such events, it did at least instruct delegates in the realities of the day.

The Czech delegate, Masaryk, almost despairingly remarked that 'the fact that we know where we stand can and should be of very great importance for the future shaping of the economic policies of the nations'. But that, of course, could mean that international co-operation in this field in future might be even harder.

After the monetary and economic discussions in London in 1933, the League's work for world finance and economics seemed to mark time in a period dominated by short-term considerations of national survival. In July 1934 the League Secretariat reported that 'there has been an increasing tendency towards economic nationalism and ... the principle of the economic interdependence of nations is being seriously challenged'.[8] The economic committee reported to the League Council shortly before the Assembly's ordinary session in 1936 that the idea of another world economic conference should be ruled out; it was more expedient, the committee thought, 'to proceed by stages'.[9] That could only mean trying to reach agreement with countries in twos and threes, rather than across the board. An example came in September 1936, when Britain, France and the United States used the occasion of the devaluation of the franc by 30 per cent to agree in their determination 'to relax the quota system and facilitate the removal of exchange controls'.[10] It was the old language, but intended to be limited in its application.

In any case, no-one could be sure that a return to the cherished free-trading world of pre-1914, even if it were possible, would not mean returning to the monetary and economic anarchy from which economic nationalism, however harsh, had rescued the world. Here was a paradox: that League supporters rejected the political international anarchy of the pre-war era, and yet wanted to return to the unmanaged world economic system (if it was a system) of that time, repudiating the attempts of governments to control it by purposive intervention. The League's work on financial and economic co-operation suffered from a backward-looking complex: its language was that of revival, recovery, return to the free system, overlooking the fact that economic disaster in 1929 and the early 1930s sprang from that system. League experts needed to inform themselves why states had abandoned that system, rather than chide them with having done so.

III

Communications and transit (that is, the movement of traffic from outside a state across its territory) had been matters of international regulation since the Congress of Vienna in 1815. Navigable rivers in Europe had been administered by international commissions since long before 1914. International waterways and canals, natural and artificial, were generally subject to conventions which aimed at striking a balance between the rights of the international community in free access and the sovereignty of local states. When the Central Powers were at the mercy of the Allied coalition after their defeat in November 1918, opportunity was taken to secure in Part XII of the Versailles Treaty, and in corresponding sections of the other treaties, the imposition of the sort of principles for communications and transit which international law had been moving towards for a century or more. The defeated states were required to open up their transport and communications systems without discrimination to the Allies. Allied subjects were to enjoy the same level of treatment on ex-enemy soil or waters as local inhabitants: any privileges extended to anyone on German, Austrian, Bulgarian or Hungarian rivers or railways were to be extended to everyone. The Elbe, Oder, Niemen rivers and the Danube from Ulm were declared international. Commissions were established for the first three and for the Rhine. The two existing Commissions for the Danube were revived, with a dominant position for the Allies in each. The League was authorised to settle disputes arising out of these arrangements, together with the right to revise them after five years from the coming into force of the treaties. By a sharp repudiation of a basic tenet of international law, Germany's consent in advance was assumed for any convention on transit, waterways, ports or railways concluded by the Allied and Associated Powers within five years of the coming into force of the treaties.

The League was thus involved from the outset in the complicated communications and transit regimes instituted by the peace treaties. It was also involved in a wider sense by Article 23 (e) of the Covenant, which committed it 'to secure and maintain freedom of communications and transit and equitable treatment for the commerce' of all League members. To make arrangements for satisfying these undertakings, the Council decided on 19 May 1920 to call a general diplomatic conference as soon as the Assembly agreed, and this would make proposals for the communications and transit organisation that would be required. The Assembly played its part at its first session in December and the conference duly met at Barcelona from 10 March until 20 April of the following year and drew up a scheme for a permanent organisation. Its core was to consist of an advisory committee made up of experts on communications and transit which would organise every few years conferences representing governments and charged with drawing up conventions for putting into effect the aims of Article 23 (e). The object of the committee's work, and that of the whole organisation, was 'to remove those artificial obstructions to transit raised by political boundaries'.[11] The organisation, in fact, was to do for transport and communications what the League's economic and financial organisation was to seek to do for trade. The communications and transit committee, too, like the economic and financial committee, provided a venue in which non-League states, especially Egypt, Turkey and the United States, could meet and talk with League members.

The committee enjoyed a vigorous and busy life until the Second World War. Naturally, it had to struggle with the reluctance of states to allow what they considered matters of domestic jurisdiction to form the agenda of international organisations, although the obvious advantages of international co-operation to facilitate movement from one country to another in a region as tightly packed with nations as Europe meant that governments were less hostile to the League in this field than, say, that of armaments or the settlement of international disputes. From first to last, of course, the League's work in the field represented, in the last resort, the utmost that member-states were ready for by way of international co-operation. The League could only take over as much as states were willing to give, although, in this field, at least, that was considerable. Some of the Committee's hopes, as for instance some movement towards the standardisation of passports of the different countries, were ahead of their time. The same was true of its inquiries into the pollution of the sea by oil, an anticipation of post-1945 developments. A committee representing Britain, France, Italy, Japan and the United States met at Geneva from 19 to 23 November to examine the problem. The Council approved the committee's recommendations on 11 March 1935, but member-states, when asked for their reactions, were dubious on grounds of the difficulty of enforcing any such agreement.[12]

A more bizarre undertaking of the communications and transit committee was, oddly enough, reform of the calendar, especially the fixing of movable feasts such as Easter. After several years' toil, the committee decided in 1937 not to proceed with the idea of calling a conference on the subject, but simply to leave it on the agenda, the objections of religious bodies having proved impossible to overcome.[13] On the whole, however, the committee on communications and transport, though achieving nothing spectacular, helped improve the circulation of people round the globe. It may be doubted whether, in itself, this did much to lessen the risk of war, but it met a need, and the need would have existed even if the League had not.

IV

As early as 1815 the British social reformer Robert Owen had pleaded, though vainly, with the Congress of Vienna to improve the conditions of labour by international action. It was not, however, until the formation of the socialist internationals in 1864 and 1882 that the idea became a practical possibility, eventually issuing in the formation in 1900 of the International Association for Labour Legislation, designed to raise the general standards of labour in the different countries. The Association sponsored a conference at Berne in 1906 which adopted conventions prohibiting night work for women in industry and the use of white phosphorus in the manufacture of matches. Since the First World War did so much to give trade unions an established footing in the belligerent states, it is not surprising that union leaders seized the opportunity of the peace conference in 1919 to enshrine the international protection of labour in the peace treaties. This was done by a commission of the conference presided over by Samuel Gompers (1850-1924), the first president of the American Federation of Labour, which drew up a charter for labour later to form Part XIII of the Versailles Treaty and corresponding sections of the other peace agreements.

Part XIII began with a declaration listing the desirable conditions of labour as understood by the trade union world, adding the cardinal rule that it was all but impossible to make work more humane in one country if others did not follow suit. Next came an outline of the form that the organisation for achieving those conditions would take: it illustrated the seriousness of purpose of the Gompers commission that this organisation, later known as the International Labour Organisation or ILO, was worked out in the fullest detail in Articles 387 to 399 of Part XIII of the Versailles Treaty, and was envisaged as coming into existence even before the League itself was fully established . There was to be a General Conference of delegates of member-states, original League members and states joining the League later being declared members of the Organisation (unlike the position in the post-1945 UNO, in which the ILO survives as a specialised agency, and in which membership of the parent body does not automatically carry with it membership of the labour organisation). The Conference, which was to meet at least once a year, was to be organised on the novel principle that each Member-state would be entitled to four delegates, two appointed by the government and one each for employers' and worker organisations in the state concerned. Delegates to the Conference would have their expenses paid by their own governments, but all other costs would be borne out of League funds, thus emphasising again the close ties between the two Geneva bodies. Secondly, there was to be an International Labour Office in Geneva intended to be part of the League system. The Office would collect and distribute information pertaining to the organisation's work, prepare studies for the Conference and draw up the Conference agenda. It would be headed by a Director, the first Director being the French Socialist and former War Minister, Albert Thomas (1878-1932), and controlled by a Governing Body of twenty-four. Twelve of these would represent governments, of whom eight would be nominated by the states 'of chief industrial importance', the League Council having to say which these were, and four selected by government delegates to the Conference, not including the former eight. Of the remaining twelve members of the Governing Body, six would be elected by employer delegates to the Conference and six by worker delegates.

The procedure of the Organisation was that the Conference would adopt by a two-thirds majority either recommendations or conventions dealing with matters within the ILO's purview. Recommendations would be submitted to member-states to decide what action they wished to take about them; conventions could be ratified if the appropriate authority so determined. In either case, some action, even the decision to do nothing, would have to be taken within one year, and in any event not more than eighteen months, of the closing of the Conference at which the recommendation or convention was adopted. The Gompers commission did not win for the ILO the law-making powers which some of its members asked for, but sanctions were made enforceable in the event of a complaint being filed against a member for not having carried out obligations it had freely accepted. The Governing Body could 'apply' (presumably to the League Council) for a Commission of Inquiry to look into the complaint and the Commission could indicate 'measures of an economic character', which it believed members would be justified in taking against the offending country. Alternatively, any member could refer any other member's failure to fulfil its obligations to the world court at The Hague, and that body, too, might propose economic sanctions. Section II of Part XIII concluded with some rather high-flown principles of labour legislation, described, not as 'complete or final', but as 'well fitted to guide the policy of the League' (Article 427). These began with the assertion that labour 'should not be regarded merely as a commodity or article of commerce' and then went on to prescribe such basic, and, in some cases, advanced rights of those working in industry as freedom of association for employers and workers, an eight-hour day or forty-eight-hour week, equal pay for men and women, and equitable economic treatment for all workers lawfully resident in a country.

The ILO was thus conceived as far more than the modest advisory committee of individual experts which was the normal pattern for the non-political work of the League. In the highly formal, and in large part governmental, nature of its system of representation, it resembled the substantial Specialised Agencies formed in 1945 to do similar work for the United Nations, of which the ILO subsequently became, and remains, one. The staff working in the office in Geneva and numbering a thousand in the twenties and thirties, was rather on the scale of the League Secretariat itself than the establishments serving other non-political parts of the League's work. The reason for these differences was, of course, the substantial interest in the ILO among trade unions in the developed countries, and the corresponding interest which this gave both to employers' organisations and to governments in ensuring that improvements in the conditions of work achieved through the Organisation should not handicap countries which accepted them as against trade competitors which might not.

The first years of the ILO were hectic with activity, symbolised by the holding of its first conference in Washington in October 1919, almost before the ink of the peace treaties was dry: it concerned hours of work in industry. The next meeting, from 15 June until 10 July 1920, concentrated on navigation and workers in the fishing industry, with hours of work again forming a central concern. A third session, held in Geneva from 24 October until 19 November 1921, was mainly occupied with agricultural work. In these three years sixteen conventions and eighteen recommendations were adopted. Then, as though to mark a pause while the outcome of these exertions was digested, the Organisation experienced a lull, lasting for several years. At the seventh session of the Conference in 1925, three conventions on workmen's compensation were adopted; in May and June of the following year came conventions on labour conditions on ships at sea, then on sickness insurance (1927), the creation and application of minimum-wage-fixing machinery (1928), the conditions of dock workers (1929), compulsory labour (1930), hours of work in coal mines, described as 'the most difficult of all the problems in the field' (1931), and protection against accidents in the loading and unloading of ships (1932). Conventions, recommendations, volumes of statistics, rolled forth. Admittedly the actual impact in the form of legislation passed and put into effect by member-states left much to be desired. But the Organisation formulated norms and standards for those concerned with working standards in the different countries to aim for. Trade unions found in the ILO an ally in their struggle to make life better on the factory floor, in the fields and forests, and at sea.

The Great Depression was inevitably a turning point, or rather a turning backward point, as for so many other aspects of the League's work. With 30 million unemployed when the Organisation's Conference met in April 1932, attention had to shift from making life better for the worker to making it possible at all. Mass unemployment is destructive to trade unionism: it means reduced membership as men and women on the dole fail to keep up with their contributions; it swells the reserve pools of labour and so threatens the living standards of those able to cling to a job. Moreover, the Depression weakened democratic systems of government and encouraged totalitarianism, which threatened free trade unions. Union leaders naturally looked to the Geneva body to help them deal with these threats. But success was not easily come by. Reducing unemployment was the primary object, and, in times of public spending in Nazi Germany on armaments and motorways and in New Deal America on government-backed ventures like the TVA, the way to do it could be through some international scheme of public investment, the kind of thing the League was well-equipped to organise. The idea won support in the Geneva Office and was backed at annual conferences of the Organisation. But few governments showed any interest. It was a matter of where the money was to come from, and how it could be ensured that contributing states would secure an equitable share in the benefits, if any. If public works could mop up the unemployed, the general feeling ran, it was better that they be left to individual states. But many doubted that they could.[14]

The ILO carried on with producing recommendations and conventions until the 1939 war rang down the curtain on its work. By that time its usefulness was well established, as shown by the absence of any doubt about its revival after the war. There had never been any question, as some trade union leaders had hoped at the beginning, of the Organisation blossoming out as a legislature to regulate the world of labour; nor would many have wanted that. If states themselves did not create tolerable working conditions for their own people, it was unlikely that they could be forced to do so through such a body as the ILO. The Organisation in effect served two purposes. Like all League bodies in the field of social and economic co-operation, it provided, firstly, an invaluable flow of information about conditions of labour all over the world. Secondly, it advertised the most favourable employer-worker relations as a model for the less fortunate countries, and thus helped to raise their standards. It acted as a spur to the trade union movement in countries in which it was only newly or weakly established. The practical service performed by the ILO is strikingly evident in the fact that states which never joined the League, notably the United States, were active members, and that other states, such as Germany and Japan, remained members of the ILO even after withdrawing from the League itself. The Organisation's work could only loosely be related to the maintenance of peace, but that did not affect its value as one of the League's many organs which helped to make life for the world's people somewhat more bearable than it otherwise would have been.

V

The ILO, born in 1919, survives today as a United Nations Specialized Agency. Another Specialized Agency, the World Health Organisation (WHO), is the offspring of the League's organisation for international co-operation in matters of health. This in its turn was the descendant of a late nineteenth-century pioneer, the Office international d'hygiene publique in Paris, which emerged in 1903 from an international sanitary conference which first met in 1851 and produced many conventions on medical questions in the 1890s. The Paris Office was one of the international bureaux placed under the League's direction with their consent by Article 24 of the Covenant. Owing to American objections, the Office did not form an integral part of the health organisation eventually created by the Fourth League Assembly by a resolution of 15 September 1923, but was always closely associated with it. The organisation consisted of three parts: a Health Bureau, consisting of a group of permanent officials within the League Secretariat; a General Advisory Council or Conference, made up of medical experts from all member-states which met twice a year and acted as the executive element; and a Health Committee, consisting of sixteen members and eight assessors, all, as usual, experts with high medical qualifications. The Committee's size was repeatedly increased as the years went on. Its job was to prepare the Council's work, carry out inquiries and ensure the efficient conduct of the operation. This threefold structure was to advise the League on the carrying out of Article 23 (f) of the Covenant, which bound members 'to take steps in matters of international concern for the prevention and control of disease', and of Article 25, dedicated to the establishment and promotion of contacts between Red Cross organisations.[15]

The most important work of the health organisation was to call conferences on the study and treatment of disease, the training of doctors and nurses, the design of hospitals and countless other such questions; the compilation and publication of statistics relating to health and medical practice in the different countries; the control of epidemic diseases; the conducting of inquiries into long-term health problems, such as the education of young people in the maintenance of sound health, and into questions raised by current conditions in the world, such as psychological stress caused by unemployment. As this almost endless list of subjects is considered, it is apparent that it is perhaps in the field of international co-operation in matters of health that the link between the League's political work for peace and its social and humanitarian work is most tenuous. But no-one could doubt the essentially international character of the struggle against disease and ill-health, viruses being no respecters of national frontiers. Moreover, the political evils which the League was formed to deal with take their toll in the form of reduced efficiency of mind and body. What the League actually contributed to man's gradually increasing mastery over disease is impossible to say. But the foundations were laid.

Closely connected with health as a League of Nations interest was control of the traffic in opium and other dangerous drugs, which was placed under the League's supervision by Article 23 (c) of the Covenant. An unofficial British society for the suppression of the opium trade had been founded in 1874. The first international conference on the subject was summoned by President Theodore Roosevelt at Shanghai, appropriately, in 1909 and represented thirteen countries. Its recommendations provided the basis for the Hague conference on opium in 1912, which devised a convention ultimately signed by forty countries, which became the foundation of the League's work in this field. By Article 295 of the Versailles Treaty all the contracting parties were deemed to have signed and ratified the 1912 convention, a remarkable example of the use of the promised benefits from one treaty in order to secure the implementation of another.

The First League Assembly decided on 15 December 1920 to ask the Council to create an advisory committee on opium and other dangerous drugs, and the Council complied on 21 February 1921.[16] The Assembly resolution also instructed the Secretariat to collect information about the arrangements made in the various countries for carrying out the opium Convention, world production, distribution and consumption of the drug, and other necessary data. The advisory committee, made up, as usual, of experts meeting as a rule in annual session, achieved its greatest success in the winter of 1924-25, with the holding of a conference in Geneva which produced a Convention extending the national control of narcotics provided by the 1912 agreement to supervision of the international traffic by means of a system of certificates authorising the import and export of drugs. The Convention was to be supervised by a Central Opium Board which collected statistics on the drug trade and acted as a lobby applying pressure on countries to sign, ratify and effectively implement the convention.[17]

At its fifty-ninth session in May 1930 the Council, taking heed of criticism in the Assembly of the little progress made up to that time in stamping out the world drug trade, decided to enlarge the committee by 50 per cent, admitting experts from non-manufacturing countries for the first time.[18] The first fruit of this reform was a conference held in Geneva in May-July 1931 which established a strong permanent supervisory body of four members with a British chairman, Sir Malcolm Delevingne. The basic principle was to limit production of the three dangerous drugs, morphine, diacetylmorphine and cocaine, strictly to amounts required for medical and scientific purposes by requiring parties to the convention to provide the supervisory body with regular statistics of manufacture and trade.[19]

By a new convention adopted at a forty-nation conference in Geneva in June 1936 after three weeks' discussion, provision was made for the punishment of illegal drug traders, loopholes for evasion, as for instance the extradition of offenders from one country to another, were closed, the international and administrative arrangements were tightened up and each party was obliged to open a central office to ensure that its commitments were properly carried out.[20] Although ratifications of the 1936 Convention were slow in arriving, it was reported in 1937 that sixty states were party to the Hague Convention of 1912, and fifty-four and sixty-one respectively to the Geneva Conventions of 1925 and 1931.[21] The outbreak of the Sino-Japanese war in July 1937, however, the month in which that report was published, was a serious setback since the Far East always played a dominant role both in the production and the consumption of dangerous drugs.

Coupled with opium and other drugs in Article 23 (c) was the traffic in women and children, another human vice brought under the League's supervision. Its method of fulfilling this commitment was the same: the creation of an expert committee, appointed by the Council and responsible to the Assembly, a conference of member-states on the subject from time to time, the adoption of suitable conventions, and the struggle to secure their signature and ratification. Again, a start had been made before the war, with the creation in 1899 of an international bureau for the suppression of the white slave traffic, and the holding of conferences, chiefly on the initiative of the Belgian and French governments, to combat prostitution and the abuse of children. A congress for child protection convened by Belgium in 1913 claimed to be the first of its kind and was attended by the representatives of forty-two states. The League called its first international meeting on white slavery on 30 June 1921, which delegates from thirty-five states attended in order to draft a convention abolishing it. The next move was the League Council's decision on 14 January 1922 to create an advisory committee of nine, assisted by five assessors, to take this work in hand. Owing partly to pressure from the International Association for the Promotion of Child Welfare, which applied for affiliation to the League in 1924, the committee was renamed the Advisory Committee on the Traffic in Women and Children. In 1930 its size was enlarged to twelve and then to fifteen in 1933. By this time it was divided into two sections, one on the traffic in women and children, and one on child welfare.

By 1933, forty-four countries had ratified the 1921 Convention on the traffic in women and children. Attention then moved to the effort to reach agreement on a world-wide ban on the trade in prostitution. A diplomatic conference with this end in view met in Geneva from 9 to 11 October 1933 and adopted a Convention for punishing 'any person who, to gratify the passion of another person, has procured, enticed or led away, even with her consent, a woman or girl of full age for immoral purposes to be carried out in another country'.[22] Such an enterprise is, of course, steeped in difficulties, especially that of interfering with a trade in which both buyers and sellers are willing partners. Many wondered whether it was right for the League, a body inevitably surrounded by controversies, to stray into a field so thickly strewn with mines.

A less doubtful area was that of slavery itself, for which there was, again, a considerable ancestry, going back to the nineteenth century at least. A conference at Brussels in 1890 had produced a General Act which treated slave trading as a criminal offence. It was signed by all the major European Powers and by the United States, Turkey, Iran and Zanzibar, the last three being especially important since they still recognised slavery as legal. After the war, the Allied Powers signed a new agreement at St Germain-en-Laye on 10 September 1919, which endeavoured to secure the complete suppression of slavery in all its forms and of the slave trade by land and sea.

A Temporary Slavery Commission created by the League in 1924 called for a new convention and this was adopted at an international conference on 10 September 1926 and thereafter recommended by the League Assembly for signature and ratification by member-states.[23] The scope of this, however, was not as wide as many had hoped. It excluded forced or compulsory labour, which was remitted for study by the ILO, which produced its own convention on forced labour in 1930. It also excluded military service in countries in which it was compulsory, normal civil obligations, prison labour, and labour imposed by the authorities on a people in times of natural disasters, such as floods, earthquakes and forest fires. In October 1932 the Assembly decided to reinvigorate its campaign against slavery by creating a new advisory committee on the subject, consisting of seven experts charged to send for and examine documents submitted by governments. Most of the committee's work up to the outbreak of the Second World War lay in urging more states to ratify and carry out the 1926 Convention. The two most blatant examples of forced labour, though it was not technically slavery, in the 1930s – the concentration camps maintained in Nazi Germany and Soviet Russia – were not, however, the subject of much investigation by the committee. They were not, of course, open to inspection.

The League's chief success in the suppression of slavery, however, was achieved through the mandates system, the permanent mandates commission always being active in pressing the administering authorities, especially those holding former Turkish and German dependencies, to co-operate in the drive against slavery. The League Assembly also secured from Ethiopia a commitment to abolish slavery and slave trading before being admitted into the League as a member in 1926. It also used financial and technical assistance to encourage Liberia to abolish inter-tribal slavery and other forms of forced labour. Thus, the campaign against the 'peculiar institution', which began at the international level in 1815, when William Wilberforce gave delegates to the Congress of Vienna no relief until they agreed to an eight-Power declaration on the universal abolition of the slave trade, was brought to fulfilment by the League.

VI

If the League of Nations itself was a brave, almost quixotic act of defiance against man's inhumanity to himself, the advisory committee of twelve created by the Council in 1922 to help it 'resume and extend' relations between the world's learned institutions, and called the international committee on intellectual co-operation, must have seemed a thing of pure fantasy to the hardened politicians of the day. Often referred to as the forerunner of Unesco (the United Nations Educational, Scientific and Cultural Organisation), the ICIC in reality belonged to a different world and age.[24] No mammoth specialised agency with vast conferences passing often highly political resolutions, without palatial headquarters in Paris, secretaries, teams of simultaneous translators, the ICIC, existing almost entirely without funds, sat for a week or two every autumn, just before the regular plenary meeting of the Assembly, a quiet seminar made up of great names in the learned world. The French philosopher, Henri Bergson, was its first chairman, succeeded in 1925 by the Oxford classical scholar, Gilbert Murray. The Polish physicist, Madame Curie, was another long-serving member; Sigmund Freud, Albert Einstein, H.G. Wells, Aldous Huxley, and other distinguished names in science and the arts took part in its work. In 1925, the French government presented the Committee with an institute in Paris (where else could such a body find a home?), with a highly individualistic director and staff, to be, in theory, its executive instrument. The British government, and, with some exceptions, the British Dominions, frowned on intellectual co-operation as a waste of money, though the sums involved were minute.

The Committee had two tasks, one technical and useful, the other high-minded and visionary, yet in some ways acutely realistic. The technical side was simply to assist the process of intellectual work around the world by putting scientists, scholars, writers, in touch with each other, and, if possible, to improve their conditions of work in much the same way as the ILO was supposed to improve the conditions of manual labour. First, of course, the Committee found that, before international relations could be forged between the world's intellectual centres, the scholarly community had to be developed within the different states: this was done through the organisation of National Committees for intellectual life. These Committees met together in an international conference held in Paris in May 1937. The ICIC was not so successful, however, as a pressure group for improving the conditions of intellectual labour, which are naturally varied from one country to another and are often too individualistic to lend themselves to organisation. The Committee's efforts, for instance, to secure recognition for intellectual property, that is, the right of scientists to have the results of their research protected against piracy, as in the case of patents, met with no success. In many other fields, however, as in the encouragement the ICIC gave to improvements in bibliographical and translating services, to joint research projects conducted by scientists in different countries, to exchanges across frontiers of scholars and library materials, the League was a valuable assistant to learning and research.

At the same time, the Committee, being made up of men and women of exceptional intellectual gifts, could not confine itself to such small change of international co-operation. It reached out towards the grandiose aspiration of helping form a general mentality among the peoples of the world more appropriate to co-operation than the nationalistic mentality of the past. The guiding idea was that the League had been launched as an emotional reaction against the horrors of the war, and before the psychological attitudes needed to keep it afloat had been shaped. A revolutionary change in the management of human affairs, such as the advent of the League, necessitated a revolutionary change in habits of thought. In the nature of things, a start must be made with the education of the young and because academic study, research and art are essentially international in character, men and women of outstanding intellect must be looked to as the artificers of the new mental life-style essential to living in a world in which men must co-operate or perish.

The ICIC could not turn itself into a team of Platonic philosophers employing schools and colleges to re-educate people for the League. In some of the most important countries, education was not even under the control of central government. But a start could be made by encouraging intellectuals to talk about problems and suggest remedies. The Committee therefore organised *Conversations* between the 'brightest and best' in the world of learning and solicited *Open Letters* from them on problems of the day, both types of communication being later published. It promoted international studies conferences as a means of keeping the League supplied with the best advice the most highly qualified experts could provide on the whole range of world problems, from the control of inflation to the eradication of race prejudice. It tried to reduce hostilities between one nation and another by asking historians to examine textbooks used in schools in order to identify passages likely to incite ill-will against other nations. It encouraged studies of the cultural bases of the attitudes prevalent in a country towards its neighbours. The work of combating the effects of centuries of sedulously cultivated nationalism was immense, well-nigh impossible. It carried with it, too, the danger that if the people of a country became unduly conscious of the partisan character of the education they had received, their will to defend themselves against aggression might be weakened. The historian, A. J. Toynbee, described the British in the 1930s as 'prematurely humanised', too tolerant for the intolerant world they lived in.

This was a risk intellectual co-operators in the League felt they had to take. As it happened, the impact they had on events of the day, for better or worse, must have been minimal. Nevertheless, the differences in the mentality of the belligerents (especially those fighting the Axis Powers) in the Second World War from those of the First World War is striking: the emphasis on the opposing government as the target, as distinct from the people and their culture, the abandonment of primitive hate slogans, the readiness to see reason in the enemy's case. Certainly, the small committee in Geneva could not, owing to its lack of resources, have done much to engineer these vast changes. But it did point in that direction. It reminded the world that safer and sounder international relations could not be enjoyed merely in exchange for some improvement in the machinery of those relations. People had to accustom themselves to the idea that they had more to gain by working together than by snatching as much as they could for themselves. The Committee was a symbol of the fact that, at the highest level of mental achievement, the human race is one, not a chaos of conflicting parts. It was right that such a symbol should have a place in the League's structure.

VII

As the bastions of international order fell under blows from the dictators in the 1930s and the League seemed more and more unable to stem the drift to war, minds turned towards salvaging all that could be saved from the Geneva institution. It was apparent that this chiefly comprised the economic and social work described in this chapter. By the late 1930s it had become the major part of the League's activities and absorbed almost two-thirds of its income. The central portions of the Covenant, dealing with the settlement of international disputes, had broken apart on the fierce ambitions of nations, which meant to work their will in the world, whatever was said at the League. The social and economic activities – control of the drug trade and the traffic in women and children, the help given to refugees and ailing economies – would go on because it had a practical, commonsense value. Countries which fought shy of the League's politics saw enough everyday benefit in social and economic co-operation to want to play the fullest part in it.

The United States, for example, while distancing itself from the League's work for peace until the bitter end, actively participated in all its important non-political sectors. Secretary of State Cordell Hull, in a letter to the League Secretary-General early in 1939, wrote that 'the League of Nations has been responsible for the development of mutual exchange and discussion of ideas and methods to a greater extent and in more fields of humanitarian and scientific endeavour than any other organisation in history'. As we have stressed in this chapter, this work was not invented by the League's founders and placed in the Covenant: most of it originated long before the League idea was conceived. The League had merely to piece together threads disrupted by the First World War that were deeply embedded in the fabric of the international system. This, together with the obvious need for economic and social reconstruction in Europe at the end of the war, precipitated the League into this field with a rush, whereas its first ventures into world politics in the broader sense were hesitant and halting, mainly because the great Powers were not keen to see a new-fangled contraption stumbling into their traditional pastures.

On the eve of the Second World War, the Secretary-General proposed to the Council on 23 May 1939 the setting up of a committee to study and report 'on the appropriate measures of organisation', to use the arid language of the Secretariat, to ensure the development and expansion of the League's machinery for dealing with technical problems, or, as the committee when finally summoned preferred to call them, 'economic and social questions'. The idea was to snatch this one surviving section of the League's work from the tides engulfing it and strengthen it against the gathering storm.

On 27 May the Council followed this advice and appointed S.M. Bruce, the then Australian High Commissioner in London and a former Australian Prime Minister, to act as the committee's chairman (the committee and its report were named after him) and to choose its members. He nominated six others: Professor Maurice Bourquin, Harold Butler, a former ILO Director, Carl Hambro, President of the Norwegian Parliament, Charles Rist, former Vice-Governor of the Bank of France, Mr Tudela, the Peruvian ambassador to Switzerland, and Mr Varvaressos,

Deputy Governor of the Bank of Greece. The committee met for five days in August in Paris and issued a brief report summarising the League's social and economic work and justifying it on the grounds that 'none of these problems can be entirely solved by purely national action' and that 'the need for the interchange of experience and the co-ordination of action between national authorities has been proved useful and necessary time after time in every section of the economic and social fields'. The committee believed that the League's work in this area needed to be developed and expanded, and considered that this could best be done by bringing it 'under the direction of an organ representative both of the authorities responsible in each country ... and of special experience in the problems'. The organ proposed should be a Central Committee consisting of representatives of twenty-four states chosen by the Assembly for one year only in the first instance to direct and supervise the activities of all League committees dealing with economic and social co-operation. The Committee could co-opt not more than eight members appointed in a personal capacity and would meet at least once a year, examine a budget for League work in this field submitted by the Secretary-General and place an annual report on its work before the Assembly.[25]

The Bruce Report was published on 22 August 1939, the day on which the Nazi-Soviet Pact was signed in Moscow and not much more than a week before German forces lifted the curtain on the Second World War by their entry into Poland. But, ironically, it was the aggressors who destroyed the League who were themselves destroyed by history, and the League, or rather the ideas underlying it, which survived. The Bruce Report was merely shelved for the duration. When the conference to frame the first draft of the new world organisation, UNO, met at Dumbarton Oaks in September 1944, it adopted the proposal for a special body, to be called the Economic and Social Council, and to act as a principal organ of the new organisation, doing precisely the work adumbrated in the Bruce Report. It is significant that in the post-1945 period the political role of the new world organisation, after an impressive start, has become attenuated, while its social and economic work has continued without abatement. This is precisely what the Bruce Committee anticipated and recommended.

9 The mandates system

We have seen in an earlier chapter how in 1919 Germany's former colonies in Africa and the Pacific and Turkey's Arab-populated territories in the Middle East came before the peace conference to have their future determined, and how the Allies adopted Smuts' idea (though he himself applied it to the successor states of Central and East Europe) of regarding them as temporary wards of the 'advanced' nations until they were able, in the words of what became Article 22 of the Covenant, 'to stand by themselves under the strenuous conditions of the modern world'.[1] The notion of wardship or guardianship had a respectable ancestry in British colonial administration, reaching back to Edmund Burke's principle of colonies being a 'sacred trust' of civilisation, as expounded, for instance, in his famous indictment of Warren Hastings on 15 February 1788.[2] In 1885 a conference on the Congo in Berlin had adopted an Act aimed at extending 'the benefits of civilisation' to the natives, the promotion of trade and navigation on the basis of equality for all nations, and the preservation of the territory from war. Seven years later another conference in Brussels on Central Africa sought to control the import of arms and alcohol, though without providing sanctions. The Berlin and Brussels agreements were abrogated by the Allied Powers in the convention of St Germain, concluded in 1919, which committed the signatories to maintain in their African territories an authority and police force sufficient to protect lives and property and freedom of trade and transit, and to watch over the native population and supervise the improvement of their moral and material well-being.

Thus, by 1919 the idea that the welfare of 'lesser breeds without the law' somehow formed a trust assigned to the maturer members of the international community had won a measure of acceptance. One familiar phrase was the 'dual mandate', adopted from the principle of *mandatum* in Roman law, under which property or persons were entrusted to responsible individuals for safe keeping. Colonial dependencies were regarded as representing a dual mandate in the sense that the administering state had a responsibility both for the welfare of the indigenous population and for ensuring equality of access to all nations to the territories in question. But to whom was the administering Power responsible? To whom was it supposed to be accountable for the administration of subject peoples and territories? Before the foundation of the League of Nations it could only be some vague entity such as 'mankind' or 'civilisation'. After 1920 it could only be the League. Article 22 of the Covenant spelled out the connection. The states to which were allotted former German and Turkish territories under mandate were obliged to report annually to the League Council on how they had complied with the terms of the mandate, which was in effect a treaty between the League and the mandatory Power.

The League mandates system was thus a device which existed in more enlightened forms of colonial administration and was resurrected to solve a dilemma, namely, how could the Allied Powers which had seized (or, in the modern jargon, 'liberated') German and Turkish dependencies be allowed to keep their gains without affronting people, especially in the United States, who wanted to break free from old-fashioned imperialism? The mandates system was an ingenious answer: it gave the Allies who stepped into Germany's and Turkey's shoes as rulers in the territories concerned assured possession within a scheme of international accountability through the League. In the words of William Rappard, the mandatory system's first secretary,

> It was impossible ... once the peace was signed to return to the *status quo ante*. Such a solution could not be adopted for practical reasons, while annexation pure and simple would have been in contradiction with the principles which secured the victory of the Allies.

'The mandates system', Rappard concludes, 'formed a kind of compromise between the proposition advanced by the advocates of annexation and the proposition put forward by those who wished to entrust the colonial territories to an international administration'.[3]

There are certain basic facts about the system to be grasped. Firstly, it applied only to specific territories which became available for redistribution as a result of the defeat of the Central Powers in the war. These were fifteen in all, covering an area of 1.1/4 million square miles and with a population of 20 million people. There was no suggestion of all colonial territories being brought under the supervision of an international organisation, as was done in Chapter XI of the United Nations Charter drawn up in 1945. Article 23 of the League Covenant did refer to the responsibilities of member-states to secure just treatment of native inhabitants in all territories under their control, and for maintaining freedom of trade for all member-states with their colonies, but there was no provision, as there was in the case of the mandated territories, for states being answerable to the League for the way in which they discharged these responsibilities.

Secondly, the allocation of mandates to the states which assumed responsibility for them was not done through the League – it was begun before the League came into existence – but by the Allied Powers through their principal organ, the Supreme Council. It was in fact the Allied Powers, not the peace conference, who wrote the mandates article (Article 22) of the Covenant. The Supreme Council distributed Germany's African and Pacific colonies at its meeting in Paris on 7 May 1919, while Turkey's former Arab territories were distributed by the Supreme Council at its meeting in San Remo on 25 April 1920, that is, more than three years before peace was finally made between the Allies and Turkey. Moreover, although we speak of the mandates being 'distributed', the Allies in reality simply doled out the mandates among themselves. This was managed by a system commonly known as 'horse-trading'; not surprisingly, the lion's share went to Britain and France, Britain receiving six out of the fifteen territories and France three. The British Dominions, as they were then known, that is, Australia, New Zealand and South Africa, were also rewarded, partly owing to the support they received from Britain, partly owing to their occupation of adjacent German territory in the early stages of the war. Japan, an ambitious and highly esteemed member of the Allied coalition, as well as being an ally of Britain, secured as mandates Germany's islands and reefs in the Pacific north of the equator, 700 islands in all with a population of 40,000. Italy, geographically distant from Germany's colonies in Africa and having no special claim to a share in the Arab lands in the Middle East, came away empty-handed. The United States, though pressed by the European allies to take over mandates for Istanbul and Armenia, declined to accept either, and even held up the process of getting the system established by putting forward claims relating to American interests in the mandated territories.

The complete list of mandates and mandatories, together with some information about their size and population, is as follows:

Mandatory Power	Territory	Area (sq. kms)	Population (1938)
UK	Tanganyika	932,304	5,287,929
	Togoland	33,772	370,327
	Cameroons	88,266	857,675
	Palestine	27,009	1,435,341
	Transjordan	Declared independent, 1946	
	Iraq	Declared independent, 1932	
France	Cameroons	429,750	2,609,508
	Togoland	52,000	780,699
	Syria and Lebanon	Declared independent, 1944	
Belgium	Ruanda-Urandi	53,200	3,752,742
South Africa	South-West Africa	822,909	292,079
Australia	New Guinea	240,864	587,625
New Zealand	Western Samoa	2,934	57,759
British Empire	Nauru (administered by Australia)	2,929	3,400
Japan	Caroline, Mariana and Marshall Islands	2,149	121,128

(Reproduced from H. Duncan Hall, *Mandates, Dependencies and Trusteeship*, London, 1948, Annex II.)

Thirdly, the League mandates, unlike the territories within the UN trusteeship system, were divided into three groups, later known, though not so described in Article 22, as A, B and C mandates, roughly in accordance with the level of their political and cultural development. A mandates, consisting of Arab territories in the Middle East, were regarded as being on the brink of independent statehood; in fact, their independence, Article 22 declared, could be 'provisionally recognised'. Iraq, a British mandate, actually became an independent state in 1932, after only twelve years of tutelage. All that was required of the mandatory in the case of A mandates, in theory at least, was to lead their charges through the last few steps to freedom. But this did not mean that the history of the A mandates was untroubled. Simply because the Arab countries had come so far towards independence, and because their leaders believed, when they rose in revolt against Turkey during the war, that the Allies would reward them with freedom at the end of it, their acquiescence in the mandates regime was far from easy.

B mandates consisted mainly of former German colonies in Africa (except for South West Africa, which was assigned as a C mandate to South Africa) and concentrated chiefly on defending them against abuses, such as slavery, the exploitation of native labour, the drugs and liquor trade, and the maintenance of the Open Door for the trade of other countries. C mandates, on the other hand, comprising South West Africa and former German islands in the Pacific, were regarded as being on such a low level of political development as to be suitable for treatment as integral parts of the mandatory Power's territory, almost, that is, as annexed domains. This separation of A mandates, on one side, from B and C mandates, on the other, reflects the notion in Article 22 that, although all the territories and their inhabitants were in theory wards of the advanced nations, which were to guide them towards independence, independence was a practicable goal only for A mandates, and countries in that group were already near enough to it that it could not be denied them. For those in the B and C groups, independent statehood was hardly within the reach of practical politics. In the United Nations system, on the other hand, the idea was firmly embedded almost from the beginning that all colonial peoples exist on a kind of escalator in perpetual motion towards full independence. Continued dependence for them is almost as much a formality as ultimate independence was for B, and certainly for C, mandates within the League system.

This raises the question of who, in reality, was the actual sovereign in the mandated territories? Where was the ultimate source of law? The question was hardly relevant in the case of A mandates. They would shortly be independent sovereign states in their own right and international law makes no provision for a short-term kind of sovereignty, to be exercised by someone else in the mandated territory, and to be extinguished when the territory became an independent state in its own right. But sovereignty in the case of B and C mandates was a different matter: there had to be a sovereign in those territories in order that issues like defence of the territory, the settlement of frontiers with other countries, the redress of damages suffered by the nationals of other states, and such matters, could be definitively resolved. The mandatory Powers, especially those responsible for C mandates, tended to argue that they were the sovereign, or at least that they exercised sovereign powers: otherwise, they claimed, businessmen would not have enough confidence in the political system to invest money in the territories. South Africa, for instance, contended throughout the League's life that South West Africa was as much a part of her domains as Cape Town or Johannesburg. J.C. Smuts, then the South African Prime Minister, was reported in *The Cape Times* of 18 September 1920 as having said that 'in effect, the relations between the South West Protectorate' (*sic*) 'and the Union amount to annexation in all but name'.[4] In 1926, an agreement was signed between Portugal and South Africa on the frontier between Angola and South West Africa which referred to South Africa as 'possessing sovereignty' over the mandated territory. The Mandates Commission repudiated the claim, its chairman, the Marquis Theodoli, contending that South Africa merely 'exercised sovereign powers' in the territory. The Mandates Commission, according to one legal authority, 'has throughout examined the reports of the mandatory on the principle that sovereignty has not been acquired and has seen to it that the principle is honoured'.[5]

But if the mandatory Powers were not sovereign in the mandated territory (we are referring, as explained, to B and C mandates only), who was sovereign? It could hardly be the League, since no legal authority has ever recognised the League as having direct rights to govern territory or people. Moreover, if the League was sovereign in the mandated territories, the implication must be that it had the right to resume control of them if one or other mandatory power failed to keep its side of the bargain. Some League officials and writers on the League sometimes expressed the League's position in that way. But, if the Mandates Commission or League Council from time to time rapped a mandatory Power over the knuckles for having failed in its duties, no suggestion was ever made that such failings might incur the penalty of the League taking back the charge it had assigned, if only for the reason that it was not the League, but the Allies, who had done the assigning. Perhaps the most that could be said about sovereignty within the mandates system was that the exact position was never precisely defined. The mandates system was entirely unique and old categories of international law did not fit the situation. Everyone knew that, wherever sovereignty lay, it did not lie with the mandatory Powers. Those Powers acted like sovereigns in the mandated territories, but on the understanding that their right so to act would somehow lapse if they failed to observe the terms of the mandate.

II

At the centre of the mandates system, and providing it with its peculiar momentum, was the Permanent Mandates Commission, the word 'permanent' suggesting that some at least of the mandated communities would always remain 'wards of court'. The PMC was a tool of the League Council, its most important task being to advise the Council on 'all questions relating to the execution of the mandates' in the fifteen territories. It did this by receiving, examining and questioning accredited representatives of the mandatory Powers about their annual reports on the administration of the territories. To carry out this task, and to exercise the necessary impartiality in doing so, the nine or ten members of the Commission needed to be experts in colonial administration and were selected by the Council on the basis of personal merit and competence. They were supposed to be independent of their own governments and should not hold any office which might place them in a position of dependence on their governments, a striking contrast to the politically based membership of the UN Trusteeship Council. All the members were men, except for Mrs Bugge-Wicksell of Sweden, later succeeded by Mme Dannevig, of the same country. Attached to the Commission was an assessor from the ILO.[6]

The Mandates Commission enjoyed more of an independent position and came to exercise more authority during the League's life than any other expert advisory committee serving the Council. It was one of the two permanent commissions actually named in the League Covenant, the other being the Armaments Commission. Its members were invariably distinguished figures who were in every sense the equals in competence of the colonial administrators usually sent by the mandatory Powers to justify their reports; for many years Sir Frederick (later Lord) Lugard, the well-known British authority on colonial administration, was an active member of the Commission. Moreover, the Mandates Commission had a peculiarly intimate relationship with the League Council, the Assembly being usually content to approve the general outline of the Commission's reports and leave the detailed work to the Council.

The Commission's leading role in the League system can also be seen in the massive scale and technicality of its work, which grew throughout the League's lifetime. Meeting at first in 1921 and 1922 for a five- or ten-day session, the Commission found in 1923 that three weeks was scarcely sufficient to cope with its work. Two sessions a year became the normal rule in 1925. Three were held in 1926 and 1927. A session might include twenty-five or thirty meetings, each sometimes lasting ten hours a day, with members carrying back to their hotels voluminous papers to read in the evening. It is no wonder that they found the work gruelling; it even told on their health. It was ill-rewarded, appeals by the chairman to the Council to compensate members for the loss of their time invariably going unheeded.

Some impression of the extensiveness and variety of the Mandates Commission's work can be gained from the following list of subjects discussed with M.M. Besson, the Chief of the First Bureau of the Political Department at the French Ministry of Colonies, during the examination on 6 November 1934 of the report for 1933 for Togoland under French Mandate:

Half-castes
Native administration
Study of native languages
Frontier between Togoland under French Mandate and
    Dahomey
Relations between the various frontier tribes
Economic equality
Public finance
The economic situation. Imports and exports
Cattle
Situation of women in the territory
Judicial organisation
Imprisonment for debt
Penitentiary system
Defence of the territory
Police
Organisation of civil status in the territory

Lomé incidents of 1932
Witchcraft
Child welfare
Labour
Freedom of conscience
Missions
Education
Cinematograph
Alcohol and spirits
Public health
Land tenure
Forests
Demographic statistics
Polygamy
Petition dated 4 April 1933 from the Chief and inhabitants of
     Woame

In the beginning, several mandatory Powers treated the
Commission with some disdain, giving insufficient or the wrong
sort of information in their annual reports, sending as reports
annual accounts by colonial officials addressed to their own
governments, despatching reports at irregular intervals,
sometimes long after the period to which they referred. It is easy to
see how the bureaucratic discipline required by the system must
have irked often over-worked officials and colonial offices.
Sometimes a mandatory Power's representative would be kept
several days before the PMC answering detailed questions about
forced labour, the number of doctors available per thousand of the
population, mortality in the mines, the incidence of venereal
disease, the training of teachers, the upkeep of the railways, and a
thousand and one other questions. But, as the years passed, the
respect of the mandatory Powers for the Commission grew. This
was reflected in the increasing orderliness in the compilation of
their annual reports and the sense of routine as the system became
established.

The Mandates Commission and its tiny secretariat, at first
headed by Rappard, who became a Commission member in his
own right in 1925, could not have worked with a more
unpretentious air. They were well aware that, since the mandatory
Powers were, in effect, in possession of the territories, the
overriding need must be to secure their co-operation: this could
never be done by putting them in the dock, so to speak, and

addressing them in an accusatory tone. The Commission had to be at all times scrupulously polite to the mandatories, congratulating them when they did well, scolding them only mildly for their faults, and at all times exercising patience and avoiding haste. After all, the mandatory Powers had the overwhelming advantage of being the only source of information about their charges: other sources perhaps existed (the secretariat circulated regularly bundles of press cuttings and other publications to members), but the Commission was always conscious of the drawbacks and difficulties of using them.

The Commission, unlike the UN Trusteeship Council, could not visit the mandated territories to see for themselves. The mandatory Powers would probably have regarded any such visits as an unwarrantable interference in their difficult enough task of governing sometimes unruly populations. In any case, money did not run to travelling to distant lands in Africa or the Pacific. The Commission could and did regularly consider petitions from interested parties, though these usually did not emanate from within the territories themselves. Moreover, as a rule, petitions had to pass to the Mandates Commission, or sometimes directly to the League Council, with the approval of the mandatory Power involved: the Commission could not retain the all-important confidence of the mandatory if it relied for its information on sources of information not acceptable to that Power.

The Commission decided early in its life that petitions reaching it should be divided into two groups: those which could be dismissed as frivolous or originating in some source lacking in authority or knowledge of the local situation, and those which had to be taken more seriously. Clearly, the attitude of the mandatory Power concerned had an important influence in the decision to which group a given petition should belong. The next question was whether petitioners should be granted a hearing before the Commission, and here again the attitude of the mandatory Powers was crucial. The League Council, on being presented with this question by the Commission in 1926, appropriately decided that the mandatories should be consulted. The response varied, but the general reaction was negative and the question was not asked again.

That the Commission and the League Council which it advised should have been so unfailingly polite to the mandatory Powers, and so uncomplaining when they refused to co-operate, is not surprising. The whole idea of the international supervision of dependent territories was revolutionary. The normal assumption was that the European Powers had a natural right to rule 'natives' without interference from third parties, save for one or two latter-day international agreements on the observation of certain standards. If that assumption was to be relaxed through the use of League machinery, the process would have to be gradual and the pressure gentle. Experience showed that the rule *suaviter in modo, fortiter in re* paid dividends. The mandatory Powers, with some exceptions, learned to play the game at Geneva with an old-fashioned courtliness, fully reciprocated by their questioners and far removed from the passionate rhetoric of the United Nations era. At the same time, it should be remembered that, although some of the mandates yielded benefits to the mandatories, often more intangible than otherwise, most of them were a burden and a drain on their resources. At least one, Palestine, was an albatross round its administering Power's neck and had to be abandoned in desperation after the League's demise.

III

We must now consider, though selectively, some of the main subjects dealt with by the Mandates Commission in its discussions with representatives of the mandatory powers responsible for the fifteen territories. Prominent among these from the start was the prohibition of slavery, specified in Article 22 as an obligation of Powers responsible for administering B, though not A and C, mandates. The existence of slavery, in the sense of the ownership of and trade in human beings, was always a subject of concern to the Commission. But there were problems of definition. What about forced labour in the sense of the inhabitants of mandated territories being legally obliged to work? When discussing the questionnaire to be answered by mandatory Powers at its first session in October 1921, the Commission did not wish to rule out what it called 'the obligation of labour', which it considered to be 'the foundation of all civilised society'. Native men, said the Portuguese member Freire d'Andrade, should not 'live in idleness off their wives'. He laid down the rule, to which the rest of the Commission agreed, that 'labour in these localities should be compulsory in this sense, that the native should not be entitled to refuse work, though he should have the right to choose freely the nature and place of his work'.[7] The question arose again a year

later, when the matter of imported labour into Pacific territories
was raised: if natives felt they had no need to work because food
was plentiful and they were not required to work, labour was
attracted into the area and that created problems because imported
labour was mainly male.[8] This solicitude for the moral health of
the 'natives' was typical of the Commission. It was reflected again
in its continuous concern for control of the 'liquor traffic', another
'abuse' liable to occur in B mandates according to Article 22. That
natives, especially males, should work hard and regularly, refrain
from strong drink and treat their wives and children with
consideration was a basic requirement in European tutelage in
Africa and the Pacific. It invariably studded the questioning of the
mandatory Powers at the Commission's table year by year.

When the 'natives' rebelled against their new masters, the
mandatory Powers, as they did from time to time, the Commission
had a special task of inquiry to perform. The system depended on
the co-operation, not to say, submissiveness, of the inhabitants of
the territories: if they spurned the hand that fed them, the
experiment in supervised colonial administration could not
succeed. In discharging this part of its responsibilities, the
Commission, sitting in remote Geneva and almost totally reliant
for information on the mandatory Power, was under a serious
handicap. The problem was illustrated by an uprising in South
West Africa in 1922, known as the Bondelzwarts affair and dealt
with by the Mandates Commission at its third session in July 1923
at the request of the League Assembly. The Bondelzwarts
uprising, according to the South African authorities, involved
between 500 and 600 rebels, 200 of whom were armed: the fighting
lasted for three days. After the suppression of the rebellion, the
authorities appointed a three-man commission of inquiry the
majority report of which, signed by two of its members,
condemned the South African administration: yet, as Sir
Frederick Lugard pointed out at the PMC's third session in July
1923, the authorities still remained at their jobs.[9]

The Commission drily reported to the League Council that its
conclusions on the affair 'are based on the assumption that the
explanation given by the representatives of the Administration of
the mandated territory' – which were contrary to the South
African government's inquiry commission's own findings – 'has
not been and will not be disputed'. The Mandates Commission
agreed that the uprising was on a limited scale, but that it was
repressed 'with excessive severity' and that it could have been

prevented by 'timely personal action by the Administrator'. Major Herbst, who gave evidence before the Commission on behalf of the South African authorities, dissented from this criticism, which he said 'would have a bad effect' in South Africa.[10]

Tensions between the South African government and the PMC continued. The Commission noted in 1926 that, although white people in South West Africa were outnumbered by 'natives' in the proportion of one to eight, spending on native education amounted only to £6,500 and on white education to £65,000 in the year under review. The South African representative, Mr Smit, explained this by the terse formula that 'accommodation for white pupils had necessarily to be more elaborate and expensive.'[11] In 1934, at the Commission's twenty-sixth session, chairman Theodoli complained that in the fourteen years of the South West African Mandate South Africa had not opened a single school for the natives, to which Eric Louw, the envoy extraordinary and Minister Plenipotentiary for South Africa, replied that education was in the hands of the missionaries. Rappard's verdict at the same meeting was that 'After watching developments for the last fourteen years ... he could not find any evidence that progress had been made in that direction [that is, towards independence].' 'Of all the native populations with which the Commission had to deal', Rappard went on, 'that of South West Africa seemed the most backward: its position was static and static on a deplorably low level'.[12]

Moreover, it was almost impossible to obtain from the South African government any definite acknowledgement that the mandated territory was not under direct South African sovereignty. As we have seen above (p.197), an agreement between South Africa and Portugal to define the border between Angola and South West Africa referred to South Africa as 'possessing sovereignty' over the latter. The South African authorities rarely, if ever, budged from that position. It was intensified with the advent of Nazism in Germany in the 1930s, when the German population in South West Africa, forming a majority of the whites, began to agitate for the return of the territory to the Reich. On 27 May 1933, the Legislative Assembly at Windhoek, the capital of South West Africa, was still sufficiently pro-Boer to vote for the incorporation of South West Africa into the Union as a fifth province.

The maintenance of law and order in mandated territories was also a matter of acute concern to the PMC in regard to two other areas, both in the Middle East and both subject to A mandates, that is, communities formerly belonging to the Turkish Empire which, according to Article 22, had reached a stage of development 'where their existence as independent nations could be provisionally recognised', subject to the rendering of administrative advice and assistance by a mandatory until they were able to stand alone. These were the joint Mandate for Syria and Lebanon, administered by France, and the even more turbulent joint Mandate for Palestine and Transjordan (now Jordan), administered by Britain. Most of the inhabitants of these territories were Arabs, with nationalistic feelings stirred by the First World War and regarding themselves as tricked out of their independence by Allied promises which were never fulfilled, such as those given to Sherif Hussein of Mecca by Sir Henry McMahon, the British High Commissioner in Cairo, in 1915. Even the legal instrument which imposed the mandates on them, the League Covenant, had been violated by the Allies since it insisted that, for A mandates, 'the wishes of these communities must be a principal consideration in the selection of the mandatory'. The commission sent to the Middle East by President Wilson in 1919, consisting of Dr H.C. King and Mr Charles Crane, found that neither Britain nor France was desired as an overlord by the local population, but that, if they had to choose, they would have preferred Britain. The United States was the country most people wanted.

This did not prevent the Supreme Council at San Remo on 25 April 1920 conferring the Mandate for Syria and Lebanon on France. It was not approved by the League Council until 24 July 1922, by which time the French had entered Damascus and other principal cities in the two territories, expelled the Emir Feisal, Sherif Hussein's son, from the Syrian throne to which the Arab notables had appointed him (the British promptly installed him as king of their mandated territory, Iraq) and proceeded to enforce their rule. Arab resistance was not long in developing, taking the form of a rebellion of the Druzes in April 1925, the defeat of French forces on 3 August and the formation of an independent government in the Jebel Druze with Sultan al-Atrash as President. The rebellion spread, but never became a properly organised national uprising and, with the appointment of Senator Henri de Jouvenel as High Commissioner to replace the intemperate General Sarrail, the troubles died down in the early months of 1927.

The Mandates Commission, at the second meeting of its

seventh session on 19 October 1925, asked the French to make a statement about the rebellion and then adjourned to await it. At the following session in February-March 1926, held in Rome, the first and only occasion when the PMC met outside Geneva, its members found themselves in a dilemma: although Arab agitation in Syria was plainly directed against the whole mandatory system and the fact that it was administered by France, the Commission could take no account of this since the award of the Mandate was an Allied affair and not within the competence of League organs to express a view about. The French government, unlike the South African in the Bondelzwarts affair, had appointed no commission of inquiry into the disorders which might have provided information about them. Nor had they produced any authoritative analysis of the situation on their own account. About all that de Caix, the French representative before the PMC at its Rome meeting, would say was that

> In a country like Syria, political movements were started by a small minority with ambitions quite foreign to those of the mass of the population, who only desired to live as happily as possible, but who at certain moments were carried away by leaders who well know how to appeal to their traditional passions which were latent in normal circumstances.[13]

This was the classic apologia of the colonial governor: it entirely ignored the massive opposition of Arab leaders to French repressiveness. As the PMC put it, 'the mandatory system in Syria has encountered the whole resisting power of Oriental traditionalism'.[14]

The Commission picked its way among blunders the French had made. Its report declared that France's Druze subjects had been ruled with a heavy hand. Captain Carbillet, the governor of the Jebel Druze, had been brutally insensitive. There were three conclusions to be drawn: there had been lack of continuity in French administration in Syria, with abrupt changes in territorial organisation during the five years in which the Mandate had been in force; the higher direction of the Mandate had been inconsistent; and staff at the disposal of the French administration was not 'a sufficiently coherent and experienced body of officials'. Note of these strictures was taken in Paris, and, with the arrival of de Jouvenel in the Levant, the Mandate took a new course. For some time, a larger vision entered into French government, the coherence in administration which the Commission appealed for was somehow achieved. At the Commission's twentieth session in June 1931, the French representative was reporting, with vast optimism, that the 'present process of evolution' pointed to a termination of the Syrian-Lebanese mandate 'at a not very distant date'.[15]

With the troubled 1930s, however, disturbances returned. When the French report on the Mandate was examined by the PMC at its twenty-ninth session on 4 June 1936, new disorders in Syria were prominently featured. Again, external causes were made the scapegoat. 'Nationalist leaders', encouraged by the riots in Cairo touched off by the negotiations for an Anglo-Egyptian treaty, had started the trouble. The disturbances had erupted at ceremonies held to commemorate Ibrahim Hanano, who died at the end of 1935; at the last ceremony on 10 January crowds had denounced the Mandate and the Balfour Declaration of 1917. Resorting to familiar tactics, the French exiled the popular Syrian leader Fakri Baroudi to Upper Jezireh, only to be rewarded by six weeks of disturbances in which the bazaars in Damascus, Homs, Hama and Aleppo were closed. On 26 January, a meeting of nationalist leaders demanded the withdrawal of the Mandate. In Geneva, the Commission could do little but wring its hands. But time was running out for French imperialism in the Middle East; within a few years the home base itself would succumb to Nazi invasion. Syria and Lebanon were moving inexorably towards self-government, though another vain effort to reassert French power was made. This took place in July 1941, when British, Free French, Australian and Indian troops ousted Vichy representatives from the Levant, and there followed an uneasy experiment in Anglo-French collaboration. This could not survive General de Gaulle's efforts, at the last moment, to get rid of the British and restore to France all the controls it had exercised since the 1920s. 'The principle', writes S.H. Longrigg, 'was, in fact, now and from now onwards adopted, both by predilection and by specific orders from de Gaulle, that the Mandate (from which, it was at this stage discovered, only the League of Nations had the power of release) was still in existence, and that, whatever had been promised, independence must follow, not precede, the signature of satisfactory treaties' – treaties, that is, safeguarding French rights and interests.[16] An intemperate attempt in November 1943 by Jean Helleu, the French Délégué Général, to challenge the demands of the Syrian and Lebanese Parliaments to run their own affairs, followed by his arrest of the Lebanese

President and all but two Ministers, led to his own dismissal by General Catroux, acting for de Gaulle, and a Franco-Syrian-Lebanese agreement on 22 December by which all power was transferred to the two states, though clashes with France still persisted until all French forces were withdrawn in August 1946. The Mandate was finally extinguished.

The quarter-century of the French Mandate in Syria and Lebanon was a story of failure and humiliation, and the causes are many. For a system like the mandatory regime to succeed, there must be some substantial degree of sympathy and goodwill between the administering Power and the ward entrusted to it. This hardly ever existed. Although French culture left a deep mark on the ruling and intellectual classes in the Levant, and many friendships were struck up between Syrian and Lebanese leaders in all walks of life and the devoted and talented officials sent by Paris to administer the Mandate, the whole idea of guardianship was in conflict with the fierce nationalism which took possession of the Arab world after the war; leading Syrians (Lebanese generally had a far greater affection for France) never accepted it. On their side, the French, wracked by fears about their security in the inter-war period, never seem to have understood or had any confidence in the mandatory system. Most of France's High Commissioners and their staffs in the territories regarded themselves as the government, with some assistance from co-operative local agents: the Arabs were not looked upon as the true and rightful rulers of their own lands, though guided towards political maturity and the problems of independence by a friendly France.

The French made other mistakes, such as their disregard for Arab pride – few French officials bothered to learn Arabic, for instance – their subordination of local needs to their own wider interests in the world, their use of African troops to control disorders, their paranoid suspicion of Britain, which they foolishly blamed for the failures of their own policies. Nevertheless, the Mandate contributed to the progress of the Levant States; economic development was substantial over the twenty-five years, certainly as compared with the times of Turkish rule, communications, roads, airfields, ports and harbours were improved, educational services advanced, officials received lessons in self-government. For this, some credit must lie with the Geneva Commission, which looked upon France's misfortunes in the Arab world with tactful sympathy, tirelessly observing and questioning, chiding her and urging her to learn from her mistakes. The French took the Commission's advice on more than one occasion; without the League machinery, the balance sheet of their work in Syria and Lebanon would have been far less impressive.[17]

In Syria, unrest was focused against the Mandate. In neighbouring Palestine, Britain's fatal incubus, the Mandate was at once the promise of freedom and security for the Jews and, for the Arabs, a guarantee that, if all went well, they would not be swamped by Jewish immigration. The fact that the Mandate could have such diametrically opposite meanings for the local inhabitants symbolises its self-contradictions. The Mandate, embodying the Balfour Declaration of 1917, enjoined Britain 'to work to place the country under such political, administrative and economic conditions as will secure a National Home for the Jewish people', by, *inter alia*, facilitating Jewish immigration and the close settlement of Jews on the land. At the same time, the Mandate required the establishment of self-governing institutions. These two desiderata could not be reconciled, and, in attempting to fulfil them, Britain, and, in undertaking to supervise their fulfilment, the Mandates Commission, faced impossible tasks. Self-government would favour the Arabs since they were numerically dominant. Yet, if they achieved it, they would certainly use self-government to rule out all prospect of Palestine becoming a National Home for the Jews.

The Executive Committee of the Palestine Arab Congress refused to accept the British offer of a Legislative Council in 1923 and boycotted elections to the Council. The Council would have given them eight seats out of a total of twenty-three, the others being ten British officials, two Christians, two Jews, and the High Commissioner; considering that the country was, in their opinion, theirs, the Arabs seemed to want the full power of running it or nothing at all. After the Arabs had also rejected a proposal for a refurbished Advisory Council which would give them ten seats, with two seats each for Jews and Christians, the British authorities decided to govern the country with a panel of their own officials. By 1925 the situation seemed to have settled down, though with the continuous shift of land into Jewish hands and Arab accusations that Britain was forcing this process. After talks with Jews and Arabs in 1923, the British accepted the formula that Jewish immigration would be permitted 'up to the full economic absorptive capacity' of the country, an expression as devoid of precision as the 'National Home' shibboleth itself. On the eve of the clashes between Jews and Arabs at the famous Wailing Wall in Jerusalem in 1929, the High Commissioner, Sir John Chancellor, was telling the Mandates Commission that relations between the two communities 'continued to improve'.[18]

The fighting between Jews and Arabs in August 1929 was so serious and the casualties so heavy as to shock opinion throughout the world. The British Prime Minister, Ramsay MacDonald, went to the League Assembly in September to speak about the disturbances, Foreign Secretary Arthur Henderson gave a report on 15 May 1930 to the League Council, the government in London set on foot two inquiries, one, the Shaw Commission, into the incidents themselves, the other, under Sir John Hope Simpson, into immigration and land settlement, and the Mandates Commission held a special session wholly devoted to Palestine between 3 and 12 June 1930.[19] The Wailing Wall in Jerusalem, the focus of the disturbances, was a place of veneration for both Jews and Arabs: for Jews because, though actually the property of Moslem religious foundations, it was the remains of the Temple; for Arabs because at the wall the muezzin called the faithful to prayer every day. The blunt conclusion of the Shaw Commission was that the outbreak in Jerusalem on 23 August 'was from the beginning an attack by Arabs on Jews for which no excuse in the form of earlier murders by Jews has been established'.[20] The Commission contended that 'the fundamental cause without which the disturbances either would not have occurred or would have been little more than a local riot is the Arab feeling of animosity or hostility towards the Jews consequent upon the disappointment of their political or national aspirations and fear for their economic future'.[21]

The Mandates Commission, departing from its normally tolerant attitude towards the mandatory Powers, blamed the British authorities for accepting without question the Shaw Report's account of the origins of the disturbances. It said that Shaw was 'too kind to Arab leaders', presumably because it exonerated them from blame for the Arab attack on the Jews, which the Report did not consider premeditated. The Commission also disagreed with the Report's finding that the Arab attacks were not directed against British authority: 'it would be a mistake to conclude that the movement was entirely devoid of any intention to resist British policy in carrying out the Mandate in Palestine'. This was an unusual argument for the Commission to use. The

PMC's function was to advise the League Council concerning all matters connected with the execution of the Mandate, and it could hardly blame the British for attempting to put into effect a Mandate which evidently drove the Arabs to revolt. But even Britain's efforts to fulfil the Mandate came under the Commission's fire. The Palestine Administration was accused of 'lack of insight' in not anticipating the gravity of the demonstrations at the Wailing Wall and in having insufficient forces on hand to control the situation. 'In Palestine, a country of 900,000 inhabitants, the maintenance of order at that critical moment was entirely in the hands of 175 British policemen, one squadron of aeroplanes and one armoured car company'. Moreover, the mandatory Power could have done more to adapt the Arabs to the influx of Jews, to bring the two sections of the population closer together, and to provide common vocational training for the youth of both communities.[22]

Acid exchanges between the PMC and the mandatory Power followed the submission of the Commission's report to the Council on the 1929 disturbances. A tart British reply to the report criticised the Commission for relying too much on a Jewish account of the affair and ignoring the evidence provided by the Shaw Report. At the Commission's ninth meeting of the Nineteenth session on 8 November 1930, Orts and Van Rees vehemently protested against the British reply: this was a 'method of discussion which could obviously not be accepted'. The matter was then allowed to drop.[23] In 1930-32 the situation in Palestine was one of calm between storms. Trouble began again in autumn 1933 with rioting in Jaffa and Jerusalem in October with the loss of twenty-seven lives and well over two hundred injured. The mandatory Power's annual report assigned responsibility for initiating the disturbances to the Arab Executive.[24] Again a lull and then the most serious clashes of all took place in mid-April 1936, just as Arab and Jewish delegations were setting out for London for a conference intended to make further efforts to set up a Legislative Council. The trouble this time took the form of widespread strikes by the Arabs lasting until October, which they at first said would not stop until Jewish immigration into Palestine, intensified by the Nazi campaign against the Jews in Germany, ended. On 6 May, the British Colonial Secretary stated in Parliament that that was impossible. Instead, the Government set up a Royal Commission, headed by Lord Peel, to inquire into the causes of the unrest and the alleged grievances of Arabs and Jews.

It was to lead to a complete reversal of British policy.

At the sixteenth meeting of the Mandates Commission's Twenty-ninth session on 4 June 1936, the British Government's report on Palestine and Transjordan for 1935 could not be properly discussed because the Government declined to answer questions about it on the ground that it related to the origins of the disturbances of 1936, and these were still under consideration by the Peel Commission. The reports for 1935 and 1936, to the PMC's consternation, would have to be considered together in 1937, a date much removed from the events of 1935. The Peel Commission's Report, however, and the British response to it, when they finally appeared, were bound to dominate all consideration of the Palestine problem, and hence the PMC decided to devote the whole of its Thirty-second session, held from 30 July until 18 August 1937, to them.[25] The Peel Report was published in London on 8 June 1937 and was almost immediately followed by a Government statement which accepted its findings.[26] These were that seventeen years' experience had shown that the reconciliation of Jews and Arabs was not possible and that there was no alternative to abandoning the hopes of Palestine becoming a unitary self-governing state and to dividing the country into three parts: the larger but less fertile zone in the east would form an Arab state attached to Jordan; the coastal region and the adjacent plain would be a Jewish state, while Jerusalem, Bethlehem and certain other enclaves would remain under British mandate and be linked by a corridor with the sea. The British Government, in its statement, made no concealment of the fact that partition meant the abandonment of the Mandate in its present form.

> In the light of experience and of the arguments adduced by the [Peel] Commission, [the Government] are drawn to the conclusion that there is an irreconcilable conflict between the aspirations of Arabs and Jews in Palestine, that these aspirations cannot be satisfied under the terms of the present Mandate and that a scheme of partition on the general lines recommended by the Commission represents the best and most hopeful solution of the deadlock.

'How long can we go on adhering strictly to the Mandate in Palestine of seventeen years ago?', the Government asked.

The Mandates Commission did not minimise British efforts to make the Mandate work. After hearing Mr W. Ormsby-Gore, the

British Colonial Secretary, it reported to the League Council that 'without British efforts, certainly, there would have been no Jewish National Home; but also there would have been, on the threshold of the 20th century, no independent Arab stage'. The Commission criticised Britain for not having taken more decisive action to suppress the disorders in 1936 at an earlier state: curiously, for a League of Nations body, the Commission took the view, whenever trouble occurred in Palestine, that the British authorities did not use enough force, at the right time, to suppress it. Nevertheless, it reluctantly accepted the partition formula on certain conditions, the most important of which was that the Arab and Jewish states contemplated in the plan would not have met the conditions laid down by the PMC at its Twentieth session in 1931, and approved by the League Council, before a mandate could be terminated: hence a further period of political apprenticeship would be needed for both states. The Council accepted these observations when it considered them on 16 September 1937 and gave Britain authority to explore a practical scheme of partition.[27]

This the British Government proposed to do by sending to Palestine yet another commission, chaired by Sir John Woodhead, to consider the practical implementation of partition. In the meantime, however, it disconcerted the Mandates Commission by suspending the principle, adopted in 1922, of the economic absorptive capacity of Palestine as determining the scale of Jewish immigration and introducing a new rule under which no more than one thousand Jews would be allowed in the country for each of the following six months. This was an 'exceptional and provisional' measure arising from the 'state of war', as the mandatory Power described it, then existing between Jews and Arabs, one incident in which was the assassination of a British District Commissioner and his police escort at Nazareth. The PMC could only hope that the period before a final decision was reached about the scheme of partition would be 'as short as possible'.[28] This hope, and many others, too, were disappointed since the Woodhead Commission, predictably, found that no boundaries could be recommended for the proposed Arab and Jewish states which afforded prospects of their viability.[29] The British Government was forced to conclude that partition, on behalf of which they had contemplated abandoning the Mandate, was as unworkable as they had previously pronounced the Mandate to be.

This melancholy return to the starting point was rehearsed by

Colonial Secretary Malcolm MacDonald when he appeared before
the Mandates Commission in June 1939, ostensibly to answer
questions on the administration of the Mandate during 1938, in
reality to explain and defend the British decision, set forth in a
White Paper on 18 May, to limit Jewish immigration into Palestine
to 75,000 a year over the next five years and to make it dependent
upon Arab agreement thereafter.[30] The White Paper also
contained proposals restricting land sales to Jews and the form of a
constitution for Palestine. Mr MacDonald argued that the rights
granted to the Arabs in Articles 2 and 6 of the Mandate would be
definitely prejudiced 'if, now that immigration has made the
Jewish population a vast proportion of the whole population, and
given it a position of economic dominance, the mandatory Power
were to continue to permit indefinitely a flow of further
immigration against a strong national protest which is supported
by every articulate section of Arab opinion'. When the Mandate
was framed, 80,000 Jews and more than 600,000 Arabs lived in
Palestine: in 1939 the Jews numbered 450,000, a third of the total
population. The National Home, the Colonial Secretary asserted,
had in fact come into being: it was now strong and prosperous. To
allow it to increase in population without restriction, he said,
would mean ultimately converting Palestine into a Jewish state,
and that had never been Britain's intention.

It was difficult for the Mandates Commission, when it came to
discuss Mr MacDonald's statement, to distinguish between the
politics of the problem, in the sense of what had gone wrong and
how it could be put right, and the more technical question whether
the new British proposals were consistent with the seventeen-year-
old Mandate. The latter, however, was the proper issue for the
Commission to consider. Accordingly, when the chairman (Orts)
asked members one by one to state their views, four of the seven
present (the size of the Commission was by this time reduced
owing to the withdrawal of the Italian and Japanese members) did
not feel able to agree that the policy of the White Paper was in
conformity with the Mandate, while the other three held the
opposite opinion. The Commission's report to the League
Council, however, tended to gloss over this division of view,
stating forthrightly that

> From the first, one fact forced itself to the notice of the
> Commission – namely, that the policy set out in the White Paper
> was not in accordance with the interpretation which, in

agreement with the mandatory Power and the Council, the Commission has always placed on the Palestine Mandate.

One fact, the Commission explained, was proof of this, that is, that in 1937, when stating its reaction to the Peel Commission's report, the British Government had declared that the Mandate was unworkable and must be abandoned, whereas in 1939, according to the British representative, the Mandate was working and still in force. 'Does not this show', the Commission's report to the Council continued, with some bitterness, 'that that instrument had at that time [that is, in 1937] a different meaning in the eyes of the mandatory Power than that which it has today?'.[31]

But these regretful comments could have little influence on British policy, which would now be implemented. The Mandate had proved unworkable in that what the Jews wanted was totally at variance with what the Arabs wanted. Had it proved practically possible to split the country, as the Peel Commission recommended in 1937 with the agreement of the British Government, that judgment of Solomon might have been, as Britain declared, 'the best and most hopeful solution'. But, according to the Woodhead Commission, no scheme for splitting it could be devised, though the United Nations did devise such a scheme in 1947. The British authorities were afraid, in the last months of peace in 1939, that further implementation of the Mandate, in the sense of continued Jewish immigration, would either 'set the Middle East aflame', in the sense of making it untenable as a British base in the event of war, or, even worse, create an alliance between the Arabs and Nazi Germany all but fatal to any British war effort. By June 1939, the coming war was the major preoccupation. When the time came for that war to end, no-one knew what would have happened to the Palestine Mandate.

Had the 1937 proposals for partitioning Palestine come into effect, the Mandates Commission would have had to consider whether the resulting Arab and Jewish states were ripe for independence; as we have seen, their provisional view was that they were not.[32] The only mandated territory which emerged from its status as such during the League's life and joined the League as a fully fledged member was Iraq, placed under British mandate by the League Council in April 1920. The British Government fully supported Iraqi leaders in their pressure for independence: France's clinging to power in Syria and Lebanon was not an impressive example to follow, and, in any case, by her treaties with

Iraq in 1922 and 1930, Britain secured the substance of her desiderata, namely air bases in the country and, through the predominantly British-owned Iraq Petroleum Company, assured access to its oil. In a letter to the League Secretary-General dated 4 November 1929, Britain proposed that Iraq should be released from the mandate and join the League as a state in its own right in 1932. The League Council therefore asked the Mandates Commission on 13 January 1930 to make suggestions about the criteria to be adopted whenever the decision had to be made whether a mandate should be terminated. The Commission thereupon appointed a sub-committee of three to study the question. Following the sub-committee's recommendations, the Commission, in its report to the Council on its Twentieth session in 1931, assumed that the country in question should be able 'to stand by itself under the strenuous conditions of the modern world', in the famous words of Article 22 of the Covenant, spelled out five conditions for satisfying itself that that state of affairs existed, and then specified seven guarantees, the most important being related to the protection of minorities, which the state in question was required to provide.[33]

Did Iraq, in the state it was in 1931, satisfy these conditions? In a special report to the League Council in November 1931 on the British proposal for bringing the mandate for Iraq to an end, the Mandates Commission, 'having no information which would justify an opinion contrary to Britain's', pointed out that Iraq did not have the military establishment capable of maintaining its territorial integrity and political independence against a foreign aggressor by means of its own national forces; on the other hand, as a League member it would have the League's protection and the support of its alliance with Britain. At the same time, the Mandates Commission, 'having no information to the contrary', could not doubt that Iraq was capable of preserving the public peace. Furthermore, Iraq had the financial resources to provide normal government services and sufficient legal and judicial organisation to assure universal justice. There was no reason to doubt Iraq's qualifications for leaving the parental home and making its own way in the world.[34] The result was that, on the basis of the PMC's findings, the Mandate was declared ended on 3 October 1932, the day on which the General Assembly unanimously admitted Iraq to League membership.

A country largely unknown to the rest of the world had graduated from dependent status to full membership of the international system in less than ten years, thanks to the supervisory arrangements provided by the League system. Doubts and questions, however, remained, especially in regard to the numerous minorities in the new state, particularly the Assyrians, Kurds and Bahais. In regard to the Assyrians, for instance, the Mandates Commission agreed that their demand for administrative autonomy could not be granted, but persuaded the Iraqi government to settle landless Assyrians in homogeneous units so that their national identity could be preserved.[35] In 1933, the Iraqi Foreign Minister, Nuri Pasha, was telling a sub-committee appointed by the League Council to investigate the Assyrian question that Iraq did not have enough land for settling the Assyrians as a homogeneous group. Orts, speaking for the Mandates Commission, contradicted this.[36] The wrangle went on, reflecting the conflict between the Commission's belief that the independence of any state must involve some deference to international standards of human rights and welfare and the nationalistic argument that to demand such deference is to compromise the principle of national sovereignty. The curious thing is that, after the Second World War, Arab states like Iraq were the first to claim that rights of self-determination cannot be subordinated to superior political and military power.

Another example, this time more successful, of the Mandates Commission's determination to assert its authority was its resistance to British policy in regard to the Tanganyika Mandate. The British view was that, if Tanganyika was to develop economically and receive investment capital from abroad, the mandatory Power's position must be secure, but the Commission could not agree that this meant treating the territory as though it were a British colony. In December 1926, the Governor of Tanganyika, Sir Donald Cameron, told the Legislative Council that he had 'repeatedly stated ... that Tanganyika is part of the British Empire and will remain so'. The Mandates Commission objected. Sir Donald retracted his statement with the extraordinary explanation that 'those are not words that I should use if addressing people of education'.[37]

Later, the British authorities climbed down again from an attempt to take liberties with their position in Tanganyika. In 1929, the Hilton Young Committee submitted plans to the British Government for an administrative federation of East Africa, which would include Tanganyika. It was a favourite theme in Whitehall, but almost universally feared among native political circles in

Tanganyika since it seemed to imply the domination of the three territories (Kenya, Uganda, Tanganyika) by the white settlers of Kenya. The Hilton Young study was followed by a report by Sir Samuel Wilson on a closer union in administrative, customs and fiscal methods between the territories.[38] Pressure for union grew stronger with the economic blizzard which swept East Africa in the early 1930s. A positive step was taken in 1932 with the setting up of conferences of the Governors of the three territories and their staffs, which were to meet twice a year in the three capitals, their purpose being 'to ensure continuous and effective co-operation and co-ordination in regard to all matters of common interest to East Africa'. A member of the Mandates Commission, M. Palacios, was given the job of studying this development and reported that the mandatory Power, Britain, did not think the time was ripe for union. At the Commission's Twenty-third session in June-July 1933, the project was discussed again, and members heard the British reassure them that the government did not intend to operate any closer union 'which would involve the creation of a political and constitutional union, with the effect of destroying or endangering for the future the existence of the mandated territory as a distinct entity in international law'.[39]

Nevertheless, the movement for administrative amalgamation between the three territories continued, taking the form later in 1933 of the introduction of a common postage stamp and the unification of postal services. The Mandates Commission's suspicions were aroused and Britain was asked to explain. The matter was raised at the League Council on 22 May 1935 by the Italian representative, who also complained about the Governors' conferences. The British delegate explained that the conferences were purely advisory and the common postage stamp merely 'a matter of practical convenience'.[40] A year later, at the Mandates Commission's Twenty-ninth session in May and June, the question was raised with the British representative again, some members doubting whether the common postage stamp was simply a matter of convenience, or whether it was meant to symbolise a closer union.[41] There was no doubt, however, that the British authorities, though they would have wished administratively to unify the three territories, recognised in the Mandates Commission an effective obstacle to doing so.

IV

The League mandates system would be regarded today as part and parcel of an imperialist age now almost universally condemned. The condescension towards the 'natives' which characterised it is no doubt insufferable, if not positively racist, by present-day standards. Many think of the system as a thin veneer of internationalism covering naked acts of annexation. Even within its own terms, the system was seriously limited in its power to control the administration of the mandated territories. The Mandates Commission's inability to visit the territories and cross-question the inhabitants, its carefully circumscribed powers to deal with petitions, the limits – as with all League organs – to its financial resources, were crippling handicaps. Its obsession with legal proprieties, arising to a large extent from the knowledge that if it overstepped the limits to its authority, the mandatory Powers might withdraw their co-operation, inhibited it in dealing with the real problems of the territories it was concerned with. Above all, the mandatory Powers were on the spot and the Commission was in remote Geneva: influence exerted by the latter over the former was necessarily in the realm of theory rather than practice.

For all that, a system was somehow established within which, year by year, the administration of fifteen widely diverse territories was painstakingly examined in all its aspects, political, economic, and social. Chiefs of administration, even high-ranking government Ministers, came to the Commission's table in Geneva, explained carefully compiled reports on their stewardship, the very form of which was prescribed by the Commission, and patiently answered questions for whole days at a time on every branch of life in the territories. Over eighteen years, the respect of almost every mandatory government for the Commission grew, even though strictures from its members often came in full spate. The Mandates Commission, it must be stressed, wielded no powers of sanction. All it could do if it considered that the obligations of a mandate were being ignored was to report back to the League Council and then leave the matter there, knowing well that if its report to the Council displeased a mandatory Power, future relations with, and hence the flow of future information about a territory from, that Power might be affected.

It is impossible to be precise about the extent to which the Commission's inquiries actually affected administration in the mandated territories. Some mandatory Powers, notably France, were highly sensitive to criticism from the Commission, after some pretence of deafness to it; others, South Africa, for instance, cared less about what the Commission thought. But the unsparing examination of the mandatory Powers' annual reports by dedicated experts in Geneva undoubtedly kept those Powers up to the mark. Men like the Marquis Theodoli, the Commission's chairman for most of its life, Professor Rappard, Lord Lugard, and the Swedish woman member, Mme Dannevig, were not easily bamboozled by dissimulating national representatives. It is likely, too, that the high standards in all services expected by the Commission in the mandated territories had some beneficial effect in other dependent territories governed by the mandatory Powers. The people of Kenya and Uganda, for instance, could not be unaware that the United Kingdom had to face strenuous questioning year by year in Geneva about how it managed affairs in neighbouring Tanganyika.

It could be argued that the mandates system had some effect in exacerbating unrest in the territories. A public body in Geneva, with ready access to the world's press, which could be appealed to over the head of the local administrator, must have had some nuisance value to trouble-makers. But this is surely overshadowed by the benefits of a system which, within the limitations of the times, brought the government of at least a portion of dependent peoples into the light of day. The mandates system was the world's first experiment in the international control of dependent territories. It helped transform the entire climate of colonialism, contributing in the end to the demise of the colonial system. Whatever we may think of the political qualities shown by the Third World of our own times, our achievement of a sense of equality between the planet's different peoples is due to no slight extent to the League's mandatory system having existed.

10   The Abyssinian disaster

I

The Japanese conquest of Manchuria in 1931-32 and the League's inability to prevent or reverse it seriously undermined its standing as an instrument for the maintenance of peace.[1] There were, however, circumstances which helped to explain, if not excuse, the League's failure, especially the distance of Manchuria from the European great Powers which dominated the League, the ambiguity of the issues from which the Manchurian conflict arose and the elements of justification in the Japanese case, the distraction confronting the world at the time in the shape of the Great Depression. If Japan 'got away with it', it need not be taken for granted that the next aggressor would do the same. Nevertheless, precisely this was to happen in May 1936, when the Italian army made its entry into Addis Ababa, capital of the East African state of Abyssinia, which it had invaded on 3 October the previous year, and the Abyssinian Emperor, Haile Selassie, made his way to the French port of Djibuti on the Gulf of Aden and thence, by way of the Middle East, to London. There he was practically ignored by a British government which, only the previous November, had won a general election on a pledge to defend his kingdom against the invader. The League was compelled to call off the sanctions it had imposed on Italy under Article 16 of the Covenant, and this on the initiative of the British Foreign Secretary, Anthony Eden, who had led the sanctions movement at Geneva.

The blow suffered by the League was instant and fatal. It departed from the struggle to maintain the peace, being ignored in the Czechoslovak and Polish crises of 1938 and 1939 respectively, which raised the curtain on the Second World War. It was convened, shamefacedly, in the winter of 1939-40 to condemn the

Union's attack on Finland, then awaited its formal demise 946. As the Abyssinian disaster drew to its close in the early months of 1936, the British government, on which the League's chief hopes rested, was canvassing support for a reform which would in effect shut down the League's machinery for collective security and create a series of regional arrangements for maintaining peace which the great Powers would manage, a return to the philosophy of spheres of interest which the League had been expressly formed to supplant.

How had this result come about? It did not seem, on the face of it, that resort to the League to frustrate Mussolini's adventure in Abyssinia was at all impracticable. Quite the contrary. Whatever the motives for Italy's act of aggression – the fascist dream of recreating the Roman Empire, which strangely captivated the Italian people, the Italian wish to atone for the shame of 1896, when Menelik II inflicted a crushing defeat on Italian forces at Addowa, Mussolini's deification of war, or more material considerations, such as the search for raw materials or the plan to build bridges between the divided Italian colonies of Eritrea and Somaliland – the Duce left no doubt in anyone's mind that his object was, if not to annex and colonise Abyssinia, at least to appropriate its non-Amharic fringe territories and then to form an Italian protectorate or mandate over the Amharic core. Talking to Sir John Simon, the British Foreign Secretary, on 3 May 1935, Count Grandi, the Italian ambassador to London, spoke of the situation in Abyssinia as 'a cancer which had to be cut out'; he conveyed 'in veiled though unmistakable terms that Senor Mussolini was contemplating a forward policy of the most serious dimensions'.[2] Mussolini himself on 21 May bluntly told the British ambassador to Rome, Sir Eric Drummond, that 'if, in order to clarify the situation and to obtain security, it was necessary for him to resort to arms, in short 'go to war', he would do so and he would send sufficient men to carry out his plan. That was his will'.[3] In June 1935, the Duce gave a quite undisguised account of his intentions to Eden, then Minister for League of Nations affairs, when the latter visited Rome with a proposal, which the Italian Dictator found thoroughly objectionable, for compensating the Emperor with a corridor from the port of Zeila in British Somaliland in return for the cession of part of Ogaden, which adjoined Italian Somaliland, to Italy. Mussolini told Eden that if he had to go to war to achieve his ends, 'his aim would be to wipe the name of Abyssinia from the map'.[4]

On 28 March of that year, Emilio de Bono had been made Commander-in-Chief of Italian forces in East Africa, with General Graziani in command in Somaliland. De Bono's instructions were to develop the Eritrean port of Massawa to make it ready for the receipt of an Italian army of 200,000 men (subsequently twice that number) and their supplies, which was undisguisedly built up throughout 1935 for the assault on Abyssinia in October. De Bono did not reveal until 1937, when his memoirs *Anno XIIII* were published, that Mussolini had personally compiled the 'Directions and Plan of Action for the solution of the Italo-Abyssinian question' as early as 20 December 1934, that is, two weeks after a serious clash of Italian and Abyssinian forces at Wal-Wal, where the border between Abyssinia and Italian Somaliland was unmarked.[5] But the massive build-up of Italian forces in East Africa made it clear that an invasion was in the offing.

Moreover, the infringement by Italy in October of the League Covenant, that is, the resort to war against Abyssinia (though no declaration of war was ever issued by either side) without complying with means of peaceful settlement was patent and unmistakable. The Japanese attack on Manchuria in September 1931, by contrast, was not a clear-cut case of aggression as defined in Article 16. Japan could, at least in the early stages of her action, be regarded as using force to defend leased territory and property, that is, the South Manchuria Railway, which she was fully entitled to do. Hitler's vastly more dangerous coup of 7 March 1936, when he remilitarised the Rhineland, was certainly a breach of treaty, or rather two treaties, and the League was fully entitled to take action (though it did not) since the Covenant enjoined respect for treaty obligations. The Locarno treaty of 1925, which embodied the demilitarisation of the Rhineland, also involved the League since signatories were obliged to refer alleged breaches of the agreement to the League Council. But there was no 'resort to war'; it is even arguable whether the Rhineland *coup* was an offence, except potentially, against the territorial integrity and political independence of another state. In any case, Germany was by this time time no longer a League member or bound by the Covenant. But Mussolini's action against Abyssinia was a massive and blatant armed attack on another League member, of precisely the kind that the Covenant was originally designed to protect the world against, accompanied by a barrage of argument, in the Italian media and at the League itself, that Abyssinia, though a League member, had no right to an independent existence owing to the inherent chaos in its administration, its lack of governmental unity, and its 'barbarism' symbolised by such practices as slavery and intermittent savagery against its own people. Italy, Mussolini told the world, had a 'civilising mission' in Abyssinia, and that justified his conquest of the country. It was a strange comment on that claim that Italian forces used all the resources of modern war in massive strength, including the aerial bombardment of undefended villages and resort to gas in violation of the Geneva Protocol of 1925 against a primitive and poorly armed people, denied weapons because of an embargo imposed by the great Powers. If the international community did not rouse itself to take action in the face of such a crime, what did the fine words of the League Covenant really amount to?

Moreover, Italy was, of all countries, most vulnerable to the sanctions the League Covenant provided. Even if military sanctions were ruled out at the outset (and there was never any suggestion that they should be applied), the idea of a blockade of Covenant-breaking states, which is the essence of Article 16, almost seems invented for the kind of country which Italy was when it embarked on the East African venture. The main complaint of Italian politicians about their country's place in the world was its lack of almost every important raw material; this was supposed to be one of the main reasons for the attack on Abyssinia, even though, once the conquest was complete and resistance ended, the Italians did nothing to develop the country's resources, or even to investigate whether they existed.[6] If the other League members really wished to excommunicate Italy from world trade and thus threaten its very existence, as they had a legal obligation to do under Article 16 of the Covenant, they were in an excellent position to do so.

It is true that some of Italy's most important trading partners were not League members. The United States never had been, Japan withdrew in 1933, and Germany on 21 October 1935, that is, two weeks after Italy's attack on Abyssinia began. United States exports to Italy expanded massively during the Italo-Abyssinian conflict, especially of oil. But Mr Roosevelt's efforts to control them, though much handicapped by a joint Congressional resolution of 23 August 1935 making mandatory an American embargo on the sale of arms to belligerents (Roosevelt wanted it to be discretionary), were robbed of effectiveness by the evident desire of the chief sanctionist states, notably Britain and France, to make a deal with Mussolini at the Emperor's expense, thus

rewarding the very aggression they were supposed to be taking
action against. As for Japan, she could not be of much direct help
in meeting Italy's economic requirements and the German
government had little wish to see Mussolini enjoy a brilliant
success in Africa. But even if the non-League states failed to play
any part in the sanctions movement, an effective system, operated
by the fifty-odd states involved in the League programme, could
have made Italy's task in Abyssinia vastly more difficult to
complete, and hence might well have imposed a limit on
Mussolini's plans.

On the other hand, it must, of course, be admitted that
sanctions undoubtedly had the effect of hardening the Italian
determination to press on with the campaign in Abyssinia in the
spirit of 'Italia contra mundum'; Mussolini's rhetoric, too, was
highly effective in strengthening the nation's morale. The original
founders of the League appeared to think that the reverse would
happen, that is, that if a country resorted to aggression and was
publicly condemned at Geneva, its people would side with the
League rather than with their own government. The Italians in
1935 and 1936 did not act like this. They donated their gold
ornaments to the war effort and suffered hardships, thus doing
something to offset the shortage of natural resources in their
country.

II

With these assets mostly working on its side, the League, or rather
the overwhelming majority of its member-states, went into action.
In the first phase of the dispute, that is, between the incident at
Wal-Wal on 5 December 1934, followed by others at Wardair and
Gerlogubi in January and February 1935, and the actual outbreak
of war on 3 October 1935, the League Council encouraged the two
states to settle their differences. By Article 5 of a treaty concluded
on 2 August 1928, Italy and Abyssinia were obliged to submit to
conciliation and arbitration disputes arising between them which
could not be settled by ordinary diplomatic means, but in no case
should they resort to force. Negotiations to settle the Wal-Wal
affair by such means, however, proved fruitless, while anxiety
grew in the Council that, if tensions between the two states
resulted in full-scale violence, members of the Council, especially
Britain and France, would be seriously affected.

Efforts to resolve the dispute were held up, firstly, by grandiose

226

Italian demands for amends to be made for their losses at Wal-Wal, such as a large monetary compensation, a letter of apology, and a salute to the Italian flag. These were in the end scaled down, but serious differences remained in the matter of the issues to be submitted to arbitration and the appointment of arbitrators. The Italians insisted that only responsibilities for the Wal-Wal incident should be investigated, whereas the Abyssinians wanted the whole question of the demarcation of the frontier, from which the incident arose, to be settled. On this issue, the Italians finally had their way. They made a concession, however, in the matter of procedure, the disagreement about this stemming from the Abyssinian wish that the two arbitrators whom they nominated should not be Abyssinians, on the ground that suitably qualified persons from their own country were not available. The Italians at first took exception to this, then relented and accordingly a Frenchman, M. A. de la Pradelle, and an American, Pitman Potter, took their places on the Abyssinian side, Count Aldrovandi-Mares Cotti and Signor Raffaele Montagna acting for Italy. Since these four could not agree either on the facts of the Wal-Wal affair or responsibilities for it, a fifth arbitrator, as provided for in the 1928 treaty, was appointed, the choice falling upon M. Politis, at that time the Greek Minister in Paris. Politis was called in on 29 August, his intervention proving decisive. With his assistance, the five arbitrators had, by 3 September, reached the unanimous agreement that the Wal-Wal affair was minor and accidental and that 'no international responsibility need be involved'.[7] It all seemed a wrangle over nothing, but, from the Italian point of view, something useful had been gained, and that was time. So long as the arguments about the Wal-Wal incident continued, the world's attention was focused on that, while Italian preparations for the major struggle continued.

The dispute over the Wal-Wal affair seemed to be satisfactorily resolved, but the breach between Italy and Abyssinia widened as the summer passed. Abyssinia professed to fear the growth in Italian military strength in East Africa, while bitterly complaining about the refusal of the great Powers to sell arms to herself, despite the existence of international agreements such as an Anglo-Abyssinian treaty signed in 1930 to do so. In September, the rainy season would come to an end and the door would be open for military operations. The League Council met in extraordinary session on 31 July at the request of the French Prime Minister, Pierre Laval, who was also Foreign Minister, then adjourned to 3

August in order that Britain and France should have an opportunity to find terms of settlement. The two disputing parties were at the same time asked to reach an agreement to bridge their differences and invited to report back to the Council on the progress they had made, if any, by 4 September. When the date of that meeting arrived and no progress had been made in either set of negotiations, Eden reported on the failure of the meetings between himself, Laval and Baron Aloisi, the Italian representative in Geneva, from 16 to 19 August in Paris to try to find a basis of discussion which might admit of a solution. Mussolini was not satisfied by the economic concessions in Abyssinia which Britain and France proposed: he insisted on having military garrisons in the country.[8] No Abyssinian spokesman participated in these talks, the argument being that Britain, France and Italy, though not Abyssinia, were parties to a tripartite agreement concluded on 13 December 1906 which provided for co-operation between them in maintaining the political and territorial *status quo* in Abyssinia.[9]

At these talks, Eden found himself taking the Abyssinian side, without much support from Laval. He agreed with the Italian argument that Abyssinia stood in need of reform, but insisted that any reform must be freely agreed to and not imposed. Aloisi, who could not agree with this, vehemently denounced Abyssinia's violation of all the conventional undertakings it had assumed both towards the League, when it joined that organisation, on Italy's initiative and in the face of British objections, in 1923, and towards Italy. 'Italy', Aloisi said, 'could no longer persist in an attitude of toleration with regard to a barbarous State incapable of controlling the populations subject to it, which populations were powerfully armed and threatened Italian frontiers'. He added that 'it would be wanting in Italy's dignity as a civilised nation if she continued to discuss within the League on a footing of equality with Ethiopia'. 'His Government would be lacking in its most elementary duty', Aloisi concluded, 'if it did not withdraw its confidence from Ethiopia and reserve to itself full liberty of action for the security of its colonies and its own interests'.

What was the Council to do, seeing that M. Jeze, speaking for Abyssinia, insisted that it must act under Article 15, that is to say, place the dispute on its agenda and take immediate steps to prevent the war that was impending? The most obvious step was to create a committee to examine the whole range of Italo-Abyssinian relations with a view to suggesting a peaceful solution. Britain and France were two inevitable members, though Italy objected since the two countries had had their chance to find a peaceful solution and had failed. Poland, Spain and Turkey then agreed, with some reluctance, to join them to make a group of five, with Salvador de Madariaga, the veteran League figure from Spain, acting as chairman. The committee's starting point was to draw up a scheme of international assistance for the improvement of economic, financial and political conditions in Abyssinia. Britain and France stated their willingness to make sacrifices at the expense of their own colonies in East Africa in order to facilitate territorial adjustments between Abyssinia and Italy; in other words, they would consider providing Abyssinia with access to the sea, if Abyssinia would do something to satisfy such Italian grievances as the insecurity of its borders with Abyssinia and the lack of connection, except by sea, between Eritrea and Somaliland. On 21 September, the Italian Council of Ministers rejected the committee's proposals since they did not provide a minimum basis for definite results which would finally and effectively define the rights and vital interests of Italy. At the same time, the Italian press adopted a warmer tone towards Britain, perhaps in order to encourage the Council of Five to make more generous proposals, which Abyssinia might reject and hence alienate world opinion against her.[10] On the following day the Abyssinian delegate indicated his willingness to open negotiations on the basis of the recommendations of the Committee of Five.[11]

By this time resistance to Italian demands had been immensely strengthened by the 'revivalist appeal', as he himself called it, issued by Sir Samuel Hoare, who had become Foreign Secretary on 6 June in succession to Sir John Simon, at the Sixteenth ordinary session of the League Assembly in Geneva on 11 September. During the summer, a totally unexpected surge of public opinion in Britain in favour of the League had taken the National Government under Ramsay MacDonald and, after 10 June, Stanley Baldwin, by surprise. The Press, the churches, and almost all varieties of opinion except for Right-wing Conservatives were almost unanimous in calling for action in restraint of an Italian attack on Abyssinia. Among Conservatives, Sir Austen Chamberlain was a strong advocate of sanctions against Italy. In a conversation with Hoare on 20 August, Chamberlain said that 'provided the action was collective and that we and the French were keeping in step, economic sanctions of some kind were inevitable'. 'British public opinion', he considered, 'would not be satisfied by a policy of inaction or despair'.[12] Public opinion was revealed in the so-called Peace Ballot, or, to give it its proper name, the National Declaration, organised by the League of Nations Union at the end of June, in which 11½ million people in Britain were asked their opinion on the continuance of British membership of the League, on disarmament and on economic and military sanctions against aggressor nations. The Ballot showed overwhelming support for collective security, 10 millions voting for economic sanctions, with only 635,000 against, and as many as 6,784,000 for military sanctions with only 2,351,000 against, though the identity of those who were expected to take forcible action was never made clear.[13]

The questions asked in the Peace Ballot were oversimplified; an obvious inconsistency existed between the apparent support for tough action in defence of the Covenant and the pacifist mood generally prevalent in the country. Nevertheless, the Cabinet had no option, since this was evidently what the electorate wanted, but to throw its weight, on certain conditions, behind the League's sanctions system, despite the scepticism of almost all its members. Unfortunately, the opportunity was not seized with sufficient vigour to remind the voter that standing up to the aggressor, if that was what he wanted, required strength and hence support for the rearmament measures the Cabinet now felt to be increasingly urgent. This, after all, was the year in which Hitler announced in the Reichstag on 21 March his denunciation of the military clauses of the Versailles Treaty and set Germany back on the road to war. It was allegedly in order to control German rearmament that one of Sir Samuel Hoare's first acts on becoming Foreign Secretary was to sign an agreement with Germany allowing her to build up to 35 per cent of the total naval strength of the British Commonwealth of Nations.[14] The French, not being consulted, were naturally shocked; they noted with dismay that the treaty was signed on 18 June, the anniversary of the battle of Waterloo.

Such was the background to Hoare's warmly applauded speech to the Assembly on 11 September, which put Britain in the forefront of League resistance to Mussolini's campaign against Abyssinia, now widely thought to be only a few days' distance from its shooting phase. The speech contained the electrifying words that 'in conformity with its precise and explicit obligations, the League stands, and my country stands with it, for the collective maintenance of the Covenant in its entirety, and particularly for steady and collective resistance to all acts of unprovoked aggression'. The Foreign Secretary was surprised, not to say taken aback, by the tumultuous applause which greeted his words. Had delegates not heard him aright? Had he not stressed that maintenance of the Covenant must be collective, meaning that Britain could only go as far in defending peace that other states were willing to go, and that the Covenant must be protected in its entirety, including no doubt Article 19, always dear to British hearts, which provided for peaceful revision of the *status quo*? As though to make the point quite clear, Hoare spelled it out:

> One thing is certain. If the burden is to be borne, it must be borne collectively. If risks for peace are to be run, they must be run by all. The security of the many cannot be ensured solely by the efforts of the few, however powerful they may be.

Furthermore, the Foreign Secretary's speech contained explicit hints that Abyssinia must expect to undergo reform – if necessary with League assistance – if it looked to the League to help it against aggression. 'We believe', he said, that 'backward nations' – words possible only in the European-dominated era of the League – 'are, without prejudice to their independence and integrity, entitled to expect that assistance will be afforded to them by more advanced peoples' – again, the notion of European tutelage – 'in the development of their resources and the building up of their national life'.[15] Could the shadowy outlines of the Hoare-Laval plan for Abyssinia, concocted in Paris four months later, be discerned in those words, even at this early stage of the game? Sir Samuel went as far as making a gesture to the Italian argument in favour of greater international justice by referring to the need for a new share-out of the world's natural resources.

Hoare's speech was followed two days later by one by Laval in somewhat similar terms.[16] Privately, however, British and French perceptions of the crisis widened alarmingly. Hoare, conscious of the implications of the dispute for the far more serious German challenge to the *status quo*, feared that, if the League failed in this test case, British people would conclude that it was certain to fail in the German case and accordingly would withdraw from Europe into isolation. Laval, equally conscious of the interconnectedness of the two situations, feared that too much talk about sanctions in Geneva would have the effect of driving Mussolini into Hitler's arms. 'There ought to be no provocative talk of sanctions and no wounding of Italian feelings', he told Hoare, though how the League could take measures against an Italian act of aggression in

Abyssinia without hurting Italian feelings, Laval did not explain: the League was supposed to roar like a sucking dove.[17] 'Mussolini ought to be made to feel economic pressure', Laval said, 'but not to have the knife presented to his throat'.[18] This applied, presumably, even when he was presenting his own knife to other people's throats.

Nevertheless, when de Bono went into action in north-eastern Abyssinia on 3 October, Italy's defiance of the Covenant was so blatant that none but states bound to that country by hoops of steel could fail to stand up and be counted on the side of the collective system. Fourteen members of the League Council (that is, all its members except Italy) decided at its meeting on 7 October to adopt the report of a committee, appointed on 5 October to study the situation, to the effect that Italy had resorted to war in disregard of its obligations under Article 12 of the Covenant, which provided for the peaceful settlement of international disputes. The Council's President, M. Ruiz Guinazu, explained that, in accordance with an Assembly resolution of 4 October 1921, this meant that fulfilment of their duties under Article 16 was now required of League member-states, that is, that they were obliged to impose sanctions.[19] It was the only time in the League's history that Article 16 was ever invoked. The question then came before the fourteenth Plenary Meeting of the Sixteenth Session of the Assembly on 9 October, the Council's minutes of 7 October having been forwarded to it; this meeting endorsed the Council's findings. Baron Aloisi, speaking in the Assembly on 10 October, denied that Abyssinia, 'a country which has no Government capable of exercising its authority throughout its territory, whose frontiers are not delimited, which not merely fails to mete out equitable treatment to conquered peoples, but exploits them, subjects them to slavery and destroys them', was entitled to the benefits of the sanctions clauses of the Covenant. He asked why sanctions had not been mentioned in the recent conflict between Bolivia and Paraguay, and brushed aside the invocation of the Briand-Kellogg Pact for the renunciation of war of 1928 since the pact permitted war in self-defence, and it was precisely self-defence that Italy was practising in Abyssinia.

There were few sympathisers with Aloisi among Assembly delegates.[20] Pflügel, representing Austria, drew attention to the 'serious dangers which sanctions will inevitably entail in the economic life of Europe, in particular for those smaller states whose capacity for economic and financial resistance has been considerably reduced by the unfavourable conditions imposed upon them'. Pflügel did not need to mention, since it was obvious, that Austria's very existence as an independent country rested upon Italian protection. The crisis in 1934, when Italy successfully warned the new Nazi regime in Germany against interference in Austria was sufficient demonstration of that; when that protection was withdrawn in 1938, partly as a result of Mussolini's having become an ally of Hitler, for which League sanctions against Italy in 1935-36 bore some responsibility, Austria was swallowed up into the German maw. Hungary, too, through the mouth of its delegate, Lázló de Velics, stood aside from the sanctions movement. So did the Albanian Frasheri, who could not endorse Assembly decisions on the subject 'due to treaty relations with Italy and economic relations'. Uruguay and Ecuador stated their reservations. Motta, speaking for Switzerland, exempted his country from participating in sanctions as exposing Swiss neutrality to 'real dangers'; it was these, M. Motta explained, 'which we must judge in the full exercise of our sovereignty'.

Otherwise, the sanctions front stood firm, though a unanimous vote was not necessary since Article 16 placed the obligation on all member-states directly and individually to subject Covenant-breaking countries to the severance of all trade and financial relations, to prohibit all intercourse between their own nationals and those of the offending state, and to prevent all financial, commercial and personal intercourse between the guilty state and the rest of the world. Potemkine, for Soviet Russia, struck a Marxist note in claiming that 'unity of action' would constitute the 'most effective means of settling a conflict which has its source in a desire for colonial expansion'. Anthony Eden, relishing his day of triumph, reiterated that the foreign policy of his government remained 'firmly based upon its membership of the League of Nations because we believe it is only by upholding this organisation that peace can be maintained'. Even Pierre Laval, though with lack of conviction, promised that his country would observe the Covenant; 'the Covenant is our international law and we can neither infringe it nor allow it to be weakened', he said. As the Assembly President, the Czech Beneš, explained, no League organ could bind member-states by declaring that one of them had violated the Covenant; members must respect the Covenant by reason of their general respect for treaties and must carry out obligations deriving directly from the Covenant without waiting for directions from League bodies. Nevertheless, fifty states, out of the fifty-four present in the Assembly on that day, did agree with the Council that Italy was in default in resorting to war in Abyssinia in violation of Article 12 of the Covenant. The sanctions they were then obliged to apply were automatic. However, they would need to be co-ordinated: this was to be done through the creation of a co-ordination committee, which began work on 11 October, each member-state having the right of representation on it. The committee worked through a smaller Committee of Eighteen, which in its turn operated with the help of panels of experts for dealing with the different sanctions measures.

The Co-ordination Committee, chaired by the Portuguese Vasconcellos, divided its programme into five parts, dealing respectively with an embargo on the export of arms and ammunition to Italy, the withholding of loans and credits, the prohibition of the import of goods from Italy, a ban on the export of certain key products to that country, and the organisation of mutual support among the sanctionist states so as to equalise as far as possible the burden of loss and inconvenience caused by the operation. By 31 October, fifty governments signified their intention to bring the first of these proposals into effect, forty-nine intended to apply the second, forty-eight the third and fourth, and thirty-eight the fifth. It was decided that 18 November should be the starting date for the sanctions system.[21]

The question then arose of the extension of the system to countries not members of the League. On 21 October the Co-ordination Committee forwarded the five proposals to Saudi Arabia, Brazil, Costa Rica, Egypt, Germany, Iceland, Japan, Liechtenstein, Monaco and the United States, none of which were League members. By the end of the month, replies had been received only from Egypt and the United States. The former telegraphed its agreement to accede in principle to the proposed economic and financial measures and to carry out as far as possible decisions of the League which covered those headings. The American reply, sent on 26 October, was favourable to the League's peace efforts, despite the neutrality legislation in force in the United States.[22] The most that President Roosevelt could do was to issue moral appeals to American oil producers not to help Mussolini with his war in Abyssinia. The United States supplied only a small proportion of Italy's oil requirements – 6.4 per cent in 1934, although this was increased to 12.5 per cent in the following year. 186.3 thousand metric tons of oil were exported to Italy from the United States in 1934, compared with 476.8 thousand metric tons in 1935.

Another question concerned the extension of the list of exports from sanctionist states to be embargoed to Italy. On 2 November, the Canadian delegate to the Committee of Eighteen, W.A. Riddell, proposed extending the list so as to include petroleum and its derivatives, coal, iron, cast iron and steel.[23] This was agreed to and governments taking part in the League sanctions system were asked for their opinions. It was common knowledge that the Italian authorities had issued repeated warnings that any such extension would be regarded as an act of war and none could be sure to what extent, if any, this was bluff. Laval took the Italian warnings seriously, or at least pretended to do so. So did the British, whose naval strength in the Mediterranèan had to be increased even before the war started. Britain bombarded the French authorities with requests to know what assistance she could expect from France if Italy retaliated against British naval vessels and even launched bombers against London, if and when the scope of sanctions was enlarged. Laval told Clerk on 15 October that France would only give assurances of help if British naval strength in the Mediterranean was reduced to normal.[24]

Eventually, on 18 October, French Ministers confirmed to Clerk that, in the event of an Italian attack on Britain resulting from the international action taken by Britain within the League of Nations, French support of Britain was 'assured fully and in advance'. But this assurance was given on the assumptions (a) that the Suez Canal could not and would not be closed and (b) that British battleships recently sent to Gibraltar would be withdrawn if Italian forces in Libya were reduced to approximate parity with British forces in Egypt. This undertaking, according to Vansittart, the Permanent Under-Secretary at the Foreign Office, was prised out of the French by 'forceps and biceps'.[25] Greece, Turkey and Yugoslavia were similarly pressed by London for undertakings to keep their ports and fuelling stations open to British shipping if trouble broke out. Czechoslovakia and Rumania were asked to give all the help they could. Nerves were strained as the pressure to apply oil sanctions grew in strength.

But it could easily be halted. Oil and other embargoed exports to Italy on the extended list were to have been discussed in the Co-ordination Committee on 29 November, but the discussion was deferred, with discouraging effects on the American government. Then the Committee of Eighteen took up the question at its meeting on 18 December, intending to reach a definite decision about oil in the light of an expert report on how the existing sanctions were working. But the Committee adjourned without reaching any conclusion about oil. Instead, the oil question was referred to yet another expert committee, and this was invited to consider, not the whole question of the advisability of an oil sanction, but merely the extent to which an embargo on oil might affect Italy's ability to cover the whole or the greater part of its oil requirements. The experts' report was delivered on 12 February 1936, by which time Italian forces in Abyssinia were achieving notable successes; the Emperor sustained severe reverses in fighting in Tigré, the Italians winning an overwhelming victory, mainly due to superior fire power, in the battle of Amba Aradam between 10 and 19 February. Abyssinian forces continued to fall back in March.

The experts concluded that Italy probably had enough reserves of oil for the next three or three-and-a-half months, in which time her forces stood a good chance of administering the *coup de grâce* to the Emperor. If the United States limited its oil exports to Italy to their pre-war level, the experts considered that sanctions would in all likelihood be effective. If no limits were placed on American supplies, oil sanctions imposed by League member-states (Rumania alone supplied Italy with 40 per cent of her needs) would probably make gas and oil more difficult and expensive for Italy to obtain, but nothing more than that could be assured. As a further measure, the sanctionist states might withhold the means of transporting oil to Italy, in which case she would face far greater expense in paying for the 50 per cent of chartered vessels she needed over and above her own capacity.[26] A Foreign Office paper circulated on 27 November had estimated that an oil embargo applied by Rumania, Soviet Russia, Iran (that is, the Anglo-Iranian oil company) and the Netherlands would deprive Italy of 85 per cent of her oil supplies and hamper her war effort in East Africa. The experts' report was due to be discussed by the Committee of Eighteen on 2 March.

Eden, at a session of the Cabinet held on 26 February, was authorised to vote in favour of the oil sanction at the meeting on 2 March.[27] Flandin, Laval's successor as French Foreign Minister in the new government formed by Albert Sarraut on 19 February, like Laval, regarded the oil embargo as dangerous and likely to be ineffective. He persuaded Eden to suspend a decision on oil at the meeting of the Committee of Eighteen on 2 March for twenty-eight hours. The purpose of this delay was to give an opportunity for the Committee of Eighteen, consisting of the League Council without the two disputing states, to cable the armies in Abyssinia with a plea for a ceasefire and prompt agreement to peace negotiations. Flandin's proposal was that the Committee of Eighteen would then adopt the oil sanction if there was no response to this appeal. To everyone's surprise, Eden then dropped out of line with the French by asserting that the appeal for peace need cause 'no undue delay' in the application of the oil sanction, in other words that it be proceeded with at once. On 5 March, Haile Selassie agreed in principle to opening negotiations with Italy. Two days later the Italian government made known their refusal to begin negotiations under threat of the oil sanction. That day, 7 March, however, was momentous in that it was the day on which Nazi Germany, after dropping hints for several weeks that it intended to remilitarise the Rhineland, at last did so. Hitler marked the occasion by a speech in the Reichstag offering a package of new proposals, including a promise to return to the League of Nations, outwardly intended to signify a new beginning in his relations with the democracies, but inwardly aimed at lulling them into acceptance of his Rhineland *coup* and damping down their fears of war.

The effects of Hitler's action in the Rhineland on the Abyssinian crisis were dramatic. They were also highly detrimental to the crisis being settled on any terms remotely favourable to the weaker party, that is, the Abyssinians. Mussolini's first reaction was to consider that Hitler had betrayed him by destroying the Locarno agreements of 1925 which reaffirmed the demilitarisation of the Rhineland by the Treaty of Versailles, and of Locarno, of course, Italy was a joint guarantor with Britain. This certainly did not reduce the Duce's determination successfully to wind up his military operations in East Africa. On France, the impact of Hitler's Rhineland *coup* was disastrous, causing Flandin to demand of Britain the same united action against a breach of international law which Britain had called for from France, though largely in vain, in the matter of the Italian invasion of Abyssinia. For Britain, Hitler's stroke in the Rhineland stimulated Cabinet Ministers and their parliamentary supporters who wanted British commitments in Abyssinia to be quickly liquidated so that their hands could be free to deal with the growing threat from Germany. Even Churchill, a strong defender of the League, had no desire to falter in support of France, even if it meant giving second place to Abyssinia's predicament. Like

France, Churchill chiefly regarded the League as an instrument for dealing with Germany. It was brutally clear that Italy had now been driven out of the group of nations which realised that the chief threat came from across the Rhine and wanted to do something about it. More pressure against Italy, such as the oil sanction, whether effective or not, must have the effect of destroying all possibility of Italy remaining an ally against Germany, even if it did not succeed in finally driving her into Germany's arms.

III

By this time, however, the League programme of action against Italian aggression in Abyssinia had come under threat from quite a different quarter, one which finally robbed it of all credibility. The fact that the Italian assault against Abyssinia in October 1935 had been preceded by ten months or more of conflict between the two countries, in which not a little blood was shed in the borderlands between the Emperor's domains and Italian Somaliland, meant that the League, and the two disputing states themselves, were preoccupied with efforts to reach a settlement on acceptable terms long before actual fighting began. In the crisis in Manchuria in September 1931, on the other hand, the attacks by Japanese troops on Manchurian towns and settlements came out of the blue. The League's task was therefore to stop the fighting and secure a withdrawal of Japanese forces first of all, and then explore the prospects for a lasting settlement. By contrast, the outlines of a settlement of the Italo-Abyssinian conflict began to emerge while Italian offensive power was still in preparation in East Africa. They ranged from frontier adjustments in Italy's favour, perhaps in exchange for Abyssinia being given access to the sea at British Zeila or Italian Assab, to schemes of international assistance to the Emperor's kingdom with the help of external advisers, who might include Italians in various proportions with other foreigners, or, as the spectrum of possibilities moved towards more Italian desiderata, an Italian protectorate or mandate giving that country some kind of economic preponderance or privileged status over all, or a substantial part, of the state in question. As we have seen, some such scheme was considered by the Committee of Five appointed by the League Council in September 1935 to try to find some basis for a settlement. Throughout the summer of 1935 various formulae for satisfying Italian grievances while preserving Abyssinian sovereignty and as much of Abyssinia's territorial integrity as possible were argued over by Britain, France and Italy within the framework of their agreement of 1906. These efforts came to nothing because Italy wanted more in the way of control of Abyssinia than that country's leaders were ready to concede. Italians, too, wanted less of a League presence in any ultimate settlement than Britain, or, to a less extent, France.

With the outbreak of war in October and the imposition of League sanctions in November, it became imperative to force the pace of efforts to find a solution to the deadlock. Laval, speaking in the Co-ordination Committee on 2 November, said that, besides agreeing on the sanctions programme, there was another duty to fulfil, namely 'to seek as speedily as possible for an amicable settlement of the dispute.'[28] Sir Samuel Hoare elevated this double approach into something resembling a distinct diplomatic philosophy, which he called 'the double line' in other words, the restraint of lawlessness going hand-in-hand with redressing the lawbreaker's grievances.[29] Hoare told the Committee on 18 November that 'on the one hand, as loyal members of the League, we feel it our bounden duty to carry out our obligations and to undertake the duty imposed upon us by the Covenant. On the other hand, we are under a no less insistent obligation to strive for a speedy and honourable settlement of the controversy'.[30] He let it be known that during the previous few days conversations had been taking place between Rome, Paris and London on the possibilities of a settlement. Abyssinia was not a participant, but the Foreign Secretary assured the Committee that nothing was further from the minds of the three states than 'to make and conclude an agreement behind the backs of the League'.

Other members of the Co-ordination Committee were not shocked by these disclosures, as they were shocked a month later by the Hoare-Laval agreement to which the three-cornered conversations finally led. After all, sanctions were costly, not to say dangerous: the mutual support provided for in Article 16 (3) of the Covenant and intended to minimise losses resulting from sanctions was not much compensation for the sacrifices that had to be made, especially for countries struggling to recover from the contraction of world trade in the early 1930s. Moreover, the risks of sanctions leading to armed action by Italy could never be ruled out. Italian national prestige, as well as that of the fascist regime, was heavily engaged in the East African enterprise; Mussolini himself was considered by many to be so irrational that a 'mad dog' act on his part, if driven into a corner, could not be excluded.

It was not therefore surprising that the Belgian Prime Minister, Van Zeeland, should have asked at the Co-ordination Committee on 18 November: 'since the responsible leaders of two great countries' – that is, Britain and France – 'have already devoted a large part of their time and their talents to this task, why should the League not entrust to them the mission of seeking under its auspices and control and in the spirit of the Covenant, the elements of a solution which the three parties at issue – the League, Italy and Ethiopia – might find it possible to accept?'.[31] The answer, of course, though no-one gave it, was that two of those parties, namely the League and Abyssinia, might, and in all likelihood would, have no difficulty in seeking a solution 'under the League's auspices and control and in the spirit of the Covenant', but Italy had made clear time and again, and would no doubt continue to do, that she wanted a solution to be sought between the parties and without League intervention. The ostensible reason for this was that, in the Italian view, Abyssinia was not fit to be a League member or entitled to enjoy the rights of League membership and the protection those rights afforded. The real reason, it could not be doubted, was that the Italian government aimed at the ending of Abyssinia's independence, if necessary by force, and such action it was the whole purpose of the League to prevent. Nevertheless, Van Zeeland's proposal found a ready acceptance in the Committee, chairman Vasconcellos observing that 'certain suggestions have been made that the great workers in the cause of peace should continue their action within the framework of the League'. It was the Committee's duty, he said, 'to take note of these suggestions in the certainty that the League itself will encourage these countries in their activities'.[32]

Britain and France, however, failed in their efforts to devise a settlement. The Council therefore decided to sit as a Committee of Thirteen – that is, the entire Council less the disputing states – and this body should try its hand with the same object in view. Then came the turn of the Committee of Five, as already explained. But Britain and France remained in the forefront of these endeavours. Laval pressed for a mandate for Abyssinia to be awarded to Italy, while Britain vehemently rejected any such idea, yet was uneasily conscious of her pleas to France for assistance if the Italians retaliated in the Mediterranean. At the end of October, when the war was in progress, Maurice Peterson, who had been in charge since 3 September of a newly created department in the Foreign Office dealing exclusively with Abyssinian affairs, was sent to Paris to help the Ambassador there, Sir George Clerk, ascertain French views on Italian offers, if any, for a settlement. Peterson's attitude towards the League was summed up by his statement that he 'detested Geneva, where the lack of realism was even more marked than in any House of Commons debate'.[33] Clerk had written to Hoare on 24 October that the French Prime Minister agreed that Peterson and his French opposite number, St Quentin, should get to work at once and 'see how far they can rearrange the map of Abyssinia'.[34]

Laval, according to Peterson, talked every day on the telephone with Mussolini, and then tried to squeeze the British team into swallowing more and more of the Italian conception of a settlement, especially the idea of an Italian mandate for Abyssinia.[35] The fact that Italy, though one of the leading Allied powers in the First World War, had not been invited to accept a former German or Turkish dependency when the mandates were distributed in 1920 particularly irked the Italians. Perhaps Abyssinia would do instead. The British authorities, fortified by a general election held on 14 November, which was largely fought on the issue of defence of the League Covenant, and which, while reducing the government's majority, still left them with a massive lead over their Labour and Liberal opponents, continued to resist.[36] At the end of November, the Foreign Office accepted in principle a package of proposals which Peterson was instructed to stand by in Paris. These included a League plan of assistance for Abyssinia, an exchange of the districts of Adowa, Denakil and most of Ogaden against a port on the Gulf of Aden and a corridor joining it with Abyssinia, and British support for Italy receiving 'the fullest possible facilities for economic development in such areas of southern Abyssinia as may be suitable'. In these areas, however, Abyssinian sovereignty would not be affected. It implied 'the creation of a special sphere for Italian economic development and colonisation' under League of Nations supervision.[37]

It was already common knowledge that Italy would find such proposals as these unacceptable, as Ambassador Grandi told Vansittart in a conversation in London on 5 December.[38] Italian forces were at that time poised in massive strength to complete their conquest of a country with which the government in Rome could then do as it wished. Oil sanctions could not prevent that happening, Mussolini told Sir Eric Drummond on 7 December, since Italy felt 'fairly safe' even if the oil embargo were imposed; sufficient precautions had been taken in time.[39] In any case, oil sanctions, the Italian Under-Secretary of State for the Interior let it be known, would cause Italy to go to war.[40] The British and French governments, as they deferred debate on the oil sanction week after week until the moment to impose it had passed, would evidently do anything rather than face that prospect. In the British case this fear concerning oil sanctions was strengthened by arguments from the Naval Chiefs of Staff that a strong Italian attack on the British Mediterranean Fleet would cripple it as a source of reinforcement – in terms of ships – for the Far Eastern Fleet.

Laval confronted Hoare with the dangers of war when they met in Paris on 7 December, when the British Foreign Secretary was on his way to Switzerland for a holiday after his heavy labours piloting the Government of India Bill through the Commons before going to the Foreign Office in June.[41] He later confessed that he was 'pulled down' by poor health, and this may explain his submission in Paris to Laval's pressure to accept the well-known plan for the virtual partition of Abyssinia which has since borne the names of the two men. The plan consisted of three parts: (1) an outlet to the sea at Zeila for Abyssinia with a corridor joining the port with the latter country, though Abyssinia would not be allowed to construct a railway through the corridor in order to safeguard French interests in Djibuti and the Franco-Abyssinian railway; the Abyssinian acquisition would be, as *The Times* described it, 'a corridor for camels'; (2) in exchange, part of Tigré and territory in the east and south-east of Abyssinia would be assigned to Italy; (3) a large zone in the south and south-west would be recognised as an Italian monopoly in respect of economic development under League of Nations supervision, though still under the Emperor's sovereignty.[42] The effect of the Hoare-Laval plan would be that, directly or indirectly, Abyssinia would lose somewhat more than one half of its territory as it stood before the Italian invasion. Hoare and Laval agreed at their Paris meeting, which at France's request was extended to include Sunday, 8 December, that Mussolini would be told of the plan first, and that afterwards, on 10 December, Haile Selassie would be informed, but only that Britain and France were seeking a solution by conciliation based on principles determined by the Committee of Five in September and already accepted by Abyssinia.[43] This, if not precisely a lie, was plainly intended to deceive the Emperor. Laval was brutal enough to tell Vansittart (who also attended the Paris meetings) that, if Haile Selassie rejected the plan, the oil sanction must be dropped.[44] It had never, of course, been applied, and never would be.

The sequel to the story is well known; how the Hoare-Laval plan was leaked to the French press and published by the journalist Madame Tabouis in Paris newspapers on 9 December, almost in full; how a storm of amazement and disapproval swept Britain – the Cabinet were told that opinion in the City regarded it as 'the most miserable document that has ever disgraced the signature of a British statesman';[45] how Geneva and the different League bodies involved in the dispute were thunderstruck; how the British Government, at their meeting on 9 December, at first approved the proposals, then, in view of the outcry, disowned them, forcing Hoare, now in a hospital bed after breaking his nose ice-skating in Switzerland, to resign and extinguishing all interest in the plan in Rome, where initial reactions had been favourable; and how Anthony Eden, now thirty-eight years old, sprang into Hoare's chair at the Foreign Office on 22 December, accepting the grudging invitation of Prime Minister Baldwin, who told him 'it looks as if it will have to be you', and set about picking up the pieces.[46]

The consequences of the Hoare-Laval plan for the sanctions front were unsurprisingly disastrous, though the plan itself had far more to be said for it than the cries of protest suggested. After all, the League's Committee of Five had openly been working on a scheme, which Haile Selassie had accepted in principle and which would in any case have much diminished Abyssinia's existence as an independent country; the Hoare-Laval proposals did not do much more than carry this process further. The League Council had itself blessed Anglo-French efforts to find a solution, and it was not to be supposed, in view of Italy's military position when 1936 began, that one could be found satisfactory to the two sides which did not involve some drastic reduction of Abyssinia's size and of its freedom to run its own affairs. Had the plan been quietly accepted by the parties and the League, the Emperor would at least have retained the Amharic core of his country: the failure of the Hoare-Laval plan meant that he lost all of it, though how long he could have held on to the core must remain a matter of speculation. Above all, the military odds in Abyssinia were entirely on Italy's side. By the end of March, the Emperor had lost

the decisive battle of Mai Chio, which led to the wholesale retreat
of his forces. On 4 May, Badoglio reached Addis Ababa and on the
same day the Emperor embarked on HMS *Enterprise* at Djibuti.
Five days later Badoglio was shaking hands with Graziani, the
Italian victor in the south, at Diredawa. Neville Chamberlain, the
British Chancellor of the Exchequer, wrote on 2 May that he was
'sure the time had not come for the League to own itself beaten'.
'All the same', he went on, 'it is beaten'.[47]

The fact is that the British and French Governments never had
any intention of using force against Italy to stop its advance in
Abyssinia, or even of closing the Suez Canal, which would have
locked Italian forces in East Africa in a trap. Nor had any other
country, though all were ready to cheer Britain and France on
from the side-lines, had they gone into action. Laval even regarded
an oil embargo as a form of military sanction since he considered
that it would have military consequences, and he opposed it for
that reason. It was equally evident that, for his part, Mussolini did
not intend to be prevented from conquering his victim by anything
short of superior force. The conquest of Abyssinia was too
important in his foreign policy; he had invested too much money,
too much of his own political future, in it. At the end of 1935, that
conquest did not look as though it would take anything like the two
or three years which most foreign military experts thought it
would. In these circumstances, what course remained for the chief
League Powers except to try to reach a compromise settlement
which might at least keep some part of Abyssinia outside the new
Roman Empire? The brutality and cynicism, the blatant
deception, of the Hoare-Laval proposals might be deplored, but
their logic was less easily condemned.

The rest of the Abyssinian story is little more than a tail-piece to
the Hoare-Laval débâcle. The Anglo-French plan, regardless of
how much common sense there was in it, struck the heart out of
the sanctions enterprise. Whereas, the day before the plan was out
in the open, the smaller countries in the League – states like
Czechoslovakia, Rumania, Yugoslavia – could feel that, after all,
there might be some safety for them under the League umbrella,
which Britain and France were bravely holding over their heads,
the news that these two erstwhile League champions had been
plotting for months to carve up the victim's body and reward its
attacker with substantial parts of it dealt the campaign for
collective action a mortal blow. When the next assault on the
international order came – and it came, almost as a consequence of

the Abyssinian crisis, in the form of Germany's armed entrance into the demilitarised Rhineland on 7 March – it was clear that survival for a small country must lie, not in Geneva, but in neutrality or some other form of isolation, or in coming to terms with the big bullies now roaming the streets. After all, the Hoare-Laval plan had shown that the bully's methods paid off, at least in the short run.

With the disappearance of Laval from the French scene in January 1936 and his replacement as Foreign Minister by Pierre-Etienne Flandin on the 27th, Albert Sarraut being the new Prime Minister, it might have been expected that the French bias against sanctions and in favour of the kind of terms which might buy off Mussolini would decline. But this did not happen. Internal politics continued to dominate French diplomacy. The French people did not want a quarrel with Italy and would not support any government which pursued one; in so far as the League meant anything to them, it was a weapon for using against Hitler's Germany. The new Germany, with its burning fanaticism, was the real threat, and who could disagree with that? Lloyd Thomas, the British Minister in Paris, had written home as early as 7 October, when the Italian attack on Abyssinia was no more than a few days old, that Laval's opinion was that 'the French would fight for France, they would fight for the frontiers of Belgium and he thought they would probably fight for England, but otherwise they would never fight outside France and in his personal opinion they would not ... even incur the risk of war for Austria or Czechoslovakia, much less for Russia'.[48] As later history showed, even that was an optimistic statement about the French appetite for fighting. However, Flandin was bound to take account of the same political realities, to drag his feet over the oil sanction and steer clear of any action likely to weaken the links with Rome. Against his repeated warnings of the dangers of adopting the oil measures, Eden struggled to keep interest in them alive. On 4 March, the British Foreign Secretary was forced into the pathetic justification of the oil sanction that, if it were applied, 'it will be less applied by reason of its probable effectiveness than as a means of demonstrating the determination of Members of the League to persist in the policy upon which they have embarked.'[49] It was another way of saying that they meant to press on with sanctions because they had made up their minds to do so.

Then came Hitler's Rhineland *coup* and the diversion of the world's attention from Africa to Europe. The French asked, with embarrassing logic, why Britain was far less enthusiastic about sanctions against Germany than against Italy. The Abyssinian affair became for many a tiresome irrelevance. British Admirals grew restive about their battleships standing on guard against a 'mad dog' act by Mussolini in the Mediterranean when the only reason he could have for mounting one was his desire to retaliate against League sanctions. On 1 April, the British Service Chiefs reported that 'if we seriously consider the possibility of war with Germany it is essential that the Services be relieved of their Mediterranean responsibilities. Otherwise our position is utterly unsafe'.[50] In face of the growing danger from Germany, Eden became increasingly isolated, disagreeing with France over Abyssinia, and now over Germany, criticised by the Government's military advisers, who scanned the narrow margins of national security, attacked by veteran Conservative leaders like L.S. Amery, who thought that Italy's Abyssinian adventure should be quietly forgotten and the far greater threat from Germany faced. By 6 May, two days after Italian troops entered Addis Ababa, Eden, of whom Churchill later wrote that he was 'the one young figure standing against the drawling tides of drift and disaster', was admitting in the House of Commons that sanctions had failed.

A month later, at a meeting of the 1900 Club, Neville Chamberlain was calling the continuance of sanctions the 'midsummer of madness'. 'Nations cannot be relied upon to go to the last extremity of war', he went on (though there was at that time no question of war for Britain, certainly not with Italy), 'unless their vital interests are threatened'. The supporters of sanctions in Britain, like Eden, had always contended, of course, that the League of Nations *was* a vital interest for Britain. Nevertheless, a week later, on 17 June, Eden himself was urging the abandonment of sanctions at a Cabinet meeting. His colleagues agreed and the Foreign Secretary proposed lifting sanctions in Parliament on the next day. On 4 July forty-four delegates from the sanctionist states approved the termination of the programme. Two days later the Co-ordination Committee met and decided that sanctions should be ended on 15 July. Abyssinia passed into the Duce's empire and the League's first and final experiment in the enforcement of international law was brought to a close. Twenty years later, with disastrous effects, Anthony Eden attempted the retaliation against another alleged breach of law which he had failed to impose on Mussolini.

IV

How had this happened? How could Britain, the world's most
powerful country at that time, together with France, second only
to Britain in the scale of importance in world affairs, be worsted
and humiliated by Italy, which suffered almost total defeat in the
First World War and fared even worse in the Second? How could
the League of Nations, the most hopeful development to emerge
from the First World War, supported by almost all countries and
widely recognised as the sole hope for the collective enforcement of
peace, suffer a reverse at the hands of Italy from which it never
recovered?

All causes of events on such a scale – if indeed there are 'causes'
of any events – are interconnected, no one cause being separable
from all the others, but the singularity and exceptional position of
Britain in the sanctions movement in 1935-36 demands special
attention. Britain was the unquestioned leader of the League
campaign against Italy, though British statesmen always rejected
accounts of the crisis which represented it as a conflict between
Britain and Italy, with other League states standing on the side-
lines. The conflict, the British said, was between Italy and the rest
of the League, though, owing to Britain's power, especially at sea,
and its world-wide political and commercial importance, it must
be in the forefront of any general attempt to apply sanctions
against an aggressor. There could be no doubt that, in leading the
sanctions movement, Britain was fighting, not on behalf of any
unilateral national interest, but on behalf of a universal interest,
namely collective security, even though it meant doing damage to
Britain's national interest. The inter-departmental committee
appointed by the Government under the chairmanship of Sir John
Maffey reported that Britain had no vital interest in Abyssinia
except Lake Tsana, from which springs the Blue Nile, vital to
irrigation in Sudan and Egypt, despite the persistent Italian claim
that Britain opposed the Italian campaign against Abyssinia
because of her own imperialist interests there.[51]

The National Government, however, formed in the financial
crisis of 1931, was too divided in its attitude towards the League to
supply the kind of lead which Britain's position demanded. About
Eden's role, there could be no doubt. He was sanctionist through
and through, believing that if maverick states were allowed to get
away with it, there could be no security for any country anywhere.
On the other hand, Eden was often overawed and swept off course
by older hands, who had been in politics much longer than he. In

the MacDonald and Baldwin Cabinets of the thirties, others, notably Neville Chamberlain, questioned Eden's dogmatic adherence to the League and argued that each case be judged on its merits and with reference to the pattern of forces in the world which sided with Britain, rather than with wholesale respect to abstract principles of collective action. Later, in February 1938, when Chamberlain was head of the government, the two men clashed over somewhat the same question and Eden resigned.

The Foreign Secretary had the backing of an almost unanimous public opinion throughout 1935, including the support of the Opposition parties (provided Britain kept in step with France), the churches, the League of Nations Union, and much of the press. But, although British opinion wanted League 'action' against Mussolini and deplored an advanced European Power's attack on a primitive people, the action was generally restricted to what would not seriously damage Britain, if damage it at all. The costs would not have to be too high. Though a substantial majority in the 'Peace Ballot' in 1935 voted in favour of military measures in restraint of aggression, it is doubtful whether the vote would have been so heavy had it been expressly stated in the question that military restraints would have to be applied by *Britain*, that *British* forces might be called upon to go to Abyssinia and shed blood ousting the Italians. The Government, though convinced by early 1935 that rearmament was inevitable if the country was to play any effective role in the rapidly deteriorating international situation, was still unwilling to make bluntly clear that, if the public wished to give Mussolini a bloody nose in Abyssinia, it would have to pay the price in terms of a bigger arms budget. The fact was that public opinion was opposed *both* to capitulating to Mussolini *and* to spending more money on arms. For the most part, the politicians seemed too dependent on the public for the votes which put them into office to wish to draw too much attention to this self-contradiction. In any case, men like Eden, who took a strong pro-League line because, among other reasons, it had, for a time, strong popular support, were apt to forget how fickle that support can be. Public opinion which cried out for sanctions against Italy in the early phases of the crisis in 1935, had something else to think about in 1936, namely the scandal arising from Edward VIII's affair with a divorcee, the American Mrs Simpson. The King's love life put the Abyssinian tragedy into the shade. Haile Selassie was ignored by the politicians when he fled to London, and Eden, hoisted into leadership of the sanctions campaign on a tide of popular enthusiasm, found himself having to explain its diplomatic implications to sceptical colleagues.

These colleagues were alarmed by Britain's tendency during the crisis to move out of line with France. 'Go as far in this sanctions business as France', Churchill advised Hoare, 'but no further'. The French were strictly limited in the extent to which they would oppose Italy at the League. France's main fear was Germany, morning, noon and night. If Italy were on Germany's side in the coming struggle for power in Europe, France's position would be parlous, it being all but impossible that she should stand on guard on two fronts, one facing Germany, the other Italy. On 4 January 1935, Pierre Laval arrived in Rome and three days later reached an agreement with Mussolini under which Italy would withdraw troops from its border with France. Four further conventions were entered into as part of the understanding: (1) frontier rectifications in Italy's favour would be effected as between French West Africa and Libya and French Somaliland and Eritrea; (2) in Tunisia, children born of Italian parents would be able to opt for French nationality after 1945 and would become French after 1965. Italian schools would be subject to French law after 1955; (3) Italy and France would recommend to all states concerned a non-intervention agreement with respect to Austria; pending its conclusion, the two countries would consult together whenever Austria's independence seemed threatened; (4) as far as armaments were concerned, no country could modify its obligations with respect to them by unilateral action. These agreements were published; there was, however, a secret agreement on armaments which did not see daylight until after the Second World War; this stated that, 'in the event of circumstances permitting the resumption of international negotiations with a view to the conclusion of a general disarmament agreement, the two governments will concert their efforts so that the figures of limitation inscribed in the agreement will ensure the two countries, in respect to Germany, the advantages which will be justified for each of them'. Though nothing about it was stated in the written agreements, it was generally assumed that France would, as a result, recognise Italian economic primacy, with perhaps a suggestion of political primacy, too, in Abyssinia.[52]

When Eden, on his own visit to Rome in June, protested that the latter agreement had nothing to do with the political realm, he reported the Duce as having 'flung himself back in his chair with a gesture of incredulous astonishment'.[53] Mussolini had joined

MacDonald and Sir John Simon, together with Laval, at a conference in Stresa from 11 to 14 April, in the immediate aftermath of Hitler's denunciation of the military clauses of the Versailles Treaty a month before, the Final Declaration issued after the meeting speaking of the three Powers finding themselves 'in complete agreement in opposing, by all practicable means, any unilateral repudiation of treaties which may endanger the peace of Europe and will act in close and cordial collaboration for this purpose'. Mussolini later claimed that the words 'of Europe' were inserted on his own initiative, the intention being to exclude Abyssinia. There is little doubt, however, that the British and French participants had clearly intended to limit the discussion to Europe.[54]

But it is hardly necessary to consider whether Britain and France maintained a conspiracy of silence about Africa at Stresa as a way of giving Mussolini the green light to carry out his plans for Abyssinia. The essential fact is that they counted on Italian co-operation against Germany, and when, along with almost fifty other League states, they banded together to punish Italy for attacking Abyssinia, a blow was inevitably struck against the Stresa front. It was equally inevitable that they, and especially France, should want to soften the effects of that blow. When Hitler remilitarised the Rhineland in March 1936, Italy was quick to make it plain that League sanctions against Italian policy in Abyssinia ruled out all prospect of herself participating, as a joint guarantor with Britain of the Locarno treaties of 1925, in measures against Germany. It was natural for the French to conclude that the British obsession about sanctions against Italy had ruined all prospect of sanctions against Germany's far more serious offence, certainly to the extent that they depended upon co-operation with Italy.

The great question – how it hung in the background throughout the Italo-Abyssinian affair! – was Germany, and what the situation in Europe would be like once Germany was restored to strength. 'Throughout the whole Abyssinian conflict', Sir Samuel Hoare told Laval on 10 September, the day before his great speech on defence of the Covenant at the sixteenth League Assembly, 'he had been thinking, not so much of the Italian dispute or a backward country, as of the reactions of the dispute on the European position, with Germany rearmed and under temptation to make a threat to European security some time during the next ten years'.[55] In a further talk with Laval on the next day, Hoare said that during his speech at the Assembly on 11 September 'he had the whole time been thinking of the German danger'.[56] That was the language that Laval, like any Frenchman, wished to hear. But what was the connection between the Italian and the German situations? British sanctionists, like Hoare, at least in the frame of mind in which he was on 11 September, thought that, if the League failed in Abyssinia, it would certainly fail if put to the test by Germany. Hitler would be immensely encouraged by Mussolini's successful defiance of the League, British public opinion discouraged to the point of being driven into a hopeless isolationism. But there was also the view adopted by the French, namely that the connection between sanctions against Mussolini and sanctions against Hitler was that the former destroyed the Stresa front, and it was in that front that the chief hopes of organising a system of sanctions against Hitler lay.

If war with Germany came, as a result, for instance, of an attempt to restrain Hitler, the French knew that they must bear the brunt of it; Britain's contribution in the shape of land forces, at least in the early stages, would be as slight as in 1914, perhaps even more so. Since 1914 the air age had arrived, as the devastating Italian bombardment from the air of undefended villages of Abyssinia showed only too well. The British authorities worried even about the bombing of London by the Italian air force during the dispute about Abyssinia: during 1935 they pursued the chimera of an 'air Locarno', an agreement with the states of Western Europe for mutual assistance in the event of an air attack on one of the signatories. France, seeing herself left to grapple with German armies in the mud, had no wish to prod Italy into throwing in her lot with Germany. Yet that might happen if sanctions were persisted in. Sir George Clerk, the British Ambassador in Paris, wrote to Hoare on 15 June 1935 that 'the sentiment of the bulk of the public is on the side of Italy; a policy of whole-hearted support of Abyssinia, with whom there is very little sympathy, would be most unpopular'.[57] After all, France herself was a colonial Power in Africa. In January, Abyssinian tribesmen had crossed into French Somaliland and killed a French official, sixteen militiamen and eighty Issas natives.

France's plight was alarming. Racked with internal unrest, torn between Left and Right, her only substantial ally was unrealistic and sentimental Britain, smitten with a League of Nations fever in defence of a backward and entirely insignificant African country against a European great Power with a most distinguished history. Clerk had written home on 22 August that 'France and Laval care little or nothing for the fate of Abyssinia, but only regard it in so far as it affects French security in Europe'. Laval, the Ambassador went on, 'will refuse for as long as he can to adopt a definitely hostile attitude to Italy and will seek a means of reaching a compromise ... In the last resort it may be possible to make him do so but only if he secures satisfactory assurances that he will have the support of HM Government in resisting German encroachments'.[58]

France watched the fires of militant nationalism stoked in nearby Germany by a practically insane leader who left no doubt in anyone's mind that he intended to turn his 70 million people into the scavengers of Europe. Britain appeared to be in no mood for taking Hitler seriously, condoned his repeated breaches of the Versailles Treaty system, and signed agreements with him, like the Anglo-German naval treaty of June 1935, which ratified Germany's illegal rearmament, without consulting France or even notifying her of her intention to do so. Yet Britain was bent on alienating Mussolini, a guardian of the Locarno regime which Britain had played a leading role in creating, and which protected the demilitarised zone of the Rhineland, imposed by the Allies at such terrifying cost less than twenty years before. It was almost in despair that the French, on 2 May 1935, signed their treaty for collective defence with Soviet Russia, a country which practically every French politician either despised or mistrusted, or both. The irony of it was that it was this agreement which was used by Hitler as an excuse for denouncing the Locarno treaties and remilitarising the Rhineland in March 1936. Such was the pretext, but the opportunity, every Frenchman concluded, was provided by the disarray in the Stresa front caused by the application of League sanctions against Italy. By far the greatest responsibility for that lay with 'perfide Albion'.

The failure of sanctions in the Abyssinian crisis of 1935-36, and hence the failure of the League, not merely in that crisis, but for all time, has been attributed to the leaders of the principal sanctionist countries, the 'guilty men', who never believed in the League system, but went along with public opinion in supporting it, as long as it won votes or averted political defeat, and then betrayed it at the first opportunity. The saying goes that it was not that the League was tried and found wanting; it was found difficult and not really tried at all. Alternatively, it could be said that democratic leaders in the 1930s were, if not intentionally guilty, at least unintentionally so. They straddled two diplomatic worlds, the *ancien régime*, which Europe had worked with throughout the nineteenth century, and the new world of the League; they tried to practise the methods of both at the same time and succeeded with neither. In the old world, the formation of alliances by acquiescing in potential allies compensating themselves at the expense of non-European peoples was the normal rule. When Laval talked with Mussolini in Rome in January 1935, the tacit agreement they reached, the price for which the Abyssinian Emperor and his people would pay, did not seem at all outrageous to them; that was how the system had always worked. They appeared to be unaware that a new climate of opinion had come into existence, at least in Britain and a few other places, with the foundation of the league, one in which nations had a right to existence regardless of the race of their people or their level of cultural or economic attainment. We see today the full maturation of that thinking in the United Nations General Assembly. The Italo-Abyssinian crisis occurred in Europe's prime, though at a late stage of it; the notion that the European great Powers had a natural right to supervise the benighted tribes of Africa and Asia was inherent in the system. Mussolini's irritation arose from the fact that his European partners, especially Britain, did not appear to think that his country was worthy of taking part in that supervision.

Human weakness, failure of the nerve, the temptations of duplicity, persistence in outmoded thought processes, and other faults, no doubt played their various parts in this phase of the League tragedy, as they do in all human affairs. But it is as well to ask whether this Abyssinian tale does not point to a fatal drawback in the League system which finally destroyed it, despite the lofty idealism of its founders, an inconsistency between the theory of collective security and the necessities of action in the anarchical international system. The law of the League Covenant was that a war against one was a war against all, and hence that a war waged against the rules (or, in the League system, without referring the dispute to peaceful settlement) must draw down upon the country or countries waging it the disapprobation of the international community. All members of the collective system are bound to sever relations with the offending state and thus bring it to heel, while supporting each other in the loss and inconvenience which such collective action entails. It is as though the business of the world community is proceeding smoothly when, on a sudden, a quarrel springs up between country X and country Y; country X (or Y) turns out on examination to be the aggressor and all other states party to the system pounce upon it, compelling it to bring its illegal action to an end. But are other states able to act in this way? Some may find themselves in a position to do so, but there are good reasons why we must suppose that more than a few cannot. And it is fatal if these few include states the co-operation of which is essential to the success of the enterprise. As Sir Samuel Hoare desperately wanted the sixteenth League Assembly to realise when he made his famous speech to it on 11 September 1935, the collectivity of League action was its essence.

In the ordinary course of international relations, friendships and hostilities develop spontaneously between pairs and groups of states. They may be ephemeral or lasting, but rarely remain at the same pitch of feeling: from day to day the temperature of inter-state relations rises and falls. The causes of these friendships and hostilities are too numerous and varied to be listed here: they range from racial or cultural affinities or differences to similarity or conflict between material interests. But of one thing we may be sure, namely that, in order to take care of its interests in dealings with opposing states, a country will as a general rule need all the friends it can muster. It is a harsh world, and to be without friends, or without enough friends, to see one through the rougher times is to expose oneself to danger.

This 'normal functioning' of the international system is then, at some given moment in history, translated into collective security arrangements in which friendships and hostilities between member-states are now dependent, not on pragmatic needs, but on the 'rules of the game'. Each member-state is required by the rules of the collective system to make friends with another state with which it may, in the 'normal functioning' of the system, have no considerable affinity, and in order to take hostile action against a third state, with which, according to the 'normal functioning' of the international system, it may be the closest of friends. It may be possible to rearrange one's friendships and enmities overnight in accordance with the 'rules of the game', but this may place such a strain on the pattern of relationships which every state builds up for itself in furtherance of its interests as to bring into question its very existence.

Nor is this a matter of abstract theory only. In the Italo-Abyssinian crisis of the mid-1930s, Mussolini's Italy was an enemy of the collective security system and was condemned by the League; but it was a friend of the security system which the *status quo* states of Western Europe tried to create for themselves, and which they had to create in order to defend themselves against the enemies of international order. In opposing Mussolini, these states weakened themselves against Hitler, or at least considered that they did. How could they avoid this dilemma? They could not condone Italian aggression in Abyssinia, if only because, as democratic countries, they could not ignore public opinion, which, in some states at least, had embraced the League idea. At the same time, their security still depended upon the *ancien régime*, and perhaps some of their leaders could be forgiven for thinking that that security was more effectively provided for under that system.

11 The final years

When the Co-ordination Committee and subsequently, on 4 July 1936, an extraordinary meeting of the League Assembly eventually decided that sanctions against Italy for its invasion of Abyssinia must be terminated, a sense of gloom enveloped the Genevan scene. Once the sanctions system, in such favourable circumstances, had failed, few believed that it could ever be mounted again. One consequence must be a decline in, if not total disappearance of, the confidence placed by states, especially the smaller countries, in the League's capacity to protect them against aggression. Another must be that hopes for future security must shift away from the all-embracing global formula towards the regional alliance, in which participating states would look for help from trusted friends and cut loose from dangerous confrontations between the greatest Powers. The future was bound to be a time of caution, of limited commitments and return to the well-tried methods of international politics.

The point was made, though somewhat obliquely, by Rivas Vicuña, speaking for Chile at the Ninety-second session of the League Council on 26 June 1936, when the Italian chair stood significantly empty. The time had come to consider reform of the Covenant, Vicuña said. His country wished 'to restrict the field of conflict to countries directly concerned' and to put an end 'to the system of world wars – military or economic – which the Covenant proposed as a sanction in the event of violation of its provisions'. Chile, he went on, 'stood outside the development of European policy – she had no desire to be a party to the consequences of actions which were independent of any steps she might take and were liable to involve her against her will in sanguinary conflicts or even struggles of a world-wide character'. M. Vicuña, without

going into detail, preferred regional to global security
arrangements and wanted the League to confine itself to functional
rather than security activities. He pressed for reform of the
Covenant to be placed on the Council's agenda, or on that of the
approaching Assembly meeting in September.[1] Two years later,
when these hopes failed, Chile gave notice of its intention to
withdraw from the League.

The speaker who followed Vicuña, Maxim Litvinov, the Soviet
Foreign Minister, naturally saw the League as a means of rallying
the smaller countries against Nazi Germany, and could not
disagree more: the League, he protested, 'as it stood and the
Covenant as it stood had not broken down'. Therefore he was 'not
sure it followed that the League needed reform'.[2] But this
optimism was not widely shared; in the end the Council resolution
recommended to the Assembly that member-governments should
be invited not later than 1 September to send proposals 'to improve
... the application of the principles of the Covenant'.[3] But this was
little more than papering over the cracks between those who
regarded the League's constitution as fundamentally unworkable,
either because the League did not include such important
countries as Germany, Japan, the United States, and now Italy, or
because the will to make it work was lacking, and those who, like
the Soviet delegation, considered that some change in the League's
modus operandi would somehow suffice to make it work. By
January 1938, the Committee of twenty-eight, to which this task
was referred, decided to adjourn *sine die* consideration of reform of
the Covenant.[4]

The trouble about making suggestions for improving the
League was that its chief weakness in 1936 was the absence from its
membership of Germany, now fervently rearming after the failure
of the world disarmament conference and safely digesting its latest
diplomatic *coup*, the remilitarisation of the Rhineland, which
began on 7 March. There was no doubt that the growing tension
between Germany, moving inexorably into alliance with a bitter
and revengeful Italy, and the much reduced coalition of the victors
of 1918 constituted the greatest threat to the peace, manifesting
itself in a blatant arms race between the two sides. On 23
September, R. F. Wigram, of the Foreign Office in London,
minuted on an account of the Nazi Party Congress in Nuremberg
by B.C. Newton that it was a 'fresh indication that we have no time
to lose in our rearmament'.[5] If League sanctions had failed
miserably to bring an end to Mussolini's aggression against

Abyssinia, there was hardly any chance of their being mounted in the event of an open conflict between Germany and the *status quo* Powers.

What then was to be done? The obvious solution, British and French Ministers considered, was to entice Germany back into the League, though how this was to be achieved, considering that the German departure from Geneva was supposedly due to Hitler's dissatisfaction with the disarmament policies of the democratic states, was obvious to no-one. The British government, however, now clearly taking the lead over France in dealing with the fascist Powers, did not believe it could be done by reforming the Covenant first and then asking Germany to return to Geneva. Lord Cranborne told the French Ambassador at the Foreign Office on 2 September that 'the last thing any of us want is to place before [the Germans] a *fait accompli* by asking them to return to a League in the reform of which they had no say'.[6] The trouble was that the Germans seemed to show no interest in joining a League committee to discuss reform of the Covenant.[7] Britain was therefore in the curious position of being the most active Power in the League, her Foreign Secretary, Anthony Eden, never losing an opportunity to stress his government's fidelity to the Geneva system, and yet on this occasion, when asked to consider how the League could in future avoid the blunders of the Italo-Abyssinian conflict, she could say nothing because she did not wish to prejudice German thinking about the invitation to return to Geneva. In a debate in the House of Commons on 27 July 1936, Eden shocked members by his failure to 'give a lead' to other League states on the question of reforming the Covenant, the subject everyone was talking about after the failure in Abyssinia and the indications of new German dissatisfaction with the *status quo* in Europe. He was compelled to make a winding-up speech in which he suggested that four 'elements' should be included in the British reply to the League inquiry about reform – 'the machinery for the peaceful settlement of disputes', 'the machinery for the adjustment of grievances', 'the creation of a deterrent to war', and 'the establishment of an international agreement for the reduction and limitation of armaments'.[8] It did not sound a very convincing table of amendments to the Covenant, and, not surprisingly, was never followed up.

The German government gave no indication of willingness to return to the League, and British and French urging that they should do so gave the Nazis the opportunity to put forward other demands, such as colonial concessions, which, if granted, would have helped to give Germany its cherished 'place in the sun': it certainly would not have been accomplished in the spirit of the Mandates system. The fact was that, Germany, by sending forces into the Rhineland in March 1936, had destroyed the Locarno agreements of October 1925, which a former German Foreign Minister had proposed, and on which Britain and France had based their post-war policies in Western Europe. Hitler's pretext had been that the French themselves had undermined Locarno by signing their alliance with Soviet Russia in May 1935. His strategy seemed to be to break down the Franco-Soviet alliance, since it threatened to encircle Germany, and, by filling Europeans with fear of communism, to get the Soviet Union entirely ostracised from European affairs. This was an attitude acceptable to much respectable opinion in Western Europe, which mistrusted the Franco-Soviet alliance as giving Moscow a voice in West European politics. One country in which these views were strong was Belgium, shocked in 1936 by the collapse of the Locarno system, which gave it a British and Italian guarantee against French or German aggression. On 14 October, King Leopold of Belgium delivered a devastating blow to British and French efforts to replace the Locarno system by new arrangements when he told the Cabinet in Brussels that the country 'must aim resolutely at keeping out of the quarrels of our neighbours'.[9] This was the prelude to a Belgian declaration of neutrality, which had not saved the country in August 1914, and which exposed France to an attack from Germany through Belgium to which the Maginot Line was irrelevant. Baron de Cartier, the Belgian Ambassador in London, told Eden on the following day that the King's speech did not affect Belgian commitments to the League. Eden was sure, nevertheless, that this change in Belgium's position must help those in Britain whom the Foreign Secretary described as the 'isolationists', those, that is, who did not support the replacement of the Locarno agreements by new security arrangements, and who did not wish to see the League Covenant strengthened.[10]

By Article 4 of the Locarno agreements, allegations by one of the parties that the pact had been violated – that is, that the frontiers between Belgium, France and Germany had been infringed, or that the demilitarised zone on the west bank of the Rhine had been militarily occupied – must be brought before the League Council, and this body, if it found the allegations valid, would authorise signatories of the treaty to help the victim state.

But, in the case of 'flagrant' breaches of the two provisions of the Rhine pact (though it was not stated who exactly would define them as 'flagrant'), parties must assist the victim state as soon as they were convinced that immediate action was necessary. In that case, the League Council would have to issue recommendations to the signatories, which must be agreed to by all the Council's members other than those states 'which have engaged in hostilities'. Thus, though it could be, and was, argued that the Locarno system was a move towards regional and away from the universal system of the Covenant (it arose as a result of Britain's rejection of the all-embracing Geneva Protocol), the League Council was without question central to it.[11]

In the discussions, which Britain and France initiated, and which began in Western Europe immediately after Germany's entrance into the demilitarised Rhineland and continued fitfully throughout 1937, the governments in London and Paris insisted that the League Council should once more be the body to give the decision in any new security system to replace the Locarno arrangements. In this way, it was thought, security in Western Europe, to which the new Germany was daily more of a threat, could be linked with efforts to pour new spirit into the League after the failures in Manchuria and Abyssinia. The British memorandum of 19 November, circulated to Belgium, France, Germany and Italy, the other four parties to the Locarno agreements, on preparations for a Five-Power conference to be held in London that winter was insistent that the League machinery must be restored to its former position as the agency to decide violations of the new convention, even though the League Covenant sanctified international treaties, which the Nazis were continuously disregarding, and even though the League had broken the tenuous links between Italy and the two Western democracies and driven Mussolini into Hitler's arms. 'Whatever changes may be introduced in the working of the League, it appears probable, and it is certainly the view of His Majesty's Government in the United Kingdom', the paper unconvincingly ran, 'that the peace-preserving function of the Council will become even more important than in the past'.[12] But that was the voice of Anthony Eden. In the following May, Neville Chamberlain, who took little account of the League, would be Prime Minister. Nine months later, on 20 February 1938, he broke with Eden and secured in Halifax, safely remote in the House of Lords, a more complacent Foreign Secretary.

The German leader, however, would not co-operate on the basis of the League Council proposal. On 31 March, after his own action in the Rhineland had created the crisis, he proposed, without going into detail, an international court of arbitration to decide the issue, presumably by looking at the legal aspects rather than the political facts.[13] This suggestion was not repeated in a German memorandum of 12 October, which merely stated that decisions on violations of the new agreements 'should be reached by the common decision of the signatories which are not parties to the conflict'.[14] The German Chargé d'Affaires in London explained two days later that his government did not consider it 'either necessary or appropriate to submit to the Council of the League the question of deciding whether an infringement of the obligation of non-aggression has taken place, and consequently whether the guarantee obligation has entered into force'.[15] The Nazis had left the League and had no wish to return to it. They would not even receive the colony, which Dr Schacht now claimed, from 'the present League, but from a reformed League or some other group of Powers'.[16] And the reasons were obvious. If Hitler was to break down the 1919 treaty system (and which German politician did not wish to do so?) solidarity among those who benefited from it must be weakened. The League of Nations was not only a product of the Allied victory in 1918, and hence the Covenant formed the first twenty-six articles of each of the peace treaties, it was also the largest political international organisation which existed. To attack it was to promote the very 'divide and rule' policy which was the essence of Hitlerism. But the League was also, by 1936, the chief instrument of foreign policy of Hitler's fiercest continental opponent, Soviet Russia. Whatever profited the League, profited Russia and *vice versa*. The ebullient Soviet Foreign Minister Litvinov never let anyone forget it.

The success of British and French efforts to persuade Germany to return to the League would depend on their ability to dilute its coercive features, to water down Article 16, and all talk of enforcement. This was also true in regard to the country now, in 1936, becoming Germany's closest European friend, Italy, even though Hitler, and no doubt most of his inner group of colleagues, despised Italy, Mussolini, and all his works. The Italo-Abyssinian conflict, League sanctions against Mussolini, and the Spanish civil war, which broke out with the Spanish Nationalist invasion of Spain on 18 July 1936, brought Germany and Italy closer together. Sir Eric Drummond was writing home from the British Embassy in Rome on 28 November that, according to Signor Attolico, the Italian Ambassador in Berlin, 51 per cent of the agreement between the two fascist Powers was due to the Spanish crisis.[17] Mussolini had scored a brilliant victory over the League and the liberal democratic states in Abyssinia, but the more he involved himself with Germany on General Franco's side in the Spanish conflict, the more his dependence on Germany grew. As each month in 1936 and 1937 passed, Germany became militarily stronger while Italy's foreign commitments expanded. Besides, from July 1937 Germany had a new friend in Japan, now in open war with China. Hitler considered Japan so important an ally that he agreed to modify some of the central themes of his ideology, namely its racist elements, to accommodate the partnership with Japan.

The common aggressive attitudes of the three totalitarian states towards the *status quo* and the increasing similarity of their policies as the international order dissolved in the 1930s looked more and more like that division of the international system into warring blocs which it had been the object of British policy to avoid. But the idea of Britain and France (for these two countries, with the hypothetical assistance of Stalin's Russia, was all that was now left of the Grand Allied Coalition of the First World War) being able to hold their own against the Gang of Three looked increasingly unlikely.[18] The United States was out of the picture, all the more so after the failure of League sanctions against Mussolini. On 5 October 1937, Franklin Roosevelt, less than a year after his great victory in the November 1936 elections, encountered a sharp blast of isolationism when he proposed, in a speech in Chicago, a vague system for 'quarantining' aggressors. In the Sino-Japanese conflict, and, after July 1937, the all-out war between them, Roosevelt had to watch his step in collaborating with Britain in any protest to Japan against her actions in the rivers of China which affected the shipping of other nations. Where did collective security now stand?

II

The obvious expedient was to try to break up the ring of fascist Powers which threatened the *status quo*, or rather at all costs to prevent it becoming stronger. Unfortunately, this involved, in the first instance, conciliating, or rather appeasing, Italy, the weakest member of the totalitarian opposition, and the one most amenable to pressures from outside. This became a sedulous object of British and French policy as soon as the war in Abyssinia ended in May 1936, even though the Abyssinian Emperor Haile Selassie consistently denied that it ever did end. Unfortunately, too, this meant that the two liberal democracies must screw the League further into the dust and practically grovel before the Italian blackshirted conquerors in order to win their goodwill. Drummond in Rome suggested to the Foreign Office on 7 October 1936 that, when he next talked with Italian Foreign Minister Ciano, he could tell him that 'neither you' (Eden) 'or any member of His Majesty's Government cherished any resentment against Italy over the Abyssinian affair. The desire of HMG was to shake hands with Italy and be friends'.[19] Eden agreed. Giving Drummond an account on 6 November of a conversation with Count Grandi, the Italian Ambassador in London, Eden said 'we should like to let bygones be bygones'. The Foreign Secretary then went on to tell Grandi that,

> If His Excellency would review the events of the past year, he would realise that in effect Italy had succeeded against the League. There was no attempt to deny that our efforts as a member of the League had been in vain. In spite of this there was no kind of rancour on our part, still less any thought of revenge.[20]

It was the Captain of Rugger congratulating with a smile and handshake a rival team on its victory over the School side that day.

The question nevertheless arose as to whether Britain or France could give Italy so soon what it wanted, namely diplomatic recognition of its conquest by force of an unoffending League member. Eden told Grandi that he hoped 'we should not be asked to recognise the conquest of the victim of aggression we had failed to protect at the price of improved relations with Italy'.[21] This was League doctrine, that changes brought about in defiance of the Covenant or the Pact of Paris of 1928 should not be rewarded with diplomatic recognition. American Secretary of State Stimson had offered it to the League on 7 January 1932 as a face-saving alternative to using force to expel the Japanese from Manchuria.[22] It was in conflict with the traditional British doctrine that the effective occupation of territory, no matter how acquired, is sufficient to confer title to the territory. But the Italians wanted a certificate of recognition from the greatest Power, certainly the greatest empire, of the day. Britain leaned towards it by reducing its mission in Addis Ababa to consular status and by public statements like Eden's reply to a question from the communist M.P., Willie Gallacher, in the Commons on 19 November, when he said that he 'wished to state categorically that he thought there were other Governments more to blame for intervention in Spain than those of Germany and Italy'.[23] This was at a time when there were believed to be 50,000 Italian soldiers fighting in Spain on Franco's side.

During the discussions between Britain and Italy for a detente based on mutual recognition of the *status quo* in the Mediterranean, the British did not press for the resumption of Italy's activities in the League: the Italian seats in Council and Assembly remained empty. Eden wrote to Drummond in Rome on 2 December that 'you need not mention the question of the League at all'.[24] The Anglo-Italian Declaration which emerged from these exchanges and was signed in Rome on 2 January 1937, together with an exchange of notes between Ciano and Drummond on 31 December, confirmed the maritime and territorial *status quo* in the Mediterranean. But a phrase in the Declaration which referred to an agreement 'to use their best endeavours to discourage any activities liable to impair the good relations which it is the object of the present declaration to consolidate' could be regarded either as directed against Italian anti-British propaganda and press campaigns, about which the Cabinet in London had complained, or fresh attempts to wipe out any remaining memories of the Abyssinian affair.[25] The sanctions episode was relegated to history.

Eighteen months later, when Eden was no longer Foreign Secretary – and his resignation had arisen partly from his disagreement with the Prime Minister, Chamberlain, on the conditions to be satisfied by Italy before its conquest of Abyssinia could be recognised – Britain placed Abyssinia on the League Council agenda with a motion which left it open to member-states to decide the question of recognition for themselves. There was no doubt how Britain herself saw the issue. Her new Foreign Secretary, Halifax, said at the Council on 12 May that it was

> the considered opinion of His Majesty's Government that for practical purposes Italian control over virtually the whole of Ethiopia has become an established fact, and that, sooner or later, unless we are prepared by force to alter it, or unless we are to live in an unreal world, that fact, whatever be our judgment on it, will have to be acknowledged.

'My government', Halifax continued, 'hopes that members of the Council will share the view that it is for each Member of the League to decide for itself in the light of its own situation and its own obligations'.[26] Haile Selassie, on the other hand, who was admitted to the Council table and spoke through his assistant, Ato Taezaz, who began with the words, 'Denied all succour, the Ethiopian people mounts its Calvary alone', contended that his country was far from defeated, that resistance to the Italians was continuing, and that the League Assembly should decide who was sovereign in Abyssinia.[27] But none of this availed to prevent the British resolution being carried. The sorry Abyssinian tale was finished, at least until the Second World War, which ended with Italy's defeat and the Emperor's return from exile. By that time, the League of Nations had all but expired.

The fact that Mussolini's Italy did not respond to these British enticements but joined Germany as the two fascist challengers of the *status quo* was largely due, of course, to the civil war in Spain, which concluded in May 1939 with the expulsion of the liberal, Republican government elected in February 1936 and the assumption of power over the whole country by General Franco and his Falangist forces. The civil war began as a conflict between Spanish parties, over essentially Spanish questions, which were not primarily those of contemporary Europe. Nevertheless, the fact that Europe itself in the mid-1930s was divided in a war between Right and Left, with fascist Germany and Italy representing the Right and Soviet Russia the Left, and with the liberal democracies split in their support for either side, made it inevitable that the struggle against the freely elected regime in Madrid should be regarded as the symbol or essence of the larger conflict which threshed the world. This was precisely how the fascist governments in Berlin and Rome and Stalin's communist system wished to have it represented, while Britain and the liberal democracies, even including France (where a Popular Front government under Léon Blum was elected into office in June 1936), strove to isolate the Spanish struggle from the wider European conflict, if that were possible. The British government especially opposed all tendencies for the Spanish tragedy to be absorbed in the wider European ideological battle: they also feared that, unless Spain were insulated against intervention from external European Powers, it would prove impossible for it not to become the Balkans of the next war.

The British authorities therefore co-operated with France (no-one can be sure which took and sustained the initiative) in working for an agreement under which European states, twenty-six in all (including Britain), would prohibit the export to Spain and Spanish Morocco of all arms, munitions and war materials, though not, at first, troops. A committee to implement the agreement met for the first time in the Locarno Room at the Foreign Office in London on 9 September 1936 under the chairmanship of W.S. Morrison, the Financial Secretary to the Treasury.[28] It had held fourteen meetings by the end of the year and normally worked in the form of a smaller committee representing Britain, Bulgaria, Czechoslovakia, France, Germany, Italy, Portugal, Sweden and the USSR, that is, the nations which mostly traded with Spain. The non-intervention agreement, then, had little or no connection with the League or the Covenant, even though Spanish Ministers frequently appealed to the League Council and the Assembly for support against alleged violations of the agreement, and both League bodies almost always advised member-states to comply with their obligations under the agreement. But how could they do more, considering that two of the greatest states repeatedly accused of intervention in Spain by European liberals and the European Left wing, Germany and Italy, were not League members and even refused to attend League meetings called to settle rather unimportant peripheral questions?

The Non-Intervention Committee was consistently criticised throughout most of its life by the Spanish government in Madrid for its alleged failure to prevent the fascist Powers giving support to the Nationalist rebels, and for intervening in Spain with their own armed forces, while they themselves were denied the opportunity to obtain supplies from abroad; by the Russians for the same reason; by European liberals who, though they began by supporting the idea, soon started to blame it for weakening the Spanish government's capacity to defend themselves; and by the fascist states, which argued that it overlooked Soviet supplies to the government, even though the government had every right under international law to receive them. The British government, however, contended that a leaky dam was better than no dam at all. They tried to organise arrangements for complaints about intervention in defiance of the agreement to be passed on to countries against which the complaints were levelled. They acted still more vigorously in September 1937 by pressing for and securing a conference at Nyon in France for counter-attacking and destroying submarines which tried to sink foreign vessels in the waters around Spain. Nine countries (Britain, Bulgaria, Egypt, France, Greece, Rumania, Turkey, the USSR and Yugoslavia) signed the agreements concluded at Nyon between 9 and 14 September, and on 21 September the President of the conference, Yvon Delbos, forwarded the conclusions to the League Secretary-General, Joseph Avenol.[29] It was the most successful of all Europe's non-intervention activities during the Spanish civil war, but was carried out almost entirely outside the League system. The League of Nations, in so far as it had any part at all, confined itself to taking note and applauding.

III

The League Council also took note of, though it did not applaud, a letter from the German government to the Secretary-General dated 18 March 1938, giving details of a law adopted by the Reich five days previously for the incorporation of the state of Austria, which accordingly ceased to be a League member-state.[30] The Anschluss was a unilateral German action in violation of the Treaty of Versailles of June 1919, which committed Germany to respect the inalienable independence of Austria, unless the League Council otherwise agreed. It was presumably taken in retaliation against the sudden decision of the Austrian Chancellor, Kurt Schuschnigg, announced on the evening of 9 March, to hold a referendum asking his people what their wishes were in regard to the future state of the country. Since German troops entered Austria on 12 March, before the plebiscite was held, it could hardly be claimed that the invasion reflected the will of the 6½ million people of the country: rather it seemed as though Hitler's action was intended to prevent Austrian opinion on unification with Nazi Germany becoming known.

But what could the League Council do about it? Britain, once again the leading state on the Council, had, from the signature of the peace of St Germain with Austria in June 1919, no wish to prevent that country joining Germany: unification might help with Austria's appalling economic problems, which tore it apart in the early 1930s, and there was much sentimental feeling in London that Austria, with its softer cultural traditions, might have a moderating effect on political extremism in Germany. It was the brutal manner in which the Third Reich acted on the Austrian question in March 1938 which was so shocking: 'Horrible! Horrible!' was how Foreign Secretary Halifax described it.[31]

Moreover, for the British, with their long-standing respect for international law, and for the Covenant and its defence of the sanctity of treaties, the Anschluss was a blow, though British support for peaceful change and the negotiated revision of treaties might moderate that somewhat. Nevertheless, Article 10 of the League Covenant insisted on respect by all member-states for the territorial integrity and political independence of other member-states. Article 10 had been watered down over and again since 1920 by interpretative resolutions and the refusal of states to apply it when aggression occurred. But it had never been amended out of the Covenant and could not be ignored. Germany was bound not to infringe Austria's independence. Austria was bound not to lose it by agreements reached with the League on economic assistance to that country in 1920 and 1921. Yet Germany had, once more, violated the Versailles Treaty by taking over Austria, and the Austrian authorities, if, as Hitler claimed, they had voluntarily joined Germany, had broken their agreements with the League.

The Mexican delegation to the League unburdened itself of its feelings on the question in a letter to the Secretary-General on 19 March. 'The political extinction of Austria, in the form and circumstances in which it has taken place', the Mexicans wrote, 'constituted a serious infringement of the League Covenant and the established principles of international law'. 'The League of Nations', continued the statement, 'should not accept the *fait accompli* without the most vigorous protests or without taking the action provided for by the articles of the Covenant'. But then it was hard to see what specific measures could follow: Austria was by that time inside the German homeland and no country strong enough to compel Germany to disgorge it was willing to try. Anthony Eden had laid down in a famous speech at Leamington on 20 November 1937 the occasions when Britain was willing to use force internationally; they were: in self-defence and defence of the Commonwealth and Empire, in defence of France and Belgium if they suffered unprovoked aggression, and of Germany and other countries against unprovoked aggression, if they entered a system of mutual guarantees in Western Europe to replace the Locarno arrangements of October 1925. But that was all.[32] Mexico could therefore only conclude its outburst of *saeva indignatio* by informing 'the public opinion of the world that in its view the only means of securing peace and preventing further international outrages such as those which have been committed against Ethiopia, Spain, China and Austria is for the nations to carry out the obligations laid on them by the Covenant, the treaties they have concluded and the principles of international law'.[33] But the League Council did nothing, and future victims of aggression were left to draw their own conclusions.

The Anschluss had two more consequences for the international balance of forces. One was to draw Germany and Italy even closer together. In June 1934, when Nazi forces threatened to take over Austria at the time of Chancellor Dollfuss's assassination, Mussolini sent two divisions to the Brenner Pass and Germany was then too weak to move against them. Austrian independence was essential to Italy because, if Austria was merged with a powerful Germany, its claims on behalf of its three million countrymen incorporated in Italy when its frontier with Austria was revised at the peace conference in 1919 would be that much stronger. In April 1935, Italy had joined with Britain and France in defence of the European *status quo* at the Stresa conference. But then, in October of that year, came the Italian attack on Abyssinia, followed by League sanctions and the alarming rift between Rome and the two Western democracies. Hitler quietly backed Italy over Abyssinia, when she was badly in need of friends, and became involved with her as a supporter of Franco in the Spanish civil war. Then, in March 1938, Mussolini reversed his stand by declining to oppose the German Anschluss with Austria. On 11 December 1937, Italy had finally withdrawn from the League;[34] with Italian co-operation with Germany over the Anschluss, the pact of steel was consolidated between them. This obliterated all likelihood of Italy ever returning to the League system, reduced the chances of her entering an arrangement for reciprocal security in Western Europe, and ruled out (though this was not at once perceived in London) all prospect of Rome becoming a channel of access between Britain and Nazi Germany.

The second major consequence of the Anschluss was to bring to the forefront the looming crisis over Czechoslovakia, which dominated the European stage during 1938 and was settled with the passage into the German Reich of its Sudeten fringe as a result of the four-Power conference in Munich at the end of September. Once the German Reich had digested Austria, the lower fang of its jaw embraced the Czech state from the south; Czechoslovakia was now held on three sides by a feverishly rearming and fanatical German power-house. Understanding of the Czech crisis and its resolution at Munich in September 1938 is, to a large extent, a study in British political psychology: its fear of another great war, especially with the prospect of saturation bombing from the air of south-east England; its misgivings since 1919 about the formation of the successor states in Eastern Europe; its feelings of guilt about the application of national self-determination in Eastern Europe in 1919, especially in regard to the treatment of Germany's borders, and the sense that these would soon have to be revised in her favour; its deep mistrust of the Soviet state and its unutterably harsh leader; its longing for a settled and satisfactory relationship with Germany; and other elements besides. But, as the Czech crisis unfolded in the summer of 1938, the League of Nations in Geneva was unreachably remote from the centre of the diplomatic storm. Only the Russians, who had detested the League since its birth in 1920 and then joined it for the frankest balance-of-power reasons in the 1930s, wanted the League back on the scene: in their offer of assistance to the Czechs in September 1938, the Russians said their help must be given with the League Council's agreement, a device presumably intended to encourage the Rumanians to give authority to fly over their territory to Soviet forces.[35] Otherwise, the four Powers at Munich, Britain, France, Germany and Italy, wanted no League interference. And why should they? They were involved in the act of partitioning a League member-state in circumstances in which its agreement to the process was presumed rather than elicited.

IV

Delegations which complained at Geneva about the ravages inflicted by strong-arm states on their territory and peoples increased in number in the 1930s, voting in favour of League action to support one another, while the aggressors against them sat outside sharpening their weapons, and the liberal democracies wrung their hands and apologised for their inability to take action. The inexhaustible Spanish Foreign Minister, Alvarez del Vayo, submitted resolutions to Assembly meetings called for Non-Intervention to be ended, so that the harassed government in Madrid could buy arms from outside. In the sixth committee of the Eighteenth session of the Assembly in 1937 he obtained thirty-two votes for a resolution to bring Non-Intervention to an end if efforts to secure the withdrawal of foreign combatants from Spain continued to fail. This included all the Council members except for Bolivia and Peru. The resolution failed, but, undeterred, del Vayo brought the question before the Council in May 1938, with a motion asking all those who voted for his previous resolution to end Non-Intervention immediately. Litvinov, for the Soviet Union, was fully in favour, but this time Britain and France were against. When the motion was put to the vote, only Spain and Russia supported it. Britain, France, Poland and Rumania were on the other side and nine countries abstained, thus defeating the motion.[36] Alvarez del Vayo continued his campaign, with the same result, later.

The representative of another victim of foreign aggression, Dr Wellington Koo of China, had much the same experience of tiring his colleagues in Geneva with endless tales of Japanese atrocities, including bombing from the air and the resort to poison gas against his countrymen and women. The Council adopted resolutions repeatedly deploring China's plight and asking member-governments to collect information about Japan's lawlessness in her war in China and to forward it to the League's Secretary-General. Poland was the only Council member to refrain from supporting such a resolution, and this applied only to Part I of the motion, which the Council adopted on 10 May 1938, but when Wellington Koo asked for more positive assistance from League members, he received no answer.[37] At the third meeting of the Council's 104th session on 17 January 1939, Dr Koo said that 'the time has come, and is in fact long overdue, for the League of Nations to take effective action in order to restrain Japanese aggression'. One such measure, he suggested, would be a boycott of Japanese exports, especially its raw silk, which was mainly sold in only a few of the world's markets; another was an embargo in supplies of war materials to Japan; then there was increased aid to China. The Council President, Mr Munters of Latvia, was in full agreement, but the resolution eventually voted by the Council was watered down to a mild appeal; it invited League members 'to examine, in consultation, should this appear appropriate, proposals made by the Chinese representative before the Council on 17 January for effective measures'. The solitary consolation for Dr Wellington Koo was an outburst of indignation at this pale language from Jordan of New Zealand.[38]

But in May 1939, as the war in Europe approached, Wellington Koo tried once again to make the conflict in the Far East meaningful to his preoccupied colleagues on the Council. 'What I wish to emphasise once more', he began, 'is that the present situation in the Far East, from whatever aspect it is viewed, is a problem of international concern and world-wide importance'.[39]

Although, once more, the Soviet delegate, Maisky, supported him, there was no doubt that the British and French representatives were running out of patience; they were oppressed by more immediate considerations. For Britain, Halifax was frank in confessing that he could hold out little hope of assistance to China in present circumstances and with heavy responsibilities resting upon HMG in other parts of the world. For France, Georges Bonnet was no more able than he was in the previous January 'to consider the circumstances favourable to new measures, more particularly the measures of co-ordination which the Chinese government has suggested'.[40]

Two such preoccupations for Britain were the crisis in Palestine and the serious deterioration in the European situation since the conference in Munich on the Sudeten problem in September of the previous year. With regard to Palestine, the British government, the Mandatory Power, had now abandoned the proposal for partitioning the Holy Land which the Peel Commission, summoned to deal with the causes of the Arab strike in Palestine in 1936, had recommended. A conference in London in the winter of 1938-39 between the British authorities and the two Palestinian parties separately had made it brutally clear that under no circumstances would the Arabs accept partition, and without their co-operation no rational proposals for dividing this troubled land was possible. His Majesty's Government were therefore now 'free to formulate their own policy', that is, the scheme for limiting Jewish immigration into Palestine to 75,000 during the next five years and in effect virtually bringing it to an end after that figure was reached by saying that further immigration would depend upon Arab consent. In referring, obscurely, to British policy in a statement on 22 May, Halifax seemed to anticipate that the Mandates Commission's reaction to it would be fairly negative.[41] But there were other problems, connected with the Palestine issue, but far outweighing it in importance. Halifax referred to these in a separate statement to the Council: he was thinking, he said, of the breakdown in the Munich process, on which the British government had reposed such hopes, by reason of the pledge Hitler, with the other three, had given at Munich to respect the new *status quo* in Czechoslovakia and to refrain from new acts of force, and which he had violated by sending German troops into Bohemia on 15 March 1939. This without question represented a distinct and threatening change in the German leader's policy: whereas, up to March 1939, he had demanded the return to the

Reich of German-speaking people and the territory they inhabited, now he was forcing the German army into other people's homelands, and there was no saying where that process would take him. After two days of what seemed like deep confusion, Neville Chamberlain, in a speech in Birmingham on 17 March, the outcome no doubt of violent emotions voiced in Parliament, at last recognised the German challenge by asking whether the Czech *coup* was not a new move of Nazi policy into an area which threatened everybody. At the end of that terrible month the Prime Minister gave his unilateral guarantee to Poland that, if it was attacked, and if it resisted by its national forces, it could count upon British assistance.

But how could Poland be helped by Britain and France (whose treaty of alliance with Poland went back to 1921) without arrangements being reached with the Soviet Union, a country widely regarded with mistrust and horror in Western Europe, but one which, consistently throughout the 1930s, had called for collective resistance, within the League or outside it, to fascist aggression? Chamberlain and French Prime Minister, Edouard Daladier, had no confidence in Russia or its ability to stand up against Axis armies. Stalin was in business only in Russia's interest, as he saw it, and would betray that of any ally he had whenever it was convenient to do so; he had moreover destroyed the morale of his own armed forces by his unprovoked campaign against its leading generals, beginning with Commander-in-Chief Tukhachevsky in 1937. If Hitler would agree to leave Western Europe and the British Empire alone, Chamberlain and his closest colleagues seemed to think, he could do what he liked in Eastern Europe and the Soviet Union. The idea of forming arrangements to defend any threatened state anywhere against aggression, as the League Covenant required, seemed to make no sense at all to Neville Chamberlain: it was the sort of world that Britain was fighting to defend that mattered to conservatives, not the fact that one country after another had been rendered prostrate by the fascist Powers. Nevertheless, after the German entry into Bohemia in March 1939, Chamberlain was compelled by Parliamentary and public opinion to find out what, if any, help there was to be had in Moscow, after years of snubbing that country's proposals. Hence, in May 1939 William Strang, a Foreign Office official, journeyed to the Soviet state looking for an ally, to be followed by British and French military teams. In Russia, they joined the French Ambassador, Naggiar, to face the wholly negative Molotov.

The Anglo-French talks in Moscow failed on 22 August, when it was announced that, for the time being at least, Stalin preferred neutrality as Hitler's friend to taking almost the full shock of the invasion when Hitler threw his forces into Poland. After all, the British had few troops, perhaps not more than, at most, three or four divisions at first, to commit to the struggle, and evidently the French meant to sit in the Maginot line, if that was possible, occasionally putting a toe into the water, but taking care not to leave it there. However that may be, these final British and French moves to avoid having to fight a second round with Germany or, if that proved impossible, merely to stay alive in the conflict, had little or nothing to do with the League, collective security or any general schemes for collective action against aggression, wherever and whenever it occurred. British defensive measures before the Nazi attack on Poland in September 1939 were not carried out through the League, Halifax frankly told the Council on 22 May 1939. That was, he said, in the circumstances impossible. This was not the occasion for a discussion of the events of that year, he said, but they 'inevitably affected the political influence and activity of the League'. His shadow, Bonnet, followed by equally frank admissions: security, collaboration, peace, he said, 'must be sought by other methods and on a different plane'.[42]

The League, however, by the greatest irony, still had a task to perform in the collective restraint of force, and that was against a country, the Soviet Union, which, outwardly, at least, had been the League's most valiant supporter during the 1930s. It may never be known with any assurance what Stalin and his colleagues really thought about the Geneva body after Russia joined it in 1934. But there is no denying that their verbal support for it was consistent and undeviating, and, considering that Russia's national interest in the 1930s evidently lay in rallying as many countries as possible in defence of the *status quo* against fascist aggression, there is no reason for thinking that this was, in whole or part, insincere. The Soviet Union's reward was that when she herself committed an act of unprovoked aggression against Finland in November 1939 (though it had an evidently defensive character about it), the League Council was hurriedly called together and a unanimous motion adopted to expel her from the League, the only League member to be driven out of the organisation.[43] The fascist states, whatever their crimes against peace, were never expelled from the League; on the contrary, when they left it of their own accord, the foremost pro-League states did their utmost to induce them to return, promising that, if they did so, the unfortunate affair which had caused the breach in the first place would never be mentioned again. The expulsion from Geneva of Soviet Russia in December 1939 was almost a vindication of the old Soviet claim that the League was an alliance of 'robber capitalist nations' against the solitary socialist state.

But the League in the Soviet-Finnish war was a pale reflection of its old self, with Powers great and small packing their bags in readiness to leave, or reducing their commitments in Geneva, or frankly declaring that the collective system had failed and must not be tried again. In May 1938, the Council adopted a resolution, with a small number of abstainers, which included China and the USSR, which allowed Switzerland to revert to its status as a totally neutral country.[44] In 1921, Switzerland had been allowed to limit its participation in any system of League sanctions to economic and other non-military measures: now it could virtually maintain what relations it wished with an aggressor and was not bound to help sanctionist states in their efforts to restrain wrong-doing governments. Comnène, the Rumanian delegate, told the League Council that 'when we look backwards and recall the brilliant prospects which the authors of the Covenant held out to those who were to accede to it, and then reflect how few of those expectations have been realised, we can readily understand the point of view of the republic of Switzerland'.[45]

Worse came later at that Council meeting, when the Chilean delegate, Agustin Edwards, stated that his country was withdrawing from the League 'solely because it has been our desire to restore to the League of Nations the life which is ebbing from it and because we have found ourselves faced with a position of impenetrable inertia in regard to reforms which can no longer be delayed'.[46] Mr Edwards was not explicit about the reforms he had in mind, but the general lack of success in the League's work was a sore point with him. 'Of forty-two political disputes dealt with by the League since its birth', he told the Council, 'eleven (relating almost without exception to matters connected with the liquidation of the First World War) were the subject of decision by the Council'. The other thirty-one had been settled by direct negotiations between the parties, or had been referred to other international organisations, or had been abandoned or left in suspense.[47] On 11 July 1938, the Venezuelan Foreign Minister wrote to the Secretary-General informing him of his country's desire to withdraw from the League.[48] On 8 April 1939 came another appeal against aggression with, once again, nothing done by the League to restore the *status quo* or punish the aggressor. The victim nation this time was Albania, bombed by Italian planes two days previously and then again on 7 April. The Albanian Chargé d'Affaires in Paris wrote to the Secretary-General, Avenol, on the 18th asking for an immediate meeting of the Council to decide on assistance to Albania 'in the present violation of its independence and the integrity of its territory'. Avenol made the extraordinary reply that the Albanian letter, though written on 8 April, had not been posted until the 11th and therefore 'could not be regarded as an appeal under the Covenant'. Nevertheless, he circulated copies of the letter to member-states, together with copies of one from Vetlaci, who described himself as head of the government and announced Albania's withdrawal from the League since it had now been incorporated within the Italian empire. Like Abyssinia and Austria, and not entirely unlike Spain, Albania had disappeared from the scene into the totalitarian camp and there was nothing the dwindling band of League members could do about it. Dr Wellington Koo joined the Soviet President in expressing sympathy for Albania.[49]

About the only crumb of comfort for those who still reposed any hopes in the League was a note from the American Secretary of State, Cordell Hull, dated 2 February 1939, which stated that his country would 'follow with interest the League efforts to meet more adequately problems relating to the health, humanitarian and economic phases of human activities'.[50] The American note chimed in with what most people were at that time thinking about the League, namely, that, as a means of consolidating peace it had clearly failed, and that new methods would now have to be applied, but that, as an agency for non-political co-operation, it still played a useful role, as the Bruce Committee report would shortly argue, at least when the imminent blood-letting in Europe ended. Typically, the Council's last session in peace-time, held in May 1939, was filled with the more humdrum labour of technical co-operation, including questions like fixing a date for a conference to be held on the unification of signals at level-crossings. Meanwhile, member-states prepared for the coming war. On 8 April, news came from Lima that Peru intended to withdraw from the League. Three days later, the same message arrived from Budapest concerning Hungary, which had in January declared its differences from other member-states by its recognition of Manchukuo.[51] The Second World War was in sight.

By March and April, Britain, France, India and New Zealand had stated that their acceptance of the General Act of Arbitration, concluded at Geneva on 26 September 1928, would not apply in disputes arising between themselves and other countries in the course of a war.[52] Other member-states followed their example. The League and its members were preparing to face the inevitability of the next world war, which would drive the Geneva organisation out of existence.

V

Thus, the League of Nations, as a system which men and women hoped might avert another major international conflict and defend the weak against attacks from the strong and ruthless, did not survive the efforts to mount collective action against the Italian invasion of Abyssinia. In September 1935, when Sir Samuel Hoare made his famous declaration at the League Assembly committing Britain to collective action against aggression, the League still commanded confidence: it *would* uphold the law and defend its member-states against armed attack. Three months later, when Hoare, an obviously sick man, reached with Pierre Laval in Paris the agreements to offer Mussolini a mutilated Abyssinia to embrace within his Roman empire, with a remnant left at the centre for the Emperor Haile Selassie, it was equally clear that the League was dead and would never revive. British and French governments might repudiate the Hoare-Laval agreements; they might protest that the dismemberment of Abyssinia was not at all what they had in mind. The truth was depressingly different.

That the League lived, flourished and died within three months is sufficient proof, of course, that its fatal weaknesses did not lie in the failings of its chief defenders, Britain and France, but in deeper faults which had lain there from the beginning, perhaps since Woodrow Wilson's battle to bring his country into the League in the early 1920s failed and left the United States to beat its ineffectual wings in vain while the aggressors did as they wished in Europe, Africa and the Far East. We have described this, and other elements in the tragic League story, at the end of the previous chapter, and more will be said on this in the next. But it would be wrong to judge the men who ran the League, and even those who tried to frustrate it, too harshly. Nothing like the League or the Covenant had ever been seen or tried before. They were a challenge to all the well-trusted methods which governments were used to; after the tragic disasters of the First World War, it was easy to make mistakes by relying upon new schemes conceived in the immediate emotional aftermath of that conflict. Governments, moreover, in almost all League member-states were dependent upon public moods and sentiments which were no doubt shocked by the events of 1914-18, but which nevertheless had had little or no time to react to the creation of the League. A most common public feeling, until about the mid-1930s, was that someone, somewhere and with some, as yet undisclosed, resources, would stop aggression and keep the peace. The League existed, held meetings, adopted resolutions, and would surely maintain law and order. When member-states realised that it was they themselves who had to act, that the League was in effect nothing more than the sum of its members, the old allurements of safety, the old methods and the old game, tended to return to the forefront. When Dr Wellington Koo and others like him confronted Halifax and Bonnet with China's appeal against Japanese bombing and other such aggressive acts at the League Council, the insoluble tragedy of the League was in the clearest perspective: the inability of the victim nations to believe that, after all the talk about collective action against aggression, they were alone, and so they must remain, and, on the other side, the determination of the established *status quo* states to confine themselves to doing what they could, both to discourage aggression by concessions at the victims' expense and by looking after themselves. The victims did not know whom to hate more – the violent aggressors or the friends who tried to appease them by offering them portions of the victims' flesh.

The curtain thus fell on the League in the aftermath of sanctions against Italy, though the League's work was not officially wound up until May 1946. The system had failed, though theories as to the reasons why were numerous and self-contradictory. The door was now open to a new arrangement, this time with all the great Powers which had survived the Second World War intending to serve as founder members. But had the basic weaknesses of the League been overcome? Were the makers of the new world aware of what they were and agreed on how to remove them? Had the League failed the nations, or the nations the League? No-one really knew.

12 Was failure inevitable?

I

When the victor Powers began to reorganise the world in 1945 after the final surrender of Axis forces, they had no doubt that something similar to the League of Nations must be formed again to maintain peace and act as an umbrella for international co-operation. It was all too obvious that the League had failed to prevent the outbreak of war in September 1939 and that the new world organisation would need to be created on vastly different lines. The League system and its history seem to have been examined in detail by none of the victorious governments. Nevertheless, it was felt that its basic faults must be corrected in the new United Nations Organisation.

One of the most serious of these was the League's lack of universality, those menacing empty chairs marked with the names of Germany, Italy, Japan and the United States for all or part of the League's history. The Soviet Union, on the other hand, had played an opposite role in the League from the first three of these absentee states. Its communist revolution in November 1917 created a rift between itself and the Entente Powers, who dominated the Geneva system, and Russia remained outside and highly suspicious of the League and its activities. When that country joined the League in 1934, however, it became one of its most enthusiastic supporters until expelled for its attack on Finland in the Winter War of 1939-40. Hence, there was no question that the ideological division, which sprang into existence between East and West almost from the moment that the Second World War ended, should not interfere with the formation of a United Nations Security Council in which the core would be provided by the five great victor states, Britain, China, France, the Soviet Union and the United States. As though to underline the essentiality of these

Powers in the UN, they were named as permanent members of the Security Council in Article 68 of the Charter, whereas in Article 4 of the League Covenant the permanent members of the Council were simply described as the Principal Allied and Associated Powers. It tended to be overlooked, or deliberately disregarded, in 1945, however, that having the five greatest military Powers named in the Charter as permanent Security Council members by no means ensured that they would co-operate.

Secondly, it was recognised at the end of the Second World War that the League, besides being weak in that its effective members were in reality only two in number, Britain and France, and these suffered from many basic differences of approach to current questions, the organisation itself was without the military and economic resources to take effective action against aggression. Part of the blame for this undoubtedly lay with Britain and the British Commonwealth, and with the Scandinavian democracies, which, for reasons of their own, opposed French proposals in 1919 and later for creating an international force to place behind League decisions. In 1945, therefore, there was a general agreement that the League had failed because it lacked 'teeth', or the means of enforcing its will. In the new world organisation this would be corrected by giving the Security Council 'primary responsibility for the maintenance of peace and security'. It would be authorised, if all five of its permanent members agreed, to define *any* situation, even an internal one, as a threat to peace, breach of the peace or act of aggression, and to initiate any measures, including the use of armed force, to restore the *status quo*. By Article 25 of the Charter, all member-states would be obliged to carry out the Security Council's decisions, and that body's own armed forces would be supplemented through special agreements under which ordinary member-states would earmark certain elements of their own armed strength for use in the international police force.

The new organisation would have much the same structure as the League: a General Assembly, representing all member-states and with competence over the whole field of international co-operation; a Security Council of fifteen member-states, five permanent and the rest elected periodically by the General Assembly; a Trusteeship Council for supervising the administration of dependent territories similar to the League's mandated areas, though representing governments and not serving as individual experts; an Economic and Social Council acting in the same way as the body proposed by the Bruce

Commission in 1939; a Court of International Justice; and a similar network of specialised agencies, though with far more funds and more elaborate structure, to replace the old functional committees of the League. But the United Nations was planned as a far grander structure than the League of Nations: in 1945, it was conceived almost as an embryo of a world state, with majority voting on legally binding decisions in place of the traditional unanimous voting and permissive recommendations of the Geneva organisation. The UN structure, as agreed at international meetings in Dumbarton Oaks, New Hampshire, in 1945, seemed to need only a formula for binding majority voting to be approved at the Big Three conference at Yalta in February for a world state to come into existence. This reflected no doubt the élan of American officialdom, which in any case had to 'sell' the new body to its own people, and also the feeling that the League belonged to an old world of limited horizons and that its successor must step out into a new age.

The major Power which did not enthuse to the same extent over these high-flown notions was the Soviet Union, which, in one of its early altercations with Washington, only agreed to send its Foreign Minister, Molotov, to the San Francisco conference to finalise the UN Charter out of respect for President Franklin Roosevelt, who had died on 12 April 1945. The Soviet Union's experience with the League, as we saw in the previous chapter, was one of frustration and humiliation. At the same time, the new United Nations body looked as though it might play a much bigger role in world affairs than the League, and the Soviet Union, having raised itself to super-Power status as a result of its victory over German forces during the Second World War, seemed to have no desire to be squeezed out of an organisation in which, certainly during its early years, it would be in a definite voting minority. For Moscow, UN membership, with a permanent seat in the Security Council, was a symbol of world status; in *that* it was interested, not in the vast parliamentary proceedings on the UN's functional side.

The Soviet conception of the UN prevailed. After a few years in which the United States tried to use the organisation to inflict voting victories over its great world rival, and to switch peace-keeping functions from the Security Council, in which Russia repeatedly applied its veto, to the General Assembly, over which the Americans exerted far greater influence, the Americans began to tire of the game and to lose interest in the UN. Both during the East-West detente during the 1960s and 1970s and in the intensification of the Cold War which marked the accession to the White House of President Reagan in January 1981, the United States looked increasingly to the protection of its own interests. As the size of the UN grew with the spread of decolonisation, the idea of the organisation being the 'town-meeting of the world', as John Foster Dulles called it in the 1950s, lost much of its appeal to Americans. The new state-members of the organisation turned against American idols, such as Iran, Israel and South Africa, would not vote so frequently for Western Cold-War motions, spoke against American intervention in the Middle East, South East Asia and Latin America. The United States was shocked by Third-World campaigns to use Unesco (the United Nations Educational, Scientific and Cultural Organisation) for its own ends, and the same was true for the prestigious ILO (the International Labour Organisation). The Americans lost their temper and gave notice of withdrawal. On one occasion, baffled with fury, an American Secretary of State, Mr Dean Rusk, blurted out in 1964 that his country and the Soviet Union 'had a common interest in not being outvoted in the UN by states which pay less than their fair share of contributions to the organisation'. It was almost the reverse of a common situation in the League, when smaller member-states felt that the Geneva organisation was run by the big Powers entirely in their own interests and to the disadvantage of ordinary countries.

The wheel has to a large extent come full circle. The League of Nations, which, in the 1930s, contained the 'peace-loving' states ranged against the revisionist, totalitarian Powers, was regarded in 1945 as having been too weak to restrain the aggressors. All that the 'peace-lovers' could do was to fight the law-breakers, and, by a sort of miracle (considering the position of the liberal democracies by, say, 1940) they won and had a second chance to organise a peaceful world. This time they changed the structure of the peace-keeping organisation, giving it authority and the resources to do the job. But the rift between '*status quo*' and 'revisionist' states remains what it always has been, and peace is kept between them, not by the collective organisation of majorities within and through the UN, but by a costly and highly dangerous system of deterrence, based, on both sides, on President Reagan's simple rule that 'nuclear war can never be won and must never be fought'. It is not so much, in the 1980s, that war is averted through aggressors fearing organised resistance from the civilised world, as Covenant and Charter seemed to suppose, but through the accumulation on both sides of military strength too awesome to challenge. In the entire history of war until the present time, it seems as though the most important driving force was the consideration that, however great the losses, the benefits of victory might be even greater. When that is almost certainly no longer true, with the advent of nuclear armaments, inhibitions on the use of force by great Powers against great Powers became virtually irresistible.

This is not to say, however, that the non-political work of the UN – in the economic and trading fields, the conquest of disease, the spread of technology from developed to developing countries, the ironing out of differences between rich and poor in the world, the development of backward areas, child and mother care, education, culture, professional training, and hundreds, perhaps thousands, of other activities – will not continue to provide fruitful supplements to what states can do for themselves. Member-countries, in the UN, as well as in the League, must ask themselves whether the benefits which they receive from this kind of co-operation are worth the cost, and the cost must include non-monetary expenditures, such as political and other losses which they must incur. They must also ask whether these activities are not better carried on in local and regional organisations rather than at the global level. Whether such co-operation can ever have desirable political consequences, in the sense of reducing xenophobia, bringing the peoples of the world together in closer contact and enhancing the feeling of a single world community, is another question requiring close study.

Nevertheless, most people would probably agree that, in a world as populous and complex as our own, with an increasing degree of interdependence at all levels between the different nations, such co-operation is inevitable. The fact that it may have no visible consequences in any political sense, whether good or bad, to add to the other benefits it brings, is irrelevant. It is its own justification, and history has shown that, whatever success the political or peace-keeping work of the League or UN, this functional non-political co-operation will continue. But why was the League so evidently ineffective in the maintenance of peace? What made it the failure which it was? That the UN, in vastly different circumstances, seems to be following much the same course raises profound questions about the collective organisation of peace through an international organisation.

II

The formulae for the collective defence of peace and the deterrence of aggression in the League and in the United Nations Organisation are, of course, vastly different from each other; the lessons drawn by the victorious Powers in 1945 from the 'failure' of the League are chiefly responsible for these differences. In 1945, the victors desired a far stronger world organisation, with definite responsibility for taking action against threats to or breaches of the peace assigned to the Security Council of the new body. The League, it was felt, had been designed as an investigative agency, which would probe into dangerous disputes and reveal the identity of the guilty party or parties. Once that had been done and the facts and responsibilities openly established by Council or world court or some other body, the assumption seems to have been that public opinion in the guilty state would do the rest: it would compel its government to withdraw from the situation. It is true that in Articles 10 and 16 the League Covenant admitted that aggression might nevertheless occur, that member-states might resort to war illegally, that is, without complying with the procedures for the peaceful settlement of disputes which the Covenant laid down; in that case, sanctions, perhaps the use of force against the aggressor, might have to be applied, but the idea seemed to be that member-states would institute them automatically and individually, without waiting for the Council to tell them what to do. The emphasis was on the separate member-state's responsibility rather than on collective action centrally directed.

When the UN Charter was drawn up in 1944 and 1945, it was recognised that such an arrangement did not take sufficiently into account the force and thrust of modern aggression. Provisions in the League Covenant for delay before action to preserve peace was taken, a response no doubt to the precipitate way in which war came in August 1914, were felt to be invitations to aggressor states to snatch and devour their victims before the League Council had had time to react. In the new system, the initiative must lie with the Security Council from the outset: it was for that body to recognise threats to or breaches of the peace and to notify other member-states and organise them for action. It would be illegal for other states to resort to force before the Security Council did so, although an exception was made for individual and collective self-defence under Article 51 of the Charter, and even actions under this head had to be reported to the Security Council and terminated when the Council took charge of the situation. The trouble was that the Security Council would be dominated by the victor Powers, especially the United States and the Soviet Union, and it was impossible, short of an attack on the system by some external body, that these two could ever agree on any definition of what constituted a threat to peace.

It is true, of course, that the drafters of the Charter were not so foolish as to assume that the two super-Powers would work in unison, and that they made this assumption the basic premiss of the organisation. They assumed that *unless* the super-Powers worked together, peace would be difficult, if not impossible, to maintain, and this assumption is as valid today as it was in 1945. Nevertheless, by making the new world security organisation stand or fall on the basis of co-operation between the two super-Powers, the founders of the UN substituted for an arrangement which might have worked one which could not. In supporting the idea of building up the General Assembly as an alternative security agency after the Security Council was deadlocked by the veto, the West seemed to be backtracking to the League of Nations formula. In reality, however, the idea was to capture the prestige of the new world organisation for the West's struggle against its major international enemy.

Nevertheless, the League of Nations formula for collective security undoubtedly failed, and we have to inquire into the reasons for this. In reviewing the League's sad history and re-examining the errors its member-states made and the overwhelming problems that confronted them, we are considering, of course, not merely the experience of an organisation, but the strains and tensions of the times in which it lived, and these we have tried to weave into the different chapters of this book. The central weakness of those times, for those who laboured to save the peace, was the break-up of the grand alliance which grappled with and defeated the Central Powers at such cost to themselves in the 1914-18 war. First Russia, then the United States, then Japan, then Italy, either withdrew into isolation from the world balance of power, or, after ten years or more of co-operation with their former allies, took the imperialist road and divided the world in a conflict which could not be resolved except through another round of blood-letting. As desperate League supporters cried to one another in the mid-1930s, it was a case of 'half a League, half a League, half a League onward!'

The predicament of Britain and France as the solitary League Powers with any strength in the 1930s was hard indeed. Divided from the start in their conceptions of what the League was supposed to do, Britain wanting to use the League to revise the excesses of the peace treaties of 1919, France seeking to use it to defend and enforce them, the two democracies were further divided by the absence of the United States and later by the withdrawal of the totalitarian countries. If a whole coalition of Allied and Associated Powers barely sufficed to defeat the Central Powers in 1918, how could Britain and France alone be sufficient to overcome an even larger group of revisionist states in the 1930s? They might have formed alliances with other countries threatened by the revisionists, instead of alienating them by their vacillating attitudes towards the Covenant, but those countries were militarily weak and, after the shocks of the First World War, afraid. It is a curious fact that, in the inter-war period, young men in the fascist states marched and paraded their arms as though they could not wait to enter the battlefields, whereas, in the democratic states, nothing was more chilling than suggestions of a return to the trenches. In 1933, young men in the Oxford Union voted against fighting again for King and Country, and this was often wrongly interpreted as though they would not fight for anything, including the League Covenant. Nevertheless, until the Second World War actually broke out, the young in the democratic countries strongly opposed the military life. Their governments remembered the First World War and how they had been accused of railroading millions of young people to their deaths. Next time, if there was to be a next time, the people must push the governments into battle.

But even if the League had included in its membership all the great powers, or a substantial majority of them, as was achieved in the United Nations in 1945, would they necessarily have co-operated in support of the Covenant? Would universal membership have meant a united League? It is by no means obvious. It was quite impossible for the United States, after its losses in the First World War and its disillusionment with the peace treaties, to send its forces all over the world in defence of those treaties. It did something like this after the Second World War, at least until disenchantment set in after the struggle in Vietnam. But that was after a great war, in which the United States had been a distinguished participant and had emerged from it as the only belligerent positively enriched by the war and more powerful than ever before. If a League member, it is impossible to say what policy the United States would have followed in Geneva: that it remained neutral for two years after the Second World War broke out in September 1939 and only entered the war when its own territory was attacked, throws doubt on the question whether it would have forthrightly defended the Covenant as a League member-state. Much the same applies to the revisionist states, Germany, Italy and Japan. The grievances which people in those states felt against the existing international order must have made them enemies of the *status quo* even had they never left the League in the 1930s, or, having left it, had returned to Geneva. As for the Soviet Union, it can hardly be said that its non-membership of the League in the 1920s was a serious factor in weakening the League. In the 1930s, on the other hand, the deep mistrust between Russia and the West showed that it was not the former's membership of the League, but the lack of the will to work together for the common good which decided the League's fate.

But how could the Axis Powers, as they later became, return to or remain members of an organisation which repudiated the whole basis of their policies? The League of Nations, for better or worse, was a fundamental part of the 1919 peace settlement: it was created to sanctify and enforce the defeat of the Central Powers in November 1918. Italy and Japan, it is true, were not among the defeated in 1918; they sat in the inner rank of peace-makers and were founder members of a League created to maintain the peace – *the* peace, not *a* peace. But the government of Benito Mussolini, which seized power in October 1922, was bitterly disappointed with the outcome of the promises made to Italy when it joined the Allied side in April 1915. The Italian appetite for territory could not be satisfied short of attacking and digesting a League member-state the territorial integrity and political independence of which Italy was bound by the League Covenant to respect against external aggression. The economic strains to which Italy was subjected and for which Mussolini's programme of expansion was supposed to provide a remedy, played a large part in Italian revisionism. But for this, the economic policies favoured by League bodies seemed entirely irrelevant: they recommended classical economic prescriptions, the de-restriction of foreign trade, balanced budgets, the reduction of government spending, the very pre-Keynesian policies which the dictator states derided and grew prosperous by defying. Italian membership of the League could not deflect the principal tendencies of Italian home and foreign policies.

Japan, another major renegade from the Allied coalition of the First World War, was projected into empire building by the same combination of economic pressures and the energies of her young people, who could not find a way of life for themselves at home. The Japanese government in 1931 wanted to break loose from the Western economic system which it regarded as responsible for the country's depressed state: they wished to create a Greater East Asia Co-Prosperity sphere which would prove resistant to Western disturbances. It would be a self-contained system, forging together the resources and manpower of China, Japan and Manchuria, and exempted from Western pressures and the fluctuations of the Western economy. It is hard to say how long, if Japan had remained aloof from the Pearl Harbour policies of December 1941, it could have survived as a self-contained empire. But the idea that it could have stayed part of a co-operative and peaceful League system seems highly improbable. Japan today, that is, in the 1980s, has shown itself capable of becoming a *status quo* Power, which it is hard to think of as returning to the brutal imperialism of the 1930s, but it must always be remembered that it is the Japan of the 1930s which we must think of when we try to speculate what its position in the League would have been had it retained its League membership after its attack on Manchuria in 1931.

That Germany, in the mood in which that country was in the 1930s, could have been a co-operative League member had she returned to her position in Geneva when Britain and France pleaded with her to do so also seems unlikely. Whether Hitler was really bent upon abolishing the multi-state system and replacing it with some form of racial hierarchy, with the Nordic people at the top, is still a matter of controversy. But that he wished to reduce most League member-states to hewers of wood and drawers of water in the Nazi system hardly admits of doubt. The balance of forces between that system and the *status quo* was such that, barring some drastic change in Hitler's policies, a violent collision between the two, which must result in the League's total collapse, seems hardly short of inevitable. It could be said, however, that this considers Germany's relations with the other League states at too late a stage. The *status quo* countries, led by Britain, were willing to make concessions to (or practise 'appeasement' with) Germany in the 1930s, when she was strong and almost bound to regard gifts from the liberal democracies merely as invitations to demand more. Why did they not appreciate Germany's argument for a 'place in the sun' during the Weimar Republic, when to do so might have strengthened liberal Germany against totalitarian pressures? It is often said that if Brüning had received more encouragement at the world disarmament conference in 1932, Hitler might not have won the support for his attacks on the Versailles Treaty system which he did.

We are once more, of course, in the realm of hypothesis. *If* the victors of 1918 had acted thus and thus, how *would* Germany have reacted? Opinion at the time differed on this: the French and the successor states had no easy-going optimism about Germany's ability to see reason and act responsibly when the justice in her arguments was appreciated. The British considered they had little to lose if Germany's eastern frontiers, imposed in 1919, were modified in her favour. But to the Czechs and Poles any such modification was a matter of life and death. Was Britain willing to join a collective guarantee of the successor states if territorial readjustments were made at their expense and in Germany's favour? It hardly seems likely.

But this brings us to an even more fundamental difficulty about the League system, which embarrassed it from the outset, and which has hampered the UN system, and would do so to any system intended to maintain the peace. As we have seen, the League Covenant's Article 10 was supposed to preserve the world's territorial and political *status quo*. The beneficiaries of the 1919 peace settlement, or most of them, liked that position. But those who suffered from the peace settlement – that is, the Powers defeated in the First World War – and some of those on whose shoulders the main burden of defending the *status quo* would fall, especially Britain, regarded Article 10 either as impossible to implement, or as a threat to peace because those not favoured by the existing *status quo* would never reconcile themselves to it. Hence, they wanted the clause diluted by devices such as Article 19, which made provision for the Assembly's periodic review of the *status quo*, with the right to make recommendations for peaceful change. Article 19 was separated from Article 10, and this tended rather to weaken its force. The chief difficulty about these two articles, however, was that they tended to divide League member-states, and world opinion generally, into two groups, a pro-Article 10 group and an opposing pro-Article 19 group. The pro-Article 10 group seemed to think that any modification of the established order in the world would open the road to ruin; the pro-Article 19 section believed that keeping the road to change permanently closed meant pushing problems underground, where they would fester and, at some future time, explode. The obvious tactics for any revisionist faced with these two groups was to play off one against the other. Germany gave France to think that Britain was secretly promising Berlin advantages at France's expense, while telling Britain that, if it were not for French intransigence, the whole problem of Germany's reintegration into Western Europe, with her rights respected, would be solved.

But this is the problem of all international organisations founded to protect the international system from violence against it. It is the problem of stability versus change, order versus social justice, equilibrium and balance as against the need for new arrangements to satisfy requirements of the times. How can people be persuaded to defend the *status quo* with their lives and belongings unless they are convinced that it reflects the ideas they have about social justice? It would be hateful if, at the end of the struggle, only the wicked stood to benefit. But situations which we are asked to defend within a given social order change from day to day, and moral judgments which we make about them – whether they are worth protecting further, whether they should be reformed, and, if so, how – must change with them. But the conditions on which broad agreement can be reached about order and change among many different countries, all with their own interests, beliefs, perspectives, are hazardous to speculate about. Choices and decisions have to be made, and if they involve the risk of having to use force, the pain of selecting courses of action can be great indeed.

Seen through the eyes of the different states, the world may seem to one group a familiar and perhaps an acceptable place, which suits their interests and accords with their sort of game; to another group, it may seem the very incarnation of wrong, a rejection of hopeful possibilities. As we saw in an earlier chapter, the ordinary course of international affairs results in the organisation of these groups into competing, perhaps also armed, camps, which, if all goes well, stand in a posture of immobility in relation to one another. But, when a collective agency is introduced into the scene, all its member-states, unless exceptions are allowed, must take action against countries which break the rules of the club. It is easy enough to say that, in such a case, we must all oppose the sinner and stand by the innocent victim.

290

Perhaps the victim *is* quite obviously innocent, and the aggressor quite obviously guilty; perhaps force may not have to be used; perhaps the mere size and strength of the sanctionist states will deter the wrong-doer. But suppose the two sides are roughly equal in strength, suppose that the rights and wrongs of the case are not so clear, and the risk arises of violent confrontation, with the possibility of defeat for either side. Could the collective security system, in such a situation, be charged with turning a humdrum difference of view into a global conflict?

An even worse situation would be if the 'wrong-doing' state were to be a 'friend' (in the day-by-day run of events) and the victim state an 'enemy'? Could member-states then rally to the 'right' side when signalled to by the collective security organisation? France could not do so when Italy attacked Abyssinia in 1935. The United States and her allies probably could not have done so if UN observers had reported in June 1950 that it was South, not North Korea, which had committed aggression. To suppose that state members of collective security organisations can and will act according to the rules rather than according to their political inclinations and interests is to imagine that in the political situation men and women are angels and will act like them. They are not and will not.

III

Does this mean that collective security, in the sense of arrangements agreed to by all or most of the world's states, combining them together in restraint of one country using force against another, is an impracticable enterprise? Has the League experience (and that of the United Nations, for that matter) demonstrated that, at the end of the day, the collective use of force against an indeterminate aggressor – meaning one the identity of whom is not known when the arrangement was made – is, and always will be, a non-starter? Of course, we have to distinguish between the use of force to stop or reverse an actual act of aggression, and peace-keeping forces, which depend upon the goodwill and freely given consent, both of the countries contributing to such forces and of the countries which admit them into their territories. The former is the function of 'fighting forces', conducting operations (as in Korea between June 1950 and July 1953) as intensive and destructive as those in the great international wars of the present century. The latter are police operations, using force only in self-defence and acceptable to the parties to the dispute because they wish to see the situation pacified and to avoid full-scale hostilities.

The existence of the League of Nations between 1920 and 1946 made the use of force by one state against another a matter of international concern. After the world had accepted the League Covenant, there could be no private wars, and this may have dissuaded some states from resorting to them. Countries making war must give the reasons which led them to fight, or the reasons they considered it politic to state, and must justify their arguments: their victims and critics must be allowed to have their say. This did not, during the League's history, deter powerful countries from attacking weaker ones. Moreover, in so far as such forms of international bullying have tended to decline in the period since the League's demise, the reason probably lies more in the general consciousness of the serious repercussions of using force as an instrument of policy than in the greater publicity given to international events as a result of the creation of general international organisations. Nevertheless, it is true to say that the wider publicity surrounding offences against international order today does act as some restraint against them, and, for that, we must confer some credit on the League-type body. But it is also true that the general collective security system, under which many states unite their efforts to control *any* state *anywhere* which breaks the peace, failed during the League's life and in that of the UN. The maintenance of peace has, on the whole, returned to traditional balance-of-power practices, which the world-wide organisations like the League were intended to supersede. It may be argued that, if this is so, the fault lay with the human beings who tried to work these organisations, rather than with the organisations themselves. But organisations are founded to produce certain effects: if they do not accord with the psychology of those who have to operate them, what purpose do they serve, apart from providing ideals by which men and women may judge their daily conduct, though that may be a function of the highest value in the increasingly interdependent world community?

It needs to be stressed once again, however, that in confining ourselves, as we have done in this book, mainly to the political and diplomatic work of the League, we are omitting activities which many have considered the most important part of its commitments, namely its contribution to the multitudinous international activities which proceed on this planet, the social and economic co-operation, the maintenance of health and satisfactory conditions of labour, the struggle against sex, religious or racial discrimination, the improvement of education at all levels, the achievement of social justice, and a thousand more activities central to modern life. The relation between co-operation of this kind and the maintenance of peace between nations is often obscure: it could be argued that, the more conscious we are of our dependence upon other people in different parts of the world, the less prone we may be to go to war with them. But it is not on this argument that the case for functional co-operation mainly rests, but on its obvious value to all of us in the world today. The political work of the League in the field of improving international relations, with all its tragedies, came and went, as did the League itself, but international co-operation to meet and satisfy basic human needs continues to flourish, and to that the League of Nations magnificently contributed. If the states of the world nevertheless wish to subject their disputes to the test of force, that is their affair. But the League of Nations and its successor, the United Nations, are reminders that such resorts to despair are unnecessary and rob us of the benefits which international co-operation can confer on all of us.

Abbreviations

DBFP	The series *Documents on British Foreign Policy, 1919-1939*, published by HM Stationery Office, London
FRUS	Foreign Relations of the United States, Washington, D.C.
LNOJ	League of Nations Official Journal
PRO	Public Record Office, London
RIIA	The Royal Institute of International Affairs, London
UN	United Nations

Notes

Note Places of publication are given only for works published outside the United Kingdom.

1 THE WORLD BEFORE THE LEAGUE

1. The member-states of the League on 1 February 1938 are listed in Appendix C.
2. The expression 'the international anarchy' was popularised by G. Lowes Dickinson in a book with that title published in London in 1926. Lowes Dickinson defined the international anarchy as the 'juxtaposition of a number of states, independent and armed'. Under that condition, he wrote, 'war is not an accident. It springs inevitably from the facts'.
3. On the European diplomatic system see Sir Harold Nicolson, *Diplomacy*, 3rd edn, 1963; Sir E. Satow, *A Guide to Diplomatic Practice*, 5th edn, ed. by Lord Gore-Booth, 1979; B. Sen, *A Diplomat's Handbook of International Law andPractice*, The Hague, 1965; Sir C.K. Webster, *The Art and Practice of Diplomacy*, 1961.
4. Carsten Holbraad, *The Concert of Europe. A study in German and British international theory, 1815-1914*, 1970, p.2.
5. Webster, *op.cit.*, pp.59, 69.
6. *Ibid.*, p.67.
7. *Key Treaties for the Great powers, 1815-1914*, Vol.I, 1814-1870. Selected and edited by Michael Hurst, 1972, p.123.
8. See Sir C.K. Webster, *The Foreign Policy of Castlereagh, 1815-1822*, 1925; H.G. Schenk, *The Aftermath of the Napoleonic Wars*, 1947.
9. See M.P.A. Hankey, *Diplomacy by Conference. Studies in public affairs, 1920-1946*, 1946; N.L. Hill, *The Public International Conference*, 1929; Sir E. Satow, *International Congresses and Conferences*, 1920.

10. On the Hague conferences, see J.H. Choate, *The Two Hague Conferences*, Princeton and London, 1913; A. Pearce Higgins, *The Two Hague Conferences*, Boston, 1908; M.L. Renault (ed.), *Les deux conférences de la Paix*, Paris, 1908; J.B. Scott (ed.), *Texts of the Peace Conferences at The Hague, 1899 and 1907*, Boston and London, 1908.

11. See Sir J.A. Salter, *Allied Shipping Control. An experiment in international administration*, 1921.

12. On nineteenth-century international arbitration, see W. Evans Darby, *International Tribunals*, 1904; Manley O. Hudson, *International Tribunals*, Washington, D.C., 1944; A. de Lapradelle and N. Politis, *Recueil des arbitrages internationaux*, 3 vols, Paris, 1905, 1923, 1954; R.C. Morris, *International Arbitration and Procedure*, New Haven, Conn., 1911; J.L. Simpson and Hazel Fox, *International Arbitration. Law and practice*, 1959; A.M. Stuyt, *Survey of International Arbitration, 1794-1970*, Leiden, 1972.

13. *Queen Elizabeth II's award for the arbitration of a controversy between the Argentinian Republic and the Republic of Chile concerning parts of the boundary between their territories*, 1966.

14. Simpson and Fox, *op.cit.*, p.10.

15. Hurst, *op.cit.*, p.336.

16. F.S.L. Lyons, *Internationalism in Europe, 1815-1914*, 1963, p.12. See also Paul S. Reinsch, *Public International Unions*, Boston, 1911.

17. *La vie internationale* was the name of a monthly review of the activities of unofficial international organisations edited by H. La Fontaine and P. Otlet and published by the Union of International Associations in Brussels from 1912 until 1914. It resumed publication for a short period in 1921.

18. Lyons, *op.cit.*, p.47.

19. On the nineteenth-century economic system in Europe, see W. Ashworth, *A Short History of the International Economy since 1850*, 3rd edn, 1975; K. Polanyi, *The Great Transformation*, Boston, Mass., 1957.

20. On the peace movements before 1914, see A.F.C. Beales, *The History of Peace. A short account of the organised movements for international peace*, 1931.

21. On the nineteenth-century alliance system, see L. Oppenheim, *International Law. A treatise*, ed. by H. Lauterpacht, 8th edn, 1955, Vol.I, Chapter III, Part I, pp.959-64; and W.L. Langer, *European Alliances and Alignments, 1871-1890*, 2nd edn, New York, 1962, *The Diplomacy of Imperialism*, 1890-1902, 2nd edn, New York, 1956.

22. Introduction to Sir G. Butler, *A Handbook to the League of Nations*, 1928, p.vii.

23. *The Geneva Experiment*, 1931, p.2.

2 FRAMING THE COVENANT

1. John H. Latané (ed.), *Development of the League of Nations Idea. Documents and Correspondence of Theodore Marburg*, New York, 1932, Vol.II, pp.703-06.
2. H.R. Winkler, *The League of Nations Movement in Great Britain, 1914-1919*, New Brunswick, New Jersey, 1952, pp.16-23.
3. Latané, *op.cit.*, Vol.II, p.790.
4. Ruhl J. Bartlett, *The League to Enforce Peace*, Chapel Hill, N.C., 1940, pp.39-42; *Enforced Peace. Proceedings of the First Annual Assemblage of the League to Enforce Peace, Washington, May 26-27, 1916*, New York, 1916.
5. Ray Stannard Baker, *Woodrow Wilson. Life and Letters*, Toronto, 1938, Vol.VI, pp.220-3; Arthur S. Link, *Wilson, Campaign for Progressivism and Peace, 1916-1917*, Princeton, N.J., 1965, pp.25-26.
6. Baker, *op.cit.*, Vol.VI, p.398; Link, *op.cit.*, p.218; *Foreign Relations of the United States, 1916*, Supplement, pp.89, 97-99.
7. The text of the Phillimore Report is in PRO,GT4454,CAB 24/50.
8. David Hunter Miller, *The Drafting of the Covenant*, Vol.II, New York and London, 1928, pp.7-11; Baker, *Woodrow Wilson and World Settlement*, New York, 1922, Vol.III, pp.79-87.
9. Hunter Miller, *op.cit.*, Vol.II, pp.12-15; Baker, *op.cit.*, Vol.III, pp.88-93.
10. Hunter Miller, *op.cit.*, Vol.II, pp.61-64.
11. J.C. Smuts, *A League of Nations. A Practical Suggestion*, 1918.
12. Hunter Miller, *op.cit.*, Vol.II pp 65-93; Baker, *op.cit.* Vol. III, pp.100-10.
13. See below, Chapter 9; Hunter Miller, *op.cit.* Vol.II pp.204-28.
14. Hunter Miller, *op.cit.*, Vol.II, pp.145-54; Baker, *op.cit.*, Vol.III, pp.117-29.
15. H.W.V. Temperley, *A History of the Peace Conference of Paris*, 1920, Vol.III, Appendix II, Part III, p.56.
16. Hunter Miller, *op.cit.*, Vol.II, pp.231-37; Baker, *op.cit.*, Vol.III, pp.144-51.
17. See report of the committee appointed by the French Government, completed in June 1918; PRO,FO371/3439.
18. Baker, *op.cit.*, Vol.III, pp.236-39.

3 THE COVENANT REVIEWED

1. The text of the Covenant including amendments in force on 1 February 1938 is given in Appendix A. A list of the Allied and Associated Powers which attended the Peace Conference and were original members of the League is given in Appendix B.

2. The Treaty of Versailles was signed by the Allied and Associated Powers with Germany, those of St Germain-en-Laye with Austria, Neuilly-sur-Seine with Bulgaria, and Trianon with Hungary.

3. The thirteen neutral states invited to accede to the Covenant were:

Argentine Republic	Norway	Spain
Chile	Paraguay	Sweden
Columbia	Persia	Switzerland
Denmark	Salvador	Venezuela
Netherlands		

4. In accordance with a resolution adopted by the Assembly on 21 September 1926 the paragraphs of the Covenant articles were numbered after that date.

5. Article 6.

6. See Manley O. Hudson, *The Permanent Court of International Justice*, New York, 1934.

7. The number of non-permanent members of the Council was increased to six by the Assembly on 25 September 1922, to nine on 8 September 1926, to ten on 9 October 1933, and to eleven on 2 October 1936.

8. Article 32 of the UN Charter.

9. Articles 4, 6 (2), 1 (2) of the Covenant respectively.

10. James Eric Drummond, 16th Earl of Perth, 1876-1951. Earldom, 1937. Educated Eton. Foreign Office, 1900. Private secretary to Asquith (1912-1915), Sir Edward Grey (1915-1916), and A.J. Balfour (1916-1918). Secretary-General of League, 1920-1933. British Ambassador, Rome, 1933-1941. Deputy Leader of Liberal Party, 1946.

11. Joseph Avenol, born 1879. French administrator, Secretary-General of League, 1933-1940. Deputy Secretary-General, 1923-1933.

12. Documents of United Nations Conference on International Organisation, San Francisco, 1945, Vol.III, Doc. 1, G/l, pp.1-23.

13. Misc. No.3 (1919), *The Covenant of the League of Nations with a commentary thereon*, Cmd. 151, p.14.

14. Treaty Series No.5 (1924), Cmd. 2036.

15. See below, Chapter 6.

16. Article 34 of the UN Charter.

17. Quincy Wright, *Mandates under the League of Nations*, Chicago, 1930, pp.137-55.

18. George Lenczowski, *The Middle East in World Affairs*, New York, 1962, pp.91-98.

19. See below, Chapter 9.

20. W. Galenson, *The International Labour Organisation*, University of Wisconsin, 1981.

21. For the League committees, see H.R.G. Greaves, *The League Committees and World Order*, 1931.

22. Official No. A. 23. 1939.
23. See James Avery Joyce, *Red Cross International and the Strategy of Peace*, 1959.

4   BEGINNINGS AND SETBACKS

1. F.P. Walters, *A History of the League of Nations*, 1952, Chapter 12.
2. See W.M. Jordan, *Great Britain, France and the German Problem*, London, 1943.
3. Carole Fink, *The Genoa Conference. European Diplomacy, 1921-1922*, Chapel Hill and London, 1984.
4. Procès-Verbal of the lst meeting of the Council of the League of Nations, League of Nations (27 A/2764/2765) (20/29/1). Records of the First Assembly. Plenary Meetings, Geneva, 1920.
5. Article 49.
6. Procès-Verbal of the 4th meeting of the Second Session, 12 February 1920, p.19.
7. See Laing Gray Conan, *France and the Saar, 1680-1948*, New York, 1950, Chapter 5; Sidney Osborne, *The Saar Question*, 1923; Jean Priou, *Le Territoire de la Saare*, Nancy-Paris-Strasbourg, 1923.
8. S. Wambaugh, *The Saar Plebiscite*, Cambridge, Mass., 1940.
9. Procès-Verbal of the Eighth Session of the Council, League of Nations, San Sebastian, July-August 1920, p.7.
10. 16th meeting of the Second Session, London, 13 February 1920, p.19.
11. Procès-Verbal of the 14th meeting of the Eleventh Session of the Council (20/29/17), p.37.
12. LNOJ, March 1923, p.231.
13. Procès-Verbal of the 2nd and 3rd meetings of the Fourth Session of the Council (20/29/7 – 10), Paris, pp.9-13, p.15, Annex 33b.
14. Records of the Third Assembly, Vol.I, Geneva 1922, pp.185-6.
15. Procès-Verbal of 3rd meeting of the Fourth Session (20/29/7 – 10), Paris, p.15, Annex 32b.
16. Procès-Verbal of lst meeting of the Third Session (20/29/6), Paris, pp.3, 9-11, Annex 23; 3rd meeting of the Fifth Session, Rome, p.19, Annex 38a.
17. Procès-Verbal of the lst meeting of the Sixth Session (20/29/12), London, pp.3-9.
18. Procès-Verbal of the 6th meeting of the Seventh Session (20/29/13), London, p.31, Annex 68h.
19. Procès-Verbal of the 4th meeting of the Ninth Session (20/29/15), Paris, pp.17-19, Annex 101.
20. Procès-Verbal of the 14th meeting of the Thirteenth Session, Geneva, pp.40-43.
21. League of Nations Treaty Series, Vol.IX, 1922, No.255, pp.211-21.

22. Procès-Verbal of 3rd meeting of the Ninth Session, Paris, pp.11-15; Procès-Verbal of the Tenth Session (20/29/16), Brussels, p.39. R.F. Leslie (ed.), *The History of Poland since 1863*, 1980, p.138.

23. Robert Machray, *The Poland of Pilsudski*, 1936, p.170; Richard M. Watt, *Bitter Glory. Poland and its fate, 1918-1939*, New York, 1979, pp.170-72.

24. Records of the First Assembly, Geneva, 1920, 9th Plenary Meeting, pp.185-91.

25. Procès-Verbal of 4th meeting of the Fourth Session, Paris, Annex 30c.

26. LNOJ, 1, No.8 (1920) 89; Quincy Wright, *Mandates under the League of Nations*, Chicago, 1930, p.95, n. 82.

27. 9th Plenary Meeting, 22 November 1920, p.191.

28. LNOJ, May 1921, pp.265-69.

29. *Ibid.*, November 1921, pp.982-83; December 1921, p.1141, pp.1220-32.

30. Procès-Verbal of 9th meeting of the Eighteenth Session, 16 May 1922; LNOJ, June 1922, Part II, pp.541-42.

31. *The Financial Reconstruction of Austria. General Survey and Principal Documents*, League of Nations, Geneva, 1926.

32. W. Goode, 'Austria', *Journal of the British Institute of International Affairs*, March 1922, pp.35-54.

33. See Elizabeth Barker, *Austria, 1918-1972*, 1973, Chapter 6; G.E.R. Gedye, *Heirs to the Habsburgs*, 1932, Chapter 5; Charles A. Gulick, *Austria from Habsburg to Hitler*, Vol.I, Los Angeles, 1948, pp.158-67.

34. Andrew C. Janos, *The Politics of Backwardness in Hungary*, New Jersey, 1982, Chapter 5; Ervin Pamlényi (ed.), *A History of Hungary*, 1975, Chapter 9 (3); *The Financial Reconstruction of Hungary. General Survey and Principal Documents*, League of Nations, Geneva, 1926; Sir A. Salter, 'The Reconstruction of Hungary', *Journal of the British Institute of International Affairs*, July 1924, pp.190-204.

35. LNOJ, June 1920, pp.134-36.

36. P.J. Noel-Baker, *Disarmament*, 1926, pp.74-96; F.B. Maurice, 'Lord Esher's Proposals for the Limitation of Armaments', *Journal of the British Institute of International Affairs*, July 1922, pp.101-12.

37. Records of the Third Assembly. Plenary Meetings, Geneva, 1922, p.291.

38. See Chapter 9, below.

39. League of Nations. Barcelona Conference. Verbatim Reports and Texts. [LN. VIII. 1921. 1.] Geneva, 1921.

40. League of Nations. Provisional Health Committee. Minutes of the First Session, Geneva, August 25-29, 1921.

41. International Financial Conference, Brussels, 1920. Proceedings of the Conference, Vol.I. Report of the Conference, Brussels.

42. ILO. *Official Bulletin*, Vol.I, April 1919 – August 1920, Geneva, 1923, Chapters 2 to 5.
43. D.F. Fleming, *The United States and World Organisation, 1920-1933*, New York, 1938, p.19.
44. See Henry Cabot Lodge, *The Senate and the League of Nations*, New York, 1925, especially Chapter 10.
45. See Chapter 8, below.
46. Records of the 12th Plenary Meeting of the Fourth Assembly, September 24, 1923, LNOJ Special Supplement No.13, pp.75-87.
47. For text of the draft treaty, see LNOJ, Special Supplement No.16, Records of the Fourth Assembly, Minutes of Third Committee, Geneva, 1923, pp.153-55.
48. See Report of the Dawes Committee, Cmd. 2105 (1924).
49. PRO,FO371/11070.
50. See P.J. Noel-Baker, *The Geneva Protocol*, 1926. The text of the Protocol is printed in Annex VIII.
51. *Protocol or Pact*, published by the Labour Party, 1925 (?), p.5.
52. Misc. No.5 (1925). Statement by the Rt. Hon. Austen Chamberlain on behalf of HMG to the Council of the League of Nations, Cmd. 2368.
53. Protocol for the Pacific Settlement of International Disputes. Correspondence relating to the position of the Dominions, Cmd. 2458 (1925).
54. PRO,FO371/9420.
55. *Ibid*.
56. Walters, *op.cit.*, Vol.I, p.291.

5 THE SYSTEM TAKES SHAPE

1. Records of the First Assembly, 26th Plenary Meeting, pp.570-77, 581-82, 582-84, 584-85, 585-86.
2. Records of the Second Assembly, Plenary Meetings, p.14.
3. Records of the Fourth Assembly, Plenary Meetings, 4th Plenary Meeting, p.24, pp.124-25.
4. Misc. No.5 (1923), Correspondence with the Allied Governments respecting Reparation Payments by Germany, Cmd. 1943, p.28.
5. LNOJ, March 1923, pp.198-201.
6. Treaty Series No.28 (1926). Treaty of Mutual Guarantee between the United Kingdom, Belgium, France, Germany and Italy, Cmd. 2764, p.9.
7. See Stresemann's letter to the former German Crown Prince of 7 September 1925 in *Stresemann's Diaries, Papers and Letters*, ed. by Eric Sutton, Vol.II, 1935, pp.503-55.
8. LNOJ, Special Supplement No.42. Records of the Special Session of the Assembly, March 1926.

9. LNOJ, Special Supplement No.44. Records of the Seventh Ordinary Session of the Assembly. Plenary Meetings, pp.31-36.
10. Records of the First Assembly. Plenary Meetings, 28th Plenary Meeting, pp.643-51.
11. LNOJ, July-August 1921, pp.469-84; Records of the Second Assembly. Plenary Meetings, 13th Plenary Meeting, pp.274-79; LNOJ, December 1921, pp.1194-1215.
12. LNOJ, February 1922, p.153.
13. Stephanaq Pollo and Arben Puto, *The History of Albania*, p.184.
14. The position of the Kurds is discussed in William R. Polk, *The Arab World*, Cambridge, Mass., 1965, 1969, 1975, 1980.
15. Treaty Series No.16 (1923), Cmd. 1929.
16. LNOJ, October 1924, pp.1291-92.
17. LNOJ, November 1934, p.1649.
18. LNOJ, October 1924, pp.1358-60.
19. *Collection of Advisory Opinions of the Permanent Court of International Justice*, Series B, No.12; S.H. Longrigg, *Iraq, 1900-1950. A Political, Social and Economic History*, 1953, p.155.
20. LNOJ, February 1926, pp.187-93.
21. LNOJ, April 1926, pp.502-05.
22. Great Britain, Treaty Series (1926), Cmd. 2679.
23. LNOJ, January 1924, pp.122-23.
24. James Barros, *The Corfu Incident of 1923. Mussolini and the League of Nations*, Princeton, N.J., 1965, pp.74-80.
25. LNOJ, November 1923, pp.1276-82, 1283-85.
26. *Ibid.*, p.1295.
27. *Ibid.*, pp.1305-06.
28. Barros, *op.cit.*, p.291.
29. LNOJ, November 1923, pp.1346-52.
30. LNOJ, November 1925, pp.1699-1700.
31. LNOJ, February 1926, pp.172-77, 196-209.

6 THE LURE OF DISARMAMENT

1. Foreign Office, *The Treaty of Peace between the Allied and Associated Powers and Germany*, 1925, p.82.
2. *Ibid.*, p.308.
3. The text of the convention is printed in League of Nations Publications IX, Disarmament, 1930, IX, 8.
4. The point was made by Lord Cecil in his Romanes Lecture, *Peace and Pacifism*, 1938.
5. See n. 36 to Chapter 4 above.
6. *The Treaty of Peace*, pp.247-51.
7. France No.1 (1924), Papers respecting negotiations for an Anglo-French Pact, Cmd. 2169.
8. See above, Chapter 4, p.121.

9. RIIA, *Documents on International Affairs, 1933*, 1934, p.293.
10. Report to the Council on the Work of the First Session of the Commission, C. 301. 1926. IX, Geneva, 24 May 1926.
11. RIIA, *Documents on International Affairs, 1930*, 1931, pp.l2-23; Cmd. 3758.
12. League Documents, CPD 292 (2) and CPD 295 (1); Cmd. 3757; RIIA, *Documents on International Affairs, 1931*, 1932, pp.l8-39.
13. League Document, 1932, IX, 63, pp.ll3-16; RIIA, *Documents on International Affairs, 1932*, 1933, pp.l60-61; Records of the Conference for the Reduction and Limitation of Armaments. Series A, Vol.I, pp.60-64. Conf. D. 56.
14. Records of the Conference for the Reduction and Limitation of Armaments, Series A, Vol.I, pp.67-70.
15. A.J. Toynbee, *Survey of International Affairs, 1932*, 1933. pp.225-26.
16. R.T. Clark, *The Fall of the German Republic*, 1935, p.311.
17. Erich Eyck, *A History of the Weimar Republic*, Vol.II, 1964, p.361.
18. DBFP, Second Series, Vol.III, No.240.
19. Sir J.W. Wheeler-Bennett, *The Disarmament Deadlock*, 1934, p.33.
20. Minutes of the General Commission, League Document, 1932, IX, 64, p.122.
21. 268 HC Deb. 5s. Cols 624-9; *Statement of the views of HMG in the United Kingdom regarding the proposals contained in President Hoover's declaration*, 1932.
22. DBFP, Second Series, Vol.III, Appendix VII, pp.613-17.
23. Ibid., No.270; Minutes of the General Commission, Vol.I, pp.186-88.
24. Wheeler-Bennett, *op.cit.*, p.55.
25. *The Times*, 17 September 1932.
26. Published as Document 146 of the Disarmament Conference.
27. RIIA, *Documents on International Affairs, 1932*, 1933, pp.227-29.
28. *The Times*, 12 December 1932.
29. DBFP, Second Series, Vol.IV, No.280 and n. 1.
30. Minutes of the General Commission, Vol.II, Geneva, 1933, p.251.
31. *Ibid.*, pp.251-62.
32. David Childs, *Germany since 1918*, New York, 1980, pp.53-54.
33. 87 H.L. Deb. 5s, Cols 897-99 (11 May 1933).
34. The Earl of Avon, *The Eden Memoirs. Facing the Dictators*, 1962, pp.30-4.
35. Minutes of the General Commission, Vol.II, League Document, 1933, IX, 10, pp.352-57; League Document, Conference D/1933; Cmd. 4279.
36. RIIA, *Documents on International Affairs, 1933*, 1934, pp.240-49.
37. *Ibid.*, pp.424-25.
38. Wheeler-Bennett, *op.cit.*, p.165.
39. *Ibid.*, pp.67-68.

40. *Ibid.*, pp.175-77.
41. Cmd. 4437.
42. RIIA, *Documents on International Affairs, 1933*, 1934, p.285; Cmd. 4437; *Frankfurter Zeitung*, 15 October 1933.
43. *Le Matin*, 17 November 1933.
44. League Document, 1934, IX. 1.
45. 286 H.C. Deb. 5s, Col 2078.
46. In accordance with the final resolution adopted on 8 June; see League Document, Conference D/C.G./168.
47. 254 H.C. Deb. 5s. Cols 956, 963 (29 June 1931).

7 MANCHURIA: THE COVENANT DEFIED

1. Treaty Series No.42 (1925), Cmd. 2517.
2. Article 6 of the Treaty of Portsmouth. *Nouveau Recueil Général de Traités. Continuation du Grand Recueil de G. Fr. de Martens*, par Felix Stoerk, Deuxième Série, Vol.33, Leipzig, 1926, pp.3-12.
3. T.E. la Fargue, *China and the World War*, Palo Alto and London, 1937, pp.241-43.
4. Treaty Series No.5 (1924), Cmd. 2036.
5. Treaty Series No.6 (1924), Cmd. 2037.
6. A.J. Toynbee, *Survey of International Affairs, 1932*, 1933, pp.452-70.
7. Freda Utley, *Japan's Feet of Clay*, 1936, p.9.
8. See R. Bassett, *Nineteen Thirty-One Political Crisis*, 1958, pp.234-36.
9. New York and London, 1936.
10. Report of the Commission of Inquiry, C.663. M. 320. 1932. VII, Geneva, 1 October 1932, p.71.
11. LNOJ, December 1931, Annex 1334, I, pp.2453-54.
12. *Ibid.*, pp.2265-74.
13. LNOJ, Special Supplement No.93, Geneva 1931, pp.161-63.
14. LNOJ, December 1931, pp.2307-09.
15. *Ibid.*, p.2514 and p.2516.
16. *Ibid.*, pp.2322-29.
17. US State Department, Press release, No.107, 17 October 1931.
18. LNOJ, December 1931, p.2358.
19. *Ibid.*, p.2365.
20. The four members, other than Lytton, were:
    Count Aldrovandi (Italian)
    General Henri Claudel (French)
    Major-General Frank Ross McCoy (United States)
    Dr Heinrich Schnee (German)
    See LNOJ, December 1931, p.2378.
21. *Ibid.*

304

22. See below, pp.210-11.
23. 262 H.C. Deb. 5s. Col 183.
24. *The Far Eastern Crisis*, p.92.
25. DBFP, Second Series, Vol.IX, p.102.
26. 262 H.C. Deb. 5s. Col 360 (24 February 1932).
27. Toynbee, *op.cit.*, pp.470-515.
28. LNOJ, March 1932, p.350.
29. 261 H.C. Deb. 5s. Col 1261 (15 February 1932).
30. LNOJ, March 1932, Annex I, p.373.
31. *Ibid.*, p.383.
32. Henry L. Stimson and McGeorge Bundy, *On Active Service in Peace and War*, New York, 1947, 1948, pp.249-54.
33. RIIA (ed.), *Documents on International Affairs, 1932*, 1933, pp.265-66.
34. LNOJ, December 1931, p.2455 and p.2280.
35. LNOJ, March 1932, p.365.
36. League of Nations, Monthly Summary, Vol.XII, 3, March 1932.
37. LNOJ, Special Supplement No.101, p.215.
38. Report of the Commission of Inquiry, Chapter IX, pp.127-33.
39. LNOJ, December 1932, pp.1869-1915.
40. LNOJ, Special Supplement No.111, Geneva, 1933, pp.21-75.
41. LNOJ, Special Supplement No.112, Geneva, 1933, pp.24-28.
42. *The Memoirs of Cordell Hull*, Vol.I, 1948, Chapters 12 and 13.
43. David Marquand, *Ramsay MacDonald*, 1977. pp.714-15.
44. R. Bassett, *Democracy and Foreign Policy. A case history. The Sino-Japanese dispute, 1931-33*, 1952.
45. 260 H.C. Deb. 5s. Col 464.
46. *Ibid.*, 270, Cols 532-33.
47. *Ibid.*, 259, Cols 201-02.
48. DBFP, Second Series, Vol.IX, p.33.
49. 275 H.C. Deb. 5s. Cols 58-59.

8 THE BETTERMENT OF LIFE

1. Ruth B. Henig (ed.), *The League of Nations*, 1973, p.153.
2. See above, Chapter 4, pp.81-82.
3. Report on the Work of the League of Nations since the Fourteenth Assembly Session, A. 6. 1934, Geneva, 5 July 1934.
4. H.R.G. Greaves, *The League Committees and World Order*, 1931, pp.48-49.
5. J.I. Knudson, *A History of the League of Nations*, Atlanta, Georgia, 1938, p.214.
6. League Document, 1933, ii, Spec. 1.
7. *The Economist*, 6 July 1933.

8. Report on the Work of the League of Nations since the Fourteenth Assembly Session, A. 6a. 1934, Geneva, 8 September 1934, p.45.
9. C. 378. M. 1936. IIB.
10. Report on the Work of the League of Nations, 1936-37, A. 6. 1937, p.102.
11. *La Conférence de la Société des Nations à Barcelone*, Lausanne, Geneva, 1921.
12. Report on the Work of the League of Nations since the Fifteenth Assembly Session, Part I, A. 6. 1935, Geneva, 6 July 1935, p.84.
13. A. 6a. 1937.
14. See H.V. Hodson, *Slump and Recovery, 1929-1937*, 1938, Chapter IX, 'National Efforts, 1933-35'.
15. LNOJ, Special Supplement No.13, Geneva, 1923, pp.54-57.
16. League of Nations, Records of the First Assembly, Plenary Meetings, Geneva, 1920, pp.537-45; LNOJ, March-April 1921, p.114.
17. Records of the Second Opium Conference, Vol.I, Plenary Meetings, Geneva, August 1925, C. 760. M. 260. 1924. XI.
18. LNOJ, June 1930, pp.525-28.
19. League of Nations, Records of the Conference for the Limitation of the Manufacture of Narcotic Drugs, Geneva, 1931.
20. A. 6. 1936, p.201.
21. A. 6. 1937, Geneva, 28 July 1937, p.184.
22. A. 6. 1934, Geneva, 5 July 1934, pp.81-84.
23. A. 13. 1927, Geneva, 1 June 1927, p.52; LNOJ, Special Supplement No.44, Geneva, 1926, pp.130-37.
24. See the author's unpublished Ph.D. thesis, 'International Intellectual Co-operation within the League of Nations. Its conceptual basis and lessons for the present', University of London, 1953.
25. Official No. A. 23. 1939.

9 THE MANDATES SYSTEM

1. See above, Chapter 2, p.37.
2. *The Works and Correspondence of Edmund Burke*, 8 Vols, 1852, Vol.VII, pp.279-320.
3. Minutes of the First Session of the PMC. C. 416. M. 296. 1921. VI, p.4.
4. Minutes of the Second Session. C. 548. M. 330. 1922. VI, Annex 6, pp.92-3.
5. Norman Bentwich, *The Mandates System*, 1930, p.20.
6. The first members of the Mandates Commission were:
    Pierre Orts (Belgium)
    Ormsby-Gore (British)

> Ramon Pina (Spanish)
> Beau (French)
> Marquis Theodoli (Italian)
> Yanagida (Japanese)
> Van Rees (Netherlands)
> Freire D'Andrade (Portuguese)
> Mme Bugge-Wicksell (Swedish)

Thus four of the nine members (Orts, Ormsby-Gore, Beau and Yanagida) came from states administering mandated territories.

7. Minutes, 6th meeting, 7 October, p.31.
8. Second Session, 5 August, pp.41-43.
9. Third Session. A. 19. 1923. VI, p.66 (26 July).
10. 27th meeting, Third Session, 7 August 1923, pp.183-87.
11. Ninth Session. C. 405. M. 144. 1926. VI, p.41.
12. C. 489. M. 214. 1934. VI, pp.52, 55.
13. Eighth Extraordinary Session. C. 174. M. 65. 1926. VI, p.51.
14. *Ibid.*, Annex IV, pp.198-208.
15. C. 422. M. 176. 1931. VI, p.35.
16. *Syria and Lebanon under French Mandate*, 1958, p.322.
17. See the verdict on the French Mandate for Syria and Lebanon in Longrigg, *op.cit.*, pp.362-68.
18. Fifteenth Session. C. 305. M. 105. 1929. VI, p.79.
19. LNOJ, June 1930, pp.549-50; Report of Commission on the Palestine Disturbances of August 1929, Cmd. 3530 (1930); Hope-Simpson Report on Immigration, Land Settlement and Development in Palestine, Cmd. 3686 (1930); Minutes of the Seventeenth Session of the PMC and Report to the Council. C. 355 (1). M. 147 (1). 1930. VI.
20. Cmd. 3530, p.158.
21. *Ibid.*, p.163.
22. Minutes of the Seventeenth Extraordinary Session. C. 355 (1). M. 147 (1). 1930. VI, pp.29, 67.
23. Minutes of the Nineteenth Session. C. 643. M. 262. 1930. VI, p.73.
24. Minutes of the Twenty-Fifth Session. C. 259. M. 108. 1934. VI, p.17.
25. See Minutes of the Thirty-Second Session. C. 330. M. 222. 1937. VI.
26. Cmd. 5479; Cmd. 5513.
27. LNOJ, December 1937, p.907.
28. Minutes of the Thirty-Fourth Session. C. 216. M. 119. 1938. VI, Annex 31, p.228.
29. Cmd. 5634.
30. Minutes of the Thirty-Sixth Session. C. 170. M. 100. 1939. VI; Cmd. 6019.
31. Annex 14 to Minutes of the Thirty-Sixth Session (n. 30, above).
32. See above, pp.282-83.

33. Minutes of the Twentieth Session. C. 422. M. 176. 1931. VI, Annex 16, pp.228-29.
34. Minutes of the Twenty-First Session. C. 830. M. 411. 1931. VI, Annex 22, pp.221-25.
35. Minutes of Twenty-Third Session. C. 406. M. 209. 1933. VI, p.14; LNOJ, December 1932, pp.1962-66.
36. Minutes of Twenty-Fourth Session. C. 619. M. 292. 1933. VI, pp.27-29.
37. Minutes of Eleventh Session. C. 348. M. 122. 1927. VI, pp.58-86.
38. For these proposals, see Cmd. 3234 (1929), Cmd. 3378 (1929), Cmd. 3573 (1930), Cmd. 3574 (1930), Cmd. 4141 (1932).
39. C. 406. M. 209. 1933. VI, pp.35-43, 45-52, 64-70, 71-74, 77-80, 120-24.
40. C. 251. M. 123. 1935, pp.125-28; LNOJ, June 1935, pp.606-07.
41. Minutes of Twenty-Ninth Session. C. 259. M. 153. 1936. VI, pp.41-2.

10   THE ABYSSINIAN DISASTER

1. See above, Chapter 7.
2. DBFP, Second Series, Vol.XIV, No.244.
3. *Ibid.*, No.281.
4. The Earl of Avon, *The Eden Memoirs. Facing the Dictators*, 1962, p.227.
5. *Anno XIIII. The Conquest of an Empire*, 1937, p.116.
6. Mussolini told Eden 'coolly' during the latter's visit to Rome in June 1935 that 'these lands were required for colonisation and for the sake of their mineral wealth'. Avon, *op.cit.*, p.226.
7. LNOJ, September 1935, pp.1351-55.
8. Avon, *op.cit.*, pp.250-51.
9. Sir E. Hertslet, *The Map of Africa by Treaty*, Vol.II, 1909, pp.436-44; BFSP, Vol.99 (1905-6), pp.486-89; Cmd. 3298 (1907).
10. DBFP, Second Series, Vol.XIV, No.607.
11. *Ibid.*, No.628.
12. *Ibid.*, No.476.
13. See Dame Adelaide Livingstone, *The Peace Ballot. The official history*, 1935.
14. Treaty Series No.22 (1935), Cmd. 4953.
15. LNOJ, Special Supplement No.138, Geneva, 1935, pp.43-46.
16. *Ibid.*, pp.65-66.
17. DBFP, Second Series, Vol.XIV, No.553.
18. *Ibid.*, No.554.
19. LNOJ, November 1935, p.1226.
20. LNOJ, Special Supplement No.138, pp.98-114.

21. League of Nations Monthly Summary, Vol.XV, No.10, Geneva, October 1935.
22. FRUS, 1935, Vol.I, Washington, 1953, p.675; *The Memoirs of Cordell Hull*, Vol.I, p.434.
23. LNOJ, Special Supplement No.146, pp.37-8.
24. DBFP, Second Series, Vol.XV, No.81.
25. DBFP, Second Series, Vol.XV, No.115, n. 12.
26. *Ibid.*, No.514; LNOJ, Special Supplement, No.148, pp.64-85; Ethiopia No.3 (1936), Cmd. 5094.
27. DBFP, Second Series, Vol.XV, No.545, n. 3.
28. LNOJ, Special Supplement, No.146, p.8.
29. Lord Templewood, *Nine Troubled Years*, 1954, Chapter 33.
30. League of Nations, Monthly Summary, Vol.XV, No.11, November 1935, p.298.
31. *Ibid.*, p.9.
32. *Ibid.*
33. Sir M. Peterson, *Both Sides of the Curtain. An autobiography*, 1950, p.123.
34. DBFP, Second Series, Vol.XV, No.139.
35. Peterson, *op.cit.*, p.119.
36. See Daniel Waley, *British Public Opinion and the Abyssinian War, 1935-36*, 1975.
37. DBFP, Second Series, Vol.XV, No.292.
38. *Ibid.*, No.314.
39. *Ibid.*, No.328.
40. *Ibid.*, No.316.
41. *Ibid.*, No.330.
42. Circulated to the Cabinet as C.P. 235 (35).
43. DBFP, Second Series, Vol.XV, No.337, Annex.
44. *Ibid.*, No.347.
45. *Ibid.*, No.365.
46. Avon, *op.cit.*, p.316.
47. Sir Keith Feiling, *The Life of Neville Chamberlain*, 1946, p.281.
48. DBFP, Second Series, Vol.XV, No.43.
49. *Ibid.*, Vol.XVI, No.16.
50. George W. Baer, *Test Case. Italy, Ethiopia and the League of Nations*, Stanford, Cal., 1976, p.47.
51. DBFP, Second Series Vol.XIV, Appendix II, The Maffey Report, 18 June 1935.
52. Geoffrey Warner, *Pierre Laval and the Eclipse of France*, 1968, pp.63-72; BFSP, Vol.159 (1935), pp.946-51; RIIA, *Documents on International Affairs, 1935*, Vol.I, 1936, pp.19-24; *The Middle East Journal, 1961*, pp.69-78.
53. Avon, *op.cit.*, p.224.
54. Misc. No.2 (1935), Cmd. 4880; DBFP, Second Series, Vol.XII, No.722, n. 43.

55.   DBFP, Second Series, Vol.XIV, No.553.
56.   *Ibid.*, No.564.
57.   *Ibid.*, No.307.
58.   *Ibid.*, No.487.

11   THE FINAL YEARS

1.   LNOJ, July 1936, p.751.
2.   *Ibid.*
3.   *Ibid.*, p.769.
4.   LNOJ, 19th Year, Nos 5 and 6, May-June 1938.
5.   DBFP, Second Series, Vol.XVII, No.233, n. 9.
6.   *Ibid.*, No.158.
7.   *Ibid.*, No.208.
8.   315 H.C. Deb. 5s, Cols 1116-1217.
9.   DBFP, Second Series, Vol.XVII, No.297, n. 1.
10.   *Ibid.*, No.518.
11.   Treaty Series No.28 (1926). Treaty of Guarantee between the United Kingdom, Belgium, France, Germany and Italy, Cmd. 2764.
12.   DBFP, Second Series, Vol.XVII, No.389.
13.   *Ibid.*, No.242; *Documents Diplomatiques Français*, 1932-39 (Paris), Series 2, Vol.II, No.2.
14.   DBFP, Second Series, Vol.XVII, No.286.
15.   *Ibid.*
16.   *Ibid.*, No.185.
17.   *Ibid.*, No.420.
18.   See Chief of Staff Sub-committee report on preparations for proposed five-Power conference, 1 September 1936, PRO [C6223/4/18]; DBFP, Second Series, Vol.XVII, No.156.
19.   PRO, No.1095 [R6015/226/22].
20.   DBFP, Second Series, Vol.XVII, No.356.
21.   *Ibid.*
22.   Henry L. Stimson, *The Far Eastern Crisis*, New York, 1936. pp.92, 133.
23.   317 H.C. Deb. 5s.
24.   PRO, No.451 Telegraphic [R7189/226/22].
25.   For the text of the Declaration and Exchange of Notes, see Italy (No.1) of 1937, Cmd. 5348. Texts are in *The Times*, 4 January 1937.
26.   LNOJ, 19th Year, Nos 5 and 6, May-June 1938, p.335.
27.   *Ibid.*, p.336.
28.   For stenographic notes see PRO [W11115/11115/41].
29.   LNOJ, 18th Year, Nos 8 and 9, August-September 1937, p.656.
30.   *Ibid.*, 19th Year, Nos 3 and 4, March-April 1938, p.237.
31.   A.C. Johnson, *Viscount Halifax*, 1941, p.435.

32. *The Times*, 21 November 1937.
33. LNOJ, l9th Year, Nos 3 and 4, March-April 1938, p.239.
34. *Ibid.*, l9th Year, January 1938, p.10.
35. DBFP, Second Series, Vól.II, p.489.
36. LNOJ, l9th Year, Nos 5 and 6, May-June 1938, p.356.
37. *Ibid.*, pp.306-08.
38. LNOJ, 20th Year, No.2, February 1939, pp.73-99.
39. *Ibid.*, 20th Year, Nos 5 and 6, May-June 1939, p.250.
40. *Ibid.*, pp.254-55.
41. See above, Chapter 9, pp.212-13; LNOJ, 20th Year, Nos 3 and 4, March-April 1939, p.256.
42. LNOJ, 20th Year, Nos 3 and 4, March-April 1939, pp.256-64.
43. Avon, *op.cit.*, pp.304-05.
44. LNOJ, 19th Year, Nos 5 and 6, May-June 1938, p.556.
45. *Ibid.*, p.370.
46. Avon, *op.cit.*, p.316.
47. LNOJ, 19th Year, Nos 5 and 6, p.375.
48. *Ibid.*, 19th year, No 7, July 1938.
49. *Ibid.*, 20th year, Nos 3 and 4, March-April, p.246.
50. *Ibid.*, pp.216-17.
51. *Ibid.*, 20th year, No 2, February 1939, p.205.
52. *Ibid.*, p.200.

Bibliography

A bibliography of the League of Nations would need to be a bibliography of almost all international affairs from 1920 until 1946. The following is merely a brief selection of sources used in writing this book. Publications of the League itself are cited in the notes, pp.294-310 above; a useful list of these is given in H. Aufricht, *Guide to League of Nations Publications. A bibliographical survey of the work of the League*, 1920-1947, New York, 1951.

Alcock, A., *The History of the International Labour Organisation*, London, 1970.

Amery, L.S., *The Unforgiving Years, 1929-1940*, London, 1955.

Ashworth, W., *A Short History of the International Economy since 1850*, 3rd edn, London, 1975.

Avenol, Joseph, 'The future of the League of Nations', *International Affairs, 13*, March-April 1934.

Avon, Earl of, *The Eden Memoirs. Facing the Dictators*, London, 1962.

Baer, George W., *The Coming of the Italian-Ethiopian War*, Cambridge, Mass., 1967.

—— *Test Case. Italy, Ethiopia and the League of Nations*, Stanford, California, 1976.

Baker, Ray Stannard, *Woodrow Wilson. Life and letters*, 6 vols, London, 1938.

—— *Woodrow Wilson and World Settlement*, 3 vols, New York, 1922.

Barker, A.J., *The Civilising Mission. The Italo-Ethiopian war, 1935-1936*, London, 1968.

Barros, James, *The Aaland Islands Question. Its Settlement by the League of Nations*, New Haven, Conn., 1968.

—— *Betrayal from Within. Joseph Avenol, Secretary-General of the League of Nations, 1933-1940*, New Haven, Conn., 1969.

—— *The Corfu Incident of 1923: Mussolini and the League of Nations*, Princeton, N.J., 1965.

312

— *The League of Nations and the Great Powers. The Greek-Bulgarian incident, 1925*, Oxford, 1970.

Bassett, R., *Democracy and Foreign Policy*, London, 1952.

Beales, A.C.F., *The History of Peace. A short account of the organised movements for international peace*, London, 1931.

Bentwich, Norman, *The Mandates System*, London, 1930.

Birn, D.S., *The League of Nations, 1918-1945*, London, 1981.

Birn, D.S., *The League of Nations Union, 1918-1945*, Oxford, 1981.

Blum, Léon, *L'histoire jugera*, Montreal, 1943.

Boca, Angelo del, *The Ethiopian War, 1935-1941*, tr. by P.D. Cummins, Chicago and London, 1965.

Bono, E. de, *Anno XIIII. The conquest of an empire*, London, 1937.

Bramsted, Ernest, 'Apostles of Collective Security. The League of Nations Union and its functions', *Australian Journal of Politics and History*, *13*, December 1967.

Brierly, J.L., 'The Covenant and the Charter', *The British Yearbook of International Law*, 1946.

— 'The League of Nations' (rewritten by P.A. Reynolds), Chapter IX, *The New Cambridge Modern History*, Vol.XII, revised edn., *The Shifting Balance of World Forces*, Cambridge, 1968.

Burton, M., *The Assembly of the League of Nations*, Chicago, 1941.

Butler, Sir Geoffrey, *A Handbook to the League of Nations*, London, 1928.

Carlton, D., 'Britain and the League Council Crisis of 1926', *Historical Journal*, 1968.

— 'Disarmament with Guarantees: Cecil, 1922-27', *Disarmament and Arms Control*, III, 1965.

— *MacDonald versus Henderson. The foreign policy of the second Labour Government*, London, 1969.

Carter, G., *The British Commonwealth and International Security*, Toronto, 1947.

Cecil, Robert, Viscount, *All the Way*, London, 1949.

— *A Great Experiment*, London, 1941.

Chaput, R.A., *Disarmament in British Foreign Policy*, London, 1935.

Charvet, J.F., *L'influence Britannique dans la Société des Nations*, Paris, 1938.

Choate, J.H., *The Two Hague Conferences*, Princeton and London, 1913.

Claude, Inis, *Swords into Ploughshares*, New York, 1956.

Coffey, T.M., *Lion by the Tail. The story of the Italo-Ethiopian war*, London, 1974.

Colvin, I., *Vansittart in Office*, London, 1965.

Conwell-Evans, T.P., *The League Council in Action*, London, 1929.

Cooper, A. Duff (Lord Norwich), *Old Men Forget*, London, 1953.

Darby, W. Evans, *International Tribunals*, London, 1904.

Davis, Kathryn W., *The Soviets at Geneva*, Geneva, 1934.

Dickinson, G.L., *The International Anarchy, 1904-1914*, London, 1926.

Egerton, G.W., *Great Britain and the Creation of the League of Nations*,

Strategy, politics and international organisation, 1914-1919, London, 1979.

Fleming, D.F., *The United States and the League of Nations, 1918-1920*, New York, 1932.

Galenson, W., *The International Labour Organisation*, University of Wisconsin, 1981.

Goodrich, L., 'From League of Nations to United Nations', *International Organisation*, February 1947.

Greaves, H.R.G., *The League Committees and World Order*, London, 1932.

Griswold, A.W., *Far Eastern Policy of the United States*, New York, 1938.

Gulick, E.V., *Europe's Classical Balance of Power. A case history of the theory and practice of one of the great concepts of European statecraft*, Ithaca, New York, 1955.

Hall, D., *Mandates, Dependencies and Trusteeship*, Washington, 1948.

Hamilton, M.A., *Arthur Henderson*, London, 1938.

Hankey, Sir Maurice (later Lord), *Diplomacy by Conference. Studies in public affairs, 1920-1946*, London, 1946.

Hardie, F., *The Abyssinian Crisis*, London, 1974.

Hardinge, Lord, 'The League of Nations', *The Quarterly Review*, No.241, January 1924.

Harris, H. Wilson, *What the League of Nations is*, London, 1925.

Henig, Ruth B. (ed.), *The League of Nations*, Edinburgh, 1973.

Higgins, A. Pearce, *The Hague Conferences*, Cambridge, 1909.

Highley, A.H., *The Actions of the States Members of the League in the Application of Sanctions against Italy*, Geneva, 1938.

Hill, N.L., *The Public International Conference*, London, 1929.

Hoare, Sir Samuel (Lord Templewood), *Nine Troubled Years*, London, 1954.

Holbraad, Carsten, *The Concert of Europe' A study in German and British international theory, 1815-1914*, London, 1970.

Hudson, Manley O., *International Tribunals*, London, 1944.

— *The Permanent Court of International Justice*, New York, 1943.

Hull, W.I., *The Two Hague Conferences*, Boston, 1908.

Joyce, James Avery, *Broken Star. The story of the League of Nations, 1919-1939*, Swansea, 1978.

Knudson, John I., *A History of the League of Nations*, Atlanta, Georgia, 1938.

Langer, W.L., *The Diplomacy of Imperialism, 1890-1902*, 2nd edn, New York, 1962.

— *European Alliances and Alignments, 1871-1890*, 2nd edn, New York, 1962.

Lapradelle, A. de, and Politis, N., *Recueil des arbitrages internationaux*, Paris, 1905, 1923, 1954.

Lasturel, P., *L'affaire Gréco-Italienne de 1923*, Paris, 1925.

Latané, John H. (ed.), *Development of the League of Nations Idea*, New York, 1932.

Lattimore, Owen, *Manchuria, Cradle of Conflict*, New York, 1932.

Livingstone, Dame Adelaide, *The Peace Ballot. The official history*, London, 1935.

Lodge, Henry Cabot, *The Senate and the League of Nations*, New York, London, 1925.

Macartney, C., *National States and National Minorities*, London, 1934.

Macartney, M.H.H., and Cremona, P., *Italy's Foreign and Colonial Policy, 1914-1937*, London, 1938.

McCallum, R.B., *Public Opinion and the Last Peace*, London, 1944.

McClure, Wallace, *World Prosperity as sought through the Economic Work of the League of Nations*, New York, 1933.

Manning, C.A.W., *The Policies of the British Dominions in the League of Nations*, Geneva, 1932.

Marquand, David, *Ramsay MacDonald*, London, 1977.

Miller, David Hunter, *The Drafting of the Covenant*, 2 vols, New York and London, 1928.

Miller, K., *Socialism and Foreign Policy. Theory and practice in Britain to 1931*, The Hague, 1967.

Millin, S.G., *General Smuts*, London, 1936.

Minorsky, V.F., *The Mosul Question*, Paris, 1926.

Morley, Felix, *The Society of Nations*, Washington, 1932.

Morris, R.C., *International Arbitration and Procedure*, New Haven, Conn., 1911.

Mosley, L., *Haile Selassie. The conquering lion*, London, 1964.

Murray, Gilbert, *From League to UN*, London, 1948.

— 'The League of Nations Movement; some recollections of the early days', *The David Davies Memorial Lecture*, London, 1955.

Nicolson, Sir H., *Diplomacy*, 3rd edn, London, 1963.

Niemeyer, G., 'The balance sheet of the League experiment', *International Organisation*, *16*, No.4, 1952.

Noel-Baker, P.J., *Disarmament*, London, 1926.

— *The First World Disarmament Conference, 1932-33, and Why it failed*, Oxford, 1979.

— *The Geneva Protocol*, London, 1926.

— *The League of Nations at Work*, 1926.

Northedge, F.S., *The Troubled Giant. Britain among the Great Powers, 1916-1939*, London, 1966.

Osborne, S., *The Saar Question. A disease spot in Europe*, London, 1923.

Peterson, Sir Maurice, *Both Sides of the Curtain. An autobiography*, London, 1950.

Petrie, Sir Charles, *The Life and Letters of the Right Hon. Sir Austen Chamberlain*, 2 vols, London, 1939-1940.

Phelan, E.J., *Yes and Albert Thomas*, London, 1936.

Phillips, Walter Alison, *The Confederation of Europe. A study of the European alliance, 1813-1823*, London, 1914.

Polanyi, K., *The Great Transformation*, Boston, Mass., 1957.

Rappard, W.E., *The Quest for Peace since the World War*, Cambridge, Mass., 1940.

Reinsch, Paul S., *Public International Unions*, Boston, Mass., 1911.

Renault, M.L. (ed.), *Les Deux Conférences de la Paix*, Paris, 1908.

Roskill, S., *British Naval Policy between the Wars*, Vol.I, *The period of Anglo-American Antagonism, 1919-29*, London and Glasgow, 1968.

— *Hankey, Man of Secrets*, Vol.II, London and Glasgow, 1972.

Salter, Sir J.A. (later Lord), *Allied Shipping Control. An experiment in international administration*, London, 1921.

— *Memoirs of a Public Servant*, London, 1961.

— *Slave of the Lamp. A public servant's notebook*, London, 1967.

Satow, Sir Ernest, *A Guide to Diplomatic Practice*, ed. by Lord Gore-Booth, 5th edn, London, 1979.

— *International Congresses and Conferences*, 1920.

Schenk, H.G., *The Aftermath of the Napoleonic Wars. The concert of Europe - an experiment*, London, 1947.

Schwoebel, J., *L'Angleterre et la Securité Collective*, Paris, 1938.

Scott, George, *The Rise and Fall of the League of Nations*, London, 1973.

Scott, J.B. (ed.), *Texts of the Peace Conferences at The Hague, 1899 and 1907*, Boston, Mass., and London, 1908.

Seymour, C., *The Intimate Papers of Colonel House*, 4 vols, London, 1926-28.

Simpson, J.L., and Fox, Hazel, *International Arbitration. Law and practice*, London, 1959.

Smith, Sarah R., *The Manchurian Crisis, 1931-1932. A tragedy in international relations*, New York, 1948.

Stimson, Henry L., *The Far Eastern Crisis*, New York, 1936.

Stuyt, A.M., *Survey of International Arbitration, 1794-1970*, Leiden, 1972.

Thorne, C., *The Limits of Foreign Policy. The League, the West and the Far Eastern crisis of 1931-33*, 1972.

Vansittart, Sir Robert (later Lord), *The Mist Procession*, London, 1958.

Verma, D.N., *India and the League of Nations*, Patna, 1970.

Walters, F.P., *A History of the League of Nations*, 2 vols, London, 1952.

Wambaugh, S., *The Saar Plebiscite*, Cambridge, Mass., 1940.

Warner, G., *Pierre Laval and the Eclipse of France*, London, 1968.

Webster, Sir C.K., *The Art and Practice of Diplomacy*, London, 1961.

Webster, Sir C.K., and Herbert, Sidney, *The League of Nations in Theory and Practice*, London, 1933.

Wheeler-Bennett, Sir John, *Disarmament and Security since Locarno, 1925-1931*, London, 1932.

— *The Disarmament Deadlock*, London, 1934.

— *Information on the Reduction of Armaments*, London, 1925.

— *Information on the Renunciation of War, 1927-1928*, London, 1928.
Williams, Roth (K. Zilliacus), *The League of Nations Today*, London, 1923.
Willoughby, W.W., *The Sino-Japanese Controversy and the League of Nations*, Baltimore, 1935.
Wilson, Florence, *The Origins of the League Covenant. Documentary history of its drafting*, London, 1928.
Winkler, H.R., 'The development of the League of Nations idea in Great Britain, 1914-1919', *Journal of Modern History*, June 1948.
Wolfers, A., *Britain and France between Two Wars*, New Haven, 1940.
Woolf, L.S., *International Government*, London, 1916.
Wright, Quincy, *Mandates under the League of Nations*, Chicago, 1930.
Zimmern, Sir A.E., *The League of Nations and the Rule of Law*, London, 1936.

List of Unpublished Theses

Henig, R.B., 'The British government and the League of Nations, 1919-1926', Lancaster, Ph.D., 1978.
Hill, C.J., 'British foreign policy, 1931 to 1935', Manchester, Ph.D., 1976.
Richardson, Richard Calam, 'The Conservative Government of 1924-1929 and the disarmament problems', London (LSE), Ph.D. (Econ.), 1983.
Roberts, A.M., 'Anthony Eden as Minister Without Portfolio, League of Nations Affairs, June to December 1935: a case study in the foreign policy of the National Government', Sheffield, M.A., 1980.
Ross, J.F.L., 'Neutrality and sanctions: Sweden, Switzerland and collective security operations', London (LSE), Ph.D. (Econ.), to be submitted in late 1985.
Shorney, D.J., 'Britain and disarmament, 1916-1931', Durham, Ph.D., 1981.
Talalay, M.A., 'British foreign policy and the Hoare-Laval Plan: a critique of the theory and practice of crisis decision-making', University College, London, Ph.D., 1979.
Turner, A.S., 'British policies towards France, with special reference to disarmament and security, 1926-1931', Oxford, D.Phil., 1978.
Uxbridge, A., 'British political opinion towards France and the German problem, 1918-1925', Sussex, D.Phil., 1979.
Yearwood, P.J., 'The Foreign Office and the guarantee of peace through the League of Nations, 1916-1925', Sussex, D.Phil., 1980.

Appendix A

THE COVENANT OF THE LEAGUE OF NATIONS
(Edition embodying Amendments in force, 1 February 1938)

THE High Contracting parties,
In order to promote international co-operation and to achieve international peace and security —
> by the acceptance of obligations not to resort to war,
> by the prescription of open, just and honourable relations between nations,
> by the firm establishment of the understandings of international law as the actual rule of conduct among Governments, and
> by the maintenance of justice and a scrupulous respect for all Treaty obligations in the dealings of organised peoples with one another,

Agree to this Covenant of the League of Nations.

ARTICLE 1.

1. The original Members of the League of Nations shall be those of the signatories which are named in the Annex to this Covenant, and also such of those other States named in the Annex as shall accede without reservation to this Covenant. Such accession shall be effected by a Declaration deposited with the Secretariat within two months of the coming into force of the Covenant. Notice thereof shall be sent to all other Members of the League.

2. Any fully self-governing State, Dominion or Colony not named in the Annex may become a Member of the League if its admission is agreed to by two-thirds of the Assembly, provided that it shall give effective guarantees of its sincere intention to observe its international obligations, and shall accept such regulations as may be prescribed by the League in regard to its military, naval and air forces and armaments.

3. Any Member of the League may, after two years' notice of its intention so to do, withdraw from the League, provided that all its

international obligations and all its obligations under this Covenant shall have been fulfilled at the time of its withdrawal.

ARTICLE 2.

The action of the League under this Covenant shall be effected through the instrumentality of an Assembly and of a Council, with a permanent Secretariat.

ARTICLE 3.

1. The Assembly shall consist of representatives of the Members of the League.

2. The Assembly shall meet at stated intervals and from time to time, as occasion may require, at the seat of the League, or at such other place as may be decided upon.

3. The Assembly may deal at its meetings with any matter within the sphere of action of the League or affecting the peace of the world.

4. At meetings of the Assembly each Member of the League shall have one vote and may have not more than three representatives.

ARTICLE 4.

1. The Council shall consist of representatives of the Principal Allied and Associated Powers, together with representatives of four other Members of the League. These four Members of the League shall be selected by the Assembly from time to time in its discretion. Until the appointment of the representatives of the four Members of the League first selected by the Assembly, representatives of Belgium, Brazil, Spain and Greece shall be members of the Council.

2. With the approval of the majority of the Assembly, the Council may name additional Members of the League whose representatives shall always be members of the Council; the Council, with like approval, may increase the number of Members of the League to be selected by the Assembly for representation on the Council.

2A. *The Assembly shall fix by a two-thirds majority the rules dealing with the election of the non-permanent Members of the Council, and particularly such regulations as relate to their term of office and the conditions of re-eligibility.**

3. The Council shall meet from time to time as occasion may require, and at least once a year, at the seat of the League, or at such other place as may be decided upon.

4. The Council may deal at its meetings with any matter within the sphere of action of the League or affecting the peace of the world.

5. Any Member of the League not represented on the Council shall be invited to send a representative to sit as a member at any meeting of the Council during the consideration of matters specially affecting the interests of that Member of the League.

* This amendment came into force on 29 July 1926.

6. At meetings of the Council, each Member of the League represented on the Council shall have one vote, and may have not more than one representative.

ARTICLE 5.

1. Except where otherwise expressly provided in this Covenant or by the terms of the present Treaty, decisions at any meeting of the Assembly or of the Council shall require the agreement of all the Members of the League represented at the meeting.

2. All matters of procedure at meetings of the Assembly or of the Council, including the appointment of Committees to investigate particular matters, shall be regulated by the Assembly or by the Council and may be decided by a majority of the Members of the League represented at the meeting.

3. The first meeting of the Assembly and the first meeting of the Council shall be summoned by the President of the United States of America.

ARTICLE 6.

1. The permanent Secretariat shall be established at the seat of the League. The Secretariat shall comprise a Secretary-General and such secretaries and staff as may be required.

2. The first Secretary-General shall be the person named in the Annex; thereafter the Secretary-General shall be appointed by the Council with the approval of the majority of the Assembly.

3. The secretaries and staff of the Secretariat shall be appointed by the Secretary-General with the approval of the Council.

4. The Secretary-General shall act in that capacity at all meetings of the Assembly and of the Council.

5. *The expenses of the League shall be borne by the Members of the League in the proportion decided by the Assembly.**

ARTICLE 7.

1. The seat of the League is established at Geneva.

2. The Council may at any time decide that the seat of the League shall be established elsewhere.

3. All positions under or in connection with the League, including the Secretariat, shall be open equally to men and women.

4. Representatives of the Members of the League and officials of the League, when engaged on the business of the League, shall enjoy diplomatic privileges and immunities.

5. The buildings and other property occupied by the League or its officials or by representatives attending its meetings shall be inviolable.

ARTICLE 8.

1. The Members of the League recognise that the maintenance of

* This amendment came into force on 13 August 1924.

peace requires the reduction of national armaments to the lowest point consistent with national safety, and the enforcement by common action of international obligations.

2. The Council, taking account of the geographical situation and circumstances of each State, shall formulate plans for such reduction for the consideration and action of the several Governments.

3. Such plans shall be subject to reconsideration and revision at least every ten years.

4. After these plans shall have been adopted by the several Governments, the limits of armaments therein fixed shall not be exceeded without the concurrence of the Council.

5. The Members of the League agree that the manufacture by private enterprise of munitions and implements of war is open to grave objections.
The Council shall advise how the evil effects attendant upon such manufacture can be prevented, due regard being had to the necessities of those Members of the League which are not able to manufacture the munitions and implements of war necessary for their safety.

6. The Members of the League undertake to interchange full and frank information as to the scale of their armaments, their military, naval and air programmes and the condition of such of their industries as are adaptable to warlike purposes.

ARTICLE 9.

A permanent Commission shall be constituted to advise the Council on the execution of the provisions of Articles 1 and 8 and on military, naval and air questions generally.

ARTICLE 10.

The Members of the League undertake to respect and preserve, as against external aggression, the territorial integrity and existing political independence of all Members of the League. In case of any such aggression, or in case of any threat or danger of such aggression, the Council shall advise upon the means by which this obligation shall be fulfilled.

ARTICLE 11.

1. Any war or threat of war, whether immediately affecting any of the Members of the League or not, is hereby declared a matter of concern to the whole League, and the League shall take any action that may be deemed wise and effectual to safeguard the peace of nations. In case any such emergency should arise, the Secretary-General shall, on the request of any Member of the League, forthwith summon a meeting of the Council.

2. It is also declared to be the friendly right of each Member of the League to bring to the attention of the Assembly or of the Council any

circumstance whatever affecting international relations which threatens to disturb international peace or the good understanding between nations upon which peace depends.

ARTICLE 12.

1. The Members of the League agree that, if there should arise between them any dispute likely to lead to a rupture they will submit the matter either to arbitration *or judicial settlement*★ or to enquiry by the Council, and they agree in no case to resort to war until three months after the award by the arbitrators *or the judicial decision,*★ or the report by the Council.

2. In any case, under this Article the award of the arbitrators *or the judicial decision*★ shall be made within a reasonable time, and the report of the Council shall be made within six months after the submission of the dispute.

ARTICLE 13.

1. The Members of the League agree that, whenever any dispute shall arise between them which they recognise to be suitable for submission to arbitration *or judicial settlement,*★ and which cannot be satisfactorily settled by diplomacy, they will submit the whole subject-matter to arbitration *or judicial settlement.*★

2. Disputes as to the interpretation of a Treaty, as to any question of international law, as to the existence of any fact which, if established, would constitute a breach of any international obligation, or as to the extent and nature of the reparation to be made for any such breach, are declared to be among those which are generally suitable for submission to arbitration *or judicial settlement.*★

3. *For the consideration of any such dispute, the Court to which the case is referred shall be the Permanent Court of International Justice, established in accordance with Article 14, or any tribunal agreed on by the parties to the dispute or stipulated in any Convention existing between them.*★

4. The Members of the League agree that they will carry out in full good faith any award *or decision*★ that may be rendered, and that they will not resort to war against a Member of the League which complies therewith. In the event of any failure to carry out such an award *or decision,*★ the Council shall propose what steps should be taken to give effect thereto.

ARTICLE 14.

The Council shall formulate and submit to the Members of the League for adoption plans for the establishment of a Permanent Court of International Justice. The Court shall be competent to hear and determine any dispute of an international character which the parties thereto submit to it. The Court may also give an advisory opinion upon any dispute or question referred to it by the Council or by the Assembly.

★ These amendments came into force on 26 September 1924.

ARTICLE 15.

1. If there should arise between Members of the League any dispute likely to lead to a rupture, which is not submitted to arbitration *or judicial settlement** in accordance with Article 13, the Members of the League agree that they will submit the matter to the Council. Any party to the dispute may effect such submission by giving notice of the existence of the dispute to the Secretary-General, who will make all necessary arrangements for a full investigation and consideration thereof.

2. For this purpose the parties to the dispute will communicate to the Secretary-General, as promptly as possible, statements of their case with all the relevant facts and papers, and the Council may forthwith direct the publication thereof.

3. The Council shall endeavour to effect a settlement of the dispute, and, if such efforts are successful, a statement shall be made public giving such facts and explanations regarding the dispute and the terms of settlement thereof as the Council may deem appropriate.

4. If the dispute is not thus settled, the Council, either unanimously or by a majority vote, shall make and publish a report containing a statement of the facts of the dispute and the recommendations which are deemed just and proper in regard thereto.

5. Any Member of the League represented on the Council may make a public statement of the facts of the dispute and of its conclusions regarding the same.

6. If a report by the Council is unanimously agreed to by the members thereof, other than the representatives of one or more of the parties to the dispute, the Members of the League agree that they will not go to war with any party to the dispute which complies with the recommendations of the report.

7. If the Council fails to reach a report which is unanimously agreed to by the members thereof, other than the representatives of one or more of the parties to the dispute, the Members of the League reserve to themselves the right to take such action as they shall consider necessary for the maintenance of right and justice.

8. If the dispute between the parties is claimed by one of them, and is found by the Council to arise out of a matter which by international law is solely within the domestic jurisdiction of that party, the Council shall so report, and shall make no recommendation as to its settlement.

9. The Council may in any case under this Article refer the dispute to the Assembly. The dispute shall be so referred at the request of either party to the dispute provided that such request be made within fourteen days after the submission of the dispute to the Council.

10. In any case referred to the Assembly, all the provisions of this Article and of Article 12, relating to the action and powers of the Council, shall apply to the action and powers of the Assembly, provided that a report made by the Assembly, if concurred in by the representatives of

* These amendments came into force on 26 September 1924.

those Members of the League represented on the Council, and of a majority of the other Members of the League, exclusive in each case of the representatives of the parties to the dispute, shall have the same force as a report by the Council concurred in by all the members thereof other than the representatives of one or more of the parties to the dispute.

ARTICLE 16.

1. Should any Member of the League resort to war in disregard of its Covenants under Articles 12, 13 or 15, it shall *ipso facto* be deemed to have committed an act of war against all other Members of the League, which hereby undertake immediately to subject it to the severance of all trade or financial relations, the prohibition of all intercourse between their nationals and the nationals of the Covenant-breaking State, and the prevention of all financial, commercial or personal intercourse between the nationals of the Covenant-breaking State and the nationals of any other State, whether a Member of the League or not.

2. It shall be the duty of the Council in such case to recommend to the several Governments concerned what effective military, naval or air force the Members of the League shall severally contribute to the armed forces to be used to protect the Covenants of the League.

3. The Members of the League agree, further, that they will mutually support one another in the financial and economic measures which are taken under this Article, in order to minimise the loss and inconvenience resulting from the above measures, and that they will mutually support one another in resisting any special measures aimed at one of their number by the Covenant-breaking State, and that they will take the necessary steps to afford passage through their territory to the forces of any of the Members of the League which are co-operating to protect the Covenants of the League.

4. Any Member of the League which has violated any Covenant of the League may be declared to be no longer a Member of the League by a vote of the Council concurred in by the representatives of all the other Members of the League represented thereon.

ARTICLE 17.

1. In the event of a dispute between a Member of the League and a State which is not a Member of the League, or between States not Members of the League, the State or States not Members of the League shall be invited to accept the obligations of membership in the League for the purposes of such dispute, upon such conditions as the Council may deem just. If such invitation is accepted, the provisions of Articles 12 to 16 inclusive shall be applied with such modifications as may be deemed necessary by the Council.

2. Upon such invitation being given, the Council shall immediately institute an enquiry into the circumstances of the dispute and recommend

such action as may seem best and most effectual in the circumstances.

3. If a State so invited shall refuse to accept the obligations of membership in the League for the purposes of such dispute, and shall resort to war against a Member of the League, the provisions of Article 16 shall be applicable as against the State taking such action.

4. If both parties to the dispute, when so invited, refuse to accept the obligations of membership in the League for the purposes of such dispute, the Council may take such measures and make such recommendations as will prevent hostilities and will result in the settlement of the dispute.

ARTICLE 18.

Every Treaty or international engagement entered into hereafter by any Member of the League shall be forthwith registered with the Secretariat, and shall, as soon as possible, be published by it. No such Treaty or international engagement shall be binding until so registered.

ARTICLE 19.

The Assembly may from time to time advise the reconsideration by Members of the League of Treaties which have become inapplicable, and the consideration of international conditions whose continuance might endanger the peace of the world.

ARTICLE 20.

1. The Members of the League severally agree that this Covenant is accepted as abrogating all obligations or understandings *inter se* which are inconsistent with the terms thereof, and solemnly undertake that they will not hereafter enter into any engagements inconsistent with the terms thereof.

2. In case any Member of the League shall, before becoming a Member of the League, have undertaken any obligations inconsistent with the terms of this Covenant, it shall be the duty of such member to take immediate steps to procure its release from such obligations.

ARTICLE 21.

Nothing in this Covenant shall be deemed to affect the validity of international engagements, such as Treaties of Arbitration, or regional understandings like the Monroe doctrine, for securing the maintenance of peace.

ARTICLE 22.

1. To those colonies and territories, which as a consequence of the late war have ceased to be under the sovereignty of the States which formerly governed them, and which are inhabited by peoples not yet able

to stand by themselves under the strenuous conditions of the modern world, there should be applied the principle that the well-being and development of such peoples form a sacred trust of civilisation, and that securities for the performance of this trust should be embodied in this Covenant.

2. The best method of giving practical effect to this principle is that the tutelage of such peoples should be entrusted to advanced nations who, by reason of their resources, their experience, or their geographical position, can best undertake this responsibility, and who are willing to accept it, and that this tutelage should be exercised by them as Mandatories on behalf of the League.

3. The character of the Mandate must differ according to the stage of the development of the people, the geographical situation of the territory, its economic conditions and other similar circumstances.

4. Certain communities formerly belonging to the Turkish Empire have reached a stage of development where their existence as independent nations can be provisionally recognised subject to the rendering of administrative advice and assistance by a Mandatory until such time as they are able to stand alone. The wishes of these communities must be a principal consideration in the selection of the Mandatory.

5. Other peoples, especially those of Central Africa, are at such a stage that the Mandatory must be responsible for the administration of the territory under conditions which will guarantee freedom of conscience and religion, subject only to the maintenance of public order and morals, the prohibition of abuses such as the slave trade, the arms traffic and the liquor traffic, and the prevention of the establishment of fortifications or military and naval bases, and of military training of the natives for other than police purposes and the defence of territory, and will also secure equal opportunities for the trade and commerce of other Members of the League.

6. There are territories, such as South-West Africa and certain of the South Pacific Islands, which, owing to the sparseness of their population, or their small size, or their remoteness from the centres of civilisation, or their geographical contiguity to the territory of the Mandatory, and other circumstances, can be best administered under the laws of the Mandatory as integral portions of its territory, subject to the safeguards above mentioned in the interests of the indigenous population.

7. In every case of Mandate, the Mandatory shall render to the Council an annual report in reference to the territory committed to its charge.

8. The degree of authority, control or administration to be exercised by the Mandatory shall, if not previously agreed upon by the Members of the League, be explicitly defined in each case by the Council.

9. A permanent Commission shall be constituted to receive and examine the annual reports of the Mandatories and to advise the Council on all matters relating to the observance of the Mandates.

ARTICLE 23.

Subject to and in accordance with the provisions of international Conventions existing or hereafter to be agreed upon, the Members of the League —

(a) Will endeavour to secure and maintain fair and humane conditions of labour for men, women and children, both in their own countries and in all countries to which their commercial and industrial relations extend, and for that purpose will establish and maintain the necessary international organisations.

(b) Undertake to secure just treatment of the native inhabitants of territories under their control.

(c) Will entrust the League with the general supervision over the execution of agreements with regard to the traffic in women and children, and the traffic in opium and other dangerous drugs.

(d) Will entrust the League with the general supervision of the trade in arms and ammunition with the countries in which the control of this traffic is necessary in the common interest.

(e) Will make provision to secure and maintain freedom of communications and of transit and equitable treatment for the commerce of all Members of the League. In this connection, the special necessities of the regions devastated during the war of 1914-18 shall be borne in mind.

(f) Will endeavour to take steps in matters of international concern for the prevention and control of disease.

ARTICLE 24.

1. There shall be placed under the direction of the League all international bureaux already established by general treaties if the parties to such treaties consent. All such international bureaux and all commissions for the regulation of matters of international interest hereafter constituted shall be placed under the direction of the League.

2. In all matters of international interest which are regulated by general conventions, but which are not placed under the control of international bureaux or commissions, the Secretariat of the League shall, subject to the consent of the Council, and if desired by the parties, collect and distribute all relevant information, and shall render any other assistance which may be necessary or desirable.

3. The Council may include as part of the expenses of the Secretariat the expenses of any bureau or commission which is placed under the direction of the League.

ARTICLE 25.

The Members of the League agree to encourage and promote the establishment and co-operation of duly authorised voluntary national

Red Cross organisations having as purposes the improvement of health, the prevention of disease and the mitigation of suffering throughout the world.

ARTICLE 26.

1. Amendments to this Covenant will take effect when ratified by the Members of the League whose representatives compose the Council, and by a majority of the Members of the League whose representatives compose the Assembly.

2. No such amendments shall bind any Member of the League which signifies its dissent therefrom, but in that case it shall cease to be a Member of the League.

Appendix B

The following Allied and Associated Powers attended the Peace
Conference and were Original Members of the League:

United States of America	Cuba	Nicaragua
Belgium	Ecuador	Panama
Bolivia	France	Peru
Brazil	Greece	Poland
British Empire	Guatemala	Portugal
Canada	Haiti	Roumania
Australia	Hedjaz	Serb-Croat-Slovene State
South Africa	Honduras	Siam
New Zealand	Italy	Czechoslovakia
India	Japan	Uruguay
China	Liberia	

Appendix C

LIST OF MEMBERS OF THE LEAGUE
1 February 1938

Afghanistan
Union of South Africa
Albania
Argentine Republic
Australia
Austria
Belgium
Bolivia
United Kingdom of
 Great Britain and
 Northern Ireland
Bulgaria
Canada
Chile
China
Colombia
Cuba
Czechoslovakia
Denmark
Dominican Republic

Equador
Estonia
Ethiopia
Finland
France
Greece
Guatemala
Hayti
Honduras
Hungary
India
Iran
Iraq
Ireland
Italy
Latvia
Liberia
Lithuania
Luxemburg
Mexico

Netherlands
New Zealand
Nicaragua
Norway
Panama
Peru
Poland
Portugal
Roumania
Salvador
Siam
Spain
Sweden
Switzerland
Turkey
Union of Soviet
 Socialist Republics
Uruguay
Venezuela
Yugoslavia

Index

Aaland Islands, successful League action in, 77-7
Abyssinia, *see* Ethiopia
Aden, Gulf of, 240
Addis Ababa, 221, 243, 245, 263
Adowa, 240
Aggressor, indeterminate, poses problem for Collective Security, 251-4
Air bombardment, of Ethiopia, 224; British fears of, 234, 250
Alabama Claims Case, 15
Albania, minorities, 76; joins League, 98; border dispute, 103-5; unwilling to back Ethiopian sanctions because of treaty and economic relations with Italy, 232; bombed and overrun by Italy but given no League aid, 275
Allied and Associated Powers, 1-4; aim to restrict League scope, 72
Allied Shipping Control, 12
Allied Supreme Council, 72, 81, 83
Ambassadors, Conference of, 11, 72, 79; Albania, 104-5, 107; Corfu dispute, 108-11
Aloisi, Baron, 127, 227, 231
America, Latin, *see* Latin American states
America, North, *see* USA
American League to Enforce Peace, 26-7
Amery, L.S., 94, 245
Anglo-French Defence Pact, fails at Cannes Conference (1922), 118
Anglo-French Military Co-operation Agreement (pre-1914), 20
Anglo-German Naval Agreement (1935), 229
Anglo-Italian Declaration (1937), 263
Anglo-Japanese Alliance (1902, 1905, 1911), 21; Britain forced to abandon by USA, 139

Anglo-Polish Alliance (1939), 272
Anglo-Saxon world and League concept, 26-45, 58, 70
Anschluss, attempts to prevent, 131-2; Hitler pushes through, 266-9
Anti-war feeling, 1-2
Arbitration, Permanent Court of, 10
Arbitrators, use of in 19th and 20th centuries, 13-16
Armaments, problem of, 55-6; plans concerning, 130
Armaments Commission, Permanent (PAC), 82-3
Armaments (Temporary Mixed Commission, TMC), 83, 117-19, 135
Armenia, dispute concerning, 79; tries to join League, 98
Arms race, blatant from 1936, 256-7; Nazi Germany speeds up with view to seizure of Czechoslovakia, 268
Assab, 237
Assembly, League, first meeting (1920), 72
Asians, position in League, 103; *see also* Japan and China
Australia, mandate over former German Guinea, 37, 64; racial discrimination, 45; assertive in League, 47
Austria, war with Prussia (1866), 3; Ausgleich with Hungary, 4-5; joins League (1920), 46, 98; minorities, 76; reconstruction of, 80-2, 170; the 3 Protocols of 1922, 81; disarmament, 113; Austro-German Customs Union, 144-45; independence dependent on Italian support, 232; conquered by Nazi Germany once Italian backing is withdrawn (1938), 232; France would not fight to defend, 244; Franco-Italian non-intervention agreement on (1935),